CALEB'S EYE:
A SPY'S JOURNEY
THROUGH GENESIS

CALEB'S EYE: A SPY'S JOURNEY THROUGH GENESIS

CARROLL W. BOSWELL

authorHOUSE®

AuthorHouse™
1663 Liberty Drive
Bloomington, IN 47403
www.authorhouse.com
Phone: 1-800-839-8640

First published by AuthorHouse   07/12/2011

ISBN: 978-1-4634-3052-8 (sc)
ISBN: 978-1-4634-3051-1 (ebk)

Library of Congress Control Number: 2011911524

Printed in the United States of America

CONTENTS

I would like to dedicate this book to Enid Newton, who made it possible. I wish she were here to read it. I remember her as a quiet woman who stayed in the background, and spoke seldom, and dispensed the kind of food and hospitality that kept college students somewhat sane, but whose wisdom and goodness is manifested now in her children. I would have been very interested in her thoughts, and even more so now that she needs no "Cliff Notes" like these.

INTRODUCTION

This book began during a brief stint at a Presbyterian seminary in St. Louis. There I encountered a book, <u>Biblical Theology</u> by Gerhardus Vos. What impressed me was not so much the book itself as the idea of the book. Vos intended to present theology as it arises chronologically from the Bible. His intent, if I remember correctly, was to show how the unity of the Scripture produces a coherent understanding of God as it unfolds over the whole history of Israel and Israel's Messiah. The book itself was an academic and scholarly book, one that was not particularly accessible to laymen. It occurred to me then that the same project could be carried out in a more "user friendly" way.

So began the first of five attempts at an adult Sunday school class. The goal was to read and discuss the whole Bible over the course of a year, and to rearrange the text in a chronological way, with the prophets in the right places and the psalms inserted where they belonged, and the two Chronicles and the two Kings shuffled together, and so on. I called it "Bible Overview". The first year I did the course, my notes consisted in a rather sparse outline, but each time I attempted the course I could not resist elaborating on the notes, correcting them, pointing out interesting passages and ideas. Although the class was only actually completed that first time, the notes continued to grow until it was brought to my attention that I had in fact written a book. This is not that book.

When it first occurred to me that it might be worthwhile making the notes into a coherent book, and I began to work toward that goal, everything expanded yet again. What we have here is what the meager outline of Genesis grew into, and the rest of the outline is gradually assuming the forms of what appears to be a series of Bible commentaries.

But this is not exactly a Bible commentary, at least not like the Bible commentaries I have seen. It is first of all not a scholarly production because I am not a biblical scholar. My professional training is in mathematics, and my understanding of the Bible has grown out of personal meditation and study over the decades. The book is not scholarly; my intent was to aim it at ordinary people, and I hope I have succeeded in doing so. But it was not my intent to write as simple a book as I could. I wanted to write a book in which the reader could watch another layman wrestling with the complex issues of theology and trying to answer the hard questions that any serious student of the Bible should inevitably encounter. It is a book for someone who wants to not set aside difficulties, even if there are no satisfying answers, and who wants to think about the Bible as hard as he or she can.

The modern age values the professional opinion, and it is right that we do so. But like all purely human values, professionalism can be a handicap as well as an aid. Do we really think that in order to contribute to a dialogue about the Bible one must be an academic? Do we mean to restrict discussion about the Bible to the scholars and have the rest of us wait in the wings until they have reached their conclusions? Are scholars always to be trusted to speak the truth so that the laymen should sit back and wait on their verdict? I have a very high opinion of the value of academic research, but the scholars are in a state of disarray these days and there seems to be room for some outside influence. I wrote this book because I thought I might have something to add.

There are other warnings I owe you before you begin to read. Where am I coming from? What are my presuppositions? Do I have "axes to grind"? Do I have intellectual or moral biases? The easiest way to try to answer these questions is to give you something of a biographical sketch, to give you my "testimony".

I have a rather patchwork denominational background. I was raised in the American South as a Southern Baptist, baptized at the age of eleven in Pelahatchie, Mississippi. Growing up in the South during the Civil Rights movement in the 1960's eventually convinced me that Christianity was the source of all evil, and by the time I graduated high school I was mostly interested in what is now called New Age ideas. But at college, in California, my interests were altered when I attended a Congregational Church out of curiosity. I had never heard of congregational churches and was unprepared. Actually, the church service itself was of no consequence; I do not have any memory of what was said or done. I merely felt the confrontation of a person, whom I intuitively knew to be Jesus, who silently demanded my allegiance. He was an emotionally tangible, almost physical, presence. At that point I realized that whatever the failings of

Christianity might or might not be, they were irrelevant; and however much I might personally dislike or despise Christianity or its history or its people, that also was irrelevant. It was on Jesus Himself that everything hinged; it was Jesus himself, and not the church, to Whom I owed a response.

My college years were spent with that congregational church, a couple of Presbyterian churches, and the Inter-varsity Christian Fellowship. It was the time of the Jesus People movement and the charismatic movement. I, like so many students, met with charismatic people who prayed for me to receive the gift of tongues. I didn't get the "baptism of the Spirit" at that time; what I did get came months later, perhaps the following year. I woke up one morning simply filled with joy. It is nothing I can adequately describe; there was no emotional room in me for anything but joy. I was ecstatic, though without the tongues or prophesying or whatever. I can't remember how long this lasted, several days I think, probably not more than a week, and then I woke up and it was gone. Just vanished with only a memory. Naturally I thought I had done something wrong and I spent a long time praying. I recall fasting for several days. The answer I got to my inquiry was very simple: you are called to live by faith, not by sight. The sort of spiritual delight I had been allowed to experience made it all too easy, but the easy way is not the way we—or at least I—have been called to live.

Thus my college years made me a Christian, and something of a charismatic: I was convinced that the gifts of the Spirit all were real and present but that they were not intended to make the Christian life groovy, like a sort of spiritual hippiedom. After college I went to St. Louis, Missouri, for graduate school and became involved in a Presbyterian Church connected to the ministry of Francis Schaeffer and L'Abri Fellowship. The pastor was Egon Middlemann, for whom I had great admiration and who taught me a great deal. In that church I learned some real theology; I got a respect for church history and for John Calvin and Martin Luther and Augustine, and many others, that I still have. And I met my wife, Kathryn, who had come to that church from a Catholic background. We were involved with the Presbyterian Church for thirteen years, and helped to establish a mission church where I became a "ruling elder" for four years. I was a seminary student for a year or so at Covenant Seminary, and then a seminary drop out as I realized that I could not fit peacefully, long term, in that denomination.

For several years Kathryn and I had both felt called to move to a rural setting and in 1986 we did so—this is a long story in itself—and ended up in upstate New York with six children. We bought a small farm from an Amish man and soon joined a non-denominational charismatic congregation. We were members at that church for about thirteen or fourteen years, and I was also an elder there for four years, until doctrinal issues made it impossible to stay. During that time we became acquainted with some Amish families and developed an permanent admiration for them as well.

In 2002 we joined the parish of Trinity Episcopal Church where we were very happy. The liturgical style is still something of a stretch for me, but I increasingly appreciate its value. In the Episcopal Church we have felt home, church-wise, for the first time. We have a total of ten children, the last being born in 1998. When our children were all older, my wife Kathryn attended an Episcopal seminary, Nashotah House. She was ordained as an Episcopal priest in December 2010 and has been called to be the rector of a small Episcopal church that is near where we live. Still, theologically I tend to fall in between the cracks: a fundamentalist/ liberal/ Calvinist/ Anabaptist/ Crypto-Catholic/ charismatic.

Wherever you may come from in your own background, this book is likely to make you alternately comfortable and uncomfortable, surprised and then perhaps angry. You will probably not find my approach to Scripture totally alien, but you will also find elements that challenge what you currently believe. I believe the theological mishmash in my viewpoint is an advantage that nearly anyone can use to their good. In this way I believe God has prepared me to be an iron that sharpens many other styles of iron. At least that is my prayer.

Other than a denominational hodge-podge, I am writing from the viewpoint of faith. I assume the Bible is a true revelation, and my default position is to believe what it says. More specifically, it is the true revelation of a Person, not a revelation of everything. Even more specifically, it is the true revelation of a Person through a series of covenants. The idea of a covenant seems to me a very useful organizational tool for understanding the Bible, and it seems to be one that the Author chose as well. Also my impulse is to organize events chronologically. The chronological organization makes sense to me because I assume the Bible is a progressive revelation. In other words, the Bible is one Person introducing Himself to other people. In that process, He doesn't tell everything about Himself all at once. He gives increasingly intimate glimpses of who He really is as people adjust to what He already said.

But there is yet another caution I owe you. I think in outlines, and that is what you will find here. I can't help but write as a mathematician and that means that sometimes I will be too organized or too abstract or too theoretical for your taste; perhaps I will be too analytical and you will find it maddening; perhaps I will speculate more than you think I should. My style may well drive you crazy. On the other hand, it is by grace that I am what I am. Minimizing who I am and how I think would also hide whatever God might intend to do through me when He made me up.

Here then is my take on what the book of Genesis says and I hope that everyone who reads this will find it irritating, offensive, challenging, interesting, helpful, and worthwhile. What good is it to read something you already agree with? You learn nothing. It may be safe but it is also boring and a waste of your time. I pray that what I say will be just irritating enough to get you thinking but not so irritating that you just go away. The individual sections will be most helpful if you read the Bible passage first and then the section and then the Bible again, back and forth. I use the New American Standard and the English Standard versions most often because they tend to be very literal translations, though they are occasionally awkward. I tried to arrange the material in "bite-sized" pieces, so that you can read it section by section without too great an expenditure of time.

I seldom consult commentaries except about technical details of Hebrew or Greek or history, so all the opinions tend to be my own and you can just blame me. There are ideas that have become such a fundamental part of my permanent mental furniture that I don't really remember where they came from. If I have inadvertently absconded with anyone else's ideas, I can only apologize in advance and congratulate you on your insights. But the one to whom I owe the most is my wife Kathryn. She has taught me most of what I understand and kept me from being stupid more times than I can remember. I respect her opinions more than anyone else's that I know, and when we have disagreed she is generally the one who has turned out to be nearer the mark. I can not give her enough credit for her good influence on me and my thinking.

Use this book, use my opinions and thoughts and speculations, as far as they are helpful to you and leave them behind when they are not. The title for this book, Caleb's Eyes: A Spy's Journey through Genesis, was suggested by Kathryn. It is, of course, a reference to the spy who, with Joshua, brought back a good report of the Promised Land. This book, and any book that follows, is my report on the Book about the Promised Land, as best I can understand it, as clearly as I can see it, hoping that you and I will be encouraged to go on in, and get out of this desert.

The Covenant of Creation

A. Establishing the Covenant of Creation (Genesis 1-2)

1. How to Read Genesis 1 and 2

There is scarcely any other segment of Scripture that has attracted as much attention as the beginning of Genesis. It has been the source of some of the most heated controversy during the last two centuries, and no wonder since it is the story of the very beginning of all things. How we think of our beginnings shapes to a great extent how we think of ourselves and of our role in the universe. When we argue about the first two chapters of Genesis, we are mainly arguing about our self-image, and that is why the debate gets so emotional.

Some argue that these two chapters must be interpreted as an historical account, that we must read this passage as a physical description of seven consecutive twenty-four hour days. Others argue that these two chapters are poetic in style and should be taken metaphorically, as a grand story not to be taken literally. I am suggesting a third possibility: that these two chapters are a presentation of a covenant between God and the universe. The idea of a covenant is no longer a common idea in our culture, and so an explanation is in order.

The so-called Covenant Theology arose in a Puritan and Calvinist context, but my approach to the covenants in the Bible is somewhat different from theirs. When the Puritans talked about the Covenant, the example they used most often was a legal or a business contract, but that is not at all the way I think about it. Nor does it seem to be the way it was usually presented in the Bible. When the Bible gets specific about covenants, it almost always has in mind two examples: the covenant established by a conquering king over the king he has just defeated is one; but more commonly, marriage is the example of a covenant that is used. Essentially, "covenant" is the word used in the Bible to mean "relationship". Whenever God establishes a close tie to some person or people, He does it in the form of a covenant. We are accustomed to think of our relationship to God as a "personal relationship" but that phrase was never used in the Bible, and it does not do justice to the biblical concept. It is better to say that we have a covenant relationship to God rather than a personal relationship to God, and as this discussion goes on I will try to explain why. Just so you can interpret me accurately, when I talk about the covenant, I am usually thinking marriage.

As a covenant, then, the purpose of these two chapters is to state the terms of a relationship. Viewing them as a covenant we need not worry about a time frame for the events described or even whether or not it is describing events. Tthe point is not when or in what order events happened, nor even if they happened exactly as pictured. On the other hand, viewing them as a covenant, we need not transform these two chapters into a collection of symbols or some allegory which can be interpreted as we wish. The point is not a mystical look into unimaginable events. From my viewpoint, the purpose of Genesis 1 and 2 was to set guidelines for the way we were to interact with each other and with God. Looking at the passage as the description of a covenant, the days of creation are not periods of time, nor imaginary realms of creative activity, but are more like the articles in a constitution. Just as the American Constitution, for example, establishes the branches of government, prescribes the duties they are to perform, and sets limits on their powers, so God partitioned His universe and set the boundaries for each realm and the rules for the interaction between the realms.

Though the word "covenant" is not used in these chapters, there are at least two other places in Scripture which describe this passage as a covenant. In Jeremiah 33:20 we read, "Thus says the Lord, 'If you break My covenant for the day, and My covenant for the night, so that day and night will not be at their appointed time, then My covenant may also be broken with David My servant that he shall not have a son to reign on his throne, and with the Levitical priests, My ministers.' "Here the Scripture refers to the ordering of the day and the night as a covenant on the order of the covenant with David that his descendents would always reign over Israel; it also compares the ordering of the day and the night to the covenant with the tribe of Levi which gave them the priesthood. Thus the establishment of the day and the night was the same kind of act on God's part as the establishment of the priesthood of Aaron, the kingdom of David and the promise of the Messiah.

Also in Hosea 6:7 we find, "But like Adam they have transgressed the covenant; there they have dealt treacherously against Me." When Adam sinned by eating the forbidden fruit he was committing the same kind of act as the later Israelites committed in breaking the Covenant of the Law. From the moment of his creation, Adam was bound to God in the same kind of relationship that would join all of Israel to God at Mt. Sinai. There were also differences, of course, but they were the differences that distinguish one covenant from another covenant, not that distinguish what is a covenant from what is not a covenant.

Finally it is right to view these chapters as a covenant because they have the right form, they contain the kind of information a covenant should contain and they are arranged like a written covenant should be arranged. Here God is portrayed not only as creating all things, but He is also described as ordering His creation, delineating the various realms of the creation, establishing rules and authorities, and setting the penalty for the violation of the rules (actually, the one rule). What He was doing here was establishing the context for the parties involved to pursue their mutual relationships and to grow in their knowledge and love for each other and for Him. No relationship is formless; there are always protocols involved. The rules of engagement, the rules of civility and decorum, are aids, not hindrances, to relationship, particularly when God Himself sets them up. Relationships are most like a dance, like the very elaborate dances from three hundred years ago with intricate patterns of coordinated movement. In these chapters of Genesis God was telling us how the dance would proceed.

Taking the first two chapters of Genesis as a description of a Covenant, there are at least six major elements, or provisions, that emerge as central to the relationship God instituted with His new creation. Here these six provisions are listed not in the order in which they are mentioned in the Scripture, nor in their order of importance, but in the order that is most convenient for discussion. Rather than considering these two chapters in order, verse by verse, we will work through the passage by considering the terms of the Covenant one at a time.

2. The Terms of the Covenant of Creation

a) The Trees of the Knowledge of Good and Evil, and of Life (Genesis 2:8-17)

The command not to eat of the Tree of the Knowledge of Good and Evil has sometimes been referred to as the **probation test** and this term does seem to represent a fairly common understanding of this part of Genesis. My dictionary defines "probation" as "a process or period of testing the character or abilities of a person in a certain role". Calling the prohibition of the Tree of Knowledge a probation test suggests that Adam and Eve's position in Eden was not secure, that they had to prove themselves in order to be granted permanent residence, as it were. This is a view that seems to be commonly held, that God meant the Tree to be a kind of job interview, an examination of Adam's and Eve's qualifications to live in paradise.

But the question must be asked: why would God test them? Didn't He know what He was doing when He made them? Was He unsure about the quality of His workmanship? Did He suspect there was some hidden flaw in His creation that needed to be checked out before He gave it His full warranty? If so, then did He not really mean it in 1:31 when He said that everything He had made was very good? Or perhaps He was trying to prove to a skeptical audience, the host of heaven or whoever, that this creation, and particularly the human part of it, was up to snuff? I hope these questions are sufficiently sarcastic to cast doubt on the concept of the Tree of Knowledge as a probation test. Further, the idea of a probation test assumes, tacitly or otherwise, that the possibility of evil had to be present in order for there to be a vindication of good; and it assumes that the perfection of Adam and Eve (the very creatures described as being created in the image of God) could not really be claimed until they had met temptation and rejected it. Let's consider these assumptions further.

If the Tree of Knowledge was a probation *test* then goodness would seem to require the existence of evil, or the possibility of evil, to be recognizable as good. Something like this belief has the authority of popular mythology, but do Christians or Jews really believe such a thing? Does the Bible intend that we believe this? Putting the question in other words: must we be occasionally miserable so that when we attain bliss it is recognizable? Does light require darkness in order to be recognizable as light? Does God require a devil in order to be fully known as God?

The Biblical view of God and of goodness requires that we answer in the negative. The goodness of God, and the goodness which He built into creation, stand on their own and do not need any contrast in order to be fully themselves. To believe otherwise is to believe that God is not complete in Himself, that evil is as much built into the foundation of reality as good is. But the God portrayed in Scripture is purely good, with no trace of evil, and yet in need of nothing to complete Him. This self-containment of God's Goodness, this independence of Goodness that renders it Good absolutely without any reference to evil, is a quality that is passed down to every level of the creation. Throughout chapter 1 God asserted the goodness of everything with no badness present and no badness necessary to reveal it as good. When God repeatedly pronounced the creation to be good, He was not using the term in a relative way as if He were saying, "This creation is really pretty good compared to others I've seen". We are accustomed to using our terms in a relative manner, but there is no reason to suppose that God does. It is one of the distinctives of the Judeo/Christian tradition that it views evil as entirely dispensable and unnecessary. Not only is evil not a necessity, but it is our hope that the day is coming when it will be eradicated without a trace. It is not only theoretically dispensable, but it is in fact to be dispensed with.

From a Scriptural point of view, evil is not a created thing at all; it has no intrinsic existence. The most revealing metaphor of the character of good and evil is the metaphor of light and darkness. Just as darkness is not a thing in itself, just as darkness is only a lacking of light, so evil is merely a defect of goodness. There is no substance to darkness and there is no substance to evil. One can never devise a switch that can be flipped on to flood the room with dark. A room can't properly be said to be full of darkness; properly we must say it is empty of light. Evil is just such a non-entity, a powerlessness, an absence of something which ought to have been there and isn't. Evil is not only an *unnecessary* thing; it is not even a truly a *thing* at all.

Furthermore, if the Tree of Knowledge is a probation test then its whole point was the temptation and the testing of the character of Adam and Eve, as if God were not sure of what He had made, or as if He did not know what they would do, or as if He had to prove Himself to a skeptical audience. It would mean that when God made the universe, He could barely hold it together, that its goodness was so fragile and uncertain that He had to take it out for a test drive, as it were, before He was willing to give a warranty on His work. In this view God wasn't *creating* the world in the biblical sense; He was experimenting, playing around, practicing the craft of universe manufacture, perhaps rehearsing for some future and better effort; He didn't really know what He was doing; the whole creation was a sort of on-the-job training, and apparently His work failed the test and proved to be of poor quality. Just as a construction worker who tests his work is really testing himself, in testing Adam and Eve, God was really testing Himself, the quality of His work. We can make excuses for Him; He was, after all, trying to do a pretty difficult thing, making a universe that was genuinely good out of nothing; His reach exceeded His grasp, that's all. In short, the view that God planted this Tree to *test* Adam and Eve undermines the way we think about God's competence.

On the other hand, if the Tree of Knowledge was a *probation* test then Adam and Eve had to justify themselves by works and were not under God's grace. No other creature had to prove its goodness; only the two in God's own image had to prove themselves. Do we believe that the closer a creature comes to God's character the less grace is involved in its relationship to Him? If we view the Tree of Knowledge as a *probation* then we would seem to imply that grace was not part of God's character until after the Fall, as if He began by using a strict moral accounting system, a Law, and then was forced into being gracious after the Fall in order to keep the whole thing from falling apart. However, if we think that the universe began by law and that our relationship to God began based on strict obedience, then we give up grace for all time. We cannot make grace grow out of law. Law is a poison soil that gives life to nothing and grace will wither every time; it becomes non-grace; it becomes another version of law. One of the major themes of the Scripture as it goes on is a repudiation of Law as the foundation of being. To believe in the probation test ultimately undermines the central meaning of the rest of Scripture.

So if we throw out the idea of a probation test as the poison pill that it is, how should we begin thinking about the Tree of Knowledge?

The most striking thing about the command not to eat of the Tree of Knowledge is that it appears unnecessary. When God planted Eden, there was no need for Him to plant a tree in the very middle of the garden where it could not possibly escape their notice and which would bear attractive fruit that He knew He was going to forbid. It begins to look as though He wanted to tempt them, as though He meant to put a stumbling block in their way, as though Eden and paradise were just a ruse which He never meant for them to enjoy for long. Have I then sought to avoid the charge of incompetence against God only to have Him brought up on charges of fraud?

I must stress that there was no need for Adam and Eve to resist temptation in order to prove that they were good; they were good in the most absolute way, pronounced to be so by God and known to be so by God, all the way to the core of their being. A better representation of God's true character and purpose in the Tree of Knowledge is this: He did not put the Tree of Knowledge in the garden to provide a possibility of sin; rather, He planted the Tree of Knowledge in the center of the garden, and made it attractive, and then put it out of their reach, in order to provide a possibility for love, to give them an opportunity to act out their love for Him. The Tree was not planted to make sin possible but to make love tangible.

This may sound strange, but I think a little reflection will show how much sense it makes. The other provisions that God had imposed on creation and on people were all matters of common sense and desire. Except for the planting of the Tree of Knowledge and the law against eating its fruit, nothing which Adam and Eve desired was forbidden and nothing was required of them that they did not already want for themselves. The curse of the Fall on Adam in Genesis 3 implies that until the Fall all of his labor had been free of painful toil. Obedience to God and love for God were no big deal; there was no opportunity for Adam and Eve to give something to God that cost them anything. It was the very arbitrariness of the command and the attractiveness of the Tree of Knowledge that gave Adam and Eve the chance to do something for God purely out of love and *for no other reason*. The fruit of this tree was the only desirable thing in all creation that was denied to them, and the only reason given for its denial was simply God's will. Hence the only reason to obey the command was to please God and to express love for God. The Tree of Knowledge was not planted as a test; it was planted as an opportunity.

The moral law prescribed in the Scripture frequently has a "for your own good" character to it. For the most part, the commandments are all things that, if we could just behave according to enlightened common sense, we would probably do anyway. We break the commandments because we are weak and because we are fools, not because God is withholding something good from us. I wonder, though, if there aren't "trees of knowledge" in each of our lives, convictions of individual consciences differing from one to another of us: places we are forbidden to go by some mysterious inner conviction, delights that others may enjoy but we are forbidden to taste, desires we are forbidden to satisfy but not because the places or things or desires are bad, for they are good and desirable and we long to reach out to them. Perhaps God gives each of us an opportunity to fully express our love for Him, to turn aside from what we want and give Him a gift that does cost, which may even cost everything we have. Perhaps not. But if so, we should be much more careful of each other. We must be careful not to foist off our "tree of knowledge" on someone else, as if our convictions were a general moral law that applied to anyone but us; and we must not despise the scruples of others which we may in our superiority regard as childish. It is exactly the seemingly unnecessary scruple whose keeping may bring us closest to God.

There is no need to think that the Tree of Knowledge was a special kind of tree. It was special in that it was forbidden, and the choice of obedience to the command, not the fruit itself, provided the knowledge of good and evil. On the other hand, the Tree of Life was a different sort of tree altogether. Its presence was strange and mysterious. After all, Adam and Eve already had life, and with no death to end it. There would seem to be no need for a Tree of Life; and to make it more mysterious, when they were in need of something like a Tree of Life after the Fall it was denied to them.

I believe part of the meaning of the Tree of Life is this: that though Adam and Eve had unending days in paradise, they did not have what would later be called "eternal life". They did have eternal life in the sense of having a life that spread out to the future forever, but they did not have eternal life in some other sense, some other sense which God clearly meant for them to possess, planting a Tree of Life beside them and leaving it for them to enjoy if they chose. They had life and joy forever in the presence of God, but there was something more, a different kind of life, a higher quality of life, that was in store for them, and that was symbolized by the Tree of Life. Thus when the Messiah brought this kind of life back within our grasp and called it "eternal life", He was not referring merely to unending days, a return to the kind of life our first parents briefly enjoyed; He meant a qualitatively different kind of life, a life beyond all imagining.

The Tree of Life is a type of Christ, a symbol of His presence. And the planting of the Tree of Life in Eden was the planting of Christ Himself in the midst of the world. For the Incarnation of God was not a late thing in history, nor was it an ad hoc method of addressing a crisis in the Creation; it was part of the original intent from the very beginning. From the moment He decided to create—whatever that means—God had intended to live inside His creation Himself, to relate to His work most intimately by weaving Himself into its very fabric, not mystically but concretely, not as a spiritual force blowing like a wind though its threads, but as one of the threads, a fellow animal with other animals, a fellow man with His people. God was never, is not, and could never be a Spectator.

b) The Image of God (Genesis 1:24-27 and 2:7,19,20)

Both our stewardship over creation and marriage could have been discussed with the idea of being in the image of God, but the discussion seems to work better if we split these three ideas up and tackle them separately. Compartmentalizing the Covenant in this way is artificial, clearly, and could be done in other ways; and the various aspects of the Covenant are so closely related that any dissection of the Covenant into pieces is liable to do damage to our appreciation of the Covenant as a whole. I have only adopted this approach in order to make my discussion a little more coherent than it would be otherwise.

The creation of human beings was peculiar in several respects and this peculiarity was highlighted by the phrase "image of God". We are the only creatures designated as being in the image of God. There have been many opinions about what exactly the image of God is. Some early Christians, under the influence of Greek philosophy, suggested that the image of God is our ability to think, our rationality. In a modern evangelical context, which stresses proper behavior and respectability, the tendency is to see the image of God as the ability to make moral or ethical choices. These understandings arise from predispositions that come from culture or upbringing or personal bias; with no clear cut definition given in the Scripture it is natural to understand the image of God in terms of what we value the most. But suppose we were to look for hints from the Bible itself as to what it means to be in God's image? Taking these two chapters of Genesis in isolation—and if the Scripture is a progressive revelation (which I think it clearly is) then it is natural to let the revelation progress. These

9

two chapters are logically intended to be taken in a somewhat isolated fashion as the very first of a long sequence—taking them in isolation for the moment, what would they imply about the meaning of the image of God?

There are at least two aspects of God's nature that are highlighted in these chapters and so it would be natural to take them as the primary ingredients in His image as well. First, and primarily, this passage reveals God as the Creator, and so it is natural to think that an important part of the analogy in God's image is that we were made to be creators like He is. Obviously we can't claim to be creators exactly as He is the Creator. It is not part of who we are now nor who we were originally, to create something from nothing. We work strictly within the limits of the created order; our creations are copies, more or less, of His ideas, but He has placed in our hands the job of making His ideas come to be. It is as if, when we create, that we are providing bodies for what He has created but left on the edge of nothingness for us to find. The truly excellent little book, An Artist by M. B. Goffstein, is a marvelous description of the artist and, by extension, any other type of human creator, in the truest biblical sense. It expresses just what it means to be a creator in the image of the Creator, to be a human in the image of God.

Consider for a moment the meaning of Genesis 1:1-5. When God began to create, initially the creation was formless and empty and dark, but He would not leave it that way. The formlessness was given form, the emptiness was filled, and the darkness was illuminated. But not all of the darkness was illumined; the light did not fill all the creation; some of the creation was left in darkness and separated from the light. It is as if, when He separated the light from the dark, He was protecting some realm of darkness, for darkness is naturally destroyed by light. What then can this mean? One possibility is that when He separated the light from the darkness on the First Day, the darkness represented a gift to us, a region of His creation that we were given to explore, to bring to light, to bring into full creation. Perhaps this is what it means to be creators in the image of the Creator. He left some formlessness so that we could join Him in giving it form.

On the other hand, the creativity inherent in the image of God is like God's own creativity in this respect: we humans are most like God when we create out of the joy of the creative impulse rather than out of necessity. God's creation of the universe was the most spectacularly unnecessary act.

God did not need the universe; He felt no lack in Himself that compelled Him to create. His creation of the universe arose from His joy, His delight, which overflowed and burst forth into stars and forests and armadillos. Our impulse to create is like His creativity in this respect—it arises without regard to necessity. Since the Fall, we are driven to creativity through the fight to survive, but such necessity does not give the clearest picture of the image of the Creator. Doubtless the creativity we exhibit in our great engineering projects also exhibits the image of God, but not perfectly. In creating the universe and all it contains God was acting more like the artist, the poet, the composer, than like the engineer or the businessman.

But when we say that the creation was unnecessary to God, we do not mean that it was unimportant to Him. On the contrary, the fact that the universe is unnecessary to Him proves how important it is; God was creating the universe for Himself, for His own pleasure, not from *need* but from *desire*. The purpose of the creation was to please Himself, to bring Himself delight and pleasure, and at every step along the road to the completion it did please Him indeed. Genesis 1 bursts with God's joy and delight in what He was making like the flavor bursts out of a perfectly ripe grape. In the same way, the impulse to create that is placed in us by virtue of being in God's image most perfectly resembles God's own creativity when it is driven by pleasure and joy in the process of creating. Furthermore, being in God's image means that the creative impulse in us brings God joy as well; He delights in our creativity and the results of our creativity add to His joy in His own creation. Part of what it meant when God pronounced each realm of the creation to be good was that each creature had its own integrity built into it in its creation, and that by pursuing its own inclinations and nature it would please God. The same was true of humanity in our original created form: when we pursued our creative impulses, pursuing our own pleasure in creativity, we would also automatically be pleasing God simply by being who He created. There was no conflict in all of the universe between the desires of the creature and the desires of the Creator.

Unfortunately we can no longer say that. Quite commonly the desires of the human creature run counter to the desires of the Creator, and this is as true in the creative area as in any other. Our own pleasure and joy in our creations are no longer a certain indicator of God's pleasure and joy in them. In addition it is now possible for us to put our creative impulses at the service of other, even alien, masters. In particular, when creativity is made to serve the pursuit of money its tendency is inevitably to degenerate into ugliness, like a sacrifice offered on a pagan altar. Our own culture provides virtually unlimited examples of the process of degeneration and uglification at work in creativity when it is turned to other ends than God's pleasure.

But the impulse and ability to create is not the only aspect of God's nature that is being revealed in these two chapters; God is also the Covenant Maker. God is not content to create; He is impelled to love, to interact with the things He makes. No sooner did He speak the creative word that brought light into existence, no sooner did the light respond by emerging from nothingness into existence, than God was playing with it, separating it, multiplying it, refracting it and making it His very own. The Deists didn't just miss the ball when they imagined the Divine Watchmaker winding it all up and then letting it go; they weren't even playing the right game. God creates and relates. There is nothing that exists that can escape His advances; and nothing that did manage to escape Him could continue to exist at all.

The image of God as a covenant maker is related to Adam's first official job assignment, the naming of the animals. God had already been engaged in the naming of the various things as He created them; the giving of names is a fundamental part of the divine nature. Adam, and all of us human beings since then, have shared this compulsion to name things. There are some who have imagined that the power to confer a name is an expression of authority over the thing being named. The argument goes that parents name their children as an expression of their parental authority; likewise people named the creatures because people had been placed in charge of creation; and likewise Adam named Eve because men hold a position of authority over women (the point the interpreter in question was trying to prove). This line of thinking misses the real point. It focuses attention on an incidental and irrelevant issue—an issue that was not present in Eden—the issue of power, and it misses the real question: what is truly being accomplished when a name is conferred?

Even among the ancient pagans it was not the *conferring* of the name that established power; it was the *knowing* of the name that did it. In the ancient world, a person's name had a magical significance. Even among the gods, letting their true names become known made them vulnerable to magic spells cast by other gods. Among the Egyptians, for example, Isis was considered an especially powerful magician. There is a myth that describes how she tricked Re into revealing his secret name to her; it was the only thing left that she did not know in heaven or earth. She made a serpent which bit Re as he took his evening walk. The venom had no remedy apart from Isis' magic, and she pointed out that she could not use it to heal Re unless she knew Re's true name. He tried to give her one of his other names but only got worse; in desperation, he finally divulged his secret name. Isis knowing his secret name meant he was vulnerable to magic for either for good or ill. She could heal him, but she could also exert magical power over him in any way she chose.

The biblical understanding of names was very different from that of the surrounding cultures. First of all, in the biblical view the person's name had nothing to do with magic; it had nothing to do with power or authority. It had to do with relationship, with intimacy. When God gave His "secret" name to Moses, it did not give Moses magical power over God, but a new level of intimacy with Him.

The act of giving a name to something is the foundational step in establishing a connection and then a relationship with the thing. We name what we recognize and seek to know better. The impulse to name arises out of the desire for a relationship, and the name provides a context in which the relationship can grow. God is not only the Creator, He is the Covenant Maker, the Relationship Maker. It was not His purpose merely to create, but to know and interact with whatever He created and that is why He gave names to the things He made. Indeed, the ultimate expression of God's anger toward someone is that He "will blot out his name from under heaven" (Deuteronomy 29:20; see also Exodus 17:14, 32:33; II Kings 14:27; Psalm 9:5, 69:28, 109:13; Proverbs 10:7; Luke 10:20; Revelations 3:5 and 13:8 for example). The blotting out of the name is not a surrendering of authority; it is an abandoning of a relationship.

Similarly, to be in God's image means to be creatures that continue His work of relating to everything He had made. We name things because we carry the Covenant with us; and by naming things we are the agents of God to bring them more deeply and more actively into Covenant with Him. When we name our children we are not asserting our authority over them; we are extending the Covenant relationship between God and ourselves to a new generation. Nicknames are common among the closest of friends because the nickname expresses the special character of the relationship, it deepens the sense of covenant between the parties involved. It is important to understand that when we think of the account of Genesis 1 and 2 as a covenant relationship between God and His creation, we ought to be thinking of a web of relationships. We are caught up in the middle of that Covenant. The covenant relationship is a transitive relationship: if I am in covenant with God and He is in covenant with you, then I am in covenant with you. When God gave Adam the job of naming the animals He was inviting him to explore the range and variety of the relationships that were his through Him.

In summary the "image of God" means that at the very core of our being we are creator/relators and the two roles are inextricably woven together. We create because we exist in a web of covenant relationships, and our creativity reveals, expresses, and extends the relationships we are responsible for. We are the bearers of the Covenant to the rest of the universe; and I think that the bearing of that Covenant was the primary meaning of our headship over the creation as well. Our job was to be the stewards of that original covenant, to foster it and extend it and elaborate it, to oversee the intricacies of how everything connects and relates to everything else, to nurture and educate the ability to love and share what one thing has with all other things.

But the image of God comes in a particular context: dust. We were created out of the dust of the earth and that dust is as much a part of who we are as the image of God is. What does it mean to be dust then? First it is a matter of humility. We are chemical and it should be no matter for surprise that the most important part of us—our thinking and our feeling and our hoping, and even our sexuality—are basically matters of chemical reactions. This does not lessen the significance of what we think or feel; God who can create the whole universe out of nothing at all can just as well endow a complex chemical reaction with the transcendental ability to love and think.

It is a trick of our culture to make us believe that if our thoughts and emotions are chemical in nature then they are not "real". Modern science has it all backwards: the scientists have been trying to understand complex biological phenomena in terms of the basic laws of physics, reducing them to their most basic components, perfectly properly, but with the sometimes tacit assumption that the significance of the complexity disappears when you can understand its pieces. The reductionist approach does not require such an assumption, but it seems to have become reductionist orthodoxy that for the truly human and complex behavior to have real meaning it must consist in nothing simpler (religion, ironically, gave them that assumption) and that once we have shown it to be merely chemical in nature then it is merely mechanical and whatever was distinctively human disappears. The molecules are the little levers and wheels and we are just machines, you see, like fancy organic computers or robots.

But the Bible has the opposite perspective, that the glory of God is to take the most humble of things and make them into something that is more significant than their parts. "The whole is greater than the sum of its parts" is true only if God is behind the organization of the parts and makes them by His Word into something greater. We are machines, yes, but we are machines fashioned by God Himself into something beyond our own imagining.

Perhaps we tricked ourselves when we adopted a belief in a dichotomy between the material and the spiritual. We have become accustomed to thinking that we must insist on some super-natural dimension to human personality in order to justify it as significant, in order to defend the belief in the image of God in us; somehow we have come to think that if we are simply genes and complex chemical interactions then spirituality is invalid. We have somehow been fooled into believing that spirit cannot be "merely" natural and that the natural cannot be spiritual.

God's viewpoint on our make-up would appear to be quite different. He chose to make us of dust and it is His good will that we be dust, that we be dust that thinks and feels and loves, dust that knows Him and knows Him truly, dust which is capable of love for God and its fellow dust. It is the glory of God that He can take such humble material and make it the bearer of His glory. We need not defend our belief in the super-natural dignity of human beings by inventing the soul as a super-natural component to our being. We believe in the super-natural dignity of human beings because God gives us super-natural dignity, and He gives it to us by entering into covenant with us, not by making us out of some particularly dignified stuff or even out of super-natural stuff.

Some think, when "[God] breathed into his nostrils the breath of life and man became a living being", that this is the creation of the soul of the man. It is possible, of course, but not necessary. In Genesis 7:15, for example, all the creatures that boarded the ark are described as having the breath of life in themselves. It would seem then that either we allow the possibility that all the creatures have souls, or that this passage does not necessarily refer to the creation of a soul as a super-natural component to our identity. In thinking about the nature of spiritual reality it is important to understand that there is no threat to a fully biblical understanding from either alternative. It is not necessary to a Christian understanding of the nature of man to maintain the existence of a super-natural component; and it is no threat to our uniqueness as the image of God if the other mere animals have souls as well.

Ultimately a biblical view is that the spiritual is the same as the material. God is the only uncreated thing, so the human soul, if it is anything at all, is a created thing. The existence and nature of the soul is a topic on which there is very little information given. However one thing should be said now more plainly than I have said it above: talk about the "super-natural" has at least one major logical problem: we cannot give the term a logically consistent meaning. First we cannot mean that the super-natural is not part of the creation. If so, then is God not the Creator of all things? Or if we are suggesting that the super-natural is created but not part of our creation, then have we gained anything? Would another creation be less subject to being analyzed into its component parts and laws than this one? Is such a thing possible or even conceivable? On the other hand, we cannot mean that the super-natural is part of the creation, for then isn't it just "natural"? Our categories of thought need some serious work here, and I can't help but feel that the natural/super-natural distinction is not very worthwhile except for the relatively unimportant use of distinguishing our created order from another one. Jonathan Edwards, a somewhat neglected theologian, made a similar point 250 years ago, I believe.

But there is a more important insight to be gained from our creation out of dust. It is God's will that we be susceptible to chemical influences. We were created to be vulnerable to chemicals, and it is part of the nature God chose to create in us that we are stimulated by caffeine, intoxicated by alcohol, and altered in various ways by the various kinds of drugs available to us. It is not true that our susceptibility to chemical influences is something that is shameful and unspiritual; we were designed that way. It is true that in our present circumstances, in the corrupted state we live in, that our own natures are a real danger to us. However, although there are drugs that are unbelievably powerful and dangerous and damaging to society, it is not a biblical idea that the root of the problem is in the drugs themselves, nor is it in our susceptibility to them. The problem of our nature is not outside of us, but inside of us. We cannot blame our difficulty with drugs on the drugs; there is nothing wrong with them. It is our own natures, our sinful and fallen condition, that is the problem.

It is a serious theological error that Christians have made: we have pushed the issue of sin onto the creation rather than taking responsibility for it ourselves. We see the issue of sin as one of avoiding the evil temptations of an evil and fallen creation all around us. We spend our time dealing with corruption "out there" in demon rum or whatever that the demon doesn't possess rum—he possesses us. It is our own fallenness where the real problem lies. We waste so much time fighting the wrong enemy.

There is one other aspect of the meaning of the image of God that is critical to how we understand the revelation. When the first man was called "Adam", a word that means merely "man", it was to indicate in part that he was representative of the human race as a whole. This is a theme that Paul expanded on greatly in the book of Romans, and it is a concept that applies as well to the meaning of the image of God. Who or what is the bearer of the image of God? We read "Let us make man in our image, according to our likeness"; but it is not the individual man, Adam, that is referred to here; it is the human race as a whole that is the focus, for both male and female are included to make it clear that the image of God is not an individual. The bearer of the image of God, the bearer of the Covenant, is humanity and not primarily the individuals within humanity. I can say, as an individual, that I am myself in the image of God; each of us individually is in the image of God. But what this means is that I am in the image of God just as I am in the human race. I am a member of the image of God. When the Christ did come to begin restoring the full image of God to us, what He created was a *collective* entity called the Body of Christ. You and I are truly in the image of God because you and I are *contained in* the image of God. You and I are truly in the image of God, but we cannot bear it alone. Only together, only in all of us together, is the image of God truly manifested.

It is difficult to emphasize enough how radically the ancient biblical idea of man's origin differs from the other ancient mythologies. Many ancient mythologies have us created out of mud, but there the comparisons end. The most ancient non-biblical mythology is the Sumerian one, in which humanity was created as the slaves of the gods. The biblical view, from its very foundation, exalts the nature of the human race, and exalts God's view of, and purpose for, humanity. There is nothing else in the ancient world that makes our status even close to the exalted status that the biblical view gives us.

c) Stewardship over the Creation
(Genesis 1:28-30 and 2:15)

"Be fruitful and multiply, and fill the earth, and subdue it; and rule over the fish of the sea and over the birds of the sky and over every living thing that moves on the earth." These are the very first recorded words God spoke to Adam and Eve, and there is no other commission He has given us that we have misused more completely. The commission includes three tasks that we can discuss separately: first, to *populate* the earth; second, to *subdue* the earth; and third to *rule* over the other creatures. The first part of the commission is best left until we discuss marriage. It is interesting though that the first word addressed to the first people was an invitation to a sexual relationship, but we will come back to this later.

We should focus on the second and third parts of the commission now. There are two key words, the one translated "subdue" and the one translated "rule over". In Hebrew the word for "subdue" has a very wide range in meanings, from those which are more gentle ("acquire control") to those which are more violent, ("rape"). When the word was translated into Greek by the ancient Jews, they used the word κατακυριευσατε, *katakyrieusate*. It is on the gentler side of the range but can also have a fairly wide range of meanings from "gain control over" to "subdue" to "tame" to "conquer". The English Standard Version chose a translation in the middle of the range.

In both Hebrew and Greek the word translated "rule over" means to "govern", in general, but the Greek word, αρχετε, *archete*, means particularly to "govern as a deputy or subordinate officer". Different English translations use other phrases like "have dominion over" but the emphasis in the original is easily lost. In the context, this first commission flows out of being the image of God and our translation should be determined by that idea.

How we understand the image of God colors how we understand our commission to the creation, and how we understand God colors how we understand the image of God. Too much of our tradition pictures God as a stern grandfather figure, and that inclines us, particularly men, to adopt such a stance as images of God: forceful men, dominant men, strong and somewhat aloof. What I have argued previously is that God is a Creator and Covenant Maker who made everything up out of His joy and enthusiasm. Being a Covenant Maker is the opposite of the stern grandfather in many ways, particularly in not being aloof. We need not, should not, understand the word subdue in its most forceful sense of subjugating, conquering. Instead we should understand "subdue" as to "gain control" and in connection with the idea of ruling as a deputy.

A newly inaugurated ruler, say a son succeeding to his father's throne, would "gain control" over his dominions as he became increasingly competent at governing and shaping the policies he wanted enforced in his realm; but he wouldn't necessarily have to "subdue" or "conquer" anything, unless there was a rebellion among his subjects. In the context of Genesis 1 there is no hint at all of force or violence in the commission God gave to Adam. The creation was good, it was perfect, it was flawless. There was no need for Adam and Eve to *subjugate* the creation. There was no indication, no hint, that the creation would be in any way reluctant to come under the direction of the first people.

The commission given to our first parents by God was to extend their control over the creation, not by *making* it submit, but by *learning how to order the world* for the good of all concerned. They were bearers of the Covenant, not bearers of an army. Their commission was primarily an educational one, from the beginning: go out and learn how to care for the creation, what it needs and how best to serve it, and then teach it what it should do. Even now, in the age of sin and death, the best of kings, the ideal of kingship, is the king who gets to know his people and learns how best to order them for the good of the nation. It is typical of the thought patterns of this world to think of the first commission to the human race as one of forcing our will on the rest of a reluctant world. But it "shall not be so among you", as the Messiah commanded in a somewhat different but related context, pointing out that in His Kingdom those who would be great would be the servants.

The best phrase used to translate the Biblical commission to rule or have dominion is "exercise stewardship over" but stewardship is a somewhat old fashioned word today. Perhaps the idea of being a deputy is more understandable than being a steward. We could also say that Adam and Eve were given the job of being pastors to the creation, the shepherds of all things. Primarily to have dominion or authority over the creation, in the Biblical context of bearing the Covenant, is to have the job of nurturing relationships among the creatures in such a way as to extend God's pleasure and joy in it all. Never at any point in the Scripture, in Genesis or afterwards, does God give us cause to think that He has signed over the title to the world, as it were, and walked away, that He has abandoned His claim on the creation. He never, at any point, made us the *owners* of the world. Every step our rule over creation is to be carried out as His agents, acting for His pleasure and His goals and not our own.

It is our greed that has re-interpreted "dominion" to mean "the right to exploit as we please with no limits". We must be very clear on this point: God did not create the universe with its profit potential in mind. He created the universe out of joy and love and for His own pleasure, and He created the various parts of creation to inter-relate in joy and love for their own mutual pleasure. We fulfill our commission when we serve His ends, when we work to enhance His pleasure in His works, and when we work toward the harmony and mutual joy of all things together. To be head over the creation does not mean to be the master over the creation; it means to be a servant to care for the creation as God wishes it to be cared for. We do not serve ourselves. The earth does not belong to us. The world was not made as raw material for our factories.

It was a good creation; it merely had no self control, no innate sense of order or beauty or love, no faculties given to it by its Creator that would help any part of it to know how to behave with kindness and respect to the other parts. Nor are we accustomed to thinking in such terms about the creation. We are so trapped in the survival of the fittest, in the competition to survive, that the circumstances in Eden are outside our imaginations. The initial creation was full of life and energy; it was not in the short supply it is now. There was no rationing of life, like creatures in a drought who divvy up the food just to get through the year with some survivors intact. There was no need for death, for competition, for struggle, in the original order, however many of the current laws of science that violates. When Adam and Eve gained control over the creation, their duties did not include keeping the carnivores from eating too many chickens. God appointed our first parents to teach each part of creation how to behave toward the other parts of creation, how and where and when to grow, how to live together to fulfill the beauty inherent in their design.

Perhaps the two words, "to subdue" the creation and "to have dominion over" it are repeating the same idea for emphasis. But I think there is a distinction in meaning between the two words that is worth thinking about. Note that in the third part of the commission our first parents were given rule over realms of the creation that, at least from the perspective of the present, would have been inaccessible to them. Presumably they could not fly, and for most of the history of the human race, we have had to stay out of the air. We can't swim much and only the fringe of the sea is available to us. Nevertheless, the third part of the commission explicitly puts all of these things under our dominion. We were charged to rule the parts that we might never even be able to visit.

And we have even now a vestigial sense of that concern with the whole creation. It is what drives us to explore, to learn to fly, to search the bottom of the sea and the top of the world and climb the highest mountain "because they are there". It is what drives some of us to seek out ways to explore the planets and makes us contemplate a journey to the stars. When I look at the photograph of the Andromeda galaxy or see it in a telescope, though it is two million years away by light, something in me knows that it too is part of me and my concerns and I have a desire to know it and feel it that is like nothing else but homesickness. Sometimes the longing and "homesickness" for the remote universe can be crushing. Perhaps this just indicates some mental aberration in me and has no theological significance. Obviously, God has not given any of us a calling to go to the stars at this point. But the urge to go to the stars is, I think, one of the echoes of that commission to our first parents. Everything God said in Genesis 1 was cosmic in scope, including this commission.

But He made the commission specific as well as general just in case later generations misunderstood His intent when He used words like "subdue" and "rule". He planted a garden, Eden, and put Adam there to "work" and "keep" it. It was my wife, Kathryn, who pointed out to me the larger meaning of this passage. The Hebrew word translated "work" also means to "serve", and the Hebrew word translated "keep" also means to "honor". This tends to support my interpretation of the commission, but I think it goes further. There is a sense in which we could say that we people in the image of God were appointed to be priests to the creation. We were intermediaries, standing between God and the rest of the world, not to coordinate repentance and forgiveness, but to coordinate worship and grace. We bring the creation into God's presence for worship, both for us to worship God and to teach the creation itself to worship God. Ultimately, the meaning of a garden is man and nature in worship together. This idea will be picked up later in the revelation by King David.

Unfortunately, we must adjust our commission to new circumstances; we do live after the Fall and violence invariably infects everything we do. Violence even taints the way we must do our gardening, poisoning or shooting the animals and bugs that "steal" what is "ours", fencing them out, scaring them away, competing for that last lettuce or even one bug-free apple. But the distinction between the commission we were given and the way that commission looks now is a crucially important one to hold on to.

We often justify the most ruthless acts of greed and cruelty in the name of subduing the creation, as if our selfishness and arrogance could be transformed into moral acts by attaching them to a Bible verse. It is true that we live and act in a morally compromised world, that our relationship to the creation is morally deficient, that we must do many things now that we ought never to have had to do. But to turn the inevitable moral compromise into an excuse for wholesale exploitation, to adopt the attitude that "well, we blew it, no use in even trying anymore", is to betray the original mandate in the most fundamental and savage way. And it is the grossest form of hypocrisy to turn around and pretend that our greed is actually a virtue, that our consumption of the creation is now the commission.

The preceding discussion leads us naturally to consider another peculiarity of human nature in relation to the world: we are the animals that work. We were the only creatures to whom God gave a job. All other animals simply live their lives and follow their instincts, but we work. Even when there is no necessity, no need to work for food or shelter or money, we are the creatures that seek out something to do. Those who have no desire to do anything are considered deficient in character; they are "slobs", "couch potatoes" and are looked down on. The impulse to work is rooted in our dominion over the creation, and so ultimately in being the image of God. To say that we are created to work is just a different way of saying that we are created to be creators.

When God gave us this commission, He was taking us into a partnership. God has created us to be little gods. What child is there who has not wanted to join in their parents' work? We all wanted to be a help when we were little and it takes a great deal of grace for the parent to let the child participate in his or her work. The child's help inevitably slows down the work and causes accidents, and may mean that much of the work must be redone. This is very much like what God did with the creation by making us the stewards over it.

The desire to work, to have a job to do, is built into our very identity. But ever since Adam and Eve ate the forbidden fruit we have lived with an identity crisis. Work has been changed into drudgery. Still we must be clear that the original meaning of work was as a glorious and divine calling. The Fall has changed the nature of work for us; it has made it nearly impossible for us to understand work in its original sense. Indeed, the Fall has twisted the built in need to work that God gave us, so that work can be a disease rather than healthful. When we talk about the Covenant of Creation, we are not talking about the way we live or feel now; it is all about what and how much we have lost.

In speaking of the commission to "fill the earth and have dominion over it and rule it", I have been careful to use the word "commission" rather than the word "command". It is a commission, as opposed to a command, because the desire to respond is built into us; as the ones who were given stewardship, there is created within us the need to be stewards. We are the stewards over the creation not because we were ordered to be so but because we were created to be so; it is who we are, not what we are obliged to do. It is an internal compulsion and not an external assignment. God does not give a commission without simultaneously creating the desires that are necessary to carry out that commission.

It is evidence that we were created to care for the world that we so strongly want and need to do just that. In the best of human nature, the best that is left to us, is the feeling toward the other creatures that they are like our children. I have heard childless couples mocked for getting a dog or a cat and treating it as a substitute son or daughter, but what could be more fitting? What could be a more natural and spiritual channel for the frustrated or delayed desire for children? To adopt other creatures as our own, as our own family, is closest to the original mandate, it is closest to the way God Himself feels about His creatures.

d) Sexuality (Genesis 2:18 and 2:21-25)

There is at least one other peculiarity of being in the image of God that needs special attention. All other animals were created male and female as a matter of course, but for human beings the creation of the male and the female was portrayed as two distinct acts. The woman, Eve, was not just created as a "female human", but had a special significance as evidenced by her special mode of creation. Sex was created first among the animals, but among human beings it was transformed into something more. While human sexuality obviously has elements in common with that of the animals, it is also something that is qualitatively different. For people, sexuality is something that involves the mind and the imagination as well as instinct, making human sexuality into something on a higher level than it can ever be among the other creatures. I suspect the two accounts of the creation of sexuality given here, in Genesis 1 the creation of male and female and in Genesis 2 the creation of Eve, symbolize the transformation of sexuality in people from something they shared with the animals to something uniquely human and spiritual.

Among the other creatures, sexuality is primarily a means of reproduction, but for human beings this is not true. Some have assumed, since the first item in God's first commission to our first parents was to be fruitful and multiply, that sex was created primarily with reproduction in view. This assumption is somewhat reasonable but fails to do justice to the delight, the relief, the joy that Adam experienced when he first saw Eve. When he said, "This at last . . ." it was not in the sense of "now I can finally have some children". From the first moment Adam perceived much more than the possibility of reproduction in Eve. The subsequent experience of the human race as well as the subsequent revelation shows that much more was intended by human sexuality than children. It is not that producing children is unimportant, but the production of children is not the central purpose of sexuality, even from God's perspective. Sexuality remains central to marriage even when there is no possibility of children. Sexuality remains central to the identity of individuals who are committed to celibacy as a lifestyle, or who have chosen not to reproduce. Reproduction is an added blessing to sexuality but is not its essence, and this is even more evident in recent years as birth control has become effective and available.

God's first commission to us in 1:28 suggests to some that birth control is forbidden, that the reproductive aspect is always to be associated with sex. Some seem to think that sex apart from the possibility of reproduction is somehow offensive to God and unclean in itself. Since God told us to be fruitful, these interpreters think that we must do all that we can to bring more children into the world, that this is a responsibility which is unending, or cannot be amended until God Himself alters it. But surely this is bad logic. If I were to tell my son to go upstairs and fill the tub for a bath, I would expect him to discern when the tub was full, and turn the water off at that point. If he left the water running so that it flooded the house, all with the excuse that I had not given him permission to ever turn the water off, I would not be pleased. God said we were to fill the earth, and it seems to me that He also gave us the common sense to discern when the earth was full and to curb our efforts at the right time. The discovery of effective birth control could be providential.

There is a fundamental dichotomy in the way our relationship to God is understood, a dichotomy that has long divided Christians: one group of Christians believe that we are permitted to do or think only what God has specifically sanctioned in the Scripture and any departure from this "straight and narrow way" is sin; another group of Christians believe that everything is permitted to us except what God has specifically forbidden. It is a question of how we think about life with God, whether our relationship with Him is based fundamentally on the rules He makes or on the freedom He gives. For the first group of Christians sexuality is unclean except where God has specifically allowed it, and the fact that it is such a strong desire in us makes it even more suspicious. For the second group of Christians sexuality is a gift from God for our joy, though in these last days it is somewhat dangerous at the same time and must occasionally be restrained for our good and our neighbor's good. Usually which group a person affiliates with is not determined by the study of the Scripture but by the tendencies of his own personality. I will argue, as we read through Genesis, that the second group are the ones who are the most biblical. No doubt my personality plays a large role in making me think as I do but I can not cease to have my personality just because I am thinking. It is better to be aware of who we are and not take ourselves too seriously than to not be aware of who we are and end up believing we speak for God.

The essential role of sexuality to the human identity need not have been; we could have been created as the animals are, with reproduction being the sole purpose of sex, all handled on an instinctual level, with no deeper level of emotional or cognitive involvement. There would have been advantages to being more animal-like. Pornography, for example, would not exist. A mere animal could never see the point in something like pornography because its sexuality has no connection to its imagination. When sexuality became corrupted, it was not merely reduced potentially to the level of animal sex; it found new open chasms to fall into lower than the animals. What was given as a gift to delight and even ennoble us became charged with the potential to reduce us lower than the lowest creatures. The more glorious the gift the more dangerous it becomes when corrupted.

25

Since there was no necessity to make sex a central theme in our nature, why did God choose to transform it the way that He did? Make no mistake about it: that sex is so central to human nature, and therefore in history and culture, is purely God's choice. Considering how much grief and misery has accompanied human sexuality through the years, would it not have been better if we had been left to be mere animals in this respect? What was God thinking in choosing to emphasize sex so strongly? These questions may be unanswerable; most theological questions are only partially answerable at best. In this instance, the Bible provides enough clues for us that we can hazard some theories. However, these clues are scattered throughout the Scripture, and so in commenting on the nature of sexuality I will be bringing in, even more than I usually do, a wider context than what Genesis alone tells us.

Ultimately, I think, our sexuality was enhanced in order to be part of God's revelation to us and this requires me to go off on a tangent for a bit. By the act of creating the universe, God posed Himself something of a puzzle. If God had not been Love, if God had not cared to relate and interact with what He made, then there would have been no problem. But how does an infinite and transcendent God make Himself knowable to a finite creation? It depends on what you mean by the word "knowable", and this opens up a whole epistemological can of worms that I cannot explore. For my limited purposes here, what I mean by "knowable" is to be "knowable by the 'average' human", a person like most of us, not trained in mathematics or the sciences or abstract philosophy, who believes that he can truly know things and does not think about the technical difficulties of what it means to really know something. How can God make Himself knowable to us ordinary people who have not yet learned how to put up sophisticated barriers against knowing things?

Ultimately, I think the answer has to be that He cheats. What I mean is that He does not try to make Himself knowable in the sense of *proving* His existence, or even of building into the creation the kind of evidence that would force us all to conclude without reservation that God exists. There is serious doubt if such physical evidence is even possible, but whether or no, He doesn't seem to have tried to provide it. Instead it seems to me that He built us with an internal understanding of His existence, a part of our make up, whether biochemical in our brains or, if you will, some innate spiritual component. We are "hard-wired" to know that He is there, and He embedded this knowledge so that it correlates with our experience of the created world. We can choose to ignore and suppress this knowledge, but we cannot delete it. It is part of being created in the image of God that we have an innate glimpse of what we are in the image of.

I know that my theory of how God is known by us will be unsatisfying to many people. For one thing, it means that our knowledge of God is not and cannot be purely rational. The idea that the existence of God, much less His character, could be proved like a mathematical theorem, was perhaps the greatest philosophical blunder of all time. We are so proud of our rationality. We think the human mind must surely be capable of ascending to the throne of God itself, a sort of internal or intellectual tower of Babel. This theory of God's knowability commends itself to me, in part, because it is so offensive to our intellectual pride. This kind of pride—the kind of pride which reveals itself in arrogance—should be offended whenever possible.

But it is not simply a matter of God "programming" us and suddenly we know all about Him; the "program" is only to make us know that He is there, to get us to seek to know Him, to open the door for further interaction. The knowledge of His existence must still be filled up with some content. Once we know that Someone is sitting over there waiting to speak with us, we will want to know something of what He is like. There are many ways to communicate with us once He has given us the eyes that can see and the ears that can hear. Then and only then we can begin to infer facts about God from the creation; then we can look inside ourselves to see how we think and feel, to see how our conscience works, and deduce from these things something about God. It is all analogy, of course, but that is the way it must be. But God does much more than sitting there waiting for us to figure things out; He actively attempts to speak with us, in words and also in other ways.

Let's consider some of the ways He communicates with us. Christians always point to the Bible first as God's way of speaking to us. This is true, but it is not detailed enough for this discussion. The Bible is rather complicated; it has parts, organization and organs, not all of which function the same way. We need to look more closely at the idea of revelation and how it is carried out.

One way is to elaborate on our internal knowledge of Him to create more specialized understanding. Another way is to speak to us audibly or visually in a dream or a vision. These are both a bit tricky, for reasons we will get to later, and they must be handled with some caution. A third way is to use our language to describe Himself through poets and prophets, either dictated or inspired by some more subtle means. A fourth way is to use history to act out plays about Himself by interfering in our affairs. And He does other things more wild and dangerous than we dream of. But the important mode of revelation for this discussing is that He builds into the creation special images of Himself, little metaphors for His character. These metaphors, once we have noticed them, elevate our imaginations to understand something new about His character.

I believe that God created human sexuality as one of these revelatory metaphors. Human sexuality was created as a little picture of who God is. That this unique and human form of sexuality was a part of the make up of the creatures that were in God's image is no accident. At some basic level, God's nature is sexual. This is to use language in an analogous way, not in a literal way, but it merits much more reflection and the Scripture is filled with such reflection and encourages us to think in this direction. I will attempt to do such thinking now.

It is marriage in particular that is given as a vehicle to carry the revelation of God in sexuality in the present age. The marriage relationship, and particularly the sexual aspect of the marriage relationship, is used in the Scripture as a picture of a covenant, as a metaphor for the relationship of God and His people. The common euphemism for sexual intercourse in the Scripture is the verb "to know". It is no accident we are called to love God and to know Him; what He has in mind for us and Him together is something analogous to sex. The ecstatic experiences in the charismatic movement, the raptures of the mystics over the centuries, are all testimonies to the sexual nature that is part of God's essence, and to the fact that we can learn about God by understanding and experiencing our own sexuality. It is the sexuality of God that gives complete meaning to the act of celibacy for those who are called to it: celibates do not leave their sexuality behind; they carry their sexuality into another realm.

But sexuality is distinct from marriage, both symbolically and in essence, and the everything was altered by the Fall. Sexuality was created as a revelation to us whether or not the Fall had happened, whether or not there had ever been an interruption in our contact with God. Even in a perfect state, a finite creation needs hooks to understand the nature of the infinite God. There would have been no cognitive or psychological or emotional or spiritual barriers to understanding the metaphors God used to reveal Himself, but revelation would still have been a necessity even in an un-fallen nature. Sexuality was one of those metaphors given to people in the un-fallen state to help them know God.

Before the Fall, there was no code of sexual morality or ethics provided in Genesis. Human sexuality was not a "problem" before the Fall; it was not described as a possible problem; it was not a realm in which rules were deemed necessary. Even after the Fall, the Bible was very slow to establish any rules for sexual behavior. We must remember, in thinking about sexual morality in this age, in which the recent traditional rules are being challenged or ignored, that the traditional rules of sexual conduct were makeshift to some extent anyway. Human sexual ethics are the sort of rules that were designed to handle a crisis situation rather than a normal and stable one. We can have no clear concept of what sexuality was like before the Fall, no more than a person born blind can have a clear concept of a rainbow.

It is possible that nothing had to be said in the Bible about sexual ethics before the Fall because the rules for right conduct were built into Adam and Eve, in much the same way that I argued the knowledge of God was built in. They might have known what was right and what was wrong instinctively. Possibly so; but these chapters were not written for Adam and Eve. They were written for us, and we have no such instincts of good behavior. If anything, our instincts tend to be rather depraved. If right instincts were ours before the Fall, it is strange that God was so casual about letting them all go without remark when the Fall happened. The instinct to know God can be discerned in the most rabid atheist, but no such instinct for sexual decency can be discerned in the sexual behavior of the average man.

Marriage, as we have it now, was not part of that original metaphor. However sexuality was expressed in Eden (and a large number of the early church believed that it wasn't expressed physically at all), there are two reasons to believe that marriage, as we now understand it, was a symbol added to sexuality after the Fall. Marriage as it developed in the sequence of revelation was particularly a redemptive image, revealing the relationship between Yahweh and Israel, the relationship between Christ and the Church. Thus marriage was a symbol designed for fallen people. Secondly, the Messiah indicated that marriage will have lost it significance after the healing of all things. Once redemption is accomplished the symbol of redemption will no longer be necessary and will vanish.

One way of looking at the institution of marriage is this: at the Fall sexuality had ceased to function in a covenantal way, as it was intended; marriage was instituted to restore and preserve some of that covenantal flavor of sexuality. Marriage enabled sexuality to continue as a bearer of revelation and not descend into mere triviality or depravity.

Whatever the case before the Fall, once the original Covenant had been broken marriage became a central metaphor of spiritual truth. Sexuality, which could exist in an unfallen state freely and with no shame or danger, became a problem. I think the problem was that the "one-ness" which sexuality was designed to express was no longer possible. Sexuality could no longer accomplish its purpose and so was inevitably turned to other channels that would invariably become destructive. Marriage was instituted, gradually over many centuries, to curb the danger and to protect some vestige of the original meaning and goodness of sex.

It is no accident that marriage is a universal custom among all cultures. One current theory to explain the universality of marriage is that it was necessitated by the competition for mates. If all men competed with all other men for all the available women, and the competition never stopped, there would be societal chaos. The cultural institution of marriage could at least limit the extent of the competition. It could put some men out of the struggle and channel their energies in more constructive directions. It was a survival trait. Evolution rears its reductionist head and the humanity of yet another aspect of life is reduced to mere survival of the species.

There is no harm admitting that this viewpoint of evolution carries some validity; without some form of marriage, human society descends to chaos. All I mean to maintain here is that a biblical view of marriage makes it more than this, and without a biblical view there is no way to elevate marriage to a higher plane. That it makes society stable is a natural result of the divine impulse to speak to us. There is in each of us, even in the most reprobate of us, at least the vestige of the idea of, and the desire for, the intimacy and commitment and stability, of the happiness, which marriage is intended to provide. There is in each of us the image of what our parents' marriage should have been and the longing for that ideal home of nurturing and safety. Even in the most wretched circumstances, where the actuality of marriage is most degraded, there is a lingering image of what might have been, of an ideal and hope that the partner will change into that ideal. The hope for this ideal keeps many a hopeless marriage together.

That the ideal of marriage runs so counter to the actuality of marriage implies to me that it comes from some higher source than the impulse to produce a new generation. Could the survival of our species depend on believing in such a cruel delusion? Or does the disjunction of marriage the ideal from marriage the reality reveal to us yet again that we are meant for a different and better world? Is the institution of marriage to make us despair or make us hope?

Though the basic pattern of marriage was nurtured in us from the beginning of our fallen state, the details were left to sort themselves out. There would be variations in the number of wives that were allowed, sometimes in the number of husbands, but in no culture was simple promiscuity the ideal for sexual behavior. As the Scripture unfolds it holds up a high standard for sexual behavior, not because sex is in any way unclean as so many "spiritual" people suppose, but rather because sex is so central and so powerful and so dangerous. Sexuality is a theme which runs through every aspect of the creation, if we have the eyes to see it, and for this reason how we behave sexually has great import, great power to heal or to damage everything we are and touch. To wield our sexuality carelessly is like being a klutz at large with a chain saw: we can kill and maim. We are all hopelessly clumsy but we all have the power of sexuality in our hands and it is a wonder that the human race has continued to exist in any sane form at all.

The modern American culture has taken sexual carelessness and made it into something of a status symbol: they are "happiest", they are "coolest", who most thoughtlessly and freely practice their sexuality before the universe. But to be *careless* of something means to *have no care* for that thing. We are only careless with what we do not value. Contrary to popular myth, contrary to superficial appearances, the true meaning of the prevalence of public sexuality and pornography in our culture is that we loathe and detest sex. Our slang reveals the same hatred: every slang expression for sex is also a curse, a term that describes what is ruined and dirty and despicable; every common word for intercourse in our culture also carries the connotations of violence and hate.

Our culture's hatred for sex is one of its most distinguishing marks. Our culture's hatred of sex is in terrible contrast to the biblical attitude, which loves and honors sexuality. It is popular in our culture for the most wanton and reckless of people to mock sexual morality and Christians as haters of sex, but it is the opposite that is the truth. Granted, there are many Christians who teach that sexuality is inherently tainted and they give rise to the stereotype; I grew up in such an environment. But it is the people of this world who are most ruthlessly contemptuous of it.

Something probably must be said here about homosexuality. This is an issue that has become extremely divisive and emotional in the present day, and it is beyond my ability to bring a resolution to the controversy. My position is that these two chapters of Genesis do not provide any conclusive argument for or against the normalcy of homosexuality. The passage simply does not indicate whether homosexuality could have been part of God's original intentions or not.

There is of course the statement that the man and the woman become one flesh, and some take these words as precluding the validity of a homosexual relationship, but in fact it seems to do nothing of the kind. It only refers to the special nature of the relationship between a man and a woman and remains silent about the nature of a possible homosexual relationship. It is presumed that there were no other people present and so there was not yet a question about such relationships. This can explain why the passage is silent on the question of homosexuality but it does not provide a way to predict what would have been said.

Those who have decided already that the Bible condemns homosexuality will see Genesis 2 as a part of that condemnation; and those who have decided already that God does not condemn homosexuality will see Genesis 2 as irrelevant. I agree with the latter, not—I think—because I have already decided that homosexuality is all right, but because I do not see the logic of the former. The sort of oneness that is described as accomplished in a heterosexual relationship would seem to be potentially possible in a homosexual relationship as well, though opponents would rightly point out that the passage does not say so.

Two points should be made however. The first point is that the oneness that was part of the goal for the heterosexual relationship is no longer attainable even in the best circumstances. The Fall has damaged sexuality too severely and it is the very rare heterosexual relationship that can even be said to be fairly good. It is therefore not at all clear that an argument based on the original intent can apply to the present circumstances.

On the other hand, a second point must be made: the symbolic meaning of a heterosexual marriage would not be at all clear in a same-sex marriage. There is a character to a heterosexual relationship that carries a symbolism of Christ and the Church in a manner that a same-sex union cannot do. At least so it appears to me. This is not an argument that same-sex marriage should be forbidden. I only mean to argue that a same-sex marriage seemingly cannot function in the same sacramental or revelatory way that a heterosexual marriage can. My hope is that at some point there will actually be a sensible dialogue about the biblical perspective on the issue, a dialogue that has so far been piecemeal and contentious.

I should also say something about celibacy. My preceding remarks might be taken to suggest that I do not regard celibacy as fully biblical, but that is not at all the case. Celibacy has a very different role in revelatory symbolism, a role that has been central in previous centuries and might be becoming central again. Celibacy, as practiced in the Christian tradition, does not deny the validity and importance of marriage; it merely carries a different message. I will discuss it at an appropriate future time.

In short, the emphasis in these two chapters of Genesis is that sex, especially as humans experience it, was a very good idea. It is specifically human sexuality that was God's answer to the only fault that He could find in all of His works—the isolation, the loneliness of Adam. The theme of sexuality only becomes more intricate as we continue to read the Scripture, but it will ultimately be summarized by Paul when he says, "This mystery is great, but I am speaking about Christ and the church".

e) The Sabbath (Genesis 2:1-3)

The Sabbath day is another metaphor that God uses for revelation, but it is a very different sort of metaphor than sexuality. Human sexuality is a metaphor built into the creation itself, internal to it. But the Sabbath is entirely artificial, external to the creation. Marriage is a metaphor that was instituted by God into human behavior as an addition to sexuality and buried in our psychology. But unlike marriage the Sabbath day did not arise from anything in nature. There is no instinct or inclination to observe the Sabbath. Except in the cultures directly under the influence of the Bible, there is no impulse to observe a Sabbath at all. Adam and Eve might have observed the Sabbath, simply because God suggested it; but if He hadn't said anything, it wouldn't have happened.

But the Sabbath is like sexuality in one important respect. They both happened because God gave the word. In the case of sex, it came into being because God said "Let there be . . ." In the case of the Sabbath, it began to be observed because of a different kind of word: a description and then a prescription; more like "Here's what happened, and what you should do about it is . . ." Nonetheless, both came about by a Word, which means that both came about directly by the will of God, of His choosing. Similarly, they are both held in existence by the Word being spoken. Sexuality as a part of human nature is maintained by God on a day by day basis and continues as long as it is in His will. The Sabbath as a part of human practice is also maintained by God on a day by day basis and continues as long as it is His will.

It may be that He didn't say anything at this point; it is not recorded that He ever spoke to Adam or Eve regarding the desirability of keeping a regular Sabbath. It could be that the oral tradition, which was begun after the Fall to keep alive the knowledge of the beginnings, was the first to mention the Sabbath, that the blessing of the Sabbath was part of the revelation given after the Fall to prepare the way for later revelation on the subject. Other peoples than the Hebrews had some traditions of a cycle of seven days, or of seven years. The Romans divided the sequence of days into sevens but they had separated the cycle of sevens from the creation of things and do not seem to have understood the seventh day as being holy. But the Romans were very late in history; two or three thousand years before the Christ, the Canaanites divided the sequence of years into sevens; this was not an idea connected to the creation of things and did not seem to invoke any special sanctity on the seventh year. Where the ancient seven-fold temporal cycles came from is not clear but it is certainly possible that the oral tradition after the Fall kept some aspects of the creation lingering in people's minds even if most of the details were lost to most people.

At any rate, the keeping of the Sabbath Day was not given in Eden as a commandment to Adam and Eve. There was no blessing offered for keeping it, and no threat of punishment for not keeping it. In fact, there was no indication of any kind at this point as to exactly how God intended the Sabbath to be honored. All that was said is that the Sabbath represented God's resting from the work of creation, and so on that day it would be natural to remember His rest. Nothing else was spelled out, and there was no indication that God would have been upset if something had happened and our first parents had forgotten to take the day off. It is not even clear what resting would have meant to our first parents since it is not clear what working meant to them. The results of sin which turned work into drudgery as described in chapter 3 suggest that the work in the Garden was not the kind of work which wears a person out, not the kind of work which would require any rest. Nor is there any reason to imagine that our first parents would have needed a day to focus their attention on God, as if He were as difficult to remember then as we find Him to be now. So the setting apart of the Sabbath was an entirely superfluous act, not required by the conditions of life, but only and purely God's choice.

But if it played so unimportant a role in Eden, then it was intended for the future; and if the future, then the ultimate future. From the beginning of the world, from the point at which Adam first opened his eyes, there was an eschatological dimension to life. Even in Eden, the Sabbath was a sign of incompleteness, not of completeness. We need only get into Genesis 2 and the creation of Eve to see that God had not stopped work on the "Seventh Day" of Genesis 1. He mentioned the Sabbath, He mentioned the Seventh Day, to reveal to us that something had been left out, and to give a hint of what had been left out. It was a hint of the future need for rest, not only for us, but for God who had not quit working yet. It was a hint of the disaster that was about to transform work into something we would need a rest from. It was a prophecy and a promise, a revelation, as sexuality was also, of meanings that would not be apparent for a long long time. It also shows that the Fall did not take God by surprise.

If the Sabbath was a metaphor of the revelation, what did it symbolize? To Adam and Eve, probably nothing. The whole text of Genesis 1 and 2 would not have existed, even as an oral tradition, until after the Fall. Only after the Fall was an oral tradition needed to keep memory alive, to preserve knowledge, to remember God. All Adam and Eve knew was that God had created, that He was happy with how it had turned out, and they were happy with it too. The Sabbath was the sign of completion only after everything began to unravel. The Sabbath then was the very first promise that the destruction of the original creation would not be allowed to stand; that indeed there would come a day when all that work of those six days was repaired and everything of God's purpose was restored. It was a commitment from God that His work would always be finished, perfected, never abandoned.

We can now make some observations about the Sabbath from hindsight. First we need not take the seventh day of creation as being a literal day. In the next section we will take up the interpretation of the days and nights of creation, but at this point there are good reasons not to think of the first Sabbath as an ordinary twenty-four day, though of course it would have to be literally observed in ordinary twenty-four hour days. We recognize the language instituting the Sabbath as metaphorical language as soon as it mentions God resting. Though it is only much later on in Scripture that it is denied that God can get tired, it is doubtful that Adam or Eve ever imagined that He could be in need of rest. Secondly, in the New Testament, in chapter 4 of his book, the author of Hebrews speaks of the Sabbath rest of God as something that is yet in the future. Finally, when the Pharisees criticized Jesus for working on the Sabbath He replied, "My Father is working until now, and I Myself am working" (John 5:17). All of these parts of Scripture together strongly suggest that the Seventh Day of creation in Genesis 2 was not a literal twenty-four hour day, nor even something that occurred in any sense in time at all. They suggest that it was a metaphor whose meaning reaches all the way to the next creation, the new heavens and the new earth.

The Sabbath was a sign of the end, the completion, the fulfillment of all of God's designs and purposes in creation. It was also a promise of completion, a promise that all of God's will would ultimately be established. The Sabbath, if it was verbalized to our first parents at all, was a hint that the Fall was coming and that God knew there would be more to be done in order to establish what He had made. He knew that the promise which the Sabbath conveyed was going to be required, that there would be days of hard labor which would grind His people back into dust unless He gave them some promise of rest. And so, without giving away the plot of history, He put His promise into the foundation of the world, ready to reassure our first parents as soon as reassurance was needed, that however hard the labor and however great the pain might become, there would be an end to it. Neither Adam and Eve nor their children for many generations would have thought it all through like this, but it was there for them to carry along until people did begin to see what it meant.

From the beginning God took a long-term approach to making Himself known. Relationships and mutual understanding cannot be hurried and God showed at every point in the creation what great care He intended to take in arranging the revelation. He was quite ready, from the very beginning, with a symbol that could not even be partially understood for thousands of years. Adam and Eve, even after the Fall, would not have had any clear idea of what the Sabbath meant, but they would have been able to feel some of the hope in it. As history unfolded, the promise became more sharply focused on the hope of the world that is to come. The Sabbath was a promise of the fulfillment of God's Creation, particularly the fulfillment of the goodness of Creation. All will be well, and all manner of things will be well. That is the meaning and promise of the Sabbath.

f) The System of Physical Law (Genesis 1)

In modern terms, Genesis 1 describes God establishing the laws of physics and biology, the pattern of causes and effects, which would govern the way things work. A biblical view of science sees the physical laws that scientists discover and formulate as expressions of God's interaction with the world. Far from the picture of the Divine Watchmaker winding up the creation and letting it run, it is more like setting up the rules before the game begins, after which we each go to our positions and commence the play. By understanding the laws of science as the provisions of a covenant, we are admitting God as a player in the game rather than as a spectator.

This suggests that there is a certain amount of arbitrariness in the rules, the scientific laws, themselves, and that seems to me to be very clear. Not only was the universe unnecessary, but the sort of universe we live in could have been different in character. In fact, Christian theology has always maintained that the rules of the game were very different in Eden than they are now in New York, and they will be different yet again in the New Jerusalem. God was free to set up the rules just as He chose, and is equally free to change them whenever and however He wishes. In fact, the physical laws apply right now only because God enforces them. This makes it sound as though the physical order of the universe stands on God's whims and that is exactly what I do mean. This also makes the activity of the scientist sound rather precarious, but so it is.

Unfortunately, the times being what they are, these two chapters of Genesis virtually demand some discussion of the Evolutionism/Creationism debate. The issue of the theory of evolution has become so emotional and deep in some circles as to preclude real thought. First, let me say that I personally reject both alternatives. On the one hand, though I am not a biologist, I am a trained mathematician with a strong background in the sciences. As such, I do not feel obligated to be in awe of the current theories of scientists. A theory is merely the best guess, at the present time, of the truth about various physical phenomena.

If I were a practicing biologist my feelings toward the theory of evolution would probably be quite different, but it has long seemed to me that the theory of evolution is neither very convincing, nor very good as a best guess. The theory of evolution lacks the two essential ingredients that make a theory convincing: it does not seem to make predictions that can be experimentally verified, and it does not seem to be open to falsification by experiment. These are all matters for the philosophers of science and the biologists to iron out; I am merely giving my *non-professional* opinion. I have no problem with someone who is convinced of the truth of evolution, except that I cannot share the conviction.

But as to the philosophical or theological thinking that arises from the theory of evolution, my antipathy goes deeper. The fundamental problem with the theory of evolution, that seems to me to be a fatal flaw philosophically, is that it is committed to understanding every biological phenomenon as a result of the struggle to survive. The theory of evolution gives us a view of the world that is ultimately as dog-eat-dog as one could fear in his worst nightmares. No longer can we enjoy a symphony or take pleasure in the beauty of nature without the lurching realization that somehow it must make us better competitors, better survivors, better killers. To thoroughly and seriously believe in the theory of evolution is ironically to simultaneously become less human. This is the price of survival?

These two aspects to the theory of evolution—the scientific theory itself and the theological uses to which it is put—must be kept carefully distinguished. There is one glaring way in which these chapters of Genesis do seem incompatible with the science of the theory of evolution. In the biblical account death played no part in the creation of the animals, and the "survival of the fittest" is out of place in these chapters. This has caused some to think that death, at least of animals, and the food chain as it now exists, are not evil in themselves and were a part of the original scheme of things. Some are confused enough that they try to rationalize death itself into being good in some sense. Others take this as a clear indication that the Bible and the theory of evolution are irreconcilable enemies. My own position on this issue is neither of these, but it is best to explain my thoughts on the subject in a future section when I discuss the Fall. For now I can only say that I do not accept death and the law of competition as part of the original creation, and I do not regard the theory of evolution as relevant to the question of origins. I hope I am being provocative enough to lure you into reading more of these pages.

When we turn to the various attempts to reconcile the theory of evolution with Christian theology, there is at least one line of thought that does it in an illegitimate way. The idea of "emergent evolution" does violence to the Christian understanding of God. However it seems more coherent to put off discussing emergent evolution until the next page on the doctrine of creation, and so I will put off discussing this idea for the moment.

As a non-biologist my opinions regarding the *science* of the theory of evolution, are surely unimportant. I only insert my suspicions about evolution here to make it more clear what I mean by objecting to creationism. The creationists I know seem to regard this debate as black and white, good versus evil, and they suggest that any Christian who does not stand with them has joined with the Enemy. It seems to me critically important that everyone, Christian and non-Christian alike, understand that creationist is not identical to Christian.

Creationism, as it is usually presented, combines bad science with bad theology. Creationism is bad science because it departs at a foundational level from the definition of science. The essence of science is to seek to understand a chain of natural, physical causes and effects leading from one point in time to the next. This is a limitation that science voluntarily assumes and which gives to science both its value and its character. Science excludes miracle and acts of God from its domain, and it is right to do so. This is not to say that miracles do not happen, or even that scientists cannot believe that miracles may occur. In fact, when a scientist does reject the possibility of miracles, it is based on an additional presupposition that is independent of science itself (which I will discuss in a future section). Nonetheless, science is bound to exclude miracles from consideration, to assume that the event it is investigating is not miraculous even if the event is in fact miraculous. The only point of doing a scientific study of an alleged miracle is to try to remove it from the category of miracle and put it into the category of a natural event. To say that we believe in the occurrence of miracles (which I do), is to say that there are events which a scientist practicing science will not be able to understand *on any level*.

A true miracle is by definition an event which is utterly and always beyond the realm of science; it is God exercising His prerogative as Creator to do what He wants to do with what is His, completely outside of the rules of the game that He Himself set up. For a scientist to admit that an event is a miracle is the same as giving up on a scientific explanation of it and quitting the game. In humility, a scientist should admit that he may be playing a losing game, that there may well come a point at which he is face to face with a direct act of God and no other cause for the effect; but he would never be able to detect scientifically that he was at that point. For a scientist to admit that some event is miraculous is the same thing as giving up on science and I do not believe God lets the scientist off the hook. Even in the face of a miracle, God does not wish the scientist to give up looking for the natural causes because He respects the art of science. Science is an expression of the image of God in us, a way that some of us pursue Him, and He does not want us to give up the chase. Creationism fundamentally is the science of quitters, and I do not think God holds such quitters in high esteem. Only He can ring the final bell (blow the final trumpet?) that signals the end of the game. Creationism either forgets this, or misunderstands it, or denies it.

As to why creationism is bad theology, if I understand creationism correctly it holds that the first chapters of Genesis are a relatively straightforward historical account of specific events and *must* be interpreted that way. Hence some Creationists, with a possible exception here and there, seem to claim that viewing Genesis 1 and 2 as an historical narrative, believing in seven twenty-four hour days of creation and a young universe, is obligatory to all who intend to submit to scripture's authority. However the Scripture, and these two chapters of Genesis in particular, do not constitute such an obligation to believers, even to believers who are committed to a conservative view of Scripture. A careful reading of these two chapters, with an attitude and desire to take them literally, leaves me entirely unconvinced of the Creationist position. Though I adopt a covenantal view in my interpretation of Genesis 1 and 2, rather than a merely metaphorical view, it seems clear that taking much of this passage as narrative violates rather than respects the Scripture.

First, the structure of chapter 1 is very much like a poem. The first three days describe the creation of three different "spheres" of reality: on day 1, the domains of light and dark were created; on day 2, the firmament, or sky, was established and the waters on the earth were collected into seas; on day 3, the dry land appeared and the vegetation. It does not matter in the least whether these domains of reality are the way we currently divide it or not. These domains were the most natural way to look at reality, not "primitive" but immediate. The last three days then revisited each sphere and established the inhabitants and rulers in each sphere: on day 4, the sun, moon, and stars to rule the light and dark; on day 5, the birds in the sky and the fish in the sea; and on day 6, the animals and humans on the dry land. The first three days state three themes, and the second three days repeat the themes in the same order with variations. It is a style that appears to be a poem rather than an historical account, even on a superficial reading. Insofar as this passage is to be taken as a description of God's activity, it is more faithful to the text to take it as a poetic account of an activity of God that probably can't be described in literal terms.

Second, the word "day" does not necessarily mean a period of 24 hours, and in this passage seems unlikely to mean a particular period of time for several reasons. As the account proceeds in chapter 2, the creation of man suggests that the days in chapter 1 overlap. The timing of the events in chapter 2 is unclear and not easy to reconcile with the order of events in chapter 1. In 2:4-8 it is suggested that Adam was created before the green plants; the suggestion in 2:18-20 is that God created the animals after He created the man, and these animals specifically included the birds which by chapter 1 were created on the previous day. In 2:4 it says, "This is the account of the heavens and the earth when they were created, in the *day* that the Lord God made earth and heaven." The use of "day" in this verse collects all of the activity of the seven days together and summarizes it as a single "day" and so it can't be taken as a twenty-four hour day at least in this one verse. Then in 2:17 we read, "but from the tree of the knowledge of good and evil you shall not eat, for in the *day* that you eat from it you will surely die." The death indicated here is not merely physical, of course; it is meant to convey all the aspects of the human personality that come under the curse of death: emotional, physical, psychological, spiritual. The death resulting from disobedience only began at the point of disobedience, and was not completed for many hundreds of years after that "day", so in this verse "day" seems to mean the indefinite period of time following a specific event during which it unfolds. This is similar to English usage, just as I might say, "In my day the cold war was going on."

Furthermore, taking the days of Genesis 1 as being twenty-four hour time periods either forces them to have an unreasonable meaning or else forces them to violate their plain meaning. Exactly what is a "day" in the time before the creation of the sun; what exactly was the "morning" and the "evening" on the first few days of creation before there was a sun to

41

rise or set? To require the word "day" to keep its usual meaning in this context seems to fly in the face of the intent of the Scripture. Further it would be strange if the green plants were created the day before the sun, as if God were an absent-minded Creator not quite remembering to put first things first. Or worse yet, duplicating His own work: for on the first day He separated the light from the dark, but on the fourth day He made the sun and the moon in order to do the same thing He had already done, to separate the light from the darkness. The creationist interpretation seems to me to be not at all a literal interpretation of the scripture, but an interpretation which forces the Scripture to say something the creationist wants it to say, and to answer questions which are alien to its context and intent. Christians must understand that taking the Bible literally does not mean taking it superficially. It is never truly a literal interpretation that forces the Bible to say what it simply does not say.

I believe that the Scripture was given as a revelation of God and of things pertaining to God. In particular, I believe that consistency with science has no part in the purpose of Scripture and furthermore is of no importance whatsoever. But suppose it were. Then exactly which century of scientific progress would we require the Scripture to support? Newtonian mechanics or quantum mechanics? Wouldn't there have been inexplicable elements in the Scripture to all who read it before the twentieth century if it were required to support the theory of relativity? Or shouldn't we have to require the Scripture to be consistent with the science of, say, the twenty-third century? After all, we have not arrived at the culmination of science, have we? And how do we know that it isn't perfectly in harmony with the science of the twenty-third century rather than with our "modern" science? These rhetorical questions are meant to show the absurdity of trying to "reconcile" science with a revelation that was intended for all people through all the centuries of our world.

The issue is not whether scripture is as true as science; the issue is whether a revelation of eternal truths about God should contaminate itself by dealing with anything so weak and ephemeral as scientific truth. I would maintain that science is neither true enough, nor reliable enough, for a revelation from God to bother with. So what if the ancients believed in a three-story universe, with hell beneath and heaven above? Do we seriously think that we do not also believe in things that will seem equally silly in a few hundred years? If we received a revelation right now from God, would we even want Him to straighten out our science to the standards of future centuries? Wouldn't it just confuse us with irrelevancies if He did? In short the Evolutionist/Creationist debate seems to me to be a waste of time arguing badly about things that should be more carefully discussed in a less emotional way. It is certainly true that God could have created all things in six 24 hour time periods; or He could have created all things in 14 billion years. We are free scripturally to believe either, but we are not free to insist that ours is the only Christian way to think.

3. The Doctrine of Creation

I do agree with creationists in one sense, however, in spite of the negative comments I made in the previous section. I do believe that the doctrine of creation is the central, the fundamental doctrine on which the rest of Christian theology rests. The polemics of the present age dictate that most works on systematic theology begin with the doctrine of revelation, but for me the doctrine of revelation grows out of the doctrine of creation. Because systematic theology is *systematic* it has to have a beginning and a middle and an end, and because it is a system it is inevitably circular and has no natural beginning or end. Each theologian will seek to present theology in the most natural progression that he can unless the world forces him to modify his style to accommodate its priorities. All I am saying is that for me the most natural place to begin the discussion of what I believe is with the creation.

The primary point of these first two chapters of the Bible is that God created everything, that God and only God is uncreated. This is an idea that is shared by Christians, Jews and Muslims, varying in some of the details, of course. Hence, the doctrine of creation serves to distinguish the eastern from the western religions. The western religions share the view of God as the Creator distinct from His creation. This concept of creation is so central to the character of western religions, and is so vividly emphasized in the Bible, that eastern and western religions cannot be made compatible on this point. Eastern and western religions may have similar looking leaves, they do arrive at similar conclusions about certain ethical dilemmas and give similar answers to some questions, but at their roots they are completely distinct organisms.

How Christians should think about other religions is a question that can be postponed to another time. We focus first on the differences between the east and the west and that will help clarify the similarities we can find. Of course there are variations within western religions on how the doctrine of creation is presented and naturally the presentation here is just one form of the Christian approach, but I present my views on the assumption that the biggest enemy to understanding each other or the truth is vagueness.

The most fundamental and profound idea regarding creation found in Scripture is that God and the creation are entirely distinct from each other. The creation is not merely some extension of God; nor is God merely the totality of what has been created, a sort of cosmic consciousness. The view that creation and Creator are just different sides of the same coin is called *pantheism* and is entirely alien to the biblical view. From a pantheistic viewpoint, if the creation ceased to exist then God would also cease to exist; but from a biblical viewpoint, the creation is utterly unnecessary to God. God did not need to create anything at all in order to be complete in Himself, and if everything that has been created simply disappeared God would go on as perfect as always. This idea is usually expressed by saying that God alone is uncreated. God alone, and no part of anything else, exists absolutely; you and I and stars and demons and crabs exist only at God's command.

To emphasize the point I just made, we believe that God made the Creation *ex nihilo*, out of nothing. He did not use some pre-existing "glop" to make the world as He is imagined doing in the ancient myths; He made it from less than scratch, creating the ingredients as well as the product. Before He made it, there was simply nothing, not even vacuum, not space, not time; these are all as much created things as atoms are. We are all made literally of nothing at all; only He exists in Himself, not depending on anything outside of Himself, not contingent.

The most ancient mythologies that we have, the Sumerian creation myths, have nothing even approaches the biblical understanding of creation. In all the most ancient myths, the gods were all part of a pre-existing, rather formless matrix of existence within which and from which they arise and make the world and stars and such like. To the Sumerians the gods and people all inhabited the same space, the same system of relationships and patterns. In person-hood, the Sumerian gods were very much like people except that the gods were immortal and more powerful. The Canaanite and Indo-European gods were very human as well, and even less mature. Before these most ancient gods created, there was a universe already existing, a boring one but a kind of existence nonetheless. The Egyptian mythology was much more sophisticated in its conception of the gods (in fact, more nearly an eastern than a western religion), but it still did not imagine the gods as creating all things. In every case, the primeval god or gods were part of some pre-existing matrix of reality.

The gods of the non-biblical ancient world, except in Egypt, were more like the super-heroes of the modern comic books than like anything Christians, Jews, or Muslims could accept as God. Among ancient literature, the Bible is utterly alone in its conception of God as standing apart from His creation. The first chapter of Genesis seems to make a point of asserting that God created all those things that the other ancients were most inclined to associate with their gods and to worship: the sun, the moon, the stars, the seas. The Bible presents all those gods as mere creatures on the same plane as we are, and emphatically not on the same level as Yahweh, the Creator. From its first words, Genesis 1 challenged paganism.

The other side of the coin to the emphasis on the distinction between creature and Creator is the emphasis on the actual existence of the Creation. The Scripture insists that the material universe is not some kind of illusion. Though we might well define existence as "the state of being in the mind of God" and though we speak of being made of nothing, the balancing side of the equation is that the universe is not nothing anymore. It is part of the glory of God that He is powerful enough to make creatures that stand apart from Himself and look back at Him. From a biblical perspective, attaining union with God, attaining "nirvana", can only be done from inside creation. Our material existence is something that the Bible describes as being fundamental to who we are, not as a delusion to be escaped.

Though eastern and western spirituality both talk about seeking a "unity with God", they are talking about very different things. The eastern form of enlightenment envisions the complete merging of the creature and the Creator, more like a cup of water uniting with the ocean as it is poured in; the individual creature ceases to be distinct as an individual. In contrast, the revelation given through Scripture portrays sexuality as an image of the unity of creature and Creator. The Christian seeks to be "one" with God, but the unity the Christian seeks is something like the unity of husband and wife, a merging of intimacy rather than a merging of identity. Fundamental to the relationship between Creator and creature is that they are two, they stand apart and come together and stand apart again. Just as in marriage, it is the distinction between the two, their "twoness", which gives meaning to their becoming one. To make the creation an extension of the Creator, or to make the Creator an extension of the creation, destroys the glory and beauty of what the Bible describes.

On the other hand, there is a lot of popular non-sense these days that overstates the significance of being physical. For example, it is common to portray angels in movies as longing to experience the senses, the sensuality, of being physical, as if God had created angels as an order of being with no joy in their own being, whose very existence was invented as an arid and shallow thing. The Bible *does* picture the dead in Christ as longing to be re-clothed in flesh (still ignoring the question of the existence and nature of the soul), to have again a physical body, but that is because we are essentially physical, to the center of our being. For us to be dead, to be bodiless, is to be deprived of a crucial part of our being. But the same is not true of angels, whatever kind of beings they are. The angels have an integrity, a wholeness, of their own; they do not envy us anything we are (though there may be exceptions to this general rule we will get to later).

Pantheism has one other form that disguises itself as a legitimate Christian belief. Emergent evolution is the idea that the creation is in a process of evolving toward God, that the universe as a whole will produce God in some sense, or attain unity with God, by the natural process of evolution. Though some prominent theologians like de Chardin have championed this viewpoint, it is alien to Christianity. It makes the Creator the one with the derivative nature, whose existence is somehow contingent on us rather than the other way around. But the really glaring disconnection between emergent evolution and Christian faith is in the area of grace. We will postpone a more careful discussion of grace, but for now the point is that the unity with God that we expect to attain is a unity that is derived from God much as our very existence is derived from God. We do not grow up into Him. He comes down to us and takes us back up with Him.

The Creation is unnecessary to God. If everything that exists simply vanished as if it had never had been, God would in no way be diminished. We assert that the Creation is unnecessary to God, but we never suppose that the Creation is therefore unimportant to God. In fact, God created things so enthusiastically that it would be more accurate to say that God made all things out of joy rather than that He made them out of nothing. God need not have created, but once He did create there was no going back for Him. The act of creation was also an act of commitment. It is only His commitment to us and to all things that keeps us from returning to nothingness.

Nihilism, if it means anything at all, assumes that things go on existing without God paying any attention to them. And Nihilists are right in their conclusions: if God has indeed ceased to heed or care for the creation, it would be better that it not exist. We know in our hearts that our meaning, our significance, our value rests in God's commitment to us; without it we are even less than vacuum. But we exist because God has named us, He has announced us as existing by the power of His word; and we cannot cease to exist as long as He calls us by name. Death is not a way out of existence, not so much because we have an immortal soul, but because we do not have God's *permission* to cease to exist. Or perhaps we could say that the soul is just God speaking our names after our bodies have died. He is the God of Abraham and Isaac and Jacob because He continues to say their names and His Word is the foundation of their present existence.

We continue to exist because God keeps creating us from nothing. Every moment is the same as the beginning of all things. Every moment God says again "Let there be light" and because of this and no other reason, you and I and all things exist right now. And then He does it again. And again. And again. The idea that He maintains by the word of His power the whole universe is another reason that Genesis 1 does not describe a particular period of seven days. Genesis 1:1 describes every single instant. Genesis 1:1 happens right now. And right now. And right now. And so on for all the nows that will ever exist. "This is the day that the Lord has made" is true at the very deepest possible level. This is what it means to say that the creation's existence is contingent. Without God's word of command it would simply collapse into nothing at all, vanish.

But the final point of distinction between eastern and western religions is decisive to my mind in showing how irreconcilable they are. The Bible says that the Creation, physical existence, as originally conceived by the Creator, is *good*. There is *nothing* intrinsically evil about material existence. It is not our physical body that prevents us from being fully spiritual; it is the fact that that we are corrupt and evil that prevents us from being spiritual. It is good that we have bodies, and the rest of scripture indicates that we hope to live for an eternity in some kind of material body. Not only does God repeatedly pronounce the Creation to be good, but also He continues to love the creation. Granted that He does not come right out and say so at this point (He does say so later), the fact that this is the description of a covenant implies that He loves it. With God, covenants are always founded on love. Where there is a covenant, there is love, and where there is love there is at least a tacit covenant.

The idea that material existence is itself tainted or unclean originally infected the Christian church from a pagan source, the Greeks. The Platonists regarded our existence in physical bodies as something to be transcended and escaped by the wise. Though the Church has always rejected this idea in its doctrine, the influence of the idea remains with us even to the present. The Fall into sin may have corrupted the whole world, but our hope of redemption is in physical terms. The uncleanness of the present physical order is not inherent to it; it is an uncleanness that we put there and that will be cleansed. In contrast, it is an essential part of eastern religions that unity with God is attained only by escaping the delusion of physical existence. The physical creation is evil in the sense that it hinders us from understanding or merging with God.

The Greek language itself can be a source of confusion on this point. The Greek word translated as "flesh" means both "the sinful nature" as well as "the physical body", and the Greek word translated as "world" means both "the human order which is in opposition to God" as well as "the created order". When we read the New Testament we must be careful to distinguish the two meanings or we will misinterpret what we read. The Bible as a whole amply shows that the two meanings are to be kept distinct.

I am now done with discussing these two chapters of Genesis. They take an inordinate amount of space for their consideration because they state most of the themes that will be elaborated in the rest of the Scripture. Genesis 3 is foundational as well, but before we move on to chapter 3 let's pause a bit to summarize what I've tried to say so far: I am suggesting a third alternative to the standard interpretations of these two chapters as history or as allegory; I am suggesting that we interpret them as the terms of a covenant. What we read here is God creating a way to relate to existence. It is not a fable; it is not a chronological narrative; it is a marriage license.

B. Breaking the Covenant of Creation (Genesis 3:1-19)

1. Introducing the Characters

I discussed the historicity of chapter 1 but left that consideration aside when I discussed chapter 2. At this point then, as we prepare to consider chapter 3 and the Fall, I want to re-open the question of the historical nature of these events. Were there in fact a real Adam and Eve, first parents of the human race? And did the events in this chapter actually occur, or is this a mythical retelling of something cosmic?

I believe that the answer to the second question should be: both. In our culture we are accustomed to thinking of myth as being the antithesis of historical narrative, but the two are not really mutually exclusive (as C. S. Lewis and J. R. R. Tolkien have argued). A myth is not necessarily a fiction, and there are good reasons to understand chapter 3 as portraying actual people and actual events, but portraying them in a mythical way. The mythical form has at least two characteristics which distinguish it from an historical narrative: first, a mythical narrative is under no obligation to be complete in any sense; and second, a mythical narrative is under no obligation to give any accounting for super-natural events. An historical narrative will typically try to account for new characters as they are introduced, and will usually try to give some explanation for super-natural events, acknowledging their unusual character and giving some reason for believing them nonetheless.

Who is this guy, who are his parents, what country did he come from, and why did he end up in this story? These are all questions that an historical narrative could be expected to address. In historical narrative, when unusual events are finally simply attributed to God as beyond natural explanation, there is at least an admission that the event does need some faith for believing it. An historical narrative is fully aware of the boundary between the natural and the super-natural, between normal experience and the transcendent, and seeks to assure the reader that, though the occurrence is hardly believable, it nonetheless did happen.

The mythical narrative, on the other hand, gives no quarter to unbelief, makes no distinction between the ordinary and the extra-ordinary, and does not bother introducing its characters unless it is necessary to do so for the sake of the story. In a mythical narrative, the focus is on the event, which is assumed to be of supreme and cosmic significance. Characters are brought in as needed and there is no obligation to account for them because it is the event that is important. The line between natural and super-natural simply disappears. If a snake begins to talk in a mythical narrative, why, then it begins to talk and you are on your own; you must take it or leave it because no explanation will be given.

By these two criteria, then, Genesis 3 is a mythical narrative from the first word. The serpent appears from nowhere, acting in a most super-natural fashion, with no introduction and no accounting for his origin or his ability to speak. In fact, though there may be hints later in the Scripture, no definitive answer is ever given to where the devil came from. The origin of the Tempter, and therefore the origin of evil, is left blank. All we are really told in this chapter about the beginning of evil is that evil did not originate with the human race. Evil is like an infection which was spread to us from the outside. Who got it first or how he got it remains a mystery. The grim but important fact for us is that we got it.

On the other hand, myth is not the same as fiction. To call Genesis 3 a myth, which I do, is not to say that Adam and Eve had no actual existence. On the contrary there are very good reasons to believe that Adam and Eve actually existed, not as metaphors for the beginning of the human race, but as two flesh and blood individuals who went on to become parents of the rest of us in the ordinary way.

A myth does not attempt to explain the events it portrays in ordinary terms. Rather, the events that it portrays are meant to explain of some other larger question of deep and abiding significance. It is very clear that the purpose of Genesis 3 is to explain how we got to the desperate condition we are in considering the perfect condition we started with. If God is so good and powerful, and the creation was so pleasing to Him, why is there so much pain and evil all around us now? This is a question which, to my mind, is at the center of the Biblical revelation and is one piece of the evidence that convinces me the Bible is a genuine revelation.

Some use the "problem of evil" as proof that Christianity must be false, but they forget it is the Bible that invented the problem of evil, that rubbed our noses in it until we had to notice it was a problem. The Bible poses the dilemma of good and evil deliberately in such an extreme way that it virtually seals off all possible answers: the Creator is absolutely good in Himself; the Creator is the absolute origin of all that exists and has absolute power over it; and the creation was absolutely good from the beginning with no hint of pain, suffering, evil, no taint of death whatsoever.

And yet now the creation has become seriously corrupted, and the picture it paints of this corruption is so relentlessly grim as to silence all suspicion that the Bible is trying to gloss over anything that doesn't fit with its main theme of the goodness of God. How then can such evil exist at all with such a good and all-powerful Creator? Yet the Bible insists on maintaining these two seemingly incompatible axioms: the goodness and power of God and the total corruption of nature. Scripture emphasizes these two themes as if it were trying to make us notice the apparent contradictions. It is so vivid that it seems to argue against itself, all the while insisting that if we are patient and willing to trust a complete answer can be given eventually. Such a plot would be inexplicable in a merely human book.

Hence when we find a myth in the Bible it follows that it must be a *biblical* myth; that is, it must be a myth that explains, or starts to explain, its conundrum in its own biblical terms. The Bible, as we read from Genesis up to the gospels, relentlessly places God in an historical context. In any pagan myth, it is the remoteness of the event in time and place that lends the mythical tone to the narrative, and that makes the blurring of the boundary between natural and super-natural more palatable. But the Bible does not allow any boundary between natural and super-natural, period. One of the over-riding themes in the biblical narrative is that the super-natural is always immediately at hand, always threatening to break through, and when the super-natural does invade it is very matter of fact and frequently cloaked in natural camouflage.

Rather than using the remoteness of time and place to make the mythical super-natural element more "believer friendly", the Bible tries to minimize that remoteness. Though Eden is lost to us geographically, some of the nearby rivers still exist and are still familiar to the general reader. And though the Fall did indeed happen in the remote past, you can see how we are linked to it by a series of ancestors that are named and whose foibles are occasionally remarked on. To think of the Fall as fiction runs counter to the whole character of Scripture.

Hence we see the myth gradually drifting into ordinary historical narrative. The central hero and heroine of the myth descend from paradise to be mere people who have children in the ordinary way, and these children fight in the ordinary way and end up as the first criminal and crime victim in the ordinary way. As the myth concludes, the resulting narrative is so depressingly ordinary, so thoroughly a narrative, as to leave no question that the myth is seamlessly and continuously joined with the history, a single fabric. Adam and Eve, who played such a larger-than-life role in ruining the universe, come down from their exalted status as the Original Myth and now carry on with such ordinary lives over their next millennium that there is nothing much of interest to say about them.

Another reason for rejecting the account of the Fall as being fictional is that myths were never intended as fiction. That our culture regards myth as equivalent to fairy tale is partly prejudice. The ancients invented many myths but they did not understand themselves as telling mere stories. The ancient myths were explanations, they were accounts that were meant to be taken seriously in a world in which "factual" could mean quite extraordinary things in remote times and remote places.

The myth was always remote in time or space, and the remoteness was to help account for the strangeness of the events it portrayed. But mythical events were meant to be taken as real events in remote time and space that explained real events in the present time and place. In this sense, mythology was the ancient equivalent of science: the myths were the theories that gave the reasons for the things in our daily experience. They were as serious as science is today. We are, naturally, prejudiced in favor of science as the preferable means of explaining the nature of reality, but the question is not whether myth is better than science or not. The point is that myths served in the ancient world as an explanation and were not meant a fiction. Nor was the account of the Fall intended to be taken as a fiction; to take it as fiction (without some other just cause) is merely to express our cultural biases.

But weren't the other myths of the ancients actually not historically true? Probably not, though some of them, such as the stories of the Trojan War, have turned out to have a surprising amount of historical content when the opportunity to check them finally occurred. But whether the pagan myths are historical or not is irrelevant to the issue here. The question is: what was the intent of the biblical myth? Did the author (the Holy Spirit, I assume, but some other ancient people if you wish) intend to say that the events were merely fiction, mere metaphors telling us cosmic truths in a purely symbolic way? Not if He were telling a myth to ancient people in the way of the ancients.

But if the Holy Spirit were revealing an historical event, why would He have chosen to couch it in a myth? For one thing, because the story was too big for a narrative. There was too much background for a straightforward story. It was a story that would require a great deal of telling to make it coherent if it were told as a simple narrative. The background of the serpent, at the very least, would demand some accounting for and that would open another story that must surely be cosmic in scale. No, the story of the Fall from Eden, by its nature, required the mythical form, not because it was fiction but because a background narrative would have only added an enormous amount of confusing and irrelevant detail. Sure we would all like to know where the serpent came from, how he became evil, and why he came to Eden in the first place, but knowing such things would only take our focus off the important facts of the event: that we are in these dire straits despite the absolute goodness and power of the Creator and the absolute goodness of the creation.

Finally, Adam and Eve should be understood as real people because covenants are not made with fictional characters; God does not enter into covenants with symbols or metaphors. If Adam and Eve were not two individual and real people, my own direct ancestors in the ordinary biological sense, then the whole point of the covenant vanishes. If there was no actual Adam or Eve then there was no actual covenant and the transition from good to evil is left as unexplained as ever, a myth that draws attention to a question and then utterly fails to explain what it forces us to confront. For the Covenant is essential to the story. The Fall makes sense only from the viewpoint of the Covenant. Why was the choice made by a single man and a single woman of such universal weight that the Bible portrays it as killing the whole universe? The answer rests entirely on the Covenant. Without the Covenant Adam was just a man acting as he saw fit and there is no reason why his choice should have anything to do with me or you.

We might as well finish the discussion of the origin and motivation of Satan as much as possible now. Disregarding the mythical mode of the passage, modern sensibilities compel us to ask who Satan was and where he came from. How can we believe in the literal existence of such a creature? Why would he bother to come to Eden with the intent of spoiling it all? These are questions that cannot be answered because the Scripture never gives more than a hint at the answers. One tradition was that Satan had been the highest of the angels, so glorious that he became proud and thought that he could himself be god. His attempted coup led to a war and in the ensuing war between the angels and the fallen angels who joined him, his forces were driven out of heaven, wherever that is. Part of Satan's strategy then became to take this bit of ground, the world we live in, as his base of operations, and us as his prisoners and his food supply.

There is nothing intrinsically unbelievable about this story. It is common to argue among the intelligentsia about the existence of extra-terrestrials and about the existence of other universes. It is not considered intrinsically unbelievable that other whole systems of nature might exist. On the contrary, it is popular in some circles to believe in such things. And here in the Bible we have a possible candidate for just such a one of these extra-terrestrials to examine. Satan is very clearly portrayed as a creature who is not of flesh and blood, not of matter in the ordinary sense, a creature who is not a part of our visible universe at all but part of a different system of existence governed by other physical laws, which for lack of any better term we call "spiritual". If one admits the possible existence of extra-terrestrials and of other universes, then one must admit the possible existence of spirits, of angels, of demons. The very materialist skeptical scientists, say Isaac Asimov as an example, who argue for the existence of other life in the universe are simultaneously making belief in the devils and angels more respectable, whether they intend to or not (and clearly Asimov didn't).

As to the serpent's motivation in the temptation, that is equally blank. One tradition from the early church taught that when God created humanity and appointed us as head over creation, He was including the angelic realm under our dominion (this might imply that the angelic realm is connected to this creation somehow rather than being an entirely different one). The tradition goes that Satan was jealous of the glorious position given to the human race and resentful of being placed in the service of such pathetic creatures. It was his jealousy and pride that led to his fall, for by this account he was second only to God in the glory of his nature, though still a mere creature.

It is as good an explanation as any. If other such creatures may exist then there is simply no way to exclude any theory regarding our relationship to them as intrinsically impossible. Our ignorance is just too great. The Scripture offers one of the few coherent possible ancient accounts of what our connection may be to such creatures. To merely dismiss the biblical account as unbelievable is simply prejudice. There may be reasons I do not know to doubt the account. Some, as their basic axiom, simply do not believe the Bible as a reliable record regardless. But given a basic belief in the possibility of revelation and the basic belief that there may be aliens in our very strange universe, there is no compelling reason to disbelieve the historicity of the Fall.

2. The Temptation (Genesis 3:1-6)

And so the serpent appears from nowhere, with no introduction and no explanation. We are not even given a description of this serpent except that he was subtle. He is the most subtle of the beasts, but his subtlety does not reside in great or deep intelligence or wisdom; rather his subtlety lies in his ability to contrive elaborate scams by which he can deceive and manipulate others into doing his will. His subtlety is psychological rather than intellectual. Later Paul will say that our warfare with the forces of evil lies in standing against the *schemes* of the devil, the psychological warfare he wages against us, the propaganda of the spirit. Spiritual warfare is not for those who are spiritually asleep, nor for those who are inexperienced. But of course Adam and Eve were exactly that: inexperienced.

With the introduction of the serpent we are encountering a metaphor. The Scripture does not say, and very few have imagined, that Satan actually *is* a snake. On the other hand, whatever Satan actually is, he is portrayed as ordinarily not visible to us; so if he were to attempt conversing with Eve he presumably had to devise some way of becoming visible to our eyes. Thus in the biblical account he chose the form of a serpent.

It is preferable to think of the serpent as a dragon rather than as a snake. He appeared as an un-named creature, a creature that was not among the ones Adam had met and named previously, a creature that neither Adam nor Eve had encountered before and with whom they had no relationship, no covenant tie, a creature over whom they had assumed no dominion. Satan came as a stranger to them and, inexperienced as they were with the creation, it did not seem strange to them that he should suddenly appear. They were like children and nothing is strange to children the way it is to an adult. Children have little idea of what they can expect from the world or what is possible and so they accept quickly whatever happens. This dragon came to speak to children, people who were presumably created as adults but were infants in experience.

Some have argued that the manner of the temptation and Fall shows that Eve was created to be under Adam's dominion. These interpreters would say that the Fall didn't happen until Adam made his choice because the woman's choice was not authoritative. She was not the head over creation; her husband was the head, and therefore any choice she made had to be ratified by him, just as later the choices of women under the Law of Moses had to be ratified by husband or father. It seems to me that these interpreters are reversing cause and effect, taking the results of the Fall and then reading them back into the conditions before the Fall.

It is more logical to view the temptation as a well-executed strategy aimed at striking both the man and the woman where they were the weakest. It was the inexperience of both Adam and Eve that was the central weakness the dragon sought to exploit. Their inexperience with respect to evil was a fact that could only be cured by encountering evil, of course. There had to be a first time and the dragon provided it; and the logical choice for the attempted deception would be the one who had the least experience, the least knowledge of the exact restriction placed on the central tree: Eve. Eve would be the easier to deceive because she had not been there when God had planted the tree and given the command; she had heard it second hand from Adam. It isn't clear how long she had existed before the dragon appeared to her, but if it were shortly after her creation she would naturally be more vulnerable to misinformation.

But Adam would be the easier one to actually tempt, and his weakest spot would be in regard to his companionship with Eve and her welfare. He had just come from the experience of naming the animals and the realization that in the whole creation he was really alone among all the other creatures; and then the overwhelming delight and relief at Eve's creation and the joy of no longer being alone, an aloneness which even God had pronounced as being "not good". To face the danger Eve was in, and the risk of losing her, was Adam's vulnerable point. Thus, when he had to choose between obeying what he knew God had commanded at the risk of losing Eve to death (whatever that was), or disobeying God and joining her in death but at least not losing her, he chose to reject God and keep Eve. Satan's method of temptation was an attack on both Adam and Eve, the joint heads over creation; but the strategy he chose happened to put the final choice to sin or not in Adam's hands.

It is important to realize what it means that Eve was deceived into eating the forbidden fruit. She was tricked; her act was foolish but was not open, willful rebellion against God. Every word the dragon spoke engaged Eve on a level for which she had had no preparation, on a level entirely outside her experience. The first question—"Has God said, 'You shall not eat from any tree of the garden'?"—would have been disorienting to one who had never encountered exaggeration or misinformation before. It would even have been difficult for a modern person, as accustomed to lies and half truths as we are daily in the television and newspapers. A well-aimed, exaggerated question is a powerful and effective tool for throwing the unwary off balance; the mind is easy to disorient, and once off balance it has a kind of inertia that carries it further off balance. It is the small thing that knocks us down, just as a small branch is more likely to trip us than a fallen tree trunk. We are easy creatures to manipulate, even when we are cynical, and much more so when we have no clue as to what might be happening. Eve would have been easy prey, as her response shows; she didn't remember the exact words of the command she had received. Her disorientation had begun.

But the dragon's second sentence would be entirely bewildering—"You surely shall not die"—a direct contradiction of what God had said. Lies, deception, exaggeration were all alien to Eve's life. What does one do with a contradiction? There had never been such a thing before and this statement from the dragon must have been very confusing. He followed it up by imputing to God motives which would be meaningless to her: that God was self-serving, jealous of His own wisdom over against theirs, and plotting to withhold a desirable thing from them for His own selfish purposes. All of these ideas were included in the dragon's statement and would strike a resonant chord in any of us.

Who among us does not instinctively feel some suspicion and distrust and fear when we hear such an accusation, even against a friend. We have all been betrayed at one time or another, and the pain of the memory makes us the more ready to entertain suspicions, to be careful even with our closest friends that we not be hurt again. No such resonant chord would have been struck within Eve. She had no experience of betrayal or selfishness or jealousy. The dragon's words were gibberish to her. He was using words that she would never have heard before and putting them together in a way that she could not have imagined, putting them together in a way that was conceptually alien but that would seem to hint at a meaning. And she had heard the word "evil" applied to the Tree, but it had no content for her, just a name for a tree. The state produced in Eve would have been one of perplexity and confusion, and in this state of mind she ate the forbidden fruit. But this is not sin, not yet.

Sin did not enter, the Covenant with creation was not broken, until Adam saw what Eve had done and chose to join her rather than obey

God. That is why later in Romans 5 Paul would say that sin entered into the world through one *man*. What would have happened then if Adam had refused to join Eve? The Fall would not have happened. Eve had not truly sinned, and I imagine that she could have been rescued from her folly by some means less than a redemption. It is easier to undo a foolish mistake than outright rebellion. But once Adam saw what she had done and perceived the clear choice before him, then a deliberate rejection of God, a deliberate choice to love Eve over God, was made. Adam became the first idolater and Eve became the first idol.

Some have argued that Adam was with her when she took the fruit, perhaps even while she was speaking with the dragon, and that the first sin was actually the sin of Adam not asserting his authority over Eve. They argue that Adam should have made her stop listening to the dragon, and that in not interfering with the temptation he had abdicated his God given authority over his wife. They argue that Adam's failure in eating the fruit began first as a failure in exercising his proper headship over Eve.

The wording of the story does suggest that Adam was with Eve during the temptation, but this interpretation of the sin of Adam reads back into Eden ideas about the nature of marriage that belong to our own corrupted condition. There is no information given on how the relationship between Adam and Eve functioned on a practical level, but reading back into Eden a worldly view of authority is unacceptable. Such an interpretation assumes that the use of force, even verbal force as opposed to physical force, in the exercise of authority would have been natural and obligatory to Adam, as it may be to us. But even if Adam was with Eve, and even if it were true that he had been given that kind of authority over her, would it have occurred to him to forcibly put a stop to the temptation, to stop her from taking the fruit by force, when no force had ever been used? To imagine that force, even gentle force, could have been a natural part of Eden is on the same level as imagining that death could have been a natural part of Eden; it gives away the goodness of creation and compromises the dilemma of our condition.

The chain of events that culminated in Adam being the one who made the fatal choice may have been something of an accident, a result of the peculiar logic of temptation, but it determined all that came after. Since a man had brought sin into the world, and death through sin, it should be a man who would deliver it. Had it been the woman who had opened the door to sin, then wouldn't it all have been set up differently when God imposed the rules which governed how death was to be administered? If sin had come into the world through one woman, then wouldn't the man have been placed in subjection to her, and wouldn't the Incarnation have involved a woman savior? This is all entirely speculation, of course; we can never know what would have happened. However, the argument that Paul later appears to use is that it was because a *man* had introduced sin into the world that a *man* came to deliver it. My view works against the pride which men take in their imagined exalted position and authority. But shouldn't any interpretation of Scripture that supports any kind of prideful attitude be automatically suspect?

It is important to understand that the dragon did not sneak in to Eden from whatever universe he came from, as if he went behind God's back and pulled a fast one on Him. The dragon got in to Eden because God let him get in to Eden, and he spoke with Eve because God let him speak with Eve. Whether or not Adam was there, whether or not you think Adam should have interfered with the conversation, God was there and He didn't interfere. It is strange how God chooses which events to meddle in. Occasionally He chose to do great and dramatic miracles when all seemed lost, but at the incipient events, when a little interference from Him would have done so much good and saved so much trouble, He seems to have typically had a hands-off policy. He goes to astonishing lengths to rescue us all from the Fall, but wouldn't a little effort on His part have prevented the whole mess right there at the beginning? Why didn't He just walk up and call the dragon's bluff, saying something like "Where do you get off telling her I'm holding out on her, you ugly old dragon?" Why is God always silent just when speaking up could do so much good?

The answer is, "I do not know"; but there are some answers that are pretty clearly false. It is not that God needed to know what they would do under temptation, whether they would fold or hold true. It is not that they had to justify themselves to God by obeying His one command. In one sense though, I think, I *think*, that God kept a hands off policy because it did not ultimately matter what they did and He wanted to show us, and perhaps the dragon as well, that it didn't matter. This sounds harsh, I know, as if I thought God didn't care what happens to us, whether we suffer or not, etc. but I do not mean it this way. What I mean is that God is so powerful, so totally in control and unflappable that whatever happened, whatever happens then or now or tomorrow, He will accomplish absolutely everything that He intends and intended.

He didn't have to hedge His bets; He didn't have to interfere with the roll of the die; He didn't have to rig the election to have the creation He wanted. But we didn't know that; the angels maybe had an inkling of it; the dragon certainly didn't know it. God wanted to display His power, the power that can accomplish whatever it will even while letting us do whatever we will. Adam could choose to love God more than Eve, or he could choose to love Eve more than God; but whatever he chose, the final outcome would be absolutely the good and perfect will of God. We can take the easy road or we can take the hard road, but we will arrive at God's planned destination, and we need to know that. He could have just told us so, but this is the kind of information that is only known by demonstration and experience. I realize my explanation is inadequate and unsatisfying, possibly even appalling, but it may be the best answer there is, and it is certainly the best I can give.

At this point Adam had broken the Covenant with God, and this carried Eve with him, and this carried the whole of our world with them. But why should this be? Why was the rest of creation the unwitting and innocent victim of Adam's choice? In part, because this is how a covenant relationship works. Or, in other words, because that is how God set it up to work. As a bearer of the Covenant, as a representative or as a ruler, when Adam sinned he brought everything down with him. It is possible that God need not have set the Creation up in this way. Perhaps He need not have set up His relationship with the creation in the form of a covenant. That He did set it up this way says a lot about who He is and what He loves, but most importantly it says a lot about how He loves. He loves people and things in a covenantal way, not in a so-called "personal" or individualistic way.

That is the kind of God He is and the rest of the Scripture fills in the details of what it all means. And one of the things that the Covenant means, one of the specifics that the Bible teaches about our relationship to God, a teaching that is begun so vividly by the results of the Fall, is that God relates to us and to the creation in a communal way rather than as separate isolated pieces. The communal aspect of the biblical view of relationships is an aspect that has been lost by our extremely individualistic society. Americans especially, but western people generally, all expect to stand alone before God, to be judged on our own with no reference to our brothers or sisters or pets or whatever, but it is not that simple. No one, from Adam on, has ever been judged in pure isolation from everyone else.

3. The Consequences and Limits of Death

a) Shame (Genesis 3:7-13)

When Adam made his choice, the covenant with creation, the whole relationship of God with His creation, was broken. We learn a lot about what a covenant relationship means and how it operates as we watch the web unravel. We also learn part of what the Bible means when it talks about death, and by contrast we learn what life was supposed to have been in the original creation.

The very first result of disobedience was shame at their nakedness. The striking thing about their shame is how quickly it appeared. They had been naked all of that time, however long it had been since Eve's creation, with no shame. It would seem that they would be able to remember just one hour before this moment. How could they go from no shame at all to hiding in the bushes in such a short time? This dramatic, and somewhat inexplicable, change shows that death is fundamentally a multi-faceted thing—physical, emotional, psychological, and mental—but first of all psychological. Physical death would wait some centuries to accomplish its slow work, but that Adam became more or less instantly ashamed of his nakedness shows that he was dead on the inside however long it might take to work its way outward.

The Scripture uses a particularly helpful phrase to explain the suddenness of the change from no shame into total shame: "their eyes were opened". Suddenly they could see something they had never seen before. They had eaten of the Tree of Knowledge of Good and Evil and now they knew evil for the first time. It would be a mistake to suppose it was their nakedness that was evil. It was their eyes that were evil, that had been transformed from lamps of the body to let in light into lamps of the body that were themselves darkness. From this point on, our eyes were the issue. From this point on the issue was making our eyes once more capable of opening to goodness: "those who have eyes to see, let them see".

Since it affects every aspect of our being, death, in the context of these few chapters of Genesis, means something like "the ruin of personhood". When Adam sinned, he died; that is, his personhood ended and only the corpse remained, and that corpse began to decay immediately. This is the origin of ghost stories, of our present fascination with zombies and vampires: they are projections, metaphors, of who we all really are, of who we know ourselves to be.

When I say their personhood died, what I mean is that they were no longer *persons* in the sense they had been created to be. They were the vestige of persons, the shadows, the ghosts of what had been persons, and those ghosts carried on like persons out of habit. Their bodies continued to live on for a while, but the process of death began at the very core, in their hearts, in their intellects, their emotions, their self-image, their wills, all the components that go into making us who we are. Nothing in them was untouched; nothing was left actually and truly alive in them.

The life that continued in their bodies was an illusion; death was in every breath that they took, as it is in us all, just as if they were on their deathbeds all their days waiting for the end to come, as are we all. When we read about Adam and Eve suddenly needing to hide in the bushes it should send chills over us, for it is ourselves we are reading about. This is not a story about those two people; it is the story of us, of what we might have been but aren't, of what we have become. We can not now know what life was like for Adam and Eve before the Fall, but the so-called life that we live now is what the Bible calls death, and the single word that captures it all is shame.

It was not so much that Adam and Eve were ashamed of their bodies; rather, the shame they showed with respect to their bodies was an outworking of the shame they felt about themselves on the whole. All the fig leaves of shame come from the same tree, the Tree of the Knowledge of Good and Evil: we feel fundamentally and at the deepest level of our being that we are creatures that should be ashamed, that any impartial judge would find us gross and disgusting. Our shame is not necessarily attached to a specific sin, nor even to a sense of guilt. We need not do anything to earn the sense of shame; we simply have it always in us, a cloud in the back of our consciousness, the mark of death.

Shame does not always appear as embarrassment about our physical bodies; sometimes the shame is centered on some other aspect of our being. In our culture the ones who are particularly physically beautiful soon learn that they can use their beauty and nakedness to achieve success or to manipulate others, and for these people shame dwells in some other area of their existence. When we call a person "shameless" what we really mean is that we think they ought to feel shame for something that they don't; but there is no truly shameless person. Usually what is going on inside us on the emotional or psychological level comes out in how we treat our bodies, but sometimes it is the reverse. Sometimes we behave toward our bodies in a way that attempts to compensate for or alter our psychological pain. A person who is outwardly "shameless" is a person who is "self-medicating", who is so overwhelmed by a sense of shame on some other level that compensation is the only alternative.

The physical dimension of our personhood is where we act out the depths of our personhood, but the connection between our internal and external selves is complex, and if shame does not express itself physically for some reason, then it will be expressed in another way. Fundamentally, to be a "sinner" means to be a creature that defines itself by shame. Shame is more fundamental than guilt, and a more accurate measure of our spiritual state. We may deceive ourselves about guilt, we can manipulate our conscience, we can rationalize nearly any behavior; but we can never truly escape shame and the fear of shame. This is why the last judgment was described in these terms: "if you are ashamed of Me before men then I will be ashamed of you before My Father."

But God created us to be naked and unashamed. Religious people sometimes discuss nakedness as if the nakedness itself were the sin, but they entirely fail to grasp what is written here. We were created to be naked; it is sin that has made nakedness impossible for us, or else has spoiled nakedness so that we cannot understand it or value it. Clothing is the result of sin, not nakedness. Clothing is the sign of sin. Nudity is not sin, but it is dishonest; it pretends that sin, that death, that shame, can be healed just by going backward, by throwing away its badge, as if acting without shame physically would be enough to cure the shame we bear in our spirits, as if acting without shame physically might make us innocent. Nudity, in the present life in this world, is a lie; it is a way of saying that we do not need God to clothe us, that we can heal ourselves, that we have nothing to be ashamed of, that we are OK without Him, that we didn't really die, that we aren't really dead.

Clothing is a symbol of all that is wrong with us and with the world, with what is still wrong with us and the world despite all we can do. Disposing of a symbol has no effect on the reality it symbolizes; it just makes it harder to think. Our hope is a resurrection in which the glory of the naked body will outshine the stars and never again will clothing have any meaning for us. Some claim that nudity now can be an eschatological sign of our hope in the resurrection, but I am skeptical. The Scripture itself chose a sign of our hope: that we put on the righteousness of Christ like we put on clothes. God made our parents their first clothes and even today He acts as the great Tailor, who clothes our shame with the glory of Christ until there will be no cause for shame left in us. Perhaps we should be content to bide our time and wait for the day when nudity is appropriate.

God took His time appearing on the scene, even after the forbidden fruit was eaten. At least Adam and Eve were able to contrive a way to sew leaves together to make some makeshift clothes, and inventing clothes and sewing would have taken some time. Why did God wait so long to confront them? Because it was not His purpose to expose them; He knew they would be ashamed and He gave them time to cover themselves so they would not be humiliated in His presence. It is not God's purpose in the world to shame sinners before the rest of the world; it is people who do that. There are no spiritual tabloids in the Kingdom of God.

The other side of the shame coin is fear. All fear is the same: the fear that some one will see us, the fear of exposure, the fear of being helpless and vulnerable because of the shame we have in our pathetic weaknesses. Adam and Eve hid from God though they had been accustomed to meeting Him and speaking and walking with Him. What were they afraid of? They were afraid, of course, that He would know they had disobeyed concerning the tree. They couldn't know what death meant, but in hiding from each other and from God, they were behaving like dead people. To fear is to be dead. Fear is not simply realizing that we must die; fear is death itself reaching back into our lives to kill us now.

God asked Adam where he was, not because He didn't know, but because Adam didn't know. When God asks questions it is obviously never because He needs the information; it is because we need the information and we do not know the right questions to ask. He asks us what we ought to be asking ourselves. Adam was in hiding because he was no longer in Eden, for Eden had died when he died. He no longer had a home, he no longer had a place he belonged; he was a trespasser. Adam's answer was all that was necessary to fully disclose the whole nature of death: "I was afraid because I was naked . . ."

And then God asked him a very peculiar question: "Who told you that you were naked?" Who had told him? Had the word ever been used in conversation before this? Surely not. Why name the condition of being without clothes when there were no clothes to be without? It is as if Adam knew the word for a condition as it made its appearance, as if the word were hanging in the air waiting to be required; or rather, hanging from a tree waiting to be plucked. He was naked, and he had never known it before, but now he did, and he knew the word for it, and this is the knowledge of good and evil.

But it is the knowledge of good and evil from the viewpoint of the evil, it is the knowledge of nakedness from the viewpoint of shame and the need to hide. If he had refused to eat, if he had preferred God over his wife, then he would still have discovered that he was naked, but it would have been the knowledge of nakedness from the viewpoint of a Beautiful One, a Glorious One, such a One who can stand before the universe and deserve only praise and admiration and awe. Now he was just such a one that all who looked on him would have to turn away their eyes in embarrassment or revulsion.

"Have you eaten from the tree of which I commanded you not to eat?" This was a rhetorical question; the answer was obvious. But it was not purely rhetorical either; it was an opportunity, if there was any real life left in Adam, to express that life and admit freely what he had done. But there was no life left in him: first the shame, then the fear, then the infinite ability for self-deception and lies and evasion. He would not admit his decision to eat the fruit: No, it was Eve that had given it to him; he really hadn't done anything but follow her lead; it was her fault. And he even tried to implicate God as bearing some of the blame. After all it was God who had given him the one who offered the fruit; if God hadn't created Eve then none of this would ever have happened, so it was really God who was to blame.

This same line has been repeated by Adam's descendants ever since. Adam's answer was simply another part of his hiding. Like all lies, it masqueraded as a truth; it even was the truth on one level of understanding, but it was a lie on the only level of understanding that mattered. The question had to be asked so that later Adam could remember it, so that his descendants could remember it through all the horrible millennia of death, so we could all understand something more of what death means. You might think that being experienced in death as we are would mean that we understand it well, but the reverse is the case. Our experience in death is what prevents us from understanding it, like being asleep prevents us from understanding sleep.

Adam is the proto-type of every fool in the world who thinks there are gods to be preferred to God. He chose his wife over God and then betrayed her the first chance he got. It is the pattern for all our collective choices since then. We repeatedly choose something we desire more than God, and then betray it. To be an idolater is to be a traitor. First betray God with some other love, some other thing to worship, and then invariably bring betrayal into every relationship we have. It becomes natural, inevitable, to us to betray whatever we choose rather than God. The bitterest seeds of our own misery are always planted by ourselves in our own desires. Thus, adultery is the most fitting model for all of sin: the one who betrays his wife will shortly betray his lover.

In contrast, Eve's answer was straightforward. Her response was the simple truth: the dragon had deceived her and she had eaten the fruit. Unlike Adam, she had nothing to hide. She had been carried into death apart from her choosing. But then God did not ask the serpent to account for himself. Why is that? Why didn't this dragon have to give some account of himself to God? Or had the dragon already answered to God, already given an account of himself and already become known by what he had previously done? The temptation was a mythical event, an event performed before the whole creation, before all other creations, but it was a sequel to what had come before, a sequel to deeds which had been played out already and which we have not seen. The dragon was an old character, familiar to the heavenly audience from the previous scenes in this super-cosmic drama, and needed no introduction; and to future generations of Adam's descendants any excuses the dragon could make would only have brought either confusion or pathological curiosity. Adam and Eve were the new characters in the play now; they needed to provide an explanation to the audience, and to their children whose lives they had ruined, for who they were and what they had done. Thus God turned to the dragon to pronounce judgment and did not seek any further explanations.

b) The Consequences for the Dragon (Genesis 3:14, 15)

We come now to the so-called curses of the Fall. But to label God's pronouncements in this passage as "curses" is to misunderstand them. A curse is a punishment; it is the sentence that a judge pronounces once the trial is over and the jury has brought in the conviction. Pronouncing a sentence is not really what God was doing here. Their sentence had already been pronounced: "in the day you eat of it you shall surely die." These so-called curses were really a way of setting boundaries for death. They spelled out the details of what death would be allowed to do, how far it would be allowed to go. Death would not be permitted simply to be infinite; it would be enclosed, contained within certain limits. These pronouncements assume, in the form they are given, that God did not accept the Fall as the last word. God was not throwing up His hands here and saying, "Oh, well. I tried to make things good, but now it will just be death forever." Hope is implicit in every one of the pronouncements, hope that there would be a point to it. The so-called curses were actually the means of setting up the environment in which redemption could be accomplished.

The alternative to the "curses" of the Fall was annihilation. If the creation was to continue to exist, to be outside of the nothing it was made from, then there must be the choice on God's part to keep the creation going, and that implies God's intention to redeem. There was never, at any point, the possibility of God simply walking away from the creation, from the Covenant, of giving up and letting it all collapse into silence; or worse, keeping it going its own way unhindered, evil and misery perpetuating themselves forever with no possibility of relief.

The logical thing to do when a project is ruined beyond repair is to tear it down and start over again. The question is whether we really believe that any of God's projects can be ruined beyond His ability to repair them. And if the creation had been ruined past even God's ability to redeem, then wouldn't He have let it return to nothingness? He would easily have let it disappear and then started over with another "Let there be light". But are the designs of God to be so easily frustrated? Are the plans of God simply to fail, to be abandoned? Do we imagine God being forced to give up? May it never be! That we exist right now, that the world exists, is proof that we are being saved. That God limited the scope of death after the Fall was an expression of mercy and commitment to put it all to rights. What Christian theology usually does is a rather pathetic compromise with total defeat: we allow Him to redeem some of it. It is not clear to me that our theology truly honors God.

But why, in this context, did God address the dragon at all? It is not commonly believed in Christian teaching that Satan will be redeemed in any manner, but the redemption of Satan is implied, not only by his continued existence as I just argued about the creation, but also by the word God addressed to him. If we take seriously that God created all things of nothing, and that He holds them in being and maintains their existence, and that God is all merciful and compassionate, then to believe that God has no intention of redeeming Satan but nonetheless preserves him in a state of evil and misery is self-contradictory. Only the most merciless and cruel among us, only someone whose intent was torture, would keep a creature alive simply to extend its misery, with no hope of cure. On the other hand, theologians are right to be restrained on the question. Of the redemption of the devil we are told nothing and we know nothing. We have enough to be concerned with involving our own plight.

Nonetheless, God spoke to the dragon and it is worthwhile listening in. From the viewpoint of God's intentions toward him, what were the consequences of the Fall for the dragon? The dragon was already evil so there was some history between God and the dragon that we are not privy to. The dragon had committed some act which had turned him to evil, but what that act was, and what the consequences of that act were, we are simply not told. However, for *this* act, for the act of entering this new world and deceiving Eve, there were consequences, which presumably were combined with the consequences the dragon already was bound by. Satan was not condemned to death here as Adam and Eve were, and so he must have already been dead in some sense, in whatever sense that kind of creature experiences death. It seems likely that it was the consequences he already was enduring that brought him to the garden in the first place.

For this act, this tempting, this infecting of a new creation with evil, the dragon was first of all cursed above all cattle. If the ancient traditions were correct, the motive of spoiling this creation was to get "revenge" on God, to get back at God somehow for assigning the angels to be ministers to the humans. The angels were among the most glorious of all God's creatures, and yet when He made the rather pitiful creatures called men, out of dirt no less, He had assigned the angels the job of serving them. Lucifer, the Light, the most glorious of the angels, had been offended by such a lowly office and had fallen into rebellion.

So goes the legend, the tradition, from outside the Scripture. It need not be taken too seriously, but it is plausible enough as far as it goes. The dragon, though he clearly hated God, was still holding on to some vestige of his former status and glory. Now he lost even that. His status was reduced lower than that of a cow, lower than that of any of the mere beasts of the field. "On your belly you will go" means that he was reduced from a dragon to a mere snake. Once he had been a Glorious One, and the form of the dragon would represent the vestigial remains of that glory, but from this point on he would be reduced to the point of begging even to be allowed to live in a herd of pigs. I will henceforth call him a snake or a serpent; dragons had become extinct.

When the serpent was sentenced to eat dust all of his life, there was a figurative meaning, a spiritual meaning; literally neither snakes nor demons eat dust. The serpent was to eat dust, and I believe that *we* are the dust that he eats. We had been made of dust, after all. The way the serpent eats us is by possessing us. This is the point at which demon possession was initiated, and it is as much a misery for the demon as it is for the person possessed. The demon seeks to possess a person, or even an animal, because it has something like a hunger to fulfill. But its hunger for the human soul is repulsive to it while simultaneously irresistible. The creature Satan, who had begun by despising these creatures whom God had exalted over him, had been reduced to feeding on them, feeding and gagging as he fed.

Perhaps there had been a war in heaven during the long ages of creation, a war between the angels and the demons, and the demons had been cast out of heaven and imprisoned on the earth. And now the army of dragons had been made into an army of snakes, writhing away in the broken world they had themselves ruined. If so, God's sentence on the serpent was proof that any such war was superfluous, that there was no question as to who was in control, that a mere word from God established whatever He chose it to establish. The serpent was, after all, just a creature; he had been made by a "let there be" command at some point. God could take him out anytime He wanted. The mystery of evil is this: that God did not and does not choose to take him out, nor apparently does He intend to. His purpose, His *good* purpose in and for these snakes, has not yet been accomplished.

There was to be enmity between the serpent and the woman and this enmity was to be permanent, handed down from generation to generation. But it means much more than perpetual conflict. As soon as the passage begins to speak of the seed of the serpent, we know that we are on symbolic grounds again. The serpent, the devil, according to the little that we know of angelic beings, does not have offspring, and so the seed of the serpent would mean something other than literal descendants.

The easiest reading, and one of the traditional ones, is that the seed of the serpent refers to that part of the human race that follows or belongs to the devil. Later Jesus would say to certain Pharisees that they were sons of their father, the devil, and perhaps He had this passage in mind. In this case, the seed of Eve would be that part of the human race that opposes and resists the devil. God would have been promising to raise up part of the human race to fight the serpent and the works of the serpent.

In some sense, once Adam had chosen to disobey God, the world had become the serpent's property, his domain, but in this pronouncement God told the serpent that he would never fully take control of his occupied territory. There would always be a state of civil war, of revolution against his rule. He would never be at peace. Further the serpent was assured that he would be defeated. The woman's seed would bruise his head, and he would bruise the heel of her seed. The picture painted here is the capturing of the snake, of the victor planting his heel on the head of the snake so that it becomes helpless, incapable of further movement and incapable of striking; it is the destruction of the snake, the destruction of his authority, the destruction of his ability to harm.

But there is still more hidden in this pronouncement. It is a singular person, not a plural group, which will inflict the final blow; *he*, not *they*, will bruise serpent's head, and be bruised in return on the heel. This is the first promise of a Messiah, a Deliverer, a Hero who will come, born of a woman, and who will deliver all of us from the works of the devil. There is a sharp difference between the way the seed of the woman and the seed of the serpent is described. The seed of the woman culminates in the single individual who will accomplish the victory. The seed of the serpent culminates not in some other individual but in the serpent himself.

The way I understand this pronouncement to the serpent is as a promise, a promise that a Mighty One would arise and destroy Satan and all his works, and that in that destruction Satan also would be delivered. The promise to kill is simultaneously the promise to redeem, and the death sentence is simultaneously the hope of rescue from death. In order for Lucifer to be redeemed, the snake he had become must be destroyed. Death was the penalty for the Fall, and that penalty was never revoked. But death need not mean merely the end; in God's hands it becomes the means to new life.

Our redemption is finally realized not by escaping the penalty, but by suffering the penalty in a redemptive way. The death of our old nature must be accomplished to leave the birth of a new nature as the ultimate reality. There is no salvation without execution; there is no resurrection without crucifixion. The consequence of Adam's choice is never to be revoked; God never cancelled the result, He will never clear the guilty. But he did transform the penalty from being a final fate to being a tool for His own purpose. When God promised warfare against Satan and promised his final destruction, He was promising his rescue as well as ours.

But there is still more. God put enmity between the serpent's seed and the woman's seed. On the face of it, this is a strange phrase to use. There will be continual warfare against evil as represented by the serpent, and apparently it will be the woman, and perhaps women in general, who are the vanguard of the battle. Why there should be a war at all is not made clear—it could be so easily settled by fiat—but setting that question aside, normally one thinks of the "seed" as belonging to the father. In general, the "seed" are the descendants, and it is common to interpret the seed of the woman as her male descendants. Certainly the ultimate seed of the woman is a particular male descendant who will crush the head of the serpent. But to specify the Messiah as the *woman's* seed rather than a man's seed is to speak in an unusual way.

To me this suggests that it is women who carry the burden of the war against the serpent. Granted, women have not played a prominent role in the record of history, but there is no reason to think that the most important warfare of all should be prominently visible in men's records of their own deeds. On the contrary, while the men have been busy with pointless wars among themselves, the seed of the woman have been waging the invisible and cosmic war. Granted also that women have not played a prominent role in the history of our redemption in the Bible. But that is also rather like God, to keep what is most important just out of view. It is yet another way in which the first shall be last and the last shall be first, I should think.

It could also be that the "seed of the woman" may refer, not only to the Messiah, but to a woman, the woman who would be God's chosen instrument to bring the Messiah into the world. When Mary said "all generations will call me blessed" she could have meant *all* of them, from the first (Eve herself) to the last. When Mary described why all generations would call her blessed in Luke 1:48, the phrase απο του νυν is usually translated "from now on". But more literally it is translated "because of this present event", or "because of this now". Perhaps Mary as well was the "seed of the woman", who crushed the serpent's head simply by being the instrument of Incarnation. Perhaps the serpent was defeated simply and completely by the Messiah being born. In this case, it was the Incarnation that defeated the power of the devil; it was the Crucifixion that defeated the power of death; and it was the Resurrection that healed all things and made a new beginning.

It is riveting, is it not, the fact that it is the seed of the *woman*, and not the seed of the *man*, whom God singled out as the enemies of the serpent. I keep italicizing the phrase because it seems so critical and yet so easy to overlook. Though the whole world was about to become patriarchal, though the genealogies were all given through the father with hardly a mention of the mother, though the whole structure of male dominated death and power and slavery was about to be instituted, nevertheless it was the *seed of the woman* that would wage war on the serpent and all his works and would win.

The world is always inside out from God's viewpoint relative to ours. Even among men, the real heroes are the fringe element of society, the people with no status or worldly position but who quietly, and with no help from the world, work to bring in the righteousness of God. The genealogies to come would all be traced through the fathers, but every once in a while God had the writers mention a woman to show how *He* was tracing the lineage. The Messiah was to be Himself a man, but emphatically He was the seed of a woman rather than the seed of a man. From the first moment of the Fall, the Messiah's father has always been a step-father. The doctrine of the virgin birth begins here. And so in the course of time, Mary was born and grew up and the angel Gabriel came to her with some very strange news.

c) The Consequences for the Woman (Genesis 3:16)

At this point God turned to the woman, following the chain of temptation back up the line. Death was to be worked out for each creature in the uniqueness of that creature, so death would be worked out for women in what was unique to women: the ability to bear children. Henceforth the bearing of children would bring pain; and the pain indicated here does not stop with the mere physical danger and difficulty and pain attendant on the process of pregnancy and labor. Rather it was motherhood itself that became painful—psychologically, emotionally, and physically. It begins with a dangerous birth, and goes on to the tragedy of raising children who are doomed to death from the beginning, who are doomed to a life of disappointment and hard labor and pain, and who will resist the care of their mother and cause her pain in their turn by their words and their foolishness and their misfortunes.

Every grief that is borne by a child is equally borne by its mother, and I think to a lesser extent by its father. It is the mother who is the primary sharer of the grief of her children. It was mothers who were to be the primary bearers of the grief of the world waiting for the Messiah; and then after He came, serving as signs of that Messiah who came and will come again.

Nonetheless, though the state of motherhood was to be full of pain, the woman was consigned to a continuing desire for her husband, a continuing desire to bear children. In a world dominated by death, it was certain that the husband would take advantage of her weakness to manipulate and rule over her. Inevitably, in a Fallen world, the rule of the husband over the wife would tend to be harsh; and inevitably, in a Fallen world, the rule of the husband over the wife would tend to expand into the rule of men in general over women in general.

The woman was consigned to be a co-dependent in her own slavery, and this co-dependency in death is visible even today every time a woman tries to shield her abusive husband from the legal consequences of his abuse. What else could explain this self-destructive behavior on the part of so many women except that it is the outworking of death in them? Even when husbands are not overtly abusive, it is a rare thing to find a happy marriage, and rare to find a woman who does not tolerate and enable any sort of behavior on the part of her husband.

And young women see it all in their own unhappy families and nonetheless still go on dreaming of their prince charming and the happy marriage waiting for them. I am always amazed at the young single women I know, the girls who want to get married and have a family, and this in spite of having virtually no examples of marriages in which there is any joy or love, in spite of parents who take so little delight in each other that they are virtually strangers who live together. They feed on the images from fiction, from romance novels, from films, from songs and this keeps their hope alive of finding happiness in this world, the world in which there is virtually no happiness at all.

But eventually people realize they are chasing a delusion, and cynicism takes over. The song "That's the Way I've Always Heard It Should Be" by Carly Simon expresses powerfully the disaster of modern marriage. The romances in fiction or film of today are trivial, offering little in the way of joy, but at least they are "realistic". Indeed it is no wonder that it is becoming the norm in present day America for couples to live together without being married. If they are to end up with the same colorless marriages as their parents, why not just skip the marriage part of it altogether? And despite the shallowness of modern American institutions, the promise and desire for the romance they hardly ever see outside of a movie lures them on into one bad relationship after another. The Creation may have put the desire for marriage into women, but the Fall made them willing to settle for pretty much anything.

I am speaking as cynically as I can about the possibility of having a happy marriage in spite of the fact that my own has been the happiest part of my life in this world, and I hope a cause of joy to my wife and to our children. There are those rare happy marriages, just enough of them that hope doesn't die completely. And yet there must be a strong warning to all that when a good and happy marriage exists it is truly a miracle, a matter of grace. It is my wish, it is the wish of every parent who is not totally jaded, that their children will find just such a joyous relationship, but they must be warned to proceed cautiously. There are landmines everywhere. It is better indeed to be single than to be entangled in misery, and the churches should be in the vanguard of the prophets warning our culture of the many disguises of death.

But death oozes out beyond the borders of marriage to the whole society. There is no use trying to maintain the pretence that the domination of the world by men is other than an outworking of death. It is ironic that such a large portion of the American Christian church has taken this result of the Fall, this embodiment of death, and "baptized" it, made it into a moral obligation, made it into a sort of badge of Christian spirituality. This is what the so-called "Christian view of marriage" common among many fundamentalists amounts to: to take a curse and call it a blessing, to take the spring of death and pretend it is a fountain of life. I have been young and now I am old and I have seen few marriages among the many fundamentalist Christians around me that have been other than a cause for grief. It is a grim mistake in the Church that we have so tightly embraced the idea of male domination as if it were good.

In our culture marriage has simply become an ugly institution and it is a wonder that the divorce rate is not higher. I do not really think the world is becoming worse; I think there is less cosmetic work done in the present age and the scars and bones are showing through. I wonder if it is not the failure of our institution of marriage that has led to unbelief generally. How can we convince anyone that Jesus is worth knowing when we tell them that the husband is the head of the wife as Christ is the head of the Church and husbands are all ugly? Marriage need not be such a cage of death, as I know from my own experience, and as the Scripture indicates when it takes marriage into the deepest part of the mystery of redemption. To recapture a fully biblical concept of marriage we must go to the Redemption rather than to the Fall for our model.

But why would God make death so bitter to the woman? I cannot give an answer to this question, and yet it is through this form of death that redemption was ordained to come for the woman. Though the bearing of children would be filled with pain, yet there was also the hope, with each child, that perhaps that child would be the Messiah, the Hero who would destroy the works of death. Even now, now that the Messiah has come and we are no longer looking for a child who will be the Deliverer for us, there is always that same hope on a smaller scale. At each new conception, each time there is a secret hope in all who can still hope, "Maybe this child will be a great one, a mighty warrior against evil, a prophet who will bring wisdom and light and turn many from their sin." God has ordained that the pain women are doomed to bear will also be the vehicle of hope. It is the real meaning of these "curses" of the Fall that the pain of death will be made to produce life.

d) The Consequences for the Man (Genesis 3:17-19)

Finally God turned to Adam, the one ultimately responsible for all the others' suffering and death, the one whose devastating choice ruined all things for all people for all time. The change in His tone of voice is remarkable. Note how differently God addressed Adam: "Because you listened to your wife and have eaten of the tree . . .". He addressed Adam in the same tone He had used with the serpent. Only with Even was there no formal accusation, no crime named. He made it clear that in Adam's case He had arrived at the root of the crisis. Unlike the woman, unlike even the serpent, Adam bore the weight of responsibility.

And the first statement God made to him was utterly devastating: "Cursed is the ground because of you." In other words, "the whole of creation has been brought into death by you". All that had been good, by God's own verdict, was now corrupted through Adam's choice, because Adam was a bearer of the covenant. The serpent himself (and demons generally) bore the consequences of his deed; the woman herself (and women generally) bore the consequences of her foolishness; but the whole creation, everything and everyone, bore the consequences of this man's crime.

This may seem unfair, that all creation should be damaged by Adam's choice, this is the nature of reality within a covenant. It is the process we see working out in all of history. No person's choices are for himself alone. What New Age people celebrate as the "circle of life" is the Covenant structure of the universe in a trivialized form. In a Covenant relationship, the evil choices of one person damage *everyone*, and the wise and good choices of one person bless *everyone*. Personal relationships in this creation are not "two way streets"; they are billion way streets, a web of cause and effect that links all things morally as well as physically. We are all of us captured by the consequences of other peoples' choices, and we all inflict the consequences of our choices on the people around us. No one ever merely suffers for his own sin; no one even mainly suffers for his own sin. We each suffer for the sins of the people around us, and they are the ones who suffer for our sins. It is the weight of death that we all participate in killing each other, just as it is the weight of glory that we all participate in redeeming each other.

It is the king who decides to go to war, but it is his people who die in the battles. It is the adulterer who chooses to break his or her promise, but it is the family, the children, the friends who bear the brunt of the pain. It is the murderer who ends the victim's life, but it is the victim's family, the bystanders, the witnesses who see the violence that walk away with the pain. And the pain is not healed by the execution, the divorce, the victorious battle. The pain subsides eventually but the damage goes limping along through all the years of our lives. And thus, when Adam sinned, the entirety of the creation, everything connected to him, was murdered. Adam's sin was against God; but it was also a sin against reality, against the fabric of the created order. It was cosmic as all evil is cosmic. But his was the first.

The death of the creation meant that Adam's work, the good gift of work that God had shared with Adam, became mere drudgery. Not only would the work be exhausting, it would be impossible. Tending the garden had been only a small part of Adam's real task. His dominion over the creation had been primarily one of supervising the Covenant and the relationships among the creatures, but now there was no working covenant. The relationship of the creation to the Creator was ruined, but also all of the internal relationships within creation had begun to unravel and they could not be retied. From this point on, people would live within a dysfunctional creation. The creatures would no longer cooperate; they would fight. The dog eat dog world had begun.

Work had been given to Adam before Eve was formed and was part of his essential nature. Work was especially a gift to Adam, not as exclusively as childbearing had been given to Eve, but more especially to him. Men have a need for work that is qualitatively different from the need women have for work. This is a generalization, and varies from individual to individual, but it is not necessarily sexist to observe that men and women are different. At the risk of stereo-typing, for women the need to work is frequently subsumed under the need and desire for family; for men, this is much less frequently the case. There are men who have little or no desire for work of any kind and are family oriented, just as there are women who have little or no desire for children and prefer to pursue a career. We are speaking in generalities here, in statistical averages, and the tendency is for women to find their identity in family and men to find their identity in work. To what extent is this socially determined? To what extent do our expectations of men and women determine what they are like? The answer is not clear, but I suspect that social conditioning accounts for a lot, but not all, of the roles we play. The tendencies are built into us and get accentuated or minimized through our lives.

At any rate, after the Fall and especially for men, death would always be mingled with the joy they might have had in their work and would taint everything they did. As Eve would give birth to children only to watch them suffer and grow old, Adam would toil away to "accomplish something" only to watch it all crumble before his eyes. In modern terms, men are subject to the fear, the inevitability, that they will be failures, losers. Our society certainly exacerbates this psychosis in men. Everything we do decays and the rubbish heaps of the world are filled with our plans, our dreams.

But it is not merely the results of work that became subject to decay; the work itself became trivial, degrading, debilitating. This has always been true, but in modern times we have refined the art of trivializing work. How many people do you know who truly love their work. Many of those who say they love their work really mean they love the lack of serious effort required by their jobs, or they love the paycheck, or they love the benefits, or they love the sense of security. There is not one man in a thousand who is fulfilled in his work, just as there is not one woman in a thousand who is fulfilled by her marriage or her children. If the work is not vacuous, leaving the man spiritless in his old age, then it sucks him dry with hard labor and leaves him empty and weary beyond the power of any rest to heal. Good work and good marriage are still the very best that this world has to offer. Good work and a good marriage were the gifts of Eden, but it is only the most blessed of us that ever gets close to such things.

However the curse on the ground goes far beyond merely spoiling our work. Part of the Covenant of Creation was God's setting up of the order, the physical laws that would govern the ways of the world. The Fall ripped apart the fabric of those laws. That the laws of nature themselves were changed is also hinted at in Romans 8 where Paul says that the creation was subjected to futility, and that it would be set free from its slavery to corruption in the end. This is what is being suggested in the next verse, that "the ground will produce thorns and thistles". This refers to the introduction of competition as the fundamental principle governing relationships among the creatures. The web of covenant relationships had been destroyed. From this point on, every creature had to compete to live. They could no longer live together, they could no longer trust each other. Now they must fight each other for the chance to live, and to live short meager lives at that. The Age of Evolution had begun.

The "circle of life" is only a spoiled shadow of the Covenant. The circle of life as we have it now is more accurately called a "circle of death". It must be fed with the deaths of its creatures just to keep it moving. It was the original Covenant that was the circle of life, without any taint of death. But at the Fall the principle of the survival of the fittest came into its own and not merely among the animals. The principle that God had built in to men to care for the creation had become a principle of competition in them. Henceforth the dominant desire in men would be for control. No longer would men represent God to the creatures; now they would insist on *being* god to the creatures. At first their drive was to control more of the world for their own comfort, but when their lives were comfortable enough, it was control for the sake of control. And when they controlled as much as they could handle, they found they needed to control more of the world than other men controlled.

The Fall had introduced the principle that would come to be called Evolution, but all of the laws of physics were altered as well. Whatever the creation is now is radically different from what it was, even down to the basic laws of matter and energy. *If* the very laws of physics changed at the Fall, there are several conclusions that follow and that ought to be considered carefully. Science assumes the uniformity of natural causes, meaning that it assumes the laws of physics do not change over the course of time, or from place to place in the universe. Some modern scientists, if I understand them correctly, allow that the laws of physics may change in a continuous and predictable way, a change that is determined by yet another law which itself doesn't change. Something like the uniformity of cause and effect is a perfectly reasonable assumption to make; otherwise science would be un-do-able. One cannot hope to capture the laws of nature unless the laws can be counted on to be laws. What I am suggesting is that, on the contrary, the Fall brought about a sudden, dramatic discontinuity in the laws of physics, and that this perfectly reasonable assumption at the foundation of science is false in fact.

Such a change in physical law would necessarily be undetectable; we can't go back in time to actually check the laws that operated in the past. Such a discontinuity is even more so undetectable because science assumes that it never happened; it is hard to find something if you don't believe it exists. What I am suggesting then is something that is essentially outside the scope of science. My interpretation of the Scripture implies that all of science concerning itself with the origins of the universe is invalid because the laws do not extrapolate back beyond a certain point. This is a bitter pill to swallow, and I cannot blame scientists for finding the idea indigestible.

Because I believe the Scripture implies that physical laws have changed since the beginning, I naturally do not expect the science of origins to "agree" with the Scripture. They could not agree with each other about the beginning of the world because they are discussing two different things. One is talking about the early universe as one with an entirely different physics than what we live under now, and the other is talking about the early universe as an extrapolation of this universe to the remote past. If I were a scientist studying the origins of the universe believing what I do, I would still continue to make as a scientific assumption what I can not make as a theological or philosophical assumption. Whether true or not, the uniformity of natural causes is necessary to pursue science, and it is worth making the assumption just to keep the game going. Science is in itself a beautiful work of human art, and I personally love what it is and how much it has done. It has a beauty and integrity that deserves the respect of everyone, Christian or not, and it seems to me to not be a fatal flaw that it cannot attain to ultimate and absolute Truth. That was an unrealistic expectation to begin with.

The point of arguing as I have done to arrive at this important observation: science requires just the sort of non-rational leap of faith that scientists have so often scorned in religion. It is important to note that each set of presuppositions, of science or of Christian theology (my version, at least), depend on faith, on trust. The scientist will subscribe to the belief in the uniformity of natural causes over time because he must if he is to do his job; he trusts in the power of human intellect, in himself. The Christian—at least the one who follows my line of thinking—will subscribe to the belief in the radical changing of the system of natural cause and effect because he must in order to submit to the revelation of Scripture; he trusts in a God who created the universe according to His absolute will. Our presuppositions always arise out of some necessity imposed on us by our ultimate commitment. Or put another away, our faith arises out of who or what we worship.

Returning to the main point, Adam along with Eve along with our whole world was condemned to a life of hard labor. We are condemned to exist in a world that had been fragmented, that is at constant war with itself and with us, until finally we dissolve back into the dust we came from. Not only is the world in a constant state of warfare, we ourselves are in a constant state of warfare within ourselves and with ourselves. Physical death was the last consequence of the Fall, but all the consequences of the Fall are actually aspects of death. Our bodies die, not because the laws of nature require death, but because we are dead people inhabiting our bodies. From the moment of conception the principle of death is in control; it just takes death a few decades to work its way out to the surface. And death is holistic. Our deaths involve every dimension of our existence: emotional, spiritual, intellectual, volitional, as well as physical.

In short what we see as the result of the Fall is that death infected every aspect of the Covenant which we enumerated previously. Here is a summary of those terms of the Covenant and how they were changed.

- Adam and Eve, and therefore we ourselves, now possessed the knowledge of good and evil, but from the stand point of evil-doers. They knew, and we know, evil from the viewpoint of natives of that realm, but we know good only as aliens.

- Creatures, including people, continue to have offspring in their own image, but the image now is not what it was created to be. Disobedience changed the relationship of humanity to God, and in so doing changed what humans are. After the Fall death became part of us, part of our genetic makeup, part of what had been the image of God; and so death spread to their descendants and down to us. When Adam and Eve had children, they had a son in their own image (5:3), in the image of the dead. And the effects of the Fall spread outward and downward like a cosmic tsunami. The word "sinner" means, not a pattern of behavior, but a particular kind of animal.

- Human authority over creation was spoiled. It was no longer "natural" nor enjoyable, but it was hard labor. The creation would be co-operative no longer, and we became abusive and exploitative toward the creation. The rule of mankind over the earth was never given as the simple right to do what we pleased with the earth, but we had become our own gods, ruthless in our greed.

- The institution of marriage was undermined; the man was given a power over the woman that inevitably became abusive, and the woman's co-dependency made it the norm. For many men and many women marriage became a prison rather than a context for companionship, and for many women it became a form of slavery. Sexual relationships became matters of manipulation and exploitation rather than of joy, and within marriage the politics of sex replaced the covenant.

- The Sabbath was changed in character. Though the Sabbath was not mentioned again in this passage, when God did choose to pick up the idea of the Sabbath once more it became the sign of a future hope that the creation would be restored and that there would be rest at the end, the sign of God's promise of a rescue of the creation from the Fall. What had begun as a sign of God's finished work, became a sign a future completion of all things.

- The very laws of nature were changed. The ground produced thorns for the first time, symbols of the new need to compete for survival. Death and entropy dominated all things.

And thus we come to the ruin of all things. The Covenant with the creation, the marriage of God and creation, had ended in divorce. More accurately there was a separation, for He was not willing to lose her. It is the first chapter in the greatest story line of all time: The boy met the girl and fell in love; they were married and unutterably happy, the perfect love story; then in the most tragic possible way she was seduced, ran away with her lovers, and he lost her. What will he do to win her back? How far is he willing to go to restore the love he had? That is how the Bible begins our story and that is what the rest of it is all about.

C. Life Without the Covenant

1. God's First Intervention: Making Clothes (Genesis 3:20-21)

We now get a view of what life was like without a covenant between God and the world. The original covenant determined relationships, person to person, people to nature, and nature to nature, but it had been abandoned. Obviously that does not mean that there were no relationships. Even between God and the creation, between God and humanity, we are not to imagine that there was no relationship at all. The restrictions placed on death after the Fall made it clear that some kind of relationship was to be maintained. That God creates and maintains us means that existence itself is a relationship of some sort. To have no relationship to God is to not exist; existence is relationship to God.

Not only did God insist on maintaining some relationship with the creation even without a covenant, not only did God promise a Hero to rescue the creation from the Fall, not only did He set limits on the expression of death, but He Himself became an active participant, eventually even a victim, in the horror of the Fall. God does not change, we are to be told later, and nowhere is this more evident than in the events succeeding the

Fall. God's commitment to His creation was unaltered. There may have been adultery, to use the most readily available covenantal language, but God never filed for divorce, as it were. He maintained communication in an uninterrupted, if not unaltered, manner.

God took three immediate steps, which we can consider one at a time, that reveal a lot about His character and intentions. His very first act was to make clothing for Adam and Eve out of animal skins. This intervention had a two-fold purpose. On the one hand, Adam and Eve needed to be taught some basic skills in order to survive in the new world that was coming to be. Things wouldn't just work out for them anymore. They would have to figure out how to get food; and they would eventually get cold and be in need of some covering. Besides, the "fig leaves" wouldn't last long. When God made clothing for them He was also teaching them how to make clothing for themselves. It was an act of mercy, helping them get started, and it showed again that death was not to be allowed to be the end. Life, albeit of a marginal and contingent sort, would go on waiting for a better. For the first time, provision had to be made for the future and God had to be the one to do it; no one else knew what was coming.

Clothing also was a symbol for redemption, corresponding to nakedness as a symbol of shame and death. God used the death of an animal to cover over the effects of death for Adam and Eve, planting a glimpse of the idea of sacrifice in their minds. It hinted that the way out of death would have to be through death. The shame of their nakedness was to be hidden under the cover of an innocent victim, an animal. The New Testament picks up on this theme when it describes us as being clothed in Christ's righteousness; and repentance, turning to Christ for salvation, is described as putting off the old rags and putting on new robes. Our spiritual shame is hidden under the cover of an Innocent Victim, the Messiah. From the beginning God has been clothing us. If we discern the truth and pay attention, merely getting dressed in the morning can be a sign to us of God's mercy and our hope, a sacrament of sorts.

God's making clothing for them was also a deliberate act of involvement in the mess that had been made of creation. Violence, death, and pain were not part of the original scheme for the creation, but if the universe was to continue to exist they were the price that must be paid. If death was not to be the final word, if all things were not simply to collapse back into nothing, then existence was going to be a dirty affair for a while; and if life was to be a messy affair from here on, then God Himself was willing to get His own hands dirty. So the very first act of violence in the world was committed by God Himself against the very creatures that He had just pronounced as good and whom He loved. It was a high price to pay, but it only hinted at the actual price God was willing to pay.

There is something that Adam did at this point which deserves some comment: he named his wife "Eve", which means "life", because she would be the mother of all the living. When Eve had been created, he had given her the name "woman", but at this point he gave her a personal, as opposed to a "generic", name. Calling her "woman" was not disrespectful, as we might imagine; after all, a personal name becomes significant only when there are many individuals of the same kind. If there were no other women in all of creation, then "woman" is a perfectly individual and personal name; as soon as there were other women, then further naming became important.

But it was not merely that now there might have been other women around (no doubt you are asking, "And where did they come from?") When Adam named his wife Eve, Life, I think he was apologizing to her. He had tried to make her his life at the Tree and by so doing he had brought everything down into death. At the very least, it is fair to say that he owed her an apology. Ironically, though she could never have been his life, now she was his hope of new life as the mother of the coming Deliverer, and her personal name would remind them both of God's promise that her seed would crush the very head of death.

Adam giving her another name does suggest that there might have been other women by this time. Since Eve was the mother of all the living, this may mean that daughters had been born to her. The revelation is silent as to whether there were other people created besides Adam and Eve or whether Adam and Eve had had children before the Fall. The fact that Adam seemed to need no personal name, but continued using his generic name, could mean he was the only male human. On the other hand, when sons were finally born to them, Adam continued using his generic name, so it is very possible that giving Eve this new name had nothing at all to do with other women being present.

So if the new name was not a numerical indicator, then what was its meaning? And were other people created than just this one couple? That Eve was the mother of all living suggests that there were no other women than a possible unmentioned daughter or two, but it might mean that only those who were descended from her were properly called human. Ancient mythology hypothesized that in Genesis 1 the female human was Lilith, and the account of the creation of Eve in chapter 2 was an entirely distinct event. In this interpretation, the "sons of God" mentioned in chapter 6 were descendants of Lilith and Adam, not fully human. What happened to Lilith? The idea is that she turned to evil before the fall happened and departed the scene; it is all rather unsatisfying. This mythology may have derived from Canaanite sources, and we do well to be cautious of ideas from outside the flow of revelation.

Perhaps the least complicated interpretation is that Eve was called the mother of all the living in a spiritual or a metaphorical, or more exactly a prophetic way, as the ancestress of the Way, the Truth, and the Life. In this view, Adam gave Eve her name because of God's promise to her through the serpent. A related interpretation hypothesizes that she was given her name because it was through her descendants alone that the warfare against the people of the serpent was to be carried on (and the people of the serpent were descendants of Lilith?).

Most interpretations, including the most likely one that she was called Eve because of the promise of the Messiah, leave room to believe that other people besides Adam and Eve were present, if not before the Fall, then very shortly afterwards. The women that Cain and Seth married could have been their sisters, of course, merely from necessity, but it is not an appealing idea that the human race began with a necessary incest. Personally I think the strongest *hint* that the original creation included more than a single couple is found in Genesis 5, which we will get to soon.

Let me add one last comment along this avenue of speculation. Hypothesizing the existence of other people than Adam and Eve does not compromise their position as covenant bearers responsible for the Fall. That the Hebrew word "adam" means "man" generically leaves open the possibility that it was a collection of people that God created in Genesis 1. It was not the uniqueness of Adam, it was not the fact of his being the one and only man, that made him the agent representing the Covenant at the temptation. We imagine that because we call him "*the* head" of the Covenant that there could only have been one like him, but that is a trick of the English translation. It is the way things work in the world of our experience but not in God's preferred order.

Our world is a world dominated by death, by the principle of competition, and by the principle of individualism. Headship in the original creation would have been untainted by such principles. Adam was the representative of the Covenant, not because he was the only one, not because he was male, but because he was human, created in the image of God. Eve was also a representative of the Covenant. And if God created hundreds of couples of people in Eden that we are not told about, they would each have been equally representatives of the Covenant. Any one of these *hypothetical* people could have been the one to ruin it all, to pull done the whole of existence; it happened to be the one we call Adam, or else he is the one we call Adam because he is the one who represented the whole Covenant in the Fall. Perhaps, after all, we have arrived at the reason Eve took a new name after the Fall and Adam did not. His name underscored that he was the representative of all mankind; it represented his responsibility. But her name underscored the future hope.

Another reason we commonly assume that Adam and Eve were necessarily the only people at the time is that it violates our sense of justice that others would have suffered death for Adam's sin. This ignores the fact that we also inconsistently allow their descendants to suffer for Adam's sin, and Eve as well. However it feels, though, the one individual is portrayed as causing the misery of absolutely everything else, and it really matters not at all if there were other independent branches of the human race or not.

Whether or not there were other people, only one person was required to make that fatal decision, and so death spread to all men, to all his descendants, to all the animals, to all the world. And because God set up the universe in a covenantal way, death would have spread to all people even if they were separate biological creations, as it did to all creation, even if they were unrelated to Adam. As descendants of Adam, we are the "innocent" victims of his choice; if there were others, they also were the innocent victims of that same choice. Indeed the whole of this creation is an innocent victim of the choice in the garden. Covenants are like webs of relationship and when the web breaks everyone tied into the web is broken with it. Even God Himself was broken by Adam's choice because God had woven Himself into the Covenant.

2. God's Second Intervention: Exile (Genesis 3:22-24)

The second thing God did—in person, as it were—was to exile Adam and Eve from the garden in order to keep them from eating from the Tree of Life. The garden would not have remained a garden for long; it would have gone wild along with the rest of creation. The real exile from paradise had already happened with the words "Cursed is the ground because of you." The point of the exile from Eden was not to throw them out of paradise—paradise was already gone—but to prevent them from eating from the Tree of Life and living forever as a result.

We must pause here to attempt again to define a term, "eternal life". I've already attempted this when I discussed the Tree of Life in conjunction with the Tree of Knowledge, but it bears some emphasis. What do we mean by "eternal life"? First, eternal life is not simply unending days, immortality; it is not simply freedom from physical death. If you believe in an after-life then you believe we are immortal in a sense anyway; the mere continuation of conscious life, physical or spiritual, is not what we mean by eternal life. Eternal life should be understood as a different *quality* of life, not merely a greater *quantity* of life. Moreover eternal life is not a return to the quality of life Adam and Eve enjoyed before the Fall. If they had already possessed eternal life there would have been no reason to plant a Tree of Life in the garden. Eternal life, as the term is used in the New Testament, refers to a higher quality of life from any that has ever been possessed by any human being, until the Messiah came. Eternal life refers to a kind of life as much beyond the life of Adam and Eve in Eden as human life is now beyond, say, canine life. It is simply impossible to describe what it means because we are incapable of knowing such things, much as a dog is incapable of knowing the quality of our lives, the beauty of a symphony or the subtlety of a metaphor.

It is not to be supposed that the Tree of Life had the power to reverse the effects of the Fall, to heal the universe from the damage done by Adam's choice. Before the Fall it would have been a pathway into eternal life from the perfection of life they already enjoyed, and in this way the Tree of Life was a sign of the Messiah's work, the purpose of His incarnation. But after the Fall, there was no longer an open way into eternal life for Adam or Eve or us because we carried within ourselves the principle of death. Even for dead people, however, the Tree of Life apparently had real power to confer a form of life—not eternal life in our Fallen state, but immortal life in the body. The Tree of Life is described as being able to undo the inevitability of physical death while leaving the principle of death untouched. This was why it was so important that God prevent them from eating it.

Physical death was the least significant aspect of the curse of death. The prevention of death on a physical level could be stopped merely by the power of the fruit of this tree, but dealing with death in the inner being would require all the rest of human history and deeds of wonder and power. In the name, "Tree of Life", "life" is not to be taken simply as the opposite of death. If the *life* conferred by the Tree of Life were the opposite of the *death* incurred in the Fall then it would have been the antidote. If it were the antidote, if just a taste of the Tree of Life would have undone the results of the Fall and we could have gone back to life as it was, if the Fall could have been undone so simply and painlessly, then how would God not have administered this anti-venom to the serpent's sting immediately?

On the contrary, the life conferred by the Tree of Life was a different sort of life altogether than Adam and Eve had been created with; it was life in a "higher plane", life that had avenues of access to God that are unimaginable to us. But while it might grant access to a higher level of existence, it would not have neutralized the principle of death. This principle of death governing us was not a disease that could be cured by plucking some other fruit and eating; it was the kind of condition that could not be cured by any action that we could take in any world with any antidote however powerful.

Eating the fruit of the Tree of Life would have conferred a higher form of life to Adam and Eve, but they would have carried the curse of death with them into that new realm, and that would only have opened up whole new vistas of suffering and pain that are as unimaginable to us now as the joys of eternal life are. It would have brought them into a realm of suffering and pain such as perhaps only the fallen angels know. In much the same way that a human suffers levels of pain—psychological, mental and emotional—beyond anything borne by an animal, we can't imagine what pain such a level of existence might hold. Any spiritual discipline that promises a short cut to bliss and bypasses the Messiah is just another way of eating the Tree of Life without being healed. It promises bliss, but it ends only in delivering new and unbelievable realms of pain. This is why the Bible so emphasizes that the occult is to be avoided.

Before He lets us experience eternity God wanted to make sure that we didn't carry death with us into that new realm. This is what the Messiah would accomplish in bruising the serpent's head: death and the principle of death would be destroyed. God's intent has always been that we partake of the Tree of Life, but only when it had been made safe for us to do so, when we had hearts that could bear the weight of eternity. The principle of death that resides in us had to be dealt with before we would be ready for immortality. Thus the afterlife as imagined by the ancients and as pictured in the Old Testament is a colorless world. It is Hades or Sheol, a place where existence may continue in its unending fashion but where the progress of death would be arrested. By exiling us away from the Tree of Life, God was *choosing* to create Sheol rather than Hell.

It is easy to get the impression that physical death was the essence of the Fall, that if we could just get around having to die that we would have it made. Such mistaken impressions account for people who, several centuries ago, would have gone off looking for the fountain of youth or followed Gilgamesh after some other magical cure for death, or who would in our generation have themselves frozen and stored for a future in which they could evade death waiting for the inevitable progress of medicine.

There are still deluded individuals who imagine that unlimited life in this world would be a good thing, but anyone who is thinking clearly can see that physical death is a mercy more often than not. The life in this world is one that is inevitably filled with pain and misery of various sorts, and an unlimited time spent in this world would be unbearable. No one in his right mind really wants to die, but the alternative is always eventually worse. Of course there are people who lead fairly nice lives, who are lucky enough to get all the breaks and enjoy good health and prosperity and good friends and live in a relatively peaceful time and place. But such luck can't last more than a few decades and eventually the luckiest would find themselves in the same plight of suffering as the rest of us. Physical death seems harsh when it ends a relatively good life, or when it separates us from those we love. But if we can keep a biblical and realistic perspective on it, we know in our hearts that facing death is preferable to facing life in this world and even a tragic death hides a darker secret it is better not to know.

Hence it was an act of mercy that God prevented unending physical life in this world because the other aspects of death are the ones that are the real problem. Escape from physical death alone is no escape from decay of the soul; to be always decaying, to be always rotting away on the inside and unable to die, to grow more and more tired, more and more twisted, year after year forever, the horrible prospect that we could become zombies such as the worst horror movie fails to depict, really is a fate worse than death, and that is what God moved to prevent. It is the dread of sliding down just such a spiral of decay with no hope of stopping the descent, that drives so many mistakenly to suicide.

For physical death does not lead to non-existence. The only way we can cease to exist is for God to quit calling our names. It is His Word that brought us into existence and only His silence can make us vanish. We have no power over it. This is our plight: to be caught up in a kind of spiritual quicksand which only pulls us deeper into decay and which only physical death can arrest—at least we think it does—and which no power in this world can reverse. It is important to see how every word spoken by God, and every act taken by Him in response to the Fall, was done out of mercy, seeking out ways to mitigate the consequences of Adam's devastating choice. There was no thought of punishment here, only the effort to limit the consequences. God was not expressing His anger over Adam's choice; He was arranging a path that would lead to deliverance. The wrath of God is nowhere visible in these chapters.

Where, then, is the concept of hell in the story of the Fall? It isn't there. If in God's mercy He was unwilling that we spend unlimited days suffering in this world, would He then turn around and create a new realm of endless torments as punishment? Indeed, unlimited life in a world like this one would have been more severe a punishment than God was willing to inflict on any evil-doer. There is no need for eternal flames; this world would serve perfectly well. If God wants a hell, all He has to do is to keep us going forever right here.

I think the Tree of Life is mysterious on any other interpretation. Why did God plant a Tree of Life in the garden when there was no death to require it, only to deny it to us when death did arrive? If what I said above is more or less correct, the mystery of the Tree of Life is the mystery of the Incarnation, for the Tree of Life is nothing less than a symbol and promise of the Messiah. He is the Tree whose fruit brings healing to the nations, in whose branches all the nations will come for shelter. The Tree of Life means that all along, before the Fall, and regardless of whether the Fall had occurred or not, the Incarnation was part of the intent for Creation. When God said "Let there be light", He wasn't just making a toy He could admire and play with; He was making a home He would inhabit. The Fall did not make the Incarnation necessary, it only altered its role in history.

The cherubim, with the sword that turned in every direction, guarded the way into Eden to make sure we would never find our way back in by that path. But he only guarded the east entrance to the garden. Are we to imagine that there was a wall of some kind encircling it on the other sides? Or that unmentioned angelic guards covered the other sides? Or perhaps Eden was removed from this universe entirely, connected only by a "wormhole" guarded by an angel, and perhaps now even this pathway has been severed entirely? Once serious people discussed other dimensions only in science fiction, but now strange numbers of dimensions have made the leap, at least tentatively, into real science and have a bit of respectability. The point is (and we should always remember this one) that we don't know much about the universe we live in, much less what is possible and what is not.

The Scripture is as silent on the nature of the cherubim as it is silent on the nature of the serpent. Interestingly, "cherubim" is not a Hebrew word but seems to have originated earlier, in even more ancient times. The sword held by the cherubim is described in an obscure way, either as a sword in constant motion or as a sword pointing in every direction at once. Perhaps it was something that moved so quickly that it did point in all directions simultaneously, but perhaps it is described this way to mean that it covered access to the garden from any direction, any physical direction or any non-physical direction, from any of the dimensions we know and from any dimensions we don't know.

If this discussion seems to be getting a bit far out at this point, I suppose it is; but this is just another way of asking whether we believe Eden was a real place or not. If Eden was a real place, and I believe it was, where is it now? My intent with the preceding remarks was to point out that biblically and logically, there is no reason to suppose that the Tree of Life and the remains of Eden are still located geographically in this world at all, even archaeologically speaking. But though the Tree of Life is a metaphor, I take it to have been at one point a literal tree as well. Perhaps it is still planted and growing in whatever other dimensions exist, still waiting for us when a new path into the garden is finally opened. Or perhaps Eden went wild along with the rest of creation, and the Tree that symbolized the Messianic work was no longer necessary in that form. Perhaps it gradually became an ordinary tree, and the angelic guards dispersed when there was nothing else to guard.

Or you could imagine Eden as a mere fiction; and the world would become all the less interesting for it. If we don't believe there was a real paradise in the past, then it is difficult to believe in any paradise in the future either. If we don't believe there was a real paradise in the past, then it is difficult to believe in any wonderful thing even in the present. Puddleglum was right.

3. Cain and Abel

a) The First Murder (Genesis 4:1-8)

With the birth of Cain and Abel we get our first glimpse of the meaning of human life after the Fall. Eve named her first-born son "Cain", which means "gotten one", because she had gotten him from God. She understood from the first the idea that children are a gift from God because He promised that through one of her children deliverance would come. By the time her second son was born, however, the full reality of their circumstances had begun to sink in. She named her second son "Abel" which means "vanity" or "nothing". The passage does not indicate why her feelings toward having children had altered so much; as usual, we are left to our imagination to fill in the details. One might almost say we are *invited* to use our imaginations, or rather our experience, to fill in the details.

Surely it was Cain himself and the experience of raising Cain (no pun intended) that had revealed to her the complete reality of parenthood. It was still true that children were a gift from God and that the hope of deliverance was in a child to come, but these gifts from God were flawed human beings, and raising them would be filled with pain and disappointment and grief. This is the meaning of death, that she would bring forth children in pain, and the pain would go on all through the life of the child. Eve had been disillusioned by the time Abel was born. Now she knew that having children in this new world meant vanity and meaninglessness. It was the first irony in history that the role of First Good Guy was played by Abel—Vanity—and the role of First Bad Guy was played by Cain, the One-Gotten-From-God.

And so Cain and Abel were born and grew up and took up different vocations and brought offerings back to God. This brings us to the third action God took immediately after the Fall to reveal His character and His intentions: He instituted the custom of bringing offerings to be burned on an altar; and with them He introduced the blood sacrifice. From nearly the beginning people had the idea that it was proper, and desirable, and beneficial to bring offerings to God, and it would appear that, if He didn't initiate the custom, then He encouraged it. The passage portrays Cain and Abel as being accustomed to having verbal interaction with God and somehow knowing that these sacrifices were appropriate. It makes sense, immediately after the Fall, that God would continue regular visitation, visually and verbally. For one thing He was getting them off to a good start, teaching them survival skills if nothing else. But as we became capable survivors, the personal visits became only a memory and then only myths told by lonely people.

It is interesting that the Bible does not picture the human race as ever existing without the accompaniment of domesticated animals, as if the domesticity of those animals had been built into their nature or else that God domesticated them for us. Nor does it picture the existence of humanity without agriculture and the tilling of the soil. If there were pockets of humanity that did not engage in agriculture or did not keep flocks and herds, then it was because they had abandoned the practice. This hypothesis is somewhat at odds with current ideas about the development of human culture and knowledge, but all archaeologists have is scattered and incomplete data and certain reasonable and logical assumptions about how things must have developed. Archaeology also must proceed on the assumption of uniformity of natural causes so we, or people like me, must be excused from accepting all their conclusions.

God's rejection of Cain's offering in favor of Abel's was not meant to be taken personally, though Cain did take it that way. The favor given to Abel's offering had to do with the symbolism God was setting up for the unfolding revelation He planned. He began to set the stage immediately for the animal sacrifices He would require under the Mosaic Law, and for the sacrifice He Himself would make through the Messiah. From the very beginning God took a long-term view both of redemption and of revelation. For God to communicate with people required the right words, but even more so it required the right metaphors, the right symbols. To a large extent, the language we actually use with each other does not consist in words with dictionary definitions, but in metaphors and figures of speech that stretch the words beyond their literal definitions. In any event, the third thing God did after the Fall, once He had taught them to make clothing and sent them away from the Tree of Life, was to begin establishing a language of symbols, the first symbol being the blood sacrifice. At the first, the blood sacrifices they brought would not have had much meaning to them except that God wanted the blood and was pleased by the sacrifices.

The metaphors necessary to understanding God and understanding His strategy for undoing death took a great deal of time to arrange. They involved customs and rituals that gradually accumulated specific meanings as they were used. This means that at any given time the people of God would always find themselves doing or saying things, reading things, that they simply could not understand completely because the full meaning lay in the future. Furthermore, the symbols were open to misinterpretation both by the people of God and by the pagans around them. The pagan ideas of the gods thirsting for blood was the calculated risk of introducing such a symbol as burnt offerings; one Sumerian myth pictures the hungry gods swarming around the sacrifices like flies or vultures, for example.

Now we Christians often assume, because the canon of revelation is closed, that we must possess the full meaning of everything we say and do, that the symbolic language is completely in place and our comprehension of the symbols is perfect. While I grant that the symbols are in place, and we do not expect any new revelation in that way, church history seems to indicate that our understanding of the symbols is not perfect. Indeed, if our understanding of the symbols were perfect, we would not disagree with each other so much and books like this one would not be written. It can be disquieting when we find pockets of ignorance in our understanding of Scripture, or when we find passages we can't agree on. It can make us afraid that we also may be missing something, and if we are missing something then it might be something important; and if we are missing something important then maybe we have missed the real point entirely. The main thing is not to let the fear of being wrong make us do absurd things to prove we are right. Let's keep our eyes on the goal: to understand the revelation as deeply and truly as possible.

Some of you reading this may think I am guilty of going to too great lengths to invent elaborate theories to explain the Scripture. Indeed, I may be guilty. But if so, that would be my flaw and not a flaw in the revelation. God's metaphors do not work like that. He does not reveal with the intent of misleading us. It is not like a human posing a riddle to see how many of his friends will be stuck and gradually adding hints until they get it. God's intent with His metaphors is to make Himself known—not all of Himself, because we could not handle such deep knowledge—but a true glimpse of Himself nonetheless. His riddles are for the purpose of drawing us in, of engaging us, of engrossing us in mystery, and when we struggle with those riddles out of a desire to know Him then He gives us Himself. He wants us to want Him, even more than He wants us to have answers. There is a subtle difference between the fear of being wrong and the love of truth and none of us, least of all me, knows his own heart very well. Wisdom and folly are next door neighbors; their houses may look identical from the street.

So what would the blood sacrifice have indicated to a discerning contemporary of Cain and Abel? I think that the sacrifices would reasonably have been understood as a means to initiate reconciliation with God, something that a human could bring that would please God and make God and worshipper closer. Thinking asymptotically, reconciliation means the undoing of death, the undoing of the Fall. If you follow the logic, then the blood sacrifices would mean that the way out of death was to be through death. It would be more like a prophetic riddle than anything else, but over the centuries new details would be provided.

Though God's rejection of Cain's offering had to do with issues impossible for Cain to know, and was not a rejection of Cain himself, Cain's reaction was one of jealousy. Now jealousy is a *diagnostic* emotion for us: the amount of love present is inversely proportional to the amount of jealousy. Even in a sexual relationship, jealousy indicates possessiveness and mistrust, not love. If Cain had loved God he would have set aside his hurt feelings and sought out ways to please God; but the one Cain truly loved was himself. What mattered to Cain was not God's preferences, not God's desires, but his own status in competition with Abel. When God approached Cain, He tried to warn him that he had not been at fault when his sacrifice was rejected, but that his jealousy toward Abel was a fault in itself that was dangerous. People had so little experience dealing with their evil inclinations at this point that God's remonstrance was as necessary as it was kind. Cain was clueless; he simply did not know how passion could lead to violence; he did not know that jealousy leads to hate and hate is murder in embryo.

It is interesting that God used the image of a beast crouching at the door intent on devouring Cain as an image of the evil in Cain. God was not speaking to Cain about the temptation to evil; the beast crouching at his door was not the desire to do something evil. Cain had already crossed the line into evil itself; he had succumbed to jealousy. God was warning him to resist this jealousy that he had already entertained like he would resist a beast intent on devouring him. The image God used here referred back to the curse on the dragon, that he would eat dust, and ever since then the dragon/serpent has been crouching at the doors of men, intent on devouring them in one way or another. First there is the temptation, the inclination and opportunity to adopt a certain attitude; then there is evil when that attitude is adopted; and then evil gives birth to death when we act on that attitude. We are accustomed to thinking of the outward action as being the evil, but really the things we do outwardly are the culmination of the process of evil, which is invisible and inward. What we are accustomed to call sins are just the outward marks of the beast tearing us apart as he eats his way out of us.

Nonetheless, though it is not the outward acts that are death in us, it is still desirable to suppress them. How much of our medicine goes toward healing disease and how much goes toward treating the symptoms to make the disease bearable? Curbing the outward expressions of evil is similar to trying to reduce the pain or the fever of a terminal disease; it is not a cure but it is still worth it. Curbing the outward expression of evil is just a way of limiting the damage evil does to the people around us, of limiting the number of innocent by-standers who suffer because of us. But curbing the outward expression of evil does not mean that there is no evil there; we are just hiding it, like we hide our nakedness, like we hide tumors or disfigurement. We are protecting the people around us from us.

The original wording of 4:8 is not totally clear. If we take the Hebrew Bible as the original, which I assume we should, then the verse should read, "Cain told Abel his brother. And it came about when they were in the field, that Cain rose up against Abel his brother and killed him." This sounds as though Cain told Abel what God had said to him, though it is not clear why. Perhaps Cain wanted to talk it over with Abel; there were presumably not many people to talk to so they might have talked about everything. Perhaps he was puzzling it out, but was still very upset by the rejection of his sacrifice. It suggests that Cain was brooding on God's words and afterwards when he was with his brother in an isolated spot he lost his temper and in a fit of anger killed Abel. Perhaps Abel was not understanding enough. This version portrays Cain as committing what we would call "second degree murder".

Other ancient versions—Septuagint, Syriac, and others—suggest that the original should be, "Cain said to Abel his brother, 'Let's go to the field.' And Cain rose up against Abel his brother and killed him." These versions make Cain's act seem like pre-meditated murder, Cain inviting Abel to a place with the intent of killing him. I don't think so, however. Evil was still too new, I think, to be planned. Later, as people became familiar with the range of possibilities for evil, they would act with deliberation. People had not learned how to scheme yet, and it is more likely that Cain behaved impulsively without thinking what the consequences might be.

In this way humanity went from stealing fruit to murder in a very short step. Indeed, there are no big steps between one kind of evil and another. They are all just different aspects of the same thing. This does show that evil behavior is not learned behavior; we do not become sinners by imitating our parents. On the contrary, we become sinners by being born, and the actual sins we commit are just the natural products of who we are. No one has to teach us the ways of evil; instinct is sufficient. It only takes a little imagination, and the whole world of evil is ours for the taking. Evil did not work its way gradually into the human heart when Adam chose to eat the fruit; it blossomed full-grown and utterly owned him from the beginning. It filled him and saturated him with its fullness. And so death and evil spread to all men because it had become who we are.

b) The Consequences of Murder (Genesis 4:9-16)

Once the murder had been committed, God gave Cain a chance to admit the crime and regain a bit of integrity, just as He had given Adam a similar opportunity. God's question as usual was a way of revealing to Cain (and to us) what was going on in Cain's heart, and in this instance it was particularly effective. Cain's reply, "Am I my brother's keeper?" has now become one of the most famous responses in history. Note how Cain's response was even *framed* from Abel's point of view as the memory of his crime against Abel burned into his conscience. Cain was the *keeper* of nothing; he was the tiller of the ground, an occupation which was the original job assignment given to people, and so an occupation with prestige and value. It was Abel who was the *keeper*, a brand new occupation, one with no pedigree. The shedding of Abel's blood had forged a link between the two brothers that was deeper than brotherhood: the bond of murderer and victim.

Cain's question was the question of a guilty man, a man who knows he has committed a crime and is trying to imply that the crime is not his problem, but his use of the word "keeper" gave it all away. He may have been denying that he was responsible for Abel, but his question betrayed even to Cain himself what he ought to have been to Abel. Cain had no one else to point to, there was no Eve in this equation, so perhaps it is not surprising that subconsciously his question pointed back to his victim. Cain's shifting eyes went to his victim, just as Adam's had gone to his victim.

But once Cain had refused the opportunity to confess, God closed in immediately. Just as Cain had related his crime to Abel's livelihood, God related the penalty of the crime to Cain's livelihood. The blood of Abel had infected the very ground as it soaked in, and was crying out against Cain. It was in the course of nature, a moral law no less forceful than a physical law, that Abel's blood would alienate Cain from that ground. For all the rest of his life the ground itself would hold Abel's blood and would cry out the accusation against him. You can interpret this from a psychological viewpoint, that the bloody ground cried out against Cain in his conscience and made a barrier between the land and himself. Or you could interpret it from a legalistic viewpoint, that God as the judge remembered Abel's blood and put a barrier between Cain and the ground as a punishment. Or you could interpret it from a mystical viewpoint, that there is a law built into nature by which the blood of Abel would itself form a kind of spiritual barrier between Cain and the ground.

The last interpretation is more in keeping with the tone of Scripture at this point. The idea that the blood of a murdered victim could poison the ground as it soaked in became a part of both the pagan, and the Hebrew, religious viewpoints. Perhaps this event—retold over the ages until it permeated the consciousness of the human race—is the source of that pagan intuition. When God announced the penalty to Cain He was not pronouncing a sentence like a judge would, but was unveiling to Cain's eyes the natural consequences of what he had done, as natural as gravity or rain. Beyond the alienation from the ground that was the result of the Fall, beyond the collapse of the Covenant that would have disconnected Cain from the earth, there was the added alienation of this witness against him. It was a personal penalty now, not the inherited grief of Adam but his own grief as a son of Adam.

It is interesting that when confronted with the first murder God prohibited the "eye for an eye" punishment. Capital punishment may seem to us to be the natural penalty for murder, but it was not so for God.

Instead, He established the rule that revenge for the murder would be met with seven times the guilt, seven times the consequence. Only later, after the Flood, did God institute capital punishment and we will discuss the reasons for it at the appropriate place. The point to notice now is that there was real reluctance on God's part to use the death penalty. In part this is because He had already used the Death Penalty for the original sin and enough was enough. His reluctance to use an additional death penalty arises from His purpose, which was not to make sure that every evil deed got punished, but to keep the results of evil in check, to keep the necessity of consequences minimized, to suppress as much as possible that long and horrible chain of moral cause and effect. God was seeking out ways to be merciful. The mark on Cain, whatever it was, was given in order to protect him and not to mark him for further abuse from other men. Some have tried to identify the mark with one racial distinction or another, as if the mark on Cain were a genetic mark rather than a superficial one. Whatever it was, the mark was a sign of God's mercy to Cain and not a sign of God's anger.

Cain's interpretation of his punishment was threefold: that he was being driven away from the earth, that he was being driven away from the face or presence of God, and that he was sentenced to death as a murderer. It is only the third of these three that God disputed, but the first two were correct to some extent. From this point on Cain apparently ceased to work the earth and verse 16 describes him as going out from the presence of the Lord. Here I believe we see the beginning of the loss of the knowledge of God by the human race generally. One question that naturally arises from the biblical account is: how did people who knew God on such a close basis lose that knowledge? Cain and Abel apparently had regular verbal interaction with God, and it was a grief to Cain, a genuine grief, that he was losing that interaction with God. From then on, among Cain's descendants, there would be no conversation with God, and all but a dim memory of God would be lost over the years.

The land of Nod was not a particular place; the name means simply a "land of banishment". The whole earth was the land of Nod to Adam, and to Cain, and to us. Cain was exiled just as his parents had been, except there was no Tree of Life he was leaving behind. The land of Nod was not a geographical place, but a spiritual place; he just happened to go east. Since he was the first person to build a city and settle down, the sentence on Cain that he would be a wanderer on the earth apparently does not refer to a nomadic existence. The wandering he was afflicted with was restlessness of spirit. Wherever he lived, however long he lived there, whether he lived in a tent or a stone house, he would never again be at home.

I wonder if rootlessness of spirit is always the spiritual consequence of violence, a moral law at work even today. There is some of the curse of Cain in many of us, and it would seem to afflict Americans with unusual frequency. How can we become rooted in a land which we took by violent means, in a land where the blood we spilled cries out against us? Part of our character as a nation, as a people, has been to wander from place to place, always further west until we finally bounced off the Pacific and had nowhere else to go. Even today we are the most rootless of all people, always moving on to something new, something different, urban nomads. The curse of Cain lies in the history and the heart of America. Our presence in this land rested on violence and therefore we cannot belong in it.

It is also true that to live away from the soil is to wander. The first job was gardening, after all, it is in our nature, our blood. To be estranged from growing things is to be estranged from a part of who we are. Building the city was a symptom of, and not a cure for, the rootlessness Cain suffered. He built a city because he had to try to live somewhere. The city was the shadow of a substance he could never have. We all of us long for that city, I think, the city whose architect and builder is God, the city where we can live, finally, and rest from all our wandering. The New Jerusalem is the city Cain was doomed to search for. When God took first Zion, then Jerusalem, and then New Jerusalem into the mainstream of His revelation, He was speaking to the children of Cain, promising them an arrival at last, a final rest in all their wandering.

4. The Descendants of Cain (Genesis 4:17-24)

We now follow the descendants of Cain and the descendants of Seth. The genealogy of Cain is not really a genealogy. There are no numbers given either for life spans or birth years. Cain and his descendants were a side line to the main story, a branch separating from the people who were charged with carrying the oracles of God. It is common to interpret the descendants of Cain and Seth as representing the seed of the serpent and the seed of the woman, but I can't fully agree. In the drama of the Messiah, the most visible representatives of the serpent are also descendants of Seth;

the warfare was to be more of an internal family feud and not inter-racial. The descendants of Cain were the rest of the human race who went out from the presence of the Lord.

Cain named his first son Enoch, which means "consecration", but the significance of this name to Cain is not clear. It is not even clear whether Enoch was born before of after Cain killed Abel, though we commonly assume Cain was unmarried until he left. If Enoch was born before Cain's banishment, the name might have been an expression of faith, but if Enoch was born after Cain's banishment, the name might have indicated defiance. But later when Cain built the first city and named it for his son, it was clearly an act of rebellion against the sentence pronounced on him to be a wanderer, as if he thought he could get out of the consequences of his crime by his own power. After all, there were no spirit police, no one to enforce the sentence. Who said he would have to be a wanderer on the earth? He would show God; he would build a city and settle down and *not* wander. And he would name both his son and his city a word which broadcast his defiance of God, claiming for himself what God had denied him and his offering. But as I pointed out previously, living physically in one place can't cure the restlessness of spirit that finds no home in the world. Whatever Cain meant by using the name, there is no indication that he or his descendants ever expressed any desire for God or admitted any weakness or homesickness or sign of regret for what had been lost.

The degeneration in these spiritual nomads came to full blossom in Lamech. Lamech was the first recorded polygamist, so we should pause for a moment to discuss polygamy. It is important to give full attention to the fact that the Scripture never forbids polygamy. Under certain conditions the Law of Moses commanded men to have more than one wife. However, while polygamy may be permissible from the legalistic viewpoint, reintroducing polygamy into our culture would be a disaster. American men, one could say western men, find it difficult to be good husbands to one wife, much less to several. The chaos that would come out of polygamy in this culture would only make bad into worse.

It might be argued that polygamy would make adultery less common (David and Bathsheba is a contra-indicator here) and perhaps stabilize our families, which seem all too prone to breaking up. None of the polygamous families detailed in the Bible were much different from the dysfunction we have in our modern monogamous families, however. The evidence seems to indicate that a man who cannot learn contentment with one woman usually can't learn contentment at all. The cause of adultery is not that men find it impossible to restrain themselves to only one woman; it's that they were never sure they wanted to in the first place. It is not the number, the quantity, of wives that is the problem, it is the quality of the commitment. It is not strong desires but weak resolve that makes us fail, whether we are talking about fidelity in marriage, in friendship, in faith.

Lamech was designated as the source of nearly all that we now consider to be the marks of civilization. His first wife, Adah, was the mother of Jabal and Jubal. Jabal was the father of the nomadic peoples who lived in tents and kept herds, but Jubal was the father of music. The name "Jubal" is related to the Hebrew word meaning "sound". This does not mean, necessarily, that Jabal and Jubal themselves personally were the sources of those innovations, though that could be what is meant. To be "the father" of something can mean that the thing originated with the descendants of that person. Once it had been invented, naturally music spread beyond the one family. The passage only says that it was Jubal or his descendants who first initiated the art of music. Lamech's second wife, Zillah, gave birth to Tubal-cain, whose descendants were credited with the first metalworking among men, which is also a kind of art. If Lamech and his wives gave these names to their children then they were giving them prophetically of what the babies would become. It would be a strange thing if a descendant of Cain were the first prophet the human race produced. But the names might have been acquired in later life by reputation, or even given to them by later generations honoring them.

Moreover Tubal-cain's sister, Naamah, is mentioned but without a reason being given. Since it is unusual for the genealogies to mention women without some particular purpose, her presence here is worth some attention. Naamah means "lovely" or "graceful". If we consider the wives' names as well, Adah means "adorned", and Zillah means something like "jingling" which creates the image of a woman wearing a lot of jewelry. Given these meanings I wonder if Naamah, Adah and Zillah were the originators of cosmetics and jewelry, and perhaps even of fashion, as the men were the originators of music and metal working. This is not stated in the passage but may be hypothesized from it.

Music has been mentioned as originating with Jubal; Lamech himself was the source of poetry and drama. Drama is the focus of this passage, and Lamech's speech to Adah and Zillah is in poetic form, making it the first recorded poem. The Hebrew of Lamech's little speech is ambiguous.

It is not clear if Lamech was confessing to a murder or if he was making a boast about what he would do if someone dared to touch him. Lamech's speech was either bragging about a murder he had committed, turning it into a Tragedy in which he was the hero as well as the criminal; or else he was bragging about what he would do to anyone who crossed him, portraying himself as a Hero whose destiny was above the rules governing common mortals. It is one of the schemes of human culture to try to ennoble our fallen condition by recasting it as great drama, and Lamech initiated this grand tradition.

It is more glorious, after all, to play the role of the tragic figure, even the victim, in the grand drama of life, than a mere fool and sinner. We are always looking for some way to make the sheer stupidity of evil less a blow to our pride, and drama is the perfect tool to do it. Formal plays and performances were many centuries down the road; the evolution of the dramatic tradition that he began was slow, but he was the first actor in the first script. The ancient myths were all in the dramatic form, and most of them were more tragedy than narrative. Lamech taught men how to dress up the results of evil choices in a palatable form, to make folly larger than life, to make it *admirable*, to make it *glamorous*, to make it *noble*. So when the earliest men began to make stories about their gods, since they could not imagine true goodness or glory, they made their gods into actors in grand plays to ennoble them as much as they could. The gods co-starred in the first great war epics. Lamech was the father of all those in our day who write about warfare as if it were noble.

Civilization and culture, I think, can be understood as "societal clothing". We wear our civilization to hide our social nakedness like we wear our coats and ties to hide our physical nakedness. The world of fashion, the world of technology, the world of art, the world of the stage—in short, the whole world we live in—is designed to recast evil and decay in a more marketable form, to dress up the process of cultural and sociological disease as something beautiful in its own way. We clothe ourselves in custom and convention and these make our mutual interactions both possible and impossible. We find it impossible to speak or work with each other without certain rules of civility, but the rules are also the means for hiding our true selves. We would no more be honest with our neighbors than we would walk into town naked, and for fundamentally the same reason.

This does not mean that people of faith are to reject the trappings of civilization any more than people of faith are to reject clothing. We can no more live without the customs of society and civilization than we can live without clothes. Consider how God responded to the inventions of the children of Cain. His answer to the development of drama was not at all to despise and reject it. On the contrary, He outplayed us at our own game. He took up drama to His own purpose. He became the starring Actor in the greatest Tragedy of all time. The greatest drama ever conceived was performed for all the world to see in the history of Israel. The rest of Scripture is God's play performed on His stage. Music was treated in the same way; whatever its original purpose, God took it as a central element in the worship of His people.

God does not despise civilization or culture because it is a result of what is left of His image operating in us. Though we are fallen and inevitably create ugliness along with beauty, it is still valued by Him who values us. The inventions of these children of Cain are expressions of the true image of God, the creative impulse that comes from Him, and God respected those inventions even when their intent was hostile. Human culture may be used to defy God, to hide our shame, to exalt ourselves in a shameless manner, but it is also the very essence of what our existence was supposed to be. The proof of my contention is that God chose to preserve in the Scripture Lamech's poem in his own praise and He didn't even give a critical response to it, letting it stand on its own. We could all take a cue from His reaction and be a little less strident and defensive when our own culture expresses itself, even when it is arrogant or deceptive or blasphemous. If God does not defend Himself from cultural attacks, He certainly doesn't need or want us to do it for Him.

To use a more biblical word, Lamech and his sons and wives and daughters invented the *world*. In the New Testament, the word that is translated "world" can mean two quite different things. First it can mean "nature", the physical world we live in. Second it can mean the human world we live in, the mindset and trappings of what we call culture. The first world is the beloved of God; the second world is invariably portrayed as an enemy of God. The relationship of the Christian to the world, the second meaning, is a bit complex, summarized by that phrase "in the world but not of it". Like so many profound phrases in the Bible, this is one that has been understood in extremely different ways by different people at different times. It has created the monastic movement, the Amish communities, the holiness movement, and modern capitalism.

Clearly Lamech and his family created a dilemma for us that we have not quite gotten a handle on even today.

So this is my take on it. I am a white, American, of the latter 20th century, strongly influenced by the 1960's toward a social and political liberalism, strongly shaped by television, books, and music, marked by the events I have lived through and the people I have lived with. These all shape me just as my genetic heritage shapes me. They were all put into the mix by God Himself when He knit me together in my mother's womb into a particular time and place and family. But unlike Lamech, He has lifted me above it all. He has given me eyes to see and a mind to judge my culture. I do not have to adopt it all. I can pick and choose which parts are helpful and which are not, which parts ought to be condemned, which parts ought to be tolerated, which parts may even be praiseworthy. In short, He has made me an outsider to my own people, my own culture, my own land. Only when we take out citizenship here in the world, only when we settle down, only when we fail to judge our own culture, but use it to judge both man and God, do we also become true children of Cain.

5. The Descendants of Seth (Genesis 4:25-5:32 and I Chronicles 1:1-4)

We now turn to the third son of Adam and Eve, Seth, whose name means something like "compensation" or "appointed one". This could signify not only that Seth was given as a replacement for Abel, but also that he was the bearer of the Appointment, the line leading to the Promised One. It is with Seth's son, Enosh, that we first hear of men beginning to call on the name of the Lord. Calling on the name of the Lord must mean something different from having daily and direct interaction with Him. It is what men do who have lost direct contact. The times of personal and frequent conversation with God had ended and people were finding it necessary to devise some kind of religion, some way to reconnect with Him. This would have been just as true for the people who carried the oral tradition contained in Genesis as for those who did not.

Enosh means "weak" or "frail" and I think this sense of frailty and human weakness is a significant contrast with the descendants of Cain. It is considered a rebuke when people call faith in God a crutch, but in fact a crutch is just what it is. It is the people who need a crutch, who are aware of their frailty, that call upon God. Enosh, "the weak one", as contrasted to Enoch, "the consecrated", introduces a theme that runs down even to the present. There are those who belong to God and represent God; these are people who are weak, who have nothing in themselves to impress people, who are "poor in spirit"; and exactly because they are nothing to boast about, God makes His boast in them. Then there are those who are "holy", who are strong or righteous, who are impressive; but they are impressive on their own and God will not make an impression on them. Seth wasn't thinking all these things when he named his son, of course, nor was Cain thinking along these lines, but the inner attitude of their hearts came through. Seth knew his weakness, the weakness of all of us, and named his son for what was in his heart; but Cain was busy hiding and blustering. It is a pattern in spiritual history: the human race divides into those who are poor in spirit and those who thank God for their own goodness.

God acted immediately to preserve true knowledge of Himself in the descendants of Seth. The account we are presently discussing of the creation of the world and the Fall was probably preserved in an oral tradition through the line of Seth. God was not willing that the memory of Him would entirely disappear and so He acted to keep the memory alive in a part of humanity while the rest of humanity walked out of God's presence and gradually drifted into rumor and myth. This does not mean that the rest of humanity, outside the line of Seth, had absolutely no knowledge of God, but their knowledge quickly became confused and vague. In the descendants of Seth, God acted to preserve an accurate, though brief, account of the origin of things, the origin of evil, and the hope of deliverance.

The two families of descendants were closer than we traditionally suppose: the descendants of Cain did not have nothing of God, and the descendants of Seth did not have much. The difference between the two does not lie in the quantity of knowledge they had or did not have; the more important difference was in their attitude toward the knowledge they had. In the long run, the most important difference between the two was God's choice. God preserved and added to the memory, the knowledge, and the understanding among the descendants of Seth in a way that He did not do among the descendants of Cain. The kind of revelation He intended was one that required a certain amount of focus, a certain amount of specialization. He had not abandoned the rest of humanity;

but He did keep them waiting, letting them choose their own path with the light they had.

A few words are appropriate about the genealogy from Seth to Noah. It was sometimes necessary, if a genealogy was to cover a large number of generations, to give only the highlights rather than an exhaustive list of each generation. The leaving out of some generations was certainly done in some of the lists in Chronicles later on, but this particular passage, this first genealogy, agrees with later lists of the same generations. This means that Genesis contains the most complete information we have about the first generations, and also the most ancient information. But it is doubtful that this genealogy is complete. When a very long period of time was being covered it was a practical necessity to leave something out.

The point is that we cannot use this genealogy as a dating tool. We do not know if the Genesis genealogy was intended as a complete list of all the generations from Creation to Flood, or if that period of time was so long that only the highlights were given here. The Hebrew language is ambiguous enough that either interpretation is possible, though most English translations make it sound more definite than it is. For what it is worth, allowing for the possibility of missing generations agrees more closely with the scant archaeological data we do have. I have previously argued that it is a mistake to reinterpret Scripture to make it agree more closely with science. I would also argue that it is a mistake to interpret Scripture to make it disagree with science whenever possible. We need not have a chip on our shoulder. My own view is that this is not a complete list of the generations, and that the length of time between the Fall and the Flood was a very great length, and we cannot know how long it was.

The life spans mentioned in this genealogy are incredibly long. Extra-biblical accounts of events before the Flood also mention long life spans as being normal. The Sumerian king list is even more incredible than the biblical account, with life spans in many thousands of years. What we are to make of it exactly is not clear. My feeling is that death was such an unnatural thing that it was "slow to catch on" in nature. The laws of nature that we live under now are not truly "natural"; they only seem to be so because they are all we've ever known. With the Fall, as I hypothesized in a previous section, the physical laws that govern us were changed, but I think the change was gradual rather than abrupt. In any case, though spiritual death was immediate, physical death seems to have been slower in taking charge of us, and this could be attributed to a gradual change in the physical laws that govern our bodies.

In the sixth generation from Adam we come to a second Enoch. Like the descendant of Cain, he was also named the "consecrated one", and he was one of only two people in the Bible who were said not to have ever physically died, but to have been translated directly from this life to a heavenly life. We don't know what that means, of course. And we don't know what motivated Jared to name his son Enoch, whether he was dedicating him to God or was speaking prophetically. Enoch was said to have "walked with God", denoting an especially close interaction, one not experienced by any other man in the millennia after the Fall. The only other individual who was said to walk with God was Noah, but he died an ordinary death.

We are given an intriguingly small amount of information about Enoch; he played no further role in God's activity on earth and that alone justifies paying some attention to him. We talk much of God's Plan for history as if that were the only thing going on. Enoch was a part of that Plan, to be sure, being one in the middle of a long chain of ancestors who bore the oral tradition and bore Noah and the future Messiah, but his closeness to God did not correspond in an obvious way to his role in the Plan. We should always remember that God is doing all manner of things in the world, and being at the center of this one plan of redeeming the world is not necessarily a mark of special holiness or intimacy with God, nor is being on the fringe of this plan a mark of God's disfavor. Of all the men who have ever lived, Enoch must have been one of the closest to God; and yet he played only a minor role in the Plan of Redemption and was not honored by more than a single verse describing him. That is the way of it; being a central character in the Play is not the same as being intimate with the Author, and vice versa. God does not arrange people or roles the way we would.

It is worth emphasizing that the genealogy in chapter 5 does not indicate the origin of the full racial diversity in the world. There seems to be a substantial portion of the world left out: Africans and Orientals at the least and probably others. The focus of the Scripture is on the ancestry of the Messiah and the people who lived in His neighborhood. All the details that weren't in the main stream were left out with no slight intended. The Messiah had to be of some race if He were to be born. Though the Bible does focus on one branch of Caucasians and Semites, it is not a mark of honor that it does. On the contrary, if the other races are absent from the biblical genealogy, as they appear to be, then it is the opposite of a slight. The ethnic groups whose account is given were not portrayed in a positive light for the most part. All we have to go on here are hints and imagination, but the hints do indicate that there may have been a lot going on in the world apart from the people in this genealogy that we do not know about.

This genealogy culminates with Noah. Noah's father, Lamech, was the first recorded prophet if we discount the possible prophetic child naming by the other Lamech who descended from Cain, or the possibility that Jared prophesied when he named Enoch. This Lamech's prophesy also occurred in the context of naming his son, but it was a full prophesy; he deliberately assumed the stance of the prophet and consciously stated what he meant by the name. Lamech prophesied concerning Noah that he would give them rest from their toil that had arisen from the land being cursed. On the surface it is not at all clear what Lamech's prophecy meant, and it certainly seems to be unrelated to the Flood. To understand the significance of his prophecy, we must look at it in the context of chapter 6 and the years immediately preceding the Flood.

My theory is that this record of Seth's genealogy is the record of the passing of the oral tradition over the millennia after the Fall, the oral tradition that was eventually written down in these first few chapters of Genesis. It would be natural if some of the individuals carrying the oral tradition added some content to that tradition over the years, possibly prophetic or possibly just recording names. Most of Seth's descendants are not listed at all, even if no generations were left out. I am assuming that there was a long period of human history before the invention of writing. This seems to be true on the whole, but we don't know with any certainty that there wasn't a written record back to the beginning. Such a possibility only becomes a possibility if we assume God acted as the teacher of the first people and gave us the gift of writing. It wouldn't be very odd that we have found no evidence of such writing considering how little total we have found, but it is not the sort of hypothesis that a serious scientist can seriously entertain without some seriously good reason. Still, the ancient myths envisioned one god or another giving some gift or another to humanity, in one case fire, in another case the plow. It would have been a great kindness indeed if God had taught us writing, even if nearly all of the ancients chose to abandon it. I don't believe He did, but it is an intriguing possibility, unsubstantiated by any evidence whatsoever, that we were literate from the beginning.

6. The End of the Beginning (Genesis 6:1-8)

To understand the conditions on the earth immediately before the Flood, I think we should note that the specific evil that is mentioned, and the only specific evil mentioned, is violence. The mercy shown to Cain had not stopped the spread of violence. Here "violence" does not simply mean one man murdering another for insulting him. Random acts of individual violence were not what was in view. Throughout human history it is when some few men become strong enough to force their will on those who are weaker that the worst violence is done. The violence of one against one had been with the human race from the first opportunity; it was nothing new. What distressed God in the days of Noah was not the quantity of the violence, lots of individuals killing other individuals, but the quality of the violence, the ruthless few who became strong and dominated and exploited the many who were weak, on an unprecedented scale.

It was this extreme corruption of violent oppression that moved God to grief. The prophecy of Lamech, the father of Noah, can be understood most easily as a reference to this pervasive violence. The most common form of such violence is the enslavement of the weak to do the hard work; the division of the world into the owners and the owned, the nobles and the serfs, the masters and the slaves, those who give the orders and those who do the manual labor of growing the necessary food and then are kept impoverished rather than rewarded. Even today this is still the most common form of violence worldwide. Lamech's prophecy can be understood as saying that with Noah there would be an end to the widespread misery that such violence produces.

The decision to destroy all living things might seem to be an extreme reaction, an over reaction. If you are thinking on a small scale, this may be true. But try to picture a world built on the model of the Nazis or the Khmer Rouge or Stalin, with nowhere to go to escape, no respite, no hope. Such a picture would be nearer to what this passage paints as the world before the Flood. But it was much worse than that. In such modern examples there have always been some few who stood against the evil, but this was a world *filled* with violence. It was not just oppression of the poor by the rich as if the poor were merely the victims. This was a world in which the poor were themselves practicing violence against each other. It was a brutal world, a dog-eat-dog world, in which violence permeated every level of society, in which the subtle line between human and animal had virtually disappeared. There were no "good guys". A world filled with such violence is a world that needs to be ended on any terms. Death, after all, is not the worst that befalls us. Long life in such a world as that, long life in a world of constant fear and hatred, is far worse than death. Physical death would be a mercy in such a world.

The passage says that the Lord was sorry that He had made man and grieved in His heart. Some have taken this, in spite of the rest of the scripture, to indicate that either God was surprised by the course of events to this point, or that God's attitude had changed. There are two things at least that should be taken into account when we read passages like this, besides the testimony of the rest of Scripture. One is that *time* matters. God respects time and does not violate it. Time is one of those good parts of creation which has been stained by the Fall, and changed in nature, but is still valued by God and is being redeemed by Him. God respects the integrity of time and that means that when He interacts with His creation, He interacts with it at particular times. It is irrelevant whether or not He knew that the world would degenerate as it did before the Flood. His grief over the violence that filled the earth would be expressed at the *time* of the violence, not before it had occurred. No doubt He could have told Adam and Eve before or after the eating of the fruit that He was grieved by what things would be like in a few thousand years, but it would have been an inappropriate and confusing and even disrespectful thing to do.

Secondly, God was expressing Himself in human terms and human terms require the use of language from inside of time. God was sorry that He had made man; this sounds like He had changed His opinions, that at one time He thought everything was going to be OK but by the time of the Flood He was ready to give up. However what this passage was really doing was expressing an eternal reaction to a condition in time to people who lived in time and had to understand things in a temporal way. God made it very clear later that He never changes; He said so outright. Nonetheless, He uses language that we can understand to explain to us what He feels, and He couches His feelings in terms of time to make them explicable to us.

It also needs to be pointed out that God's feelings toward the world before Noah were those of grief and not those of anger. We should not think of the coming Flood as God's wrath against the evil in the world, an outburst of fury against a human race which had become disgusting to Him. Rather His feelings were feelings of grief, and that means they were feelings of compassion toward people and the misery they had brought on themselves. It may seem hard to think of the Flood as expressing compassion, but I believe that is exactly the case. The Flood was the first mercy killing. It is possible that death and pain and misery can become so acute and so inescapable that physical death is the only merciful end. We can see it every day in the nations ravaged by drought and war; we can see it every day in the hospitals in our own neighborhoods. Before the Flood the whole world had been brought that low. God simply could not let the suffering and misery go on, so He ended it, and I think the suffering that was common in the world at that time was beyond our present experience, as horrible as that is.

The idea of the wrath of God, as we usually think of it, is not present in Scripture up to this point. There is another sense in which wrath is portrayed here, but I must put that off to a later discussion. Of course this absence does not mean that God did not feel anger. It is impossible for me to imagine the world I am trying to describe without also feeling anger, outrage of the kind that the stories of the Nazis inspire, or the stories of brutality in American history or in the other genocides of the present day. "Every intent of the thoughts of his [mankind's] heart was only evil continually," it says in 6:5 and we all know what that looks like on a small scale, and we all know what a deep sense of grief and shame and fear and disgust and hatred it fills even us with. Such emotions, I think, are an echo of the sorts of emotions God feels. And yet with Him it is different. Our anger is not like His, just as our ways are not like His, and we have only an echo in our hearts of what He is thinking in His heart so that the sound is muffled and distorted. It is easy to imagine that God feels as we do, that His anger is just like ours but bigger, but it would be a mistake to do so. To understand what His anger is like requires more revelation than we have had so far in these six chapters.

There are some final loose ends to consider before we go on to the Flood. As mentioned above, no one knows who the "sons of God" were in 6:2. It is unlikely that these sons of God were angels or demons, as some have suggested; Luther understood the "sons of God" as great rulers and tyrants, which is in line with what I have just said about the nature of the violence on the earth. Besides the sons of God there were the Nephilim.

"Nephilim" is just the Hebrew word for giant, but it is not at all clear what is being referred to, whether this was a tribe of giants or merely individual giants or giants in a metaphorical sense, another name for the "great men". Later Goliath is said to be a vestige of the Nephilim so my inclination is to believe that there were a race of very large people from some unknown source. No one has found any fossils of such giants but that should not lead us to think too quickly that the Nephilim are merely fictional. The world is a big place and so much of the ancient world has been lost.

It might seem that giants would be most likely to come from some kind of hybrid human/angel, the offspring of the sons of God and the daughters of men, but it seems highly unlikely that that kind of creature is biologically possible. There is nothing intrinsically impossible that there was a race of men that were giants like Goliath, ten feet tall or so, and that we have just not found their remains yet. Such a size would not be a survival trait, biologically, and it would be no wonder that they became extinct, just as lions are too large to be competitive and are also becoming extinct even without human help.

Another possibility is that the sons of God were the half of the human race that was at war with the children of the serpent, and they were here committing apostasy with the daughters of men, the seed of the serpent. The inter-marriage and resulting corruption of the people of God with pagan peoples is a constant theme through the Bible. This interpretation of the sons of God as opponents of the serpent fits well with that one theme, but otherwise seems unlikely on the face of it.

An intriguing possibility is that it was these Nephilim, whoever they were, that gave rise in the course of time to the pagan myths of gods and goddesses and that the myths of the ancient world had some historical basis. There is no way to be sure. The most ancient mythology of the Sumerians told of the gods being the first builders of the cities in Mesopotamia. The myths say that it was these gods that invented the plow and other technology, and gave it to men to make them better slaves for the gods. On the whole, the Sumerian gods do sound a bit like the descendants of Cain, and the Sumerian myths describe a world roughly like the picture I tried to paint of the world before the Flood. The Sumerian gods were pictured as living in the cities and mingling with people in their ordinary lives; then the gods went away to some other place. It is interesting that the Bible may lend some credence to those myths; it does not help much in answering who or what the Nephilim/Sumerian gods were, but it does suggest that the ancient myths were based on something other than mere imagination. The Sumerian myths said that these gods created the human race to be slaves for themselves. It is not hard to imagine a society built on oppression by the powerful, in which the rulers invented such myths to keep the peasants subjugated.

It would certainly be a mistake to run too far or too fast with such speculations as I have just made, as if they mattered. You may find some comfort in being frustrated with the Spirit and complaining to Him about the gaps in the revelation He gave us. If He was going to mention the Nephilim why not give us enough information to quench our curiosity a bit? Or, if that would have been too complicated, why not just leave them out of the revelation entirely? Ultimately, it is His fault that His revelation contains what it contains and did not give us all the answers we want; but then He never promised that He would tell us *everything*. Indeed, perhaps the Spirit's point in including a reference to the sons of God with no explanation is to underline the fact that we don't know much. Perhaps it is a desirable thing for us to know how little we know. Humility is always in short supply, if we can just be wise enough to let the Scripture make us more humble.

II

The Covenant of Preservation

A. The Flood

1. Where Noah Fits in the Flow of Revelation (Genesis 6:9-13)

Except among the one line of descendants of Seth the human race was left to drift, to preserve whatever it wanted to preserve of the knowledge of God and to keep whatever parts of the knowledge of good and evil it chose to keep. The result was disaster. When left on its own, the human race chose to keep very little knowledge of God beyond the vague idea that He existed. We preferred a comfortable idea of His remoteness and were content to drift morally. We carried along the knowledge of good and evil, but consider what it means for a sinner to "know good and evil": it means that evil is vividly before us requiring little or no creativity to practice, while goodness becomes increasingly like a dream or a mystical vision, a divine dissatisfaction with what we are doing. We had no clear grasp of what real goodness is; only a vague sense of loss and desire, of grief and sometimes guilt. The clear vision of true goodness, in the rare moments when it has been given, was devastating.

By far the most devastating result of not having a formal covenant was that people were left spiritually adrift. Not only did they have no formal connection to God, but their relationships to each other and to nature were no longer functional or reasonable. They had to work out their mutual relationships on their own, and what they did work out was the worst possible. Even the most dog-eat-dog world has some pack-like structure, some community, some family that keeps the individual from being entirely lost; but structure only comes from an over-arching covenant, some network of order and due process. Before the Flood there was no such over-arching covenant. It was anarchy. It was the perfect embodiment of a ruthless world, a world in which everyone was in it for themselves and themselves alone and there was no affectionate tie to anyone to make their lives more than the lives of animals. This is the meaning, as I make it out, of the world being filled with violence; though some translations use the word "wickedness", what is in view here is not mere immorality but the sort of behavior that best fits the word "bestial". The picture is not of a world that had become one large frat party; it was grim and demonic, more similar to Tolkien's vision of Mordor. Violence and hatred so permeated the world that the only adequate word to name it is hell.

And the culmination of the moral degeneration before the Flood was that, when God looked around the world to find a righteous man, He found exactly one. We are sometimes given to think that God had come to the point of despairing over the pervasiveness of evil and was literally on the point of destroying it all when fortunately He happened to notice there was still one good man left; and for the sake of that one good man and his family He arranged a deliverance from the destruction He had been planning. This is not an accurate picture, however.

If you think about it a little, you will see that this can't be an accurate description of the situation. How can we interpret this passage in a way that portrays God as being on the verge of failing to keep His promise? Sending a Flood to destroy absolutely every living thing would have gone against God's previously stated purpose. He had committed Himself to defeat the serpent through a man of His own choosing. He had promised to deliver the world from the plague of death through one of Eve's descendants, and there is no where any hint that He ever considered giving up in defeat. It should be unthinkable to suppose that God would fail in anything He decides to do. So whatever is going on in this passage, it cannot be that God had come to the point of despair regarding the world but luckily found Noah who gave Him an out from destroying it.

It is more accurate to say that God chose Noah and preserved the man Noah for Himself in order to preserve His creation through Noah and keep His word to the serpent. In other words, when God makes a promise He actively fulfills it. He was not just waiting around hoping that someone like Noah would come along. It was a sovereign act of God's grace in Noah that made Noah the right man at the right place at the right time. Nor did God need a righteous man to give Him an excuse for saving the world; He would have been justified in taking a total derelict and saving the world through him simply because He had promised He would.

"Noah was a righteous man, blameless in his generation." We should not imagine that Noah was a truly good man in himself, a saint as we typically imagine them to be. We should not suppose that it was on the basis of Noah's righteousness that the delivery was accomplished. Noah's righteousness, like the righteousness of any other man, was "filthy rags". The phrase "in his generation" in the quote is key to correctly understanding Noah. There is no doubt in my mind that good and evil are absolute matters, that there are absolute and universal standards of right and wrong, but absolute righteousness was not what was in view here. Noah was not credited as righteous by absolute standards, not by the standards of Jesus, nor by the standards of Moses, not by the standards of twentieth century American Christians. He was blameless *in his own generation*, a generation heir to a long sequence of generations in which there had been little revelation and less knowledge. God had planted a little root of something desirable in his heart, and soon we will consider what that root was. He had planted a little root of something gracious in Noah's heart as part of His revelation to us, to bring into focus those ghosts of goodness that haunt our best dreams. He had planted a little seed of something good in Noah and used that seed as an excuse for choosing him.

Very little is actually said in this passage about the character of Noah; it has all been left to the imagination of the readers. Thus we usually paint Noah as a sort of super-hero. We are given a man who took a hundred and twenty years to build an ark (based on taking 6:3 as a prophecy of the coming Flood and assuming God spoke to Noah immediately after He said it); who built the ark in the middle of a desert, or at least far inland, and had to endure the ridicule of all his neighbors (it is not stated where Noah lived nor where he built the ark nor even that his neighbors ridiculed him); and who had the additional task of rounding up all those animals himself. We shouldn't minimize the great thing that Noah did, of course. He believed that the Flood was coming, and that shows great faith. He built the ark, a long and expensive work that must have taken his attention away from attending to his own affairs. And he probably did have to endure much in the way of ridicule and opposition, possibly danger, during the construction. Given the state of the world at that time as I have pictured it, the personal danger could have been great—unless he was wealthy, for in all societies the wealthy can usually do what they want.

But, we ought not make him into some kind of spiritual giant. It is we who demand that God pick "good guys" to be His messengers and prophets. It is the parents and writers of Sunday School curricula who insist that God only use estimable people for His servants. It is as if we thought that, if our children saw the true character of the people God chose to use, they would be encouraged to be bad. "I don't have to be a good little boy or girl because Samson wasn't," and our understanding of the gospel is so defensive that we would have no answer for them. Thus we are always sanitizing the Bible before we let our children see it. If God did not have us to clean up His messes, where would He be? But God was not and never would be in the habit of using the "good" men of the earth to accomplish His work. The men God habitually chose, and still chooses, were not so impressive morally, and were only impressive spiritually when pious people colored them in, larger than life. God chose fools and weaklings to accomplish His purposes, people like you and me. No, Noah was a man like we are, but God was gracious to him and did this great thing through him.

At this point, when the pain we were in was unbearable to God, the time was ripe for Him to act, to reverse the tide of evil, and to rescue a remnant of everything. The rapid degeneration after the Fall had gone on long enough and had served its purpose and the time had come to raise up a deliverer. At the right moment He sent a prophecy to Lamech to foretell the role Noah would perform. "Noah found favor in the eyes of the Lord" before he was born. Noah was not the Hero promised to Eve, but certainly Noah was the first of a long series of heroes raised up to rescue the world and the people of God, leading ultimately to the promised Savior.

2. God's Call to Noah (Genesis 6:14-22)

When God called Noah He was careful to communicate three distinct things. The first was to convey to Noah exactly what he was commissioned to do in some detail, not only to build an ark, but an ark of a specific size, with a specific design, out of a specific material, etc. We don't know where

Noah lived when he was called. He might have lived near the coast and possibly knew something about building ships. The earliest evidence for sails and sailing ships suggest they were invented between 3000 and 4000 b.c., many millennia after Noah. Even if Noah were familiar with ships—or more likely boats—this one would have been enormous, probably larger than any that had ever been built. It could not have been rowed; its only purpose was to stay afloat.

Secondly, in 6:17 God said, "And behold, I, even I am bringing the flood of water upon the earth, to destroy all flesh in which is the breath of life, from under heaven; everything that is on the earth shall perish." This is a very emphatic way of taking the responsibility for what was about to happen, and it deserves some consideration. The destruction of the earth in the Flood was an act that God deliberately and voluntarily entered into. He was not forced into it by the overwhelming evil of mankind; nor was He forced into it by His strong emotional revulsion to the violence and evil in the world. His grief was certainly real, but the decision to send the Flood was His own. Our understanding of death is limited by our perspective, and it is difficult for us to appreciate that there are times when death is the lesser of an assortment of evils. I am not speaking here of how we may think death is preferable for someone we hate, an enemy who has done something wicked to us. Death was preferable at this time because of God's desire for mercy, the desire to make the suffering cease.

Death is an evil thing; death is an enemy to us and to God. But there comes a point in moral degeneration in which the suffering is simply too great to be allowed, and physical death becomes the most merciful option. Moral degeneration is most like a cancer. As long as it can be held in remission, as long as the symptoms and the pain can be controlled, we can live with it. But when it gets out of control, when the pain goes beyond the reach of the drugs we use, then we look to death as the best that life has to offer. I am not an advocate of physician-assisted suicide because I assume that death is an option that only God can be trusted to choose. When does it come to the point that we give up hope in God's healing? How can we have the wisdom to know what God might do in a terminal illness? This is an issue that we struggle to think through clearly. The first thing we must come to grips with in thinking about euthanasia is that the advocacy for euthanasia frequently springs from a very Godly desire, the desire to be merciful. Is it the right position to restrain the impulse to mercy on the grounds that we lack the wisdom, or on the grounds that the impulse to mercy may just be a disguise for the impulse to murder? Perhaps so, but we must be very careful how we think about this issue.

But moral degeneration is worse than cancer and God sometimes does what we dare not permit ourselves to do. With cancer, though the pain may become unbearable, it will end eventually on its own; but there would seem to be no end to how far moral degeneration can go, no end to the depths of pain that humans can bear as the result of evil, and no limit to the scale of the suffering. The twentieth century gave a glimpse of how deep the misery can go in a world of wars and mass murder and genocide. If it is mercy to contemplate helping a man with cancer to die, if we remember the horrors of Cambodia or Germany or Russia or Rwanda or a hundred other places, then we understand a little of how God felt before the Flood and why He did it.

In taking such pains to assume responsibility for the Flood, God was also admitting that He had done nothing to prevent the necessity of the Flood. It was God's choice to let us go, to allow our degeneration to proceed to the point that a mercy killing was desirable. It need not have been like that; God could have intervened to restrain the expression of evil, and after the Flood He did take specific steps to inhibit the spread of evil. As horrible as the Flood was, God felt that it was important for us to see the effects of unrestrained evil, the results that come from our own hearts running rampant. We needed to understand that apart from God's grace restraining our evil impulses the whole human race would end up in perpetual horror. We needed to know, to experience, how desperate our situation is, that without God's *active* intervention in human affairs we have no chance of surviving in anything like a human condition. As horrible as the conditions must have been and as the Flood was, God felt that we needed the symbol, the revelation, that the Flood conveyed.

The days before the Flood were a time, the first and only time in history, that God gave us up to our own desires. In the New Testament letter to the Romans St. Paul defines the wrath of God as God "giving us up", letting us have what we want, letting us experience the natural moral consequences of our evil desires. The days before the Flood was a time in which the world was under the wrath of God. We reside in hell whenever we are left on our own. Correspondingly whenever the human race makes steady progress toward civilization or justice or social decency it is because it is riding piggyback on God. We absolutely cannot do anything good on our own, individually or collectively. Henceforth all around the world people would have stories of the destruction of the earth in a Flood, and they would know that man's place on the earth was precarious, that evil was crouching at the door of the world like a lion to eat it alive.

Third and finally, though God emphatically took responsibility for the Flood, He was quick to add in the very next verse, "But I will establish My covenant with you; and you shall enter the ark—you and your sons and your wife, and your sons' wives with you." Though it was His choice to destroy the world, He made it clear that things were going to be different starting at that point. One purpose of the destruction was to put everything into better circumstances for a second go at it, this time with a formal relationship, a covenant between the world and God. The mere mention of a covenant conveyed that God had no intention of letting things go on as they had before the Flood. The degeneration that had been allowed before the Flood had served its purpose. God, of course, can do as He wishes. Having a covenant is not a way of giving God permission to interfere, it is not some trick He uses to get around our otherwise impermeable defenses. Having a covenant is the way God tells us *how* He is going to interfere. "Covenant" means "relationship". He was going to spell out exactly how our new relationship with Him was to proceed. There would be a covenant again that God would use as a bridge to interfere in world events, and that would provide a mechanism to restrain the unbridled growth of evil.

It was going to be very typical as covenants go. Though Noah alone was pronounced righteous in his generation, God rescued his whole family. The language is emphatic that it is Noah who was in favor and Noah only. In Genesis 7:1 the word for "you" is singular: "Then the Lord said to Noah, 'Enter the ark, you and all your household, for you alone I have seen to be righteous before Me in this time.' "Noah's wife, his sons, and also his sons' wives were all saved from the Flood because of Noah, not because they were righteous in their generation but because Noah was righteous in his generation. It is completely typical of grace, it is completely typical of covenants, that they always splash when they hit, covering not only the recipient of grace, but all those who are near him.

Though God did not establish the Covenant formally until after the Flood, the way He chose Noah and his family to rescue was a covenant-like act of mercy. God always behaves toward us in a covenantal way because His character is covenantal. Since His intent was to establish a covenant, He called Noah and rescued him and all those connected with him. Covenants are never personal in the sense of "this is mine; you get yours". It is typical of God throughout the Scripture to bestow favor on an individual, not because of what that individual did, but because of what someone else connected to him did. If every sin makes victims out of innocent bystanders, then grace makes lucky winners out of guilty bystanders, but even more so. No one ever acts for himself alone in anything he does and this is why the phrase "personal relationship" does not adequately describe our connection to God.

Noah was to take a pair of every animal so that they would repopulate the earth, but he was to take seven pairs of every clean animal. So far as the Bible says anything, the distinction between clean and unclean animals was not spelled out until the Law of Moses thousands of years after Noah. Possibly when Moses wrote down this oral tradition (as I assume he did), knowing the difference between clean and unclean animals, he simply pointed out what God was doing, and as far as Noah knew God was choosing some animals to come in fourteens for unknown reasons. The clean animals were the ones that would later be required as sacrificial animals but, being also domestic animals, it would be natural that they would have become the typical sacrifices from the earliest date, and so the inclusion of extra sheep and goats would not have seemed odd to Noah regardless of whether God called them clean or not. But possibly there had been some other revelation to people in general as to what were acceptable sacrifices. The concept of cleanness in relation to dietary laws would have been out of place before the Flood for other reasons.

Using Noah to rescue not only his family but also the creatures sets this new Covenant squarely in line with the original Covenant of Creation. It was not only people God was rescuing in the Flood; it was everything, all the other creatures on the earth. It was not only people God planned to redeem but the whole creation. It was a cosmic covenant. The animals taken on to the ark were stand-ins, proxies, for all of it: the stars, the depths of the sea. When God makes something, He is committed to it. He never abandons even an earthworm to death.

3. The Flood (Genesis 7:1-8:19)

Before we consider the historicity of the Flood, let's look at the details given in this account. The ark was approximately 450 feet long, 75 feet wide, with three decks each 15 feet tall. As a building project for one family of four men working alone, it was enormous. They must have been good carpenters, and spreading such a project over as much as one hundred and twenty years may have been necessary. We need not suppose that Noah took a pair of every species of animal and bird in the world, particularly if the Flood was local (I'll discuss this shortly). On the contrary, the idea seems more likely to have been to preserve every type of animal and bird in a more general sense, a kind of owl, a kind of bear, a kind of deer, etc. The ark came to rest in the mountains of Ararat, not necessarily on Mt. Ararat itself. Babylonian tradition, for example, claims that the ark came to rest on Mt. Nisir. Noah was given as being 600 years old at the Flood and 500 years old by the time his three sons had been born, with no information about the relative ages of Shem, Ham, and Japheth. These numbers are clearly rounded off. The sons were all about a hundred years old, all married and at the normal age, in those days, for begetting children, though apparently all still childless.

Noah and his family were in the ark for just over a year. The Flood began on the 17th day of the 2nd month and Noah finally left the ark on the 27th day of the 2nd month of the following year, Noah's 601st. It is odd that calendar dates were given for the Flood. We don't know how early in human history the sky was used to organize the year and name its parts. This passage of Genesis implies that astronomy predated the Flood, and that some human knowledge was preserved through the Flood. The account given here could not be using a later calendar system extrapolated back to Noah's life; it must have been a calendar developed before the Flood and preserved in the oral tradition through Noah's own knowledge. Furthermore, verses 7:11 and 8:3,4 show that the calendar he used divided the year into months of thirty days each. This was not a lunar calendar like the early Sumerian calendar, the oldest calendar known. A lunar calendar must have months averaging 29½ days, from new moon to new moon. The Sumerians, and the Hebrews after them, alternated 29 day months with 30 day months and in addition, to make the calendar match the sky, they varied the number of months in the year, sometimes 12 and sometimes 13. The Egyptians, who came much later in a distant land, did use a month of 30 days, but then made it match the sky by inserting five extra days named for five of their gods. Hence the dating given in this part of Genesis appears to be using a less sophisticated calendar, something older than the more accurate later calendars of recorded history.

For 40 days it rained, and for another 110 days the world was covered in water, 20 to 25 feet above the tallest mountains—whether the whole world or only the Middle East we will discuss shortly. After this the ark came to rest and there were about 220 days after the ark landed until everyone finally went out. It was not until the 1st day of the 10th month, 73 days after the ark landed, that they could see other mountains in the distance. Forty days later, on the 10th day of the 11th month Noah sent out the raven and then the dove for the first time and the dove returned with nothing. He sent it out again on the 17th day of the 11th month and this time it brought back an olive leaf. Finally he sent it out on the 24th day of the 11th month and it did not come back at all. We will consider why he sent the birds out later on.

Still he waited another 36 days before removing the covering from the ark and looking at the dry ground. The covering was probably a door on the roof of the top deck so they could stand on top of the ark in the open air. Even so, knowing the ground to be dry, he did not leave the ark for another 57 days. This is an oddly important fact that we will consider more closely later. All of these details may have had a larger metaphorical meaning, but it would require a much larger book and a different author to explore. The early Christians believed that all of the details were symbolic. Though I do believe symbolism is critical to understanding the Bible, it would go against my purpose to get too carried away with it, and it should never be allowed to hide the more literal meaning in any case. It is the literal meaning I am aiming at, both the factual aspects and the more obvious metaphorical aspects of the literal meaning.

There is some variety in ancient flood stories and it is enlightening to consider them along with the biblical account. The Sumerians had three or four versions, and other nations had their own versions. One of the Sumerian versions is the most interesting and detailed non-biblical account. In it, there was a council of gods that decided to destroy mankind, a decision bitterly contested by a minority of them. Enki and a few other gods saw that people were much too valuable as slaves to lose; without us the gods would have had to go back to hunting and preparing their own food. So Enki warned the king, Ziusudra, to build a big boat. This flood lasted seven days. In one version, the sin of mankind, for which the whole race was to be destroyed, was that we were so noisy that we kept one of the older gods awake; he decided to kill us all to get some peace and quiet. Ziusudra was chosen because of his piety (he was a good slave, attentive to his god's needs) to save a few people and animals. Afterward, Ziusudra was rewarded for his piety and obedience with the gift of immortality and a permanent home in paradise.

This story is typical of the ancient myths. Except for the common idea of a great flood, there is little similarity between the myths and the Bible, but the differences between the two are particularly revealing. First, only the Bible gives anything like a legitimate reason for sending a Flood; the myths always credit it to some trivial reason. Only the Bible portrays God as other than a selfish and petty man. Only the Bible portrays the hero/deliverer as an ordinary man. Ziusudra (the Sumerian hero) and Utnapishtim (the Akkadian hero) were kings and priests; after the flood, they were rewarded for their piety with the appropriate god-like gifts of immortality and a home in paradise. In contrast, Noah had no status worth mentioning. The Bible portrays Noah as simply a good man (without detailing what made him good) building the ark and an altar and then lapsing into an embarrassing episode of drunkenness; not the stuff of dramatic fiction, certainly not inspiring or noble. And then, confounding our expectations, no particular reward was given to him after the Flood; he just got off having to drown. Lastly, the Bible insisted on including the boring details: measurements, dates, ages, the sort of stuff that good stories and myths are not interested in. The biblical version of the Flood is the most matter of fact and unadorned of all the accounts. On the face of it, if there was a Flood to describe, the Bible is the most straight-forward and least super-natural account of the facts. Setting aside the question of when and where the Flood may have occurred for the moment, what can we make of the question: did the Flood occur at all?

First it must be stated that there is no evidence geologically for a world-wide Flood, though I don't consider the lack of evidence conclusive of anything. There is some evidence of a catastrophic flood over a large portion of the Middle East. The lack of proof will not dissuade those who are inclined to believe the Bible and will seem more conclusive than it is to those who are inclined to disbelieve the Bible. What about the widespread occurrence of Flood stories in mythology? Again, those who are inclined to disbelieve the Bible will conclude that the biblical account is just one of many and therefore no more to be taken seriously than they are; those who are inclined to believe the Bible will argue that multiple versions of the same story indicate that something occurred to cause them all; they would then point out the differences between the biblical and mythical accounts (as I have done) and conclude that the Bible is by far the most believable. In other words, our conclusions are our assumptions; we believe or we disbelieve as we did when we began to think about the question.

I follow the second line of thinking. Multiple accounts do suggest a common source for the stories, but they do not imply that they are all fictional. The simplest hypothesis for a common source to the stories is that something like a Flood did happen and the tradition of it was handed down in stories around the campfires for dozens or hundreds of generations. And if something like the Flood did happen, then one account or another is the closest to the facts of the matter. If nothing like the Flood did happen, then the invention of the story of a Flood was the earliest of myths and its near universality in mythology over so many cultures is unique in the ancient world. Where could such a story have come from? What is the source of its hold on the human imagination? How did it get so widespread? The possibility that all the stories derive from an actual event is too easily dismissed, and too casually dismissed, to have been carefully considered.

Clearly I am working on the assumption that the Flood actually occurred, so we should now briefly consider the time and place of the Flood. First there is no reasonable way to date the Flood or the time span from Adam to Noah using the genealogical data in Genesis. If you assume the genealogy in chapter 5 leaves no gaps and gives an exact account of all the generations from Adam to Noah, then there were just over a thousand years from the Fall to the Flood. However, genealogies in the Old Testament, particularly ones covering long periods of time, sometimes left out generations, mentioning only well-known or representative ancestors. This was a practical necessity whether the records were written (clay tablets get heavy and papyrus was an invention from much later) or oral (long lists of names are tedious to memorize or recite around a campfire). Further, the phrase "and he begat" is sometimes used in a very loose way to mean "he became the ancestor of". So a biblical dating of either Adam or of the Flood is impossible with any degree of certainty. There is some geological evidence that a major flood, covering a lot of the Middle East, occurred in about 8000 b.c. but it is only speculative whether that flood is the same as the one in the Bible.

There is disagreement over the extent of the Flood, obviously. Some hold that the Flood was world-wide while others hold that the Flood covered only a portion of the Middle East; the Hebrew language in the biblical account is ambiguous enough for either. There are several arguments in favor of a local Flood from within the Bible itself. First, the genealogy of Noah's descendants in Genesis 10 does not seem to include Africans, Asians, or Native Americans. The names in that genealogy are frequently plural and probably indicate tribes of people rather than individuals and it seems that non-Middle Eastern peoples either were simply left out of the genealogy or else were descended from people before the Flood who weren't destroyed in the Flood. Second, the Bible seems to mention specific tribes who lived before the Flood and yet were not destroyed by the Flood. In Genesis 6:4 the Nephilim are mentioned as living before the Flood, and later the Nephilim are mentioned in Numbers 13:33 as living in the Promised Land when Israel arrived there. However it is true that "Nephilim" simply means "giant", so it is not clear whether the Nephilim were a particular tribe or were merely giants who might be born into any tribe. A third biblical argument for a local Flood is the genealogy of Cain. In what sense can Jubal have been the father of those who do music if the descendants of Cain had all perished in the Flood? It would have been as if Cain had never existed, and all his descendants would have been simply forgotten and irrelevant. Music, metal-working, the nomadic life style, would all have had to be re-invented by one of Noah's descendants. The whole genealogy of Cain would have been pointless.

On the whole then it seems to me that the Bible does not claim that the Flood was a universal one. The Bible only apparently teaches a universal Flood because of the way this passage has been translated over the years. It is more internally consistent with the rest of Genesis, more faithful to what the Scripture actually says, to believe in a local Flood over most of the Middle East.

Now if the Flood was not universal, then that suggests that the moral degeneration was not as great among the peoples who were more distant, the peoples not mentioned in the genealogy of Noah's descendants. If the rest of the world was not so evil that it had to be destroyed, were the people from whom Noah derived more evil than all the other people of the world? Perhaps, but it may be that God had somehow hindered the expression of evil in the rest of the world, and that for His own purposes He had allowed the people of the Middle East to degenerate to the point where they were no longer tolerable. When the descendants of Cain wandered away from their brethren and went out from the presence of God, God did not let them simply go their own way with no divine presence whatsoever. He loves His creation too much to abandon it. Rather, He may have imposed restraints upon the expression of evil among the descendants of Cain so that they were spared the necessity of something like a Flood. As we will shortly see, He was about to do exactly this with Noah's descendants to prevent the necessity of a future Flood. In view of what comes after the Flood in the biblical narrative, it becomes more plausible that God had simply not hindered the moral degeneration in Seth's line as He had elsewhere.

But why not? Why would He allow the descendants of Seth to deteriorate but not the descendants of Cain? If this is what happened, I believe the explanation lies in the burden God had placed on the descendants of Seth: they were chosen to suffer the Flood because they had been chosen to bear the revelation, the oracles of God, the oral tradition. The purpose of the moral degeneration that led to the Flood was revelation. Carrying God's revelation to a corrupted world is an honor, but not necessarily a pleasant job. The bearers of revelation don't just carry a scroll or a stone tablet; they carry the revelation in their bodies, their families, their history, their interactions with an interfering God. God speaks to the world through the events of their lives, lives which are no longer their own.

By this interpretation, Caucasians and Semites and Hamites are the remnant through Noah of a people too ruthless and violent to be permitted to live on the earth, and they got that way because God allowed them to get that way, and He allowed them to get that way as a tangible manifestation to the rest of the world of how horrible the corruption of evil can get if it is not curbed. This is the nature of revelation.

To restrain the expression of evil is to disguise it, to make it appear more benign than it is. God's intent was to cloud the knowledge of good and evil, to anesthetize us spiritually. He did not wish us to bear the pain of knowing the true horror of the evil in us, so He blunted it. But He wanted to warn us about what He was doing so that we could understand the truth about ourselves without fully experiencing it. He left us the memory of the Flood, a sign like a nightmare, of a greater horror that lurks just beneath the surface of our hearts.

From this point on, the forces of nature, and especially the sea, were objects of awe to all the ancient people of the Middle East. They would identify the ocean with Chaos, the forces of disorder and destruction. It was not just that they worshiped the forces of nature, but they recognized those forces as being beyond human power, as threats to the very existence of humanity, as forces that only God had it in His power to control. The sea was an object of fear among the ancient Hebrews, a tangible reminder that the chaos of the oceans had once invaded the land and overwhelmed it, and only the authority of God kept it restrained in its boundaries. And thus the ocean became the symbol of the evil nature in men's hearts.

To conclude my discussion of this passage we must consider what exactly there was good about Noah? What made him so special? Why was he alone righteous? In fact the Bible almost seems to hide any particular reason for Noah's favor with God. You have to carefully watch the details to see it, and even then it is only as the revelation unfolds in the ensuing millennia that it becomes clear. The key to answering the question, the crucial detail to notice, is that Noah did not leave the ark until he had received specific permission to do so. When he removed the covering of the ark in Genesis 8:13 he could see that the ground around the ark was dry, but he still waited in the ark nearly two more months until God told him he could leave. He must have had the worst case of "cabin fever" in all time. Why didn't he just use his common sense and get out?

One way to answer this question is to say that Noah had humility. He understood that God Himself had sealed them into the ark; Genesis 7:16 says, ". . . and the Lord closed it [the door] behind him." *Did he have the right to open what God had closed?* It is a question that perhaps not many of us would think to ask, but it is the question that Noah knew the answer to without having to ask. I think it is his knowing the answer to the question that is the clue to the favor he found in God's sight. The general principle Noah knew instinctively, and that was the source of his favor with God, might be summed up in this way: *only God can fulfill the promises of God; it is not my job to make His decisions happen.* It was Noah's unwillingness to usurp God's place, to make God's choices or to do God's work for Him, that is the quality which God sought out, which God looked for around the world, and which Noah alone possessed.

This specific quality could be called humility, but we might also call it faith. And yet it is more basic than simply believing in God and more vivid than simply trusting in God's care. But it is exactly trust in God that is the issue, a trust in God so total that there is a willingness to simply wait on God to do what He promised however long it takes, even when we could make it happen, even when waiting itself seems silly. This quality, the willingness to obey God combined with the unwillingness to act in His place, becomes a theme that is repeated throughout Scripture. Note that the quality I am suggesting as the root of God's favor toward Noah did not make him a righteous man by any moral standard. We don't know what other personal traits Noah had (except that he liked wine a lot), and it is too much to assume that Noah was an all around good guy super-hero with virtues God just happened to want to keep hidden. God's partiality to Noah was meant to highlight one and only one desirable trait. The blamelessness that Noah had was this quality of character: a respect for God, a humility that allowed God to be God and Noah not to be God. There is no intrinsic merit in respecting God; it is merely what we owe Him. Merely to do what we ought to do is no great and virtuous deed, as the Messiah would later say in Luke 17:10. When Noah found favor in God's sight, it was because God was counting his faith as righteousness just as He would later do with Abram. Righteousness in this world is always and has always been by grace through faith whether it was explicitly stated or not.

If Noah had no intention of leaving the ark without God's express permission, then why did he send out the birds, first the raven and then the doves? The information they brought him about conditions outside the ark did not affect his actions in any way, so why do it at all? I think he sent them simply out of curiosity. He was not accumulating information in order to make more informed decisions since he wasn't planning to make any decisions; he was just curious. He knew he would be allowed out of the ark eventually and he was content to wait, but he wanted to know what was going on out there. Some people, with the best intentions, take the insight of Noah to an extreme and are afraid to so much as blink without God's permission. But God does not intend that we be paralyzed in life by fear of Him; that is not true humility; that is the servant who hides his talent under a rock. We are to be careful not to take over God's work, to not try to do what only He can do, but everything else is left to our initiative. We must learn to fear where fear is appropriate and to be fearless everywhere else.

B. The Covenant of Preservation

1. The Terms of the Covenant (Genesis 8:20-9:17)

The first thing Noah did after leaving the ark was to sacrifice some of the clean animals he had brought. Doubtless one of the reasons for bringing seven pairs of the clean animals was to have such sacrifices, but since the clean animals for sacrifices were also the domestic animals, they would have wanted extras of those to build up their herds more quickly as well. The bringing of sacrifices dates back to Cain and Abel, to the very beginning of fallen humanity. The innovation in the Law of Moses was the dietary restrictions on unclean animals, not on the requirement of sacrifices. Moses would build on a tradition long established in the world. Part of the process of revelation occurs when God inserts certain ideas in advance into the general culture where they can be adopted and elaborated for His purposes. Whether certain pagan ideas were dim memories passed orally through the generations from our first parents, or were inserted by God into pagan culture, or were ideas they came up with but which He then adopted for His own ends, He used them to speak to us. General revelation, as a theological term, should not be understood as God speaking to us in the natural world only, but as God speaking to us in everything. In this way, God's work of self-revelation proceeds in a less formal way in the world in general; His focus on the Bible did not exclude revelation to everyone.

But the next verse is peculiar. Genesis 8:21 says: "And the Lord smelled the soothing aroma . . .". The idea that the smell of the smoke of the burnt offering had a soothing effect on God is an idea that had crept into people's religious superstition, and it was an idea that God took into His own revelation. Is it merely a superstition that the smell of a burnt offering is a soothing aroma to God? Absolutely. Why then would God allow mere superstition into His revelation? For the same reason He was so careless about including science. Because His revelation is exactly a revelation to man, a seriously ignorant and unteachable creature. God could have made an issue of the truth at this point, but it would have been fruitless. Too much truth too fast is as bad as no truth at all. In this case, it was a superstition that was useful in leading to other and more accurate information later when the time was ripe. "The Lord smelled the soothing aroma" becomes a metaphor to mean that God took notice of the burnt offering, and that it was soothing conveys that He was pleased with Noah's offering and wanted his descendants to continue bringing such offerings. That people would take such a statement at face value, literally, and imagine God with a nose smelling the smoke and being placated and calmed down by it, was an error that could be tolerated until such a time as God chose to make a point of what He was really like. And people did think wrongly. In the Sumerian account, for example, when Utnapishtim offered sacrifices after the flood the hungry gods swarmed around it like flies. The Bible's language is again subdued and respectful in comparison with how the story evolved among the pagans.

There are various kinds of superstition, of course. Some superstitions are vicious by nature and not to be tolerated under any circumstance, but some are more benign, and some are even useful as a means for expressing something deeper that is true. We should not assume, because the canon of Scripture is closed, that we know everything. The Bible contains all that we need to know, not everything there is to know. We need to be made ready to hear from God before we can hear from God; and because the revelation of Truth about God is so critical God took great care to tell us only what we ready for. There is no contradiction in this. Any parent experienced with teaching children knows that timing is critical. We can't tell our children all of the truth when they are three years old; nor when they are four; nor when they are any particular age. We must be content that they do not understand some parts of the truth until they are ready; we must even be content that they believe things that are not strictly true for a time. The Bible is a progressive revelation of God's character to God's children. God has tolerated ignorance and misinformation in us for long ages. Doubtless He is tolerating it as we speak.

The way I understand it, God's plan of salvation was executed in a series of covenants, the covenant in this passage being the first. This is the same as saying that the plan of salvation is a series of relationships, a series of increasingly intimate relationships. It is something like the process leading to marriage: first the friendship, then dating and courtship, then romance, betrothal and marriage. Each phase of the relationship builds on the foundation of what came before. Or let's use a different image. The series of covenants is like treating a critical illness with a medical procedure that requires several stages to effect the complete healing. Each covenant extended the healing accomplished by the previous stage and built on the progress that had been made. Each covenant was a step in patching up the universe, a step toward that Tree in the book of Revelations whose leaves bring healing to the nations.

The first covenant is the foundation on which all the others rest. Thus it was important and right that this first covenant be between God and the whole creation. God's purpose was and is to redeem the damage done to the whole creation, and so of course the first step was to re-establish a covenant framework for all relationships through the whole creation. God's redemptive purposes have always had in view the rescue of the whole creation and not merely mankind. He loves us; but more widely, He loves everything He made. All the other covenants that would come later should be understood as extensions built onto this foundational covenant. This covenant sets the tone, establishes the priorities and character, of what would come later. I will call this one the Covenant of Preservation for reasons that will be clear shortly. Covenants set the terms for how a relationship will be worked out. This one established the following terms:

1. On God's part: the promise to protect the creation from a future destruction like the Flood.
2. On man's part:
     a) permission to eat animals, excluding their blood;
     b) and permission to execute murderers.
3. The sign of the Covenant of Preservation would be the rainbow.

This covenant is much more sweeping than it may appear. What was in God's heart here was to protect the creation and man himself from the effects of man's evil (see 8:21,22), to hinder the degeneration that had led to the Flood. But His words are superficially odd: "I will never again curse the ground on account of man, for the intent of man's heart is evil from his youth . . ." Did He mean that, after all, we couldn't help being evil and so evil would not be punished anymore? Did He mean that next time He would just let us wallow in our misery and violence with no mercy? Did He mean that He no longer cared so much about the presence of violence on the earth? Those are all rhetorical questions. On the contrary, the promise never to send another such Flood must be read as containing the tacit promise to intervene to prevent humanity from degenerating so far that another such Flood would be necessary or desirable. As I read it, this covenant commits God to restrain evil on the earth.

The world before the Flood was what happens when God allows us to proceed according to our nature with no restraint. This tacit promise to restrain evil is perhaps part of the background for understanding the strange comment in II Thessalonians 2:6,7: "And you know what restrains him now, so that in his time he will be revealed. For the mystery of lawlessness is already at work; only he who now restrains will do so until he is taken out of the way." It is this commitment to restrain evil that makes it the Covenant of Preservation. How exactly this Covenant would help restrain evil we will consider in the next section, and there were other means that God used as well. Meanwhile we will conclude this section by considering what the sign of the Covenant means.

Normally covenants are accompanied by signs. A sign is simply some tangible physical object or ceremony or event that is chosen to remind us of the covenant. It is a natural impulse, seemingly built into us, to use signs. Everything human is performed by means of signs. Language itself is just an elaborate and detailed system of signs: the words are signs of ideas and the sentences are signs of thoughts. Fundamentally, abstractions are not easy for us and we have to anchor them in the world somehow. Everything that is important to us is enshrouded in signs, and the more important it is the more signs we use, and the more honor we bestow on the signs themselves. Marriage is an abstraction, for example, an ideal of a relationship between two people, and so we link it to signs that help us remember and honor it: first a more or less elaborate ceremony and then the tangible physical sign in the wedding rings. Patriotism is another abstraction, usually embodied in a flag and the reverence the citizens show it. So it is completely natural that God would tie His covenants to particular signs.

According to its habit, the Scripture talks about the rainbow from a peculiar viewpoint, one calculated to communicate an idea but which seems to not entirely make sense at first. Putting God's perspective into human terms means that everything He says floats on the surface of our rational minds like an iceberg: only the tip of it shows. The Scripture says, "It shall come about, when I bring a cloud over the earth, that the bow will be seen in the cloud, and I will remember My covenant . . ." We must read this carefully. God of course does not need reminding because He doesn't forget. What happens is that we forget or doubt that He remembers. The rainbow was really a reminder to us, a reassurance to us, that God does remember His promise, and when we see it today we are still reminded that God remembers His promise even now.

This is humility. It ought to be enough that God has promised to preserve the world, and we should believe Him and trust Him simply on that basis. God deserves to be believed, but He does not stand on His own merits. He remembers our weaknesses and accommodates Himself to us. That God is humble is an idea that could never have entered our imaginations unless it had been put there from the outside. The revelation of the humility of God is probably the biggest surprise, the most shocking and unique idea, in all the Bible. It ought to jolt us into paying attention.

2. The Restraints on Evil (Genesis 6:3, 9:2-6)

As I see it, God used at least four measures to restrain evil: one He began concurrently with the Flood; two were terms of the Covenant of Preservation; and one other was added much later. I will consider the first three of these now.

The account of the introduction of the rainbow as the sign of the Covenant of Preservation suggests that rainbows did not occur before the Flood. If so, this could mean that the Flood was another pivotal point in history at which God chose to change the laws of nature. In this light, possibly Genesis 6:3 "My Spirit shall not strive with man forever, because he also is flesh; nevertheless his days shall be one hundred and twenty years" should be taken as a decree dramatically shortening the average human lifespan. Life spans did begin to shrink at this point. Perhaps the change in physical law after the Fall was done incrementally, an initial change at the time of the Fall, a change at the time of the Flood, and perhaps other steps in between that weren't noted. In any case I think the shortening of our life span was an important first step in limiting evil. Certainly a man who is feeling pretty slow by the time he is seventy years old is going to do less damage than one who is pretty hearty at five hundred.

The second strategy for curbing evil was more complex and subtle. At first Genesis 9:3 sounds as though God were introducing meat into the human diet at this point, and that before the Flood we were largely vegetarian. But Abel was a shepherd, and eating domestic animals seems to go naturally with keeping them. The really new element here was hunting. The hunting and eating of meat can be understood as a way to provide an outlet for our impulse to violence. Those who are out hunting game will not be out hunting people as quickly, nor will their lust for violence be as sharp. If institutional violence was the primary problem leading to the Flood, then channeling such aggression would naturally be the first priority in hindering our tendency to degeneration. Archaeological evidence shows hunting to be a very early human activity, so I am putting the Flood as earlier still.

Genesis 9:2 says, "And the fear of you and the terror of you shall be on every beast of the earth and on every bird of the sky". God made it a point to protect the animals from the slaughter that would come about if they trusted us. The passage suggests that animals were tamer before the Flood, at least in the sense of not fearing people. Perhaps there was relatively little effort involved in domesticating animals initially; perhaps the animals we currently keep as domesticated animals and livestock are just the ones we were able to keep in control when the rest went wild after the Flood. But if the human race was to become a race of hunters, some protection for the animals would be necessary to prevent their annihilation. This is a protection which we have managed to circumvent to a large extent. Consider how close we have come to destroying all wild things even when they are wild; what chance would they have had if God hadn't shielded them from our ruthlessness?

At this point God did not restrict us to eating only the clean animals. The important point here was not dietary restrictions in general but the one critical restriction: blood. This is the very first time recorded at which something was set apart as taboo, forbidden. In Genesis 9:4, "Only you shall not eat flesh with its life, that is, its blood", the word translated "life" could also be translated as "soul". There are at least two points in view here.

First God meant to emphasize that He was not turning over the creation to us as if we owned it. There were limits to how far we were permitted to exploit the creation. We might use it to provide for our own needs, for food, for clothing, and even for profit to some extent, but we could not consume the soul of Creation. Its soul, its life, belongs to God alone. The Creation itself is in a Covenant relationship to God, and because of the Covenant the Creation, every part of it, has a standing before God, an integrity that we are not to violate. The Covenant restored the status of the Creation and all its parts.

Our violation of the Covenant of Preservation is a major ethical problem in our society. When we raise animals, even something as lowly as chickens, in a factory setting, a setting in which the chicken never has the chance to actually live like a chicken, aren't we eating its soul as well as its flesh even though we are careful to drain out the blood? Modern people do not believe that animals have souls, and so we feel free to consume every vestige of their life; we may as well drink their blood. How shallow we are to have retained as a meaningless custom the draining of the blood when we have no regard whatsoever for the life the blood signifies. Indeed, it would be inconvenient to our profit margins if things in nature did have souls and had to be respected. How much of our economy would be overturned if we believed that God loved even chickens? So much of our prosperity and wealth depends on blurring the lines of biblical ethics.

It is equally a violation of the Covenant of Preservation when we hunt to extinction any species of animal or plant. Noah was afraid to open a door that God had closed, but we are not afraid to destroy, to un-create, what God has created. Thus our real god is our economy, our leisure, our recreation. But we equally drink the blood of the creatures by cruelty. The instincts of those who stand for animal rights are more biblical than the instincts of Christians who don't even bother wiping the blood from their mouths before they mock them. What then shall become of our culture that has learned to drink the blood of all things? How will God long endure us?

The second point to the ban on consuming blood is poetry. God has written poetry with the creation, and blood was made a major theme in His great poem. To effectively convey revelation, the physical nature of blood was invested with a symbolic meaning beyond its natural meaning. It had to be made into a symbol of a spiritual reality. Blood became the symbol for the breath of life itself, the metaphor for the essence, the soul, that a creature has by virtue of its creation. The first step in establishing such a metaphor is to make a rule concerning our behavior, so that we are made to act in a certain way without knowing why. Our behavior then shapes our attitudes and feelings. God put blood outside the realm of what we could use to make us reverence it. Blood was the first *holy* thing; it belonged to God and to Him only; it emphatically did not belong to us. By setting it beyond our reach it became a symbol of something beyond nature. Once we began thinking of blood as connected to something more than physical, it became a vehicle God could use to reveal truths beyond the physical.

The third restraint on evil was the adoption of human government and law in 9:5,6: ". . . And from every man, from every man's brother I will require the life of man. Whoever sheds man's blood, by man his blood shall be shed, for in the image of God He made man". What God had avoided with Cain He now endorsed. Why the change? In part, it came about because He had invested special meaning in blood. If the blood of animals was holy, then the blood of men in the image of God was even more emphatically a holy thing after the Flood, and the deepening of the perspective required a stricter behavioral standard. I have pictured the world before the Flood as a world in which government existed in a particularly hellish form. I believe that in the Covenant of Revelation, God took human government into His service to be used for His purpose. In other words, He decided to take up a much more active role in civic affairs, in all governments everywhere. Invisible though His involvement may be, that governments work at all to our benefit is a sign of His grace operating in them.

To understand what was really going on, however, we need to consider the nature of the covenants. The biblical view of evil is a covenantal view. Not only does everyone suffer the consequences of what you or I choose, but also everyone bears the responsibility for what you or I choose. To be sure, if you or I commit a crime, from stealing to murder to telling a little white lie, there is a private individual component to it. I myself choose to do the evil. But the Bible also recognizes that the society I live in nurtured my choice by providing opportunity or even encouragement for the choice I made. Whenever any one does evil, it is all of us who have chosen to do it in him or her as well. We all share in creating the context for the expression of that evil, we all share in creating the situations that foster rather than control our darkest impulses. We are not only all addicted to evil, we are all codependents with each other, enabling and abetting each other in the evil inclinations of our hearts. This is important to understand, particularly with regard to capital punishment.

Since we live in communities, which are really informal covenant groups, all that we do is related to our connections to that community; our choices all flow out of the relative health or pathology of our inter-relationships. A man who commits a murder obviously has the murder in his heart, but that murder got into his heart by the sins of omission or commission of his community. The murder in his heart was nurtured, even planted, by failures in his upbringing and family, by conflicts with his neighbors, by patterns of behavior he learned as he grew up. All of these influences combine with the natural inclinations of the heart and opportunities as they arise to bring forth the crime. Every man's sin is also my sin in proportion to how well I know him and the extent to which I have either built him up or torn him down.

To understand what God intended here, since the passage is so terse, we must borrow ahead from the Law of Moses, the way God arranged public executions to work among His people and the way they were conducted in the ancient world. The capital punishment instituted after the Flood was not a casual thing; it was a careful ceremony involving the whole community. The executions in the ancient world were serious ceremonies dramatizing that the guilt of the murder was shared by the whole community. All had been accomplices in the shedding of blood, and the execution made their involvement visible. In this way a public execution was both a public confession and a renunciation of the evil.

In modern American society there is little sense of corporate guilt; the suggestion of corporate guilt is viewed with suspicion and offends our individualism. There is no sense of our need to repent when we execute our murderers; there is little reverence for the blood, the soul, of the criminals involved. The modern execution of the murderer lacks all of the biblical meaning in the ancient practice. Ironically in our individualistic society, the concept of the holiness of blood, of the life, of the individual has been replaced by a pseudo-biblical concept of justice. We carry out a "just sentence" on an individual whom we imagine bears his own guilt alone. We imagine we are innocent as we are given the guilty what he deserves. Thus we show no reverence for his blood and we *perpetuate* rather than *expiate* his crime in the act of punishing it. His blood testifies against us. In America every execution is a form of perjury against ourselves.

We cynically execute criminals in the name of God, but we are not truly destroying the guilty because we believe in God nor because we take seriously how He feels about us and our society. We execute to rid ourselves of a nuisance, or to get revenge on a person who has offended us, or to try to scare others into submission to our rules. Execution in our day has become a matter of social policy to dispose of the unruly elements of the society so that we can evade the question of why there are unruly elements of society. We execute criminals to avoid facing our own guilt. Once execution is divorced from the knowledge of corporate guilt, it becomes a kind of hypocrisy and has no real connection to the biblical practice. We dress up capital punishment as justice but for us it is an evil and unbiblical thing.

It is a modern argument for capital punishment that it will deter men from violence (this is based on misunderstanding Romans 13), that it will restrain the expression of evil through fear, but the biblical view is more complicated. Execution of murderers was not given as a deterrent to violence, except possibly to deter revenge. What deterred violence was the cultural awe of blood, the reverence for the man created in the image of God. The reverence for human life extended both to the victim of the murder and the murderer himself. God sought to imbue people with the kind of reverence for life that would make them afraid, even superstitiously afraid, of shedding blood. The ancients would execute a murderer because God, or the gods, had been offended and demanded such a public show of guilt and repentance, but they would execute him out of fear and not out of any imagined moral superiority.

The only laws mentioned immediately after the Flood were the laws against murder and against consuming blood. But the consumption of blood had no stated penalty for its violation. That there was no penalty for the eating of blood does not mean it was considered as relatively less important than murder; on the contrary it shows how deeply God was building the rule into the hearts and minds of people. There would be no penalty needed to enforce the rule because it would become simply a part of what it meant to be human. It would become unthinkable to consume the blood of an animal. The law, as a thing external to us that accuses or directs or punishes certain behavior, was never a desirable thing in God's sight, though it was to be another tool He would adopt for His own ends. Even in the Law of Moses, some of the most serious sins had no punishment prescribed, because punishment alone could not fill us with the loathing that God wished us to have. What He really desired was internal transformation, which no law and no punishment can ever accomplish. What He really desires is that we come to know good and evil from His point of view, that we begin to *think* of evil as *unthinkable*.

Permission for society to execute murderers did not mean that there was no evil involved in the execution; the words said to Cain were unchanged as expressing God's ultimate attitude toward capital punishment. If you will, capital punishment was a moral compromise on God's part. It may seem strange to say that God was willing to compromise morals, but that is the way of it. By accepting what is inadequate in the short term He accomplishes His perfect will in the long term, and it will astonish our hearts when we see it happen. We will see many more examples as we keep reading in the Bible, even in the Law itself.

And so the Messiah would fulfill—establish, confirm, perfect—the Covenant of Preservation. The blood we had been forbidden to drink became His own blood given to us to drink to renew life. And as He ended death by submitting to death, so He would end all human government by submitting to human government, so He would end all capital punishment by submitting to capital punishment in the place of a murderer. The Covenant of Preservation was put in place just for Him to act out, like the scenery on the stage for the greatest actor to play His greatest role. It was all about Him.

C. Life under the Covenant of Preservation

1. Noah's Drunkenness (Genesis 9:18-29)

And so the Flood was over, the Covenant had been made, and life returned to "normal". The information about dates, ages, and people given here is all approximate. Noah was just over six hundred years old when the Flood ended, and according to Genesis 5:32 Shem, Ham, and Japheth were all born in the century before the Flood. We must assume they had no children of their own until after the Flood. This is consistent with the genealogy in chapter 5 in which most of the men born are to fathers over a hundred years old. That Shem, Ham, and Japheth were born so late in Noah's life is unusual and raises the possibility that Noah had older children who had families of their own and who had moved away. It's all speculation of course. If they existed and moved far enough they may have been out of the region of the Flood, of course.

We must go on now to a story that is difficult to interpret from any viewpoint: the story of Noah's drunkenness, the sin of Ham, and the subsequent curse placed on Ham's son Canaan. Clearly, a lot of time had passed between the burnt offering and this episode with the wine. At least one son, and probably four, had been born to Ham. Canaan is listed in the position of the youngest son in Ham's genealogy, but he might have been the oldest and demoted to a lower rank for an unspecified reason. There are other problems connected to Ham and Canaan and this genealogy that we will consider later. The story makes a bit more sense if Canaan were grown up, to some extent, rather than a child. Further, it would take a good number of years for a vineyard to grow up and become fruitful. Thus the span of time between the Flood and this episode of drunkenness was probably a matter of two decades, possibly more.

Since this is the first description of drunkenness in the Bible, and in an effort to protect Noah's reputation as an exemplary character, some have hypothesized that the yeast that causes fermentation did not exist before the Flood and that Noah got drunk at this time because alcohol was new to his experience. This suggestion is made by those who cannot imagine a man "blameless in his generation" drinking wine at all, and so they imagine him thinking he was only drinking grape juice as usual. Quite a surprise, but the hypothesis gets us into as much real trouble as it gets us out of imaginary trouble. It would be odd that God gave him no warning about the change he would find in his beverage of choice. If Noah did not intend to get drunk, if Noah did not even know that he could get drunk, then either God did not consider it a problem or else it was a serious oversight on God's part not to warn him about it. This is the sort of difficulty caused by trying to be holier than God.

On the other hand, if it were the case that fermentation was something new in nature after the Flood, a side effect of the changes in physical law that I hypothesized, then the invention of alcohol could be considered as another step God took to prevent the spread of evil. It may seem strange to say so considering how much evil all around us is caused by "demon rum", how many marriages are ruined and how many children are damaged just by alcohol. Obviously alcohol does cause a whole spectrum of evil, but I think that the most horrendous evil deeds are nearly invariably done by sober people.

I do not wish to minimize this evil: the violence and foolishness and damage to the families of alcoholics. But for large scale mischief there is just no substitute for a man in his right mind with violence and hatred and greed in his heart. The pain caused by drunkenness tends to be localized rather than global. It would have been better for the whole world if Hitler, for example, had been an alcoholic. None of the notorious serial killers or mass murderers were drunk when they killed their victims. Terrorists do not drink. Much of the evil done in the world today is done by CEO's in board rooms acting on greed alone untinged by scotch. By all means, let all those of evil heart drink and be drunk, and let the rest of us keep our distance; the world will be a safer place.

However, it seems doubtful that alcohol made its first appearance at this point. Wine has been such a central fact and force in history that if it had made its first appearance here it would almost demand some comment. Occasional drunkenness is not inconsistent with Noah being blameless in his generation, but it is inconsistent with God's character to pop something as powerful as alcohol out of the hat with no warning. It seems much more likely that Noah knew all about alcohol and its effects from his own experience.

Noah was at least discrete in his drunkenness; he was inside his tent. His nakedness was not public, though there was presumably not much public to be had at that time. Noah did live another 315 years after the Flood so we could believe the event occurred after perhaps hundreds of years. A tent, of course, does not provide much privacy. And the one who is drinking usually does not think about the consequences when he begins to drink, or remember the consequences of the last time he was drinking.

And so Ham went to visit his father and encountered him in a rather compromising and embarrassing state. And then Ham just went away. Could this have been done to save Noah the embarrassment of knowing that someone had found him naked in his tent? Could Ham have just gone away and done nothing about it thinking no one would be hurt? It doesn't seem so. The main danger for embarrassment to Noah would have been if he had been conscious enough to wander outside but not conscious enough to know better; or that someone else would have wandered into the tent. Ham either did not think of these possibilities or did not care. It would seem that Ham was not concerned with protecting Noah from embarrassment. He told his two brothers who were outside the tent and seemingly not far off. Why did he tell them? The only reasonable explanation is that he thought the situation was hilarious and thought they would too. It was as if he had opened the tent door and invited everyone else to come and see. The way this story plays out, it is impossible to attribute any good motives to Ham. It was Shem and Japheth who did what Ham should have done to protect their father from the possibility of future shame. They took care not to look at him so that he would be spared any embarrassment on that account as well.

It is not at all clear how Noah ever found out what Ham had done, nor what Shem and Japheth had done. Perhaps the alcohol had only made him unable to speak or move about, but had not totally robbed him of his sensibilities, or perhaps Shem or Japheth told him. And so he recovered from his drinking and knew what Ham had done. Naturally he was angry. The puzzling aspect of the account is: why did his natural anger toward Ham cause him to curse Canaan—not Ham himself or the sons of Ham in general, but only the youngest son?

Several theories have been advanced, all of them, I think, inadequate. One suggestion is that Noah was speaking prophetically at this point, that God opened a window to him to see both what Ham had done and what the descendants of Canaan would become, as if Ham's sin was symbolic of the moral and spiritual condition of the descendants of Canaan in the future. Several times in Genesis, the future of a tribe is linked to some event in the life of its progenitor. In essence this is the "sins of the fathers visited on the children", the idea that not merely the sinful nature but also the behavioral consequences of sin were passed on to succeeding generations.

Perhaps this is the most straightforward understanding that we can find for this strange passage. The name "Canaan" means "submissive one", and Noah picked up on the meaning when he made Canaan the "servant of servants". However, this answer becomes more puzzling when we consider some of the other descendants of Ham. One of the later descendants of Ham through his son Cush was the man Nimrod, the founder of Babel. The Philistines, a major future oppressor of Israel and enemy of God, also are listed as descendants of Ham through his son Mizraim. Clearly Canaan would not be the only problematic line descending from Ham. Why would the consequences of Ham's sin be bequeathed only to the youngest son and not to the others?

Others have suggested that this story was inserted by later generations of Hebrews who wanted some excuse for the extermination of the Canaanites as they were entering the Promised Land. At first the theory might sound plausible (if you set aside the question of the Scripture's integrity). But this interpretation has more problems than the preceding one. It projects a modern dilemma back on to ancient peoples. When the Hebrews did enter the Promised Land there was no qualm of conscience concerning the violence involved. In fact, the invasion of Canaan is more offensive to the modern mind than to the ancients. Western people, despite the recent history of Europe, are offended by other people's butchery, perhaps to escape thinking of their own. The ancients regarded it as unsurprising, the typical way of nations. The idea that this story was inserted by later generations of Hebrews is wishful thinking on the part of some who want people, particularly the "good guys", to be more delicate in their feelings than the ancients were, or who want God to judge ancient lives by modern standards, and put it in writing so we can hold Him to it. It means that we feel we can judge God, both what He says and what He doesn't say.

But ultimately I have no more satisfactory alternative interpretation to propose. The idea of a prophetic word about the future role of the Canaanites in revelation history may be the best we can do for now. But there is one other problem with the descendants of Ham listed here. Linguistically, it is wrong. The Canaanites spoke a Semitic language, a language that was most like the languages spoken by the descendants of Shem, and not like the languages that are called Hamitic. We will get to the confusion of languages in the next section, but for now it is enough to point out that the languages need not to have been arranged according to family, at least not at the beginning.

If this episode was recorded simply to teach us a lesson, then surely it teaches that God wishes us to protect each other from exposure. We will be exhorted later in Scripture to protect each other's reputations, to avoid gossip, to refrain from the stories that only hurt the standing of someone. Ham's betrayal of his father was exactly the kind of betrayal that is so common in daily life; it is exactly what we do to each other whenever we gossip; it is exactly what those vicious magazines do whose only purpose is to expose the shame of the famous or to invent shame if there is none to expose. Whenever we take delight in someone's embarrassment, even if the person is not our parent, we are committing the sin of Ham. The most infamous example of the sin of Ham in recent years was the Congress of the United States acting to publicly expose and humiliate the President of the United States when he was caught in a compromising situation. That Congress was not content to snicker to the American people that the President had been caught in his tent; they brought the whole country, the whole world, into the tent itself to see it, to revel in it. And they did it all in the name of "righteousness". Politics makes sinners of us all.

It is the godly thing to do to protect other people from the consequences of their own foolishness and sin. So often God is portrayed as the One who is the great Muckraker, the One who searches out sin and turns on the lights, making sure that no scandal goes unexposed, that no fool goes un-humiliated. It is true that God does sometimes expose shameful deeds for the whole world to see, but this is not His general practice. Perhaps we imagine Him being like this because that is the way we would be if we were Him. God only exposes foolishness when He must. Normally He is the great Concealer, intent on covering up the shame of the sinner as He covered up the shame of Adam and Eve, intent on making clothing to hide them, intent on patching up what can be patched and avoiding the humiliation otherwise. God takes no pleasure in the death of a sinner, we will be told, and that means that He takes no pleasure in their embarrassment either. In this respect Shem and Japheth behaved like God and Ham behaved like a snake.

2. Babel and the Nations
(Genesis 10:1-11:26 and I Chronicles 1:5-27)

The fourth means of restraining evil was the confusion of language at the Tower of Babel. The background of Babel is given in Genesis 10:8-12. Nimrod was a descendant (the number of generations being unspecified) of Ham through his eldest son, Cush. Comparing 10:7 and 10:8 illustrates how the word "fathered" or "begat" is used in the general sense of "became the ancestor of" and why the genealogies cannot be counted on for dating purposes. Nimrod was not a son of Cush, but Cush fathered Nimrod as his ancestor. Nimrod became a mighty one on the earth, what we would call a tyrant, and the list of the cities that he founded suggests that after the Flood he was the first of the emperors, the first of the kings of men who was not content with his own kingdom but wanted all the surrounding kingdoms as well. His example would inspire many followers among the city-states of Mesopotamia.

The name "Nimrod" comes from a word that means "we will revolt". The phrase in 10:9 that became a proverb, "Like Nimrod, a mighty hunter before the Lord" is misleading. The meaning of the proverb is more nearly, "Like Nimrod, a might hunter against (in opposition to) the Lord." He was a hunter not willing to hunt mere animals; he hunted men and subjugated them and made himself a mighty name in the earth; and I think it means that he hunted God like he hunted game. Nimrod was the first of that pattern of men who exalt themselves to be equal to God, following the example of the serpent he belonged to, which stretches down to Napoleon and Stalin, perhaps even to us. In particular Nimrod was the founder of Babel.

It is not stated when the division of the languages happened, whether it was in the time of Nimrod or later, but it is consistent with the character of Nimrod, the little we glimpse of it, that he inspired or instigated the building of the tower into heaven. His intent, their intent, was not so much to exalt themselves to heaven, as to attack heaven, to storm its gates, to make it their own. From the tower of Babel to the end of Revelations, Babel, and its successor Babylon, became the standard name for the power of this world arrayed against God and against His kingdom.

There is a natural process of evolution of language; once a tribe with a single language splits up, the language they had shared grows into distinct dialects as a result. The descendants of Noah and any peoples that might have migrated to other parts of the world before the Flood would have already begun to form distinct languages. But whatever dialects grew up before the Tower of Babel would have been related, perhaps closely enough to be mutually intelligible, certainly closely enough to be recognized as the same linguistic family. Linguistic evolution explains how Italian and Russian diverged but it is not clear that it can explain how Italian and Chinese could come from a common root. The linguistic diversity in the world today, containing languages that have nothing in common with each other whatsoever, suggests that language originated from many different sources independently. This could have come from language itself arising in different human contexts without divine intervention; or from the confusion of language at Babel, a real event at which the different linguistic families arose by divine decree. Linguists, as scientists, are of course committed to finding a purely natural explanation; it is enough for my purpose to point out that, assuming a meddlesome God, Babel as an actual event is plausible.

Linguists can not look far without the confirmation of written records, which do not exist from before 3000 b.c. They must make their inferences on the assumption that the linguistic evolution we observe in the present is substantially the same as it has always been. The parent language, Indo-European, from which nearly all the European, Iranian and Indian languages sprouted, is believed to date to about 4000 b.c. but could have been earlier. Thus current linguistic theory maintains that 6000 years of migrations and natural development was sufficient to produce the enormous variety of language that we see in Europe, Iran and India out of a single language. This may seem a surprisingly short length of time to account for such diversity, but just consider how much trouble you have understanding Shakespeare and multiply that by fifteen. Thus, assuming Indo-European to be a result of the confusion of languages at Babel, if something like Babel happened around 4000 b.c., it accounts for what we have. The city of Uruk (Erech in the Bible, also attributed to Nimrod) dates very nearly that early.

There are a few miscellaneous observations to be made. The division of language into various types did not necessarily coincide with genealogical relations. Descendants of Ham were not all speakers of Hamitic languages, as they are now classified, and descendants of Shem were not all necessarily speakers of Semitic languages, though there is a high degree of correlation. And there is no reason to think that any modern language is related to the language before the Flood. For example, Sumerian seems to be unrelated to every linguistic family currently existing; perhaps Sumerian was the original language, or any of a number of ancient languages that are now dead and not like anything else in the world. The confusion of language was worldwide, I think, and not restricted to the neighborhood of Babel. Linguists do not have a clear idea of how many families of languages, on the level of Indo-European, there are because the many languages of Africa, Asia and the Americas are not well known, but there may be hundreds of families of language that exist today or that have become extinct, and that are unrelated to one another.

"Come, let us build for ourselves a city, and a tower whose top will reach into heaven, and let us make for ourselves a name; lest we be scattered abroad over the face of the whole earth." Their goal was the usual arrogant one, to make something which would challenge heaven, to raise themselves to the level of God and stand face to face with Him. Generally when people wish to look God in the eye it is not because they love Him but because they despise Him; those who love Him are too much in awe to dare try to look at Him, however much they might desire to. But secondly, the goal of Babel was to *name* themselves. In other words, they wanted to define themselves apart from their relationship to God; they wanted to give themselves a name, a name which would not express relationship, would not open up the possibility of relationship, but would express a lack of relationship to God or other people or to nature. Don't miss the irony of their punishment. They wanted to give themselves a name, so God essentially replied, "Go ahead. Give yourselves hundreds of names." This is what an ethnic group essentially is, a people who name themselves out of relationship to their neighbors.

But God "came down to see the city and the tower which the sons of men had built". Nimrod may have planned to attack God or the gods to hang them on his wall like trophies, but there was no serious danger here. They may have planned to build a bridge to heaven and attack God on His throne, but in the end all our bridges get no where, like all our religions. Heaven is always still a long way off. So God had to take a journey to see their puny tower. Such a pretence of being eye to eye with God is one that is just asking to be challenged. History is full of other examples of "towers of Babel" since then; nation after nation has exalted itself in just such a way, including perhaps our own. Didn't the Puritan settlers come here with the intent of establishing a righteous kingdom, a kingdom of God on earth? Even good people with the best of intentions, as no doubt the Puritans were, can suddenly turn out to be working for a different master with different priorities. It is a scheme of the devil that hell would be assembled brick by brick by the servants of God. Babel takes on a Christian disguise whenever it can.

Genesis 11:6,7 says, "And the Lord said, 'Behold, they are one people, and they all have the same language. And this is what they began to do, and now nothing which they purpose to do will be impossible for them. Come, let Us go down and there confuse their language, that they may not understand one another's speech.' "The suggestion here is that the purpose of ethnic groups is to prevent the evil which we would be capable of if we were to be united. As long as we are fighting each other we will not be cooperating in evil. It would seem to be God's opinion that we must be divided into uncooperative and warring nations in order to minimize the evil that we are capable of when we do cooperate. The Messiah pointed out that a house divided against itself cannot stand, and one of the first tactical maneuvers God made in the long warfare of the spirit was to make sure the kingdom of hell, a.k.a. the kingdom of this world, was exactly that, divided against itself.

Let's briefly considering the genealogy of Shem, Ham, and Japheth. The genealogy is probably incomplete. In order to focus on the tribes of immediate concern to the history of the Jews, many that could have been included may have been left out. Here are the most important identifications that can be made in the genealogy in chapter 10; some of the identifications are more in dispute than others:

- The descendants of Japheth are generally the Europeans: Gomer, (the Cimmerians) leading to Ashkenaz (traditionally the Germans); Riphath (the Celts); Togarmah (the Armenians); Magog (the Scythians); Madai (the Medes); Javan (the Ionian Greeks) leading to Elishah (the Aeolian Greeks); Tarshish (possibly the Etruscans); Kittim (?); Dodanim (the Illyrians); Tubal (?); Meshech (?); and Tiras (the Thracians).
- The descendants of Ham were Cush (the Ethiopians); Mizraim (the Egyptians) leading to Ludim, Anamim, Lehabim, Naphtuhim, Pathrusim, Casluhim (the Philistines), and Caphtorim; Put (the Libyans); and Canaan leading to Sidon, Heth (the Hittites), and the various tribes of the Canaanites.
- The descendents of Shem were Elam (the Elamites); Asshur (the Assyrians); Arpachshad leading to Shelah (the Hebrews, Arabs, and others); Lud (the Lydians); and Aram leading to Uz, Hul, Gether, and Mash.

The section concludes with a more detailed account of the genealogy of Shem leading to Abram. In this genealogy the shortening of the lifespan is quite evident. This genealogy also provides the only data for when the sons of Noah began having children of their own, Shem having a son two years after the Flood. Otherwise this genealogy needs no further comment except to point out that Shem bore the oral tradition that had been preserved from the beginning to the time of Noah. Ham and Japheth would also have been heir to that tradition, but apparently did not choose to preserve it for whatever reason. Note however that the Epic of Gilgamesh and the pagan accounts of the creation and the Flood originated with the Sumerians, whose ancestry is unknown but who were not listed as descendants of Shem.

It is a hard thing to think that a united and peaceful human race is undesirable, but this seems to be the view here: the present condition of war and national strife is the lesser of two evils. Despite the horror of human history, we have little concept of what evil fate would have been ours if the world had been united. It would have been something like a repeat on a larger scale of whatever the world was like before Noah. On the other hand, it is only in recent years that the strife between nations has become worldwide in scope and capable of doing permanent and irreversible damage to the whole world. Perhaps this means that ethnic boundaries have outlasted their benefits and are now a liability. Perhaps this means that we are now at a time in which Babel will be undone and we will have to face the alternative it was meant to prevent. Perhaps it means we are nearing the end of the Covenant of Preservation, when all of the Covenants will be swallowed up in the final redemption.

In fact, the Messiah has already completed the curse of Babel by acting Himself to reverse it. The so-called Great Commission is exactly the undoing of Babel, the reunification of all the tongues of the world into a single people under the headship of the Messiah. The gift of tongues at Pentecost was another sign that the Kingdom of God was taking the world back to before Babel. The Church has always had the mission to make disciples of all nations, to make them into one body, one new man. And if God is dismantling the restraints He imposed on evil, it can only mean that He is preparing to dismantle evil as well. The picture presented in the Bible is complicated. The promise was that the head of the serpent would be bruised, not that he was to be merely restrained forever. Babel is being undone because evil itself is to be undone.

But the serpent is also eager to dismantle Babel and the other restraints he is under. It is not surprising that he would have his own schemes competing with the Body of Christ; he is still the spirit of Nimrod, storming heaven. But he has learned a thing or two and uses more subtle and less repulsive means. To turn Paul's phrase on end, "Why not do good that evil may come?" The rise of science as a common language, a common ideology, is a good thing, but works toward helping all the nations cooperate in evil. Indeed, it has enabled us to make war and ethnic strife so destructive that we can kill the whole world. Thus we are forced to create things like the United Nations to circumvent the destruction, hopefully, but simultaneously make us better able to cooperate in other kinds of evil; the Economic Monetary Fund and the world wide economy is not purely good.

From this viewpoint, the existence of the United States is a troubling one. There is no other nation that is making the effort to undo Babel the way we are. America is a single nation drawing all the peoples together with the purpose of being a "melting pot", a single nation. What will happen if racism and prejudice are actually overcome and America does become what it sometimes intends? Won't we then become the unBabel to the world? If we do regard the curse of Babel as a form of God's mercy in restraining evil, then America, by accomplishing it highest goals, may be the key to restoring the kingdom of evil that was the main threat before the Flood. America is being set up as the principle competitor to the Kingdom of God. A rivalry is being established between America and the Church, each one imitating the other. America may be Satan disguising himself as an angel of light.

III The Covenant of Revelation

A. Abraham

1. The Early Years

a) Abram's World (Genesis 11:27-32)

With Abram we are getting to the edge of datable history, though the precision of the dating is not very great. In my discussion of Genesis I will state precise dates for events, but they are not really much better than guesses. I derive my guesses from trying to honor the statements in Scripture as accurate and from fitting Genesis into the rest of the Bible, so sometimes the dates I assign things derive from much later parts of Scripture and it may not be apparent where they come from. Just to be clear, the date of Solomon's reign forms a baseline and I date events backward from there. There is a lot of room for error. These dates are to be taken lightly, as possible dates that may have to be adjusted as our knowledge of the ancient world and the Bible increases.

As to our present knowledge of the ancient world outside the Bible, the experts disagree about most dates; this is justification enough to give only approximate dates, to the nearest century or so. On the one hand, that is a more strictly truthful thing to do. On the other hand, I believe there is much to be gained from fitting everything into a careful and precise chronology, and it is no less truthful if we are clear that the dates are hypotheses rather than facts. By assigning precise dates, we open the biblical narrative to correlation with the rest of history, we gain a greater sense of the vividness of the events, and the secular history provides some added dimensions to the stories. Assigning precise dates here plays a role similar to a scientist making precise predictions with his theories. It is always helpful to have statements that are falsifiable, even if they are ultimately falsified.

First, let's sort out Abram's family. His father Terah was 70 when he fathered Abram, Nahor and Haran. Like the account of Noah's children, they are all telescoped into a single event, but these were not triplets. Terah died at age 205 just before Abram left Haran at age 75, so Abram was born when Terah was 130 or a bit later. Thus the three sons were born over a sixty year time span. Abram was the youngest of the three, though he is listed first because he was the star of the show. Haran was probably the oldest, partly because he died first and partly because one of his daughters married his brother Nahor. Haran had at least three children: Lot, Milcah, and Iscah. His daughter Milcah was the one who married her uncle Nahor. So Lot could have easily been older than Abram, but since Abram assumed guardianship of Lot when Haran died this isn't likely. Lot was a son of Haran's old age, more than likely. Finally Abram married Sarai, his half-sister, the daughter of Terah by a different woman.

So I suggest the following chronology: Abram was born in approximately 2159 b.c. probably in Ur. This means that Haran was born about 2219 b.c. Abram's and Terah's ancestors seem to have been one of the Amorite tribes that were settling around Mesopotamia in those centuries. Abram's nearest relations came from the area around the city of Haran (his brother being named for the city, apparently) in what is now Syria near Turkey. There is evidence that immigrants from the region of Haran had participated in the founding of Ur in the previous millennium. Hence it is possible there were close ethnic ties between Haran and Ur that led Terah to go from Haran to Ur before Abram was born and then to return to Haran as an old man. Haran was their real home, as the use of place names for sons indicates. It was business that took them to Ur, and successful business at that.

Around the time of Abram's birth, civilization was at a low ebb in the Middle East. The Old Kingdom of Egypt had fragmented into two minor, inglorious states, the First Intermediate Period; it was the northern one of these that Abram would visit in chapter 12. The Akkadian empire, founded by Sargon the Great, fell just as Abram was born. It was destroyed by a barbarian tribe, the Gutians, who then dominated much of Mesopotamia in a informal sense. The most important city in Mesopotamia at the time was Lagash, which the Gutians adopted as their base of operations. But in 2112 b.c. when Abram was about forty seven years old, Utu-khegal, the king of Uruk, defeated Lagash and the Gutians and made Ur-Nammu the governor of Ur. This Ur-Nammu soon set himself up as king of Ur and founded the famous Third Dynasty of Ur. Ur shortly became the center of an empire, and the center of one of the great civilizations of the ancient world; and Abram and his family were right there to see it happen.

It would appear that Ur was at the pinnacle of its glory when Terah, Abram, and Lot left it to return to Haran. The young Abram would have seen the founding of one of the great civilizations of the ancient world, and perhaps saw its second king, Shulgi, one of the most successful and dynamic rulers in Mesopotamian history. It may have been the death of his oldest son, Haran, that motivated Terah to return to his relatives. At this point, Nahor and Milcah do not seem to have returned to Haran with him, but sometime in the next few decades they did. In Acts 7:2 Stephen quotes a tradition that says God appeared to Abram first in Ur; Genesis doesn't mention that appearance, but it does say that Terah left Ur intending to go to Canaan. Whatever his intentions, however, Terah died in Haran.

When Abram was 75 years old, in 2084 b.c., God appeared to him (maybe for the second time) and told him to leave his relatives in Haran to go on to . . . somewhere. It is likely that Terah was a man of high social standing in Haran before he went to Ur and that Abram had high status there before he left. Abram seems to have been fairly wealthy even at that time, and therefore politically important. That Abram took his half sister as his wife would not have been unusual if Abram was of a noble family, or a family imitating the customs of the nobility. The title "sister-wife" was an honorific among the rulers.

Terah may have intended to go to Canaan, but it is not clear that Abram knew it and God did not specify the destination in this passage. God only said, "the land which I will show you". In Acts 7:2 Stephen states that the call to Abram came while he was in Ur before he went to Haran. Was Stephen's understanding of Genesis given as an authoritative one, or was he simply speaking from memory with no endorsement from the Spirit being implied? I must go with the latter. For one thing, in Acts 7:16 Stephen remembered Abraham as buying a field from the sons of Hamor in Shechem but we find in Genesis 33:19 that the field in Shechem was actually bought by Jacob, not Abraham. Stephen misremembered; he was filled with the Spirit, but the Spirit did not correct his mistake and, of course, was under no obligation to do so. We should be cautious interpreters.

The call to leave Haran came near the beginning of Shulgi's reign in Ur. The early years of Shulgi's reign are not well documented, possibly because the Elamites were disrupting things for a while. The Elamites were a tribe native to Iran who had long harassed the Mesopotamian cities. They may have tried to take advantage of the inexperience of the young Shulgi and increase their raids in the area. They were unable to take Ur itself at this point, but they went around it and attacked the fringes of its empire. The Elamites extended their influence over much of the Middle East and as far as the land of Canaan and collected tribute wherever they could. Their rule was not direct. They were not creating an empire, just extorting tribute. It was more like gangsters controlling a neighborhood by collecting protection money. It is doubtful that they would have taken much notice of a nomad like Abram, even a rich one.

Abram was in the line of people who had been preserving an oral tradition that we now have in the first eleven chapters of Genesis. There is no indication, however, that Abram had previously heard directly from God. God's call to Abram seemingly came out of the blue, but God Most High was familiar to him in his traditions. It is worth thinking about what Abram did and did not understand about God. It is a mistake to read back in to him much of what we understand. He was from the culture of that time and only had that knowledge of God that God had preserved in the world and in the oral tradition of his family. Basically what we have in the first eleven chapters of Genesis is what he would have heard, but he would not necessarily have had a deep or mature understanding of his tradition. He was also a product of the culture of that time and place.

As far as we can tell, with no written records, the very earliest religions were monotheistic. This is based on the assumption that the modern Stone Age tribes are similar to the ancient ones. It was a "primitive" monotheism, of course, not like the sophisticated monotheism of Genesis 1-11. Only with the rise of the cities did ancient religions become polytheistic. Each city was the home town of its own god, and the authority of the city's god was generally localized to that city. The Sumerians and other Mesopotamians understood the gods as being organized into a governing council of gods with no single god in absolute control of the world. They imagined earthly events mirroring heavenly events, so that when one city became politically dominant its god had just won a corresponding spiritual dominance over the other gods. The people of Ur belonged to Nanna-Sin who was believed to live in their city. Nanna-Sin was the god that was identified with the moon.

God (Elohim) or God Most High (El Elyon)—the two names were used interchangeably—was not a Sumerian god, nor part of the Mesopotamian religion at all. There were no myths about Him in the Mesopotamian tradition though the Canaanites, who came much later, would tell myths about the god they called El. The only stories about God Most High in Abram's day were the oral traditions contained in these few chapters of the Bible, and so far as we know these were not written down in the only existing form of writing, cuneiform. Though no city-state belonged to God Most High as His particular home (except that Salem under its king, Melchizedek, may have had an unusual devotion to God Most High), plainly God Most High was known to some extent in that general culture if only among some of the nomadic Amorites scattered through the area. It is noteworthy: Cain built cities, and his gods lived in them, but the Creator of the world chose to associate with the nomads from the beginning.

God had contrived to keep knowledge of Himself alive but without tying Himself down to a single place. To tie Himself to a particular city would have been to join in the human religious game that was going on. It would have been to acknowledge the other gods as really existing entities, as His peers. One principle that God adheres to in His self-revelation: He does not compete. The God disclosed in the Bible never presented Himself as one among many. He did not engage in what we might call *apologetics* with the ancient world. There was no argument from God, no attempt to prove that He alone was the real God, no persuasive speech to win their allegiance away from Nanna-Sin, no logical treatise to show them that Nanna-Sin must be false. Instead God had preserved a fairly minimal and general knowledge of Himself in the culture and otherwise ignored their gods entirely.

Why didn't He set Himself up with a city state of His own, like Salem, and proceed to conquer the whole world using Melchizedek or Abram as his general? That would have shown everyone who the real God was. Why all of this wasted time, all this fooling around over the millennia, when He could have accomplished everything with a few spectacular military victories? That God did not, and never does, behave in that way proves that He was and is trying to do something very different than merely asserting His authority. To do such a thing would perhaps have proven that He was the only true God, but in the process He would have become a different God. He would have been untrue to Himself.

On the other hand, in a millennium or so after calling Abram, He would seem to do just what I have maintained that He did not do. He would establish Israel as His own nation among the nations of the world. Why then and not with Abram? Why would it have been untrue to His nature to conquer the Middle East through Abram and not have been untrue to His nature to conquer the Middle East through David? I must put off a more complete answer until I can discuss David more thoroughly. At this point I can only suggest two points. First, establishing the kingdom of David was something that God did with some reluctance, in something of the same manner that he allowed executions of murderers; it was a compromise. Second, His purpose in establishing the kingdom of David was not to compete with the other nations in any way that we could recognize; the kingdom He established was unlike any other kingdom and carried out a completely different agenda in the overall scheme of the revelation. It is a question that deserves more careful consideration in the future.

We imagine that the process of self-revelation for God would have been straightforward. He need only give us a series of propositions, like a creed, do a few miracles to get our attention and intimidate us into believing, and then we would know Him. In fact a series of propositions/miracles is exactly what He did not give us, and therefore we ought to realize that such a revelatory style can never reveal who He really is. The truth is that the way we think had become so alien from God, our minds had become so crippled and corrupted, that self-revelation was (and is still) a tricky thing, one that had to be accomplished over millennia and at great cost. The kingdom of God is so unlike any kingdom in this world, so unlike what any kingdom in this world can ever be, that He could not assume the role of god to some city and proceed to show His superiority. It would have been automatically false. God simply cannot speak or act in terms of this world and remain true to Himself.

b) Abram's Call (Genesis 12:1-3)

Abram is one of the three most important people in the Hebrew Bible, along with Moses and David. What these three have in common is that God chose each of them as the beginning points for new covenants. The introduction of a new covenant means the introduction of a new level of relationship between God and His people, so naturally those people are important. New covenants are therefore naturally always accompanied by a period of intense revelation. The pattern of God's self-revelation is episodic: a fairly brief period in which a lot of information is introduced at once, followed by a much longer period in which the people "do their homework"—that is, they get used to the new information and begin to absorb it into their lives. This is the way people normally learn: we discover a new concept in a flash, but then spend a long time mulling it over, internalizing it, fitting it in with what we already know, learning how to look at the world in a new way. So with Abram, God began lesson two (Noah should be consider lesson one) about Himself and us.

This lesson naturally sets the tone for future lessons. It will be worthwhile to spend some time reflecting on what the nature of the revelation must be. What kind of information do we get? The Protestant branch of Christianity traditionally emphasizes propositional truth. This means they emphasize that the revelation was primarily intended to convey statements, facts about God and spiritual things. I personally have enormous respect for the value of propositional truth, but I am no longer convinced that it is the primary content of the revelation. Propositional truth should never be swept aside or neglected, but if we make it the exclusive focus of our attention then we will end up with a distorted understanding of what the Bible does.

Getting to know a person is not entirely like getting to know organic chemistry. In the sciences, propositional truth is virtually everything, but with people it is secondary. Getting to know my wife certainly does involve propositional truth: her birthday, important invents from her childhood and how they have affected her, her favorite colors and foods, her style of clothing, the things that I might do that would drive her crazy. But this kind of knowledge only goes so far. It doesn't make a marriage; it doesn't even suffice for a friendship. An intimate relationship with a person requires time, lots of it, a long period in which the two live together, enjoy each other, argue and reconcile, plan together, suffer and celebrate, cooperate, discuss, and basically care for each other. Revelation in marriage includes sex but it also includes much more, and covenants are more like marriage than anything else.

So when God called Abram, this is the general sort of revelation He had in mind. He chose a family for Himself. They would be His family and He would be, by and bye, their Son. He was choosing a family, a people, to have an extended conversation with, to share with, to argue with, to rejoice and suffer with, to care for and be cared for. It had to involve time, and lots of it. This was no "one night stand"; God is not like the stereotypical pathetic American male, afraid of being tied down. When He chose Abram and Sarai, He was making a lifetime commitment, *His* lifetime, generation to generation. Terah had received the oral tradition from his father, and his father before him, all the way back to Noah and beyond, and Terah passed on that oral tradition to his sons. But this time something weird happened. The Most High God of their tradition spoke to Abram, perhaps in Ur, but certainly in Haran. It was the first time He had spoken in thousands of year, so far as we know, since before the Flood.

So how exactly did He speak to Abram? A voice from the sky? In a vision or a dream? It hardly matters. Everytime God spoke to people, He did it differently. What is important is what He said. As the first verbal communication in a long time, we should pay attention to the wording of God's call to Abram in some detail. In Genesis 12:1-3 we read, "Go forth from your country, and from your relatives and from your father's house, to the land which I will show you; and I will make you a great nation, and I will bless you, and make your name great; and so you shall be a blessing; and I will bless those who bless you, and the one who curses you I will curse, and in you all the families of the earth will be blessed." We will consider the call to Abram in reverse order.

The last phrase was the most important one. It was the central promise that is behind all of the other promises God would make to Abram in the ensuing years. He promised that in Abram all the families of the earth would be blessed. Abram could hardly have understood it, but God's purpose in calling him was cosmic in scope: the blessing of the whole world. This could only mean that Abram was to bring forth the Messiah, the One who had been promised to deliver the world from the power of the serpent, but this is hindsight speaking. Abram would not have thought it obvious to associate this promise to him with the promise given to the serpent in the traditions he had inherited. One of the difficulties of a progressive revelation is that it doesn't completely make sense for the people in the middle of it. There are always loose ends that are hanging. We still have a few loose ends we haven't got sorted out even today.

Working our way backward through the call, God said He would use Abram as a vehicle of judgment on the nations: they would be blessed or cursed according to how they responded to Abram. Those who blessed Abram and his descendants would in turn find God's favor and those who cursed Abram or his descendants would in turn find themselves the objects of God's disfavor. But ultimately the curses on those who cursed him would be only temporary. There would be no one who cursed him in the end, not one single nation, because God promised that all of the families of the world would be blessed. Therefore all the families will eventually bless him. The threat of God's curse on the nations that curse Abram will never be fully or permanently realized. It is partially realized on a temporary basis, but in the end there is to be only blessing. This is a pattern with God that should be carefully noted as you read through the Scripture: the threat of God's curse is always subordinate to His promise of blessing. Every family on earth will be blessed through Abram; some of them may have to go through a curse to get there, but ultimately the blessing wins out. There is no hint of how such a promise could ever be accomplished. It had to be enough, it has to be enough, that God makes absurd promises and leaves us to believe them or not.

But more remarkable than the promise of blessing to all nations is the intimate identification God made with Abram. Essentially He said that He would take personally any attitudes directed at Abram, that He and Abram would be so closely associated as to be inseparable, nearly indistinguishable. Henceforth, no one could be God's friend without also being Abram's friend; and vice versa: to become Abram's friend was to become God's friend. To encounter Abram inevitably led to encountering God. But the most remarkable thing about this promise is how vulnerable God allowed Himself to become. God was to be so closely associated with Abram that God's reputation was at stake along with Abram's reputation. God virtually invited the world to judge Him through Abram. This is what it means that God has revealed Himself in history: we see God as an actor among Abram's family, and by this family we know and judge Him. It is impossible to describe what a remarkable commitment this was on God's part, to connect Himself so closely with an individual and his descendants. He took Abram's name as His own; henceforth the world would know Him as "the God of Abram".

Continuing to work backward through the call, the next preceding statement was the promise to bless Abram himself, to make him a great nation, and to give him a great name. Now to "make his name great" does not mean what we think of as fame and celebrity, except perhaps indirectly. For the ancients, the name expressed the relationship between the person and God and the world. "To make Abram's name great" meant that the relationship between Abram and God would be great, that it would be made central to God's relationship to the whole world. To have a great name from God is to be great in God's affection, to be great in God's sight, to be great in God's thoughts, regardless of whether the world hears of it or not, regardless of whether there is fame among men. Abram was to become the pattern for how God related to the whole world, then and forever.

We Christians sometimes talk about our "personal relationship" to God as if it were a completely new thing, as if such a relationship had never existed before. On the contrary, our relationship with God is a fulfillment of God's promise to Abram, it is a continuation of God's relationship with Abraham. It is true that we have more understanding of how it all works than Abram did, we have several millennia of additional revelation to stand on, there is a deeper level of intimacy now than then, but fundamentally we stand before God just as Abram did. His name is as great among us now as it ever was, and the coming of the Messiah only made it greater. In fact, it was the Messiah that made Abram's name great, just as God had promised.

Along with having a great name God promised Abram that he would become a great nation. The two promises are not the same. One can become a great nation without having a great name, and one can have a great name without becoming a great nation. The promise to make him a great nation squarely placed this call as a covenantal call. The promise was not merely to Abram but to his descendants after him. It was not a personal relationship in the way we understand the word "personal". God was not connecting Himself to an individual, but to a people that did not even exist yet. For two thousand years the Most High God had not chosen any nation, any city, to be His own. He had spurned them and their gods. Now he chose a man who lived in a tent, with no city, no land, no status, no glory of his own, no children, to be His nation. What a perfectly odd and typical thing for Him to do. He chose a nation in just such a way that it was simultaneously a rejection of nations.

Finally the call began with an order to leave all that was familiar and go into the unknown. Apparently the destination turned out to be the one that Terah had planned originally, but at this point God did not let on to Abram where he might be going. Abram was to give up everything he knew and, in trust of God's call, simply cast off into the unknown. In fact, Abram took all of his living relatives who were close to him. Doubtless he was living among relatives in Haran, but they were relatives he had not grown up with, that he hardly knew. What he was really sacrificing when he left was status, from the high status he enjoyed as Terah's son to no status at all among a people he did not know.

Here Abram's life itself was being used as an example of the way He calls each of us. It is the nature of God's call, whether it be to Abram or to you or to me, to be a journey to an unknown land. To be called by God is to be called to leave all that gives us our identity and place in this world and to cast off into . . . something, whether we actually move geographically or not. To answer God's call is always an emotional and psychological—and sometimes even a geographical—adventure to a new world even when it happens to coincide initially with plans we had already. To answer God's call means to travel toward a land that He cannot describe to us ahead of time. It leads to a place we can only recognize by arriving.

Most basically, God's call changed Abram's life down to its roots. He seems to have lived in a manner that was civilized, in the mainstream of the culture of the Middle East, settled into that life, but also the heir of the tradition of revelation, a spiritual nomad in the world's wilderness of religion. When God called him the two dimensions of his life traded places: he became a nomad in his lifestyle but he settled into devotion to the Most High God. Once God had spoken to Him, all other gods became secondary. The One that actually spoke to him was the obvious choice to be his God. Indeed, the sort of devotion the other gods wanted did not require anything from the gods. They didn't have to talk and they didn't give directions. But the sort of devotion the Most High God wants cannot come without His calling, without His speaking, without further directions along the way. For us to know the Most High God the way He wants to be known requires that He speak.

It is crucial to note that the call to Abram arose entirely from grace, as all covenantal events do. It was begun by grace, it proceeded by grace, and it ended with grace. There was no reason given for God's call. It was not that Abram was a better man than the others in his generation. It was not that Abram had known God more intimately and thus was a natural person for God to call. It was not that Abram was less caught up in idolatry than others—he and his children do not seem to have imagined that idolatry might be offensive to God. The whole Mesopotamian religious mindset imagined a community of gods that shared mankind's devotion like a family shares food at dinner, and a God who demanded undivided allegiance was outside their framework. The call came out of the blue, with no preparation or reason given.

Further, God did not make any conditions on His promises. He did not require Abram to be obedient to some set of laws or rules. He did not threaten to go back on any of the promises should Abram fail to deliver a specified amount of righteousness or worship. He did not leave any doubt as to the certainty that the promises would be fulfilled regardless of Abram's deserving them or not. The promises were absolute, without justification, and without condition.

So what would have happened if Abram had refused to leave Haran? We are not told, of course, so we don't know. The legalists among us must imagine that God would then reject Abram and find someone more obedient. This seems to me an absurd and ultimately unbelieving interpretation. The idea that God would fail to carry out what He promises for any reason ought to be unthinkable. If my choices and stupidity and stubbornness can gum up God's promises then they were not really promises to begin with. God does not make promises unless the fulfillment of those promises depends on God's own power alone. Clearly, refusal to leave Haran would have had some serious consequences for Abram of some nature. But whatever Abram did or did not do, he would still have become the blessing to all the nations, and his name would have been great because God had promised it. As Paul would say in the Romans 11:29, ". . . the gifts and the calling of God are irrevocable." It is not the one who is called who makes the call irrevocable; only the Caller has the right or the power to do that.

c) Arrival in the Land of Canaan (Genesis 12:4-9)

Abram and Lot traveled more than four hundred miles to the land of Canaan. We call it the land of Canaan but in fact Abram and Lot got there first, several hundred years before the Canaanites moved in and made it their own. At this time the land was inhabited by a miscellany of tribes including some Amorites, distant cousins of Abram. The Canaanite people lived to the north and along the coast, in Byblos and Tyre and Sidon. A few Canaanites doubtless lived in the land, but mainly not. It was a journey of several weeks for people who are not in a hurry and have large herds to control. Since there was no large empire keeping the peace in that land at that time, it was a journey that was somewhat dangerous on the mainly unguarded roads. Doubtless they followed the main trading route that linked the north with Egypt.

Their first stop was Shechem (the modern city of Nablus) and the oak of Moreh. This particular tree must have been unusually impressive and therefore an important place of worship for some local god, a place of worship for a cult that was well enough known in that land to be identified by this tree. If so, then God chose that place for His second appearance to Abram to make a point. Whatever god might be the local god of that land, the God who had called Abram, God Most High, was also there and even had the authority to give away that god's land to whomever He chose. In His speech with Abram, the Most High God did not make any claims directly against the gods of the land; on the contrary, He ignored them out of existence, reducing them to irrelevance by never giving them so much as a nod. If Abram had theological questions concerning the presence or authority of God Most High in a foreign land among rival gods, then God's appearance and promise of land was a direct answer.

This point deserves repeating. The promise to give Abram and his descendants the land of Canaan only came after he had arrived in the land. The original call was to go to a land, not take possession of it. It could be argued that ownership of the land was tacit in the original call, but here that tacit promise was being made explicit. In promising to give the land to Abram, God was making a clear assertion of His authority, and Abram would have naturally understood Him this way. Although the land belonged to other gods, nonetheless He had the power and the right to take their land and give it to whomever He chose. The promise of land was one way of revealing to Abram that God Most High was God over the whole world. This was a truth that Abram was not quick to understand but this claim to authority is the main point of the gift of the land.

There was a different religious mentality in Canaan than there had been in the great city of Ur, and they were both different from the religious mentality Abram would encounter in Egypt. Ancient religion was all about survival in an unpredictable world. But the world of Mesopotamia and Egypt was somewhat less unpredictable than the world of Canaan. The Mesopotamian and the Egyptian civilizations depended on the annual floods of their main rivers. Occasionally the floods would fail, but those rivers drew water from a very large area. Only a major, extensive drought in a large region of the world would be devastating. But the land of Canaan, the hill country around Mesopotamia depended on rain and punctual seasons. So the religion that grew up in the more barbaric hill country was a fertility religion, a religion of agriculture and weather gods who were much more erratic that the more "civilized" gods of Mesopotamia, and the more esoteric gods of Egypt. Abram was entering the land of more sinister gods, smaller and more immediate than the gods he had left behind. Possibly God Most High appeared to him at the oak of Moreh to emphasize that even in this different religious environment, He was still not just "one of the guys", the Chairman of the Heavenly Board. He was the Boss.

Abram and Lot led nomadic lives, but appear to have spent a fairly long time at Shechem and then near Bethel (which was called Luz at that time, being renamed Bethel much later). In those two places they stayed long enough that Abram built altars; otherwise, Abram and Lot gradually wandered toward the south arriving at last in the southern part of Canaan called the Negev (which meant "the South"). This section of Scripture probably covers a couple of years of wandering in the land. Abram and Lot were already fairly rich when they left Haran, and grew richer as they lived in Canaan.

d) The Visit to Egypt (Genesis 12:10-20)

Life in the ancient world was much more closely linked to the vagaries of the weather than modern life, particularly in Canaan. There was no regional system of food distribution; each city had to be self-sufficient. Since agriculture was fairly inefficient, and since it was very difficult to store up a large surplus in the good years for use in the bad years, drought and famine were the greatest threats and were not uncommon. One dry year, or one year with a disastrous storm at just the wrong time, could severely reduce the local food supply. The only option in a time of famine was to eat a skimpy diet or to kill off a portion of your animals or to go elsewhere in search of food. Abram's possessions were very great and a drought which made pasture scarce would have forced him to seek new pasture land for his animals. Egypt was relatively immune to such droughts and so Egypt was a common refuge for hungry neighbors in times of trouble. Thus it was not remarkable that within two or three years of his arrival in Canaan Abram was forced to seek shelter in Egypt.

The Egypt that Abram visited was the northern half of two rival Egyptian kingdoms in what is known as the First Intermediate Period, between the end of the Old Kingdom and the beginning of the Middle Kingdom. He came there late in the First Intermediate Period around 2080 b.c. The pharaohs of the northern kingdom, centered at Hierakleopolis, were in decline, gradually succumbing to their rivals from Thebes. The ruler of the southern branch of the Old Egyptian kingdom was Intef II, an aggressive ruler who pressed hard against the northern kingdom at about this time. The Pharaoh Abram visited is not known or knowable at the present. There were something like eighteen pharaohs in the north and only three or four of them are known by name; this one would not be remembered. Presumably Lot and his wife and two daughters would have gone with Abram and Sarai. They would not necessarily have stayed in close proximity to each other in Egypt since their possessions were great, and perhaps Lot did not know of the deception Abram and Sarai practiced on the Pharaoh.

Abram thought of having Sarai pose as his sister when they first set out from Haran (Genesis 20:13), but it was in Egypt that he first used the trick. Sarai was in truth Abram's half sister (20:12) so he told the pharaoh a half truth. Such marriages were not uncommon in the ancient Middle East, and became routine for Pharaoh's later in Egyptian history. The goddess Isis was both sister and wife to Osiris, and it was a wide spread custom among the gods to marry brother and sister. Thus, it would not have been thought a strange thing if Abram had told the truth, but it might have carried with it an implicit claim to more status that he wanted to claim. The Egyptian religious mentality was different from either the primitive religions in Canaan or the civilized religions of Mesopotamia. It was esoteric, mysterious, difficult for an outsider to comprehend. The Egyptians were the ones who most closely identified their gods with their human rulers. It was an age in decline, but talking to a Pharaoh in any age was something like talking to a god, and it may have been all the more emphatic to compensate for the decline in political power. It was a dangerous age, an unstable age, and rulers had to be ready to fight for whatever status they claimed. Perhaps Abram adopted the half-truth in order to avoid possible conflict on a more political level.

So how did Abram come to meet Pharaoh at all? As a wealthy unknown foreigner, meeting Pharaoh may have been inevitable, a legal obligation to obtain the necessary permits or whatever, especially in a time of war. It is not that Abram's fears of rulers wanting his wife were groundless. What other Pharaoh or king has been hesitant to take another man's wife, especially if she is the wife of a foreigner? Even the great King David, the man after God's own heart, would not hesitate to steal another's wife and murder the husband; why would the god-king of Egypt hesitate?

Still it is difficult to understand how Abram could have asked Sarai to assume such a compromising role, and even risk losing her. Pharaoh summoned her and intended to take her as one of his wives, as a concubine, and Abram was apparently going to let him have her. What exactly did he plan to do then? Just leave her behind when he left, or stay in Egypt and wait for the Pharaoh to die? What was he thinking? Was there *any* scenario in which this scheme could end well? And what was Sarai thinking she would do? Did she really intend to marry Pharaoh, stay in the Egyptian court and lose Abram forever? The modern reader of this story has to think that the marriage between Abram and Sarai was very strange. And it would seem that Abram did not have much faith in God Most High to stoop to such a scheme to protect himself from an imagined danger. It does not seem to have occurred to Abram that God could protect him from Pharaoh, who was, after all, a god himself.

But God sent great plagues against Pharaoh, though their exact nature is unspecified. And though the passage does not say how, in some manner Pharaoh discerned that the calamities befalling his household were due to Abram's deception. Plainly, though Pharaoh was naturally offended by Abram's deception, he had reason to respect Abram and even to fear him. Pharaoh felt powerless to do anything to punish Abram. Perhaps God Most High had impressed on Pharaoh, in some manner, that he had better not hurt Abram, or perhaps political circumstances made retribution impossible. At this point, though, the Pharaoh seems to have been more sensitive to God's purposes and presence than Abram was. Certainly we can't blame Pharaoh for throwing Abram out of the country; Abram was too dangerous.

God's treatment of Pharaoh does not seem entirely fair, though. Pharaoh had done nothing wrong. If anyone did anything wrong it was Abram, and Sarai as his accomplice. Yet God never rebuked Abram for deceiving the Pharaoh, for misusing Sarai, or for having such weak faith that he didn't trust Him to take care of him. What God did was bless Abram materially, rescue Sarai, and punish Pharaoh. God's behavior was more inexplicable than Abram's. But blessing Abram, in spite his questionable behavior, is part of the covenant aspect of their relationship. Whoever cursed Abram, even if his curse were justified, would find himself cursing God. It may seem unreasonable to think it, but God was right behind Abram even when Abram was stupid and unethical. That God did not speak some private word of rebuke to Abram goes beyond the Covenant, however, and we will consider this strange silence later.

Not only did God not rebuke Abram when any of us might have said something, His eventual behavior is more problematic that that. Such marriages of a man with his half-sister would later be forbidden in the Law of Moses. In Leviticus 20:17 we find, "If there is a man who takes his sister, his father's daughter or his mother's daughter, so that he sees her nakedness and she sees his nakedness, it is a disgrace; and they shall be cut off in the sight of the sons of their people. He has uncovered his sister's nakedness; he bears his guilt." Thus, by God's later standards of morality Abram would have been cut off from his own people. This has a lot to say about how we are to understand the Law of Moses and sin but we can only consider briefly here.

There are two seemingly inconsistent choices God made. First God chose Abram and his sister-wife to be the foundational marriage to produce His covenant people. Second, He chose to forbid such marriages in the Law He gave their children, a law that branded Abram and Sarai as sexually impure, as a disgrace. Either the Bible is simply internally inconsistent and therefore not to be taken seriously, or else the Law of Moses was not the absolute standard of morality we usually take it to be, or else God does not care about sexual purity as much as we were taught that He does. Or perhaps it is all a bit more complicated that any of these alternatives suggest. I believe His purpose in choosing Abram and Sarai and then labeling their marriage disgraceful was to show us that His purpose was to involve Himself in our disgrace. He chose a "tainted lineage" to be His own so that He could rescue all of us, who are all also children of such a lineage.

The episode in Egypt was revelatory on several levels. First we have another glimpse of the nature of the Covenant relationship. When God binds Himself to a person in a covenant, He chooses to be blind to that person's faults (to some extent, anyway) and to bless that person in preference to others who are not in the covenant. In short, God is *biased* toward His covenant people. This may seem strange at first, but if we think for a moment we know exactly what such bias feels like from the inside. It is the most natural thing in the world to be biased in this same way toward our own family, biased in their favor and biased against those who are outside the family. As a father I give special favors, special attention, to my own children that I do not give to other people's children. When my children do something wrong, I find it easier to make excuses for them or give them the benefit of the doubt than when other people's children do the same thing. It is part of the ideal of the good parent, the ideal we measure ourselves by, that, while we may be harsh to our children ourselves in private, we defend them equally strongly to the outside world. Failing to be biased in this way toward our own children would be considered a defect in a parent. God had adopted Abram as His child in a peculiar way that did not apply to Pharaoh. On the contrary, the Pharaoh claimed descent from his own god. He and Abram were simply from different spiritual families. The issue was not one of fairness but of loyalty. Abram had not realized how intimately God identified with him, and it took yet more time for him to realize it better.

Secondly, the episode is another illustration of grace: God did not feel the need to correct every mistaken idea Abram may have had, nor discipline every fault of Abram's character, nor punish every one of Abram's sins. Looking at this same idea from the other direction, being under God's blessing is not proof that we are right in what we think and do, nor does it prove that others are wrong if they are not blessed by God. God does not send down blessings or calamities for the purpose of settling theological arguments. He has more important things to reveal to us than the answers to our questions; He is answering the questions we should have asked.

Thirdly, the episode makes it clear that God took care to keep His name known in the world, and the knowledge He preserved there was not, and is not, insignificant. Even this lame Pharaoh of a dying kingdom knew more about God Most High than we give him credit for. Egypt, the rest of the Middle East, and the rest of the world, did not have access to that knowledge of God that provided the hope of the Messiah and salvation, but the knowledge God did give out was the knowledge He chose to give out, and would accomplish His purposes in their lives. God was content that virtually the whole world remained in relative darkness while He slowly got to know and be known by a single family, so either God did not care about the desperate plight of a world dieing without the knowledge of God, or else their plight was not as desperate as we thought.

Finally the episode shows us that God did not choose Abram because he understood God better than others, nor that he had more faith than others, nor that he was more righteous than others. Abram's limitations and weaknesses were the common ones. So why did God choose Abram? As we shall soon see, the first part of the answer is that Abram was very similar to Noah in one critical respect: he did not try to do God's job for Him. Abram was a man who knew his limits and he was able to wait for God to accomplish His own promises in His own way. But this is only half of the answer, and it was only half of the answer with Noah as well.

The other half of the answer is that God loved him, with no further explanation. But Abram had so little going for him! Can't we narrow the focus to some specific character traits that God valued in Abram? Perhaps so, but even if we do we would be all wrong to think that those traits caused God to love him. It is similar to what we call "falling in love". We may be able to specify what we like in the beloved: beauty, kindness, intelligence, punctuality, whatever. But none of these are the actual reasons we love them. Indeed we can always find others who are more beautiful, more kind, more intelligent, more punctual, than the beloved but they do not attract the way the beloved does. The chemistry of such things cannot be explained. Similarly God never offers any explanation for why He chooses one but not another. If such love is a mystery for humans, it is more so for God. We must take care to remember what it felt like to fall in love. It is not a matter of reason, it is not a matter of being fair, it is not a matter of rationally evaluating the candidates objectively. Of course God does not "fall in love" exactly like we do. But He gave us the experience of falling in love to give us a glimpse of how He feels about us. In short, God loved Pharaoh but He was in love with Abram.

e) Abram and Lot Separate (Genesis 13)

As soon as he was shown the door in Egypt, Abram moved back to the Negev and gradually retraced his route back northward to his altar near Bethel. The famine was largely over but it takes some time to recover from such things, so either because the drought was not quite over or because his visit to Egypt had been quite lucrative, the land did not have the resources to support both him and his rich nephew Lot. There was conflict between their servants over pasture and water. Abram was a man of peace, but especially as an alien in the land he did not want to quarrel with those closest to him. For the sake of peace they must separate, and Abram let Lot choose the direction he preferred. Lot chose the valley of the Jordan River to the east and eventually ended up living in Sodom, and Abram turned to the west to the hill country.

Agriculture began in the hill country surrounding the Middle East, but civilization—cities—began in the river valleys. By this time in history, cities had spread everywhere in the Middle East, but the sophisticated cultures were still to be found in the river valleys, even in a backwater like Canaan. Lot chose the richer, faster urban life to the relatively primitive rural life. Some cultural distinctions never change. Some commentators fault Lot for choosing Sodom as his home; some fault him for separating from Abram at all, but I can't agree with them. Lot showed poor judgment in choosing to live in the most notoriously wicked city in the region, but the evidence is that he kept himself relatively unstained from it all; that says a lot about his integrity and faithfulness to his heritage. That he separated from Abram is presented as a necessity, and not a moral choice. God had not chosen him as part of His people, not through any fault of Lot's but simply out of God's prerogative.

Though Abram had apparently feared the jealousy and lust of powerful men even before he began to travel with Sarai—possibly based on his experience with city life in Ur—he was not a fundamentally fearful man. While Abram may have been afraid of the power of desire, he had no concerns over his own welfare, no need to see to it that his economic interests were protected. What did it matter if Lot chose the best of the land? The insecurity of a wealthy man who feels the need to guard his wealth was something Abram just didn't have. As the elder, and as the more powerful man, Abram had the right to choose which part of the land he preferred and leave Lot with what was left. Furthermore, God had promised to give all the land to Abram. There was no indication that God had spoken to Lot nor that Lot was privy to God's plans for Abram. Based on God's promise to him, Abram could have simply told Lot to leave. That he gave Lot the choice is important. Abram may have doubted that God's authority extended into Egypt or to god-kings, but he had no doubts at all about God's care for his material well-being. It didn't matter if Lot took the best of the land because God was giving Abram everything he wanted. We all have our peculiar weaknesses, we all have situations or events or people that we are afraid of, that test our courage and faith to the breaking point. For Abram, the fear of rulers coveting his wife was simply too much, but the dread of being cheated or getting the short end of the stick had no hold on him, even though he lived as an alien nomad vulnerable to weather and forces beyond his control.

Shortly after splitting up with Lot, God appeared to Abram the third time and repeated His promise to give him the land. This time the promise was broadened to include descendants, as "the dust of the earth". It must have sounded a bit too good. Abram was about eighty years old by this time and Sarai was over seventy. Children were unlikely and every year they were a bit less likely, but life spans were still shortening and God's promise of children was still just believable. When God invited him to roam about in his future inheritance, he did so. By and by Abram arrived at the oaks of Mamre, near Hebron, about thirty miles south of Bethel. This was probably another major cult site for the local gods, but it became the long-term home for Abram. The local Amorite chieftain, Mamre, became his close ally and except for brief absences, Abram seems to have stayed in this area for the rest of his life.

f) The Battle with the Elamites (Genesis 14:1-16)

The Elamites were a tribe of people who lived in what is now Iran, in the mountains on the eastern fringe of Mesopotamia. They had long been a military nuisance in Mesopotamian history, but for thirty years Ur had been the dominant power in Mesopotamia; its empire was extensive, the greatest empire the world had yet seen. Shulgi, son of Ur-Nammu, had become the second king of his dynasty at roughly the time Abram left Ur, but his reign seems to have gotten off to a rough start. The first twenty years are not well-documented. If it actually did get off to a shaky start, the cause was probably the Elamites. They may have resumed aggressive raids on the city-states scattered about the Middle East as soon as Ur-Nammu died. Sodom, Gomorrah, Admah, Zeboiim, and Bela had been vassals of the Elamites since before God had called Abram, even though they were on the opposite side of Mesopotamia from Elam. It is a remarkable thing that the Elamites could have so much power over city states 600 miles away with a strong empire in between unless Shulgi was slow to establish his control. Although the Elamites exercised power over parts of Canaan, it was not truly an empire they founded. It was more like a gang extorting protection money.

Shortly after Abram and Lot separated, Sodom and the other four city-states at the southeastern end of what is now the Dead Sea rebelled against the rule of the Elamites and their allies. Chedorlaomer was the leader, though Amraphel was initially listed first in 14:1. Amraphel was the king of Shinar and was probably listed first to tie this episode with the preceding events at Babel. Shinar was the land around Babel (I would place the Tower of Babel event thousands of years before Abram, however). Amraphel had possibly taken advantange of Shulgi's disarray to take power in that part of Ur's empire, but if so he did not last very long. Chedorlaomer, king of the Elamites, led Amraphel, Arioch and Tidal, his loyal vassals, down the eastern side of the Jordan River, proceeding as far as what is now the Gulf of Aqaba. Apparently their intent was to attack six other tribes south of Canaan to extend their influence even further, and then turn back to deal with the rebellious kings around Sodom. Chedorlaomer made short work of these new conquests as well as the rebels. The soldiers of Sodom who were not killed in the battle or trapped in tar pits fled to hide in the hills, and Bera the king of Sodom escaped as well. Lot was in Sodom when Chedorlaomer came by after the battle and took everyone into slavery. Frequently the men would have been killed but this time perhaps the Elamites wanted some male slaves or perhaps Lot was too old to be a threat. Doubtless the same fate had overtaken the people of Gomorrah, Admah, Zeboiim, and Bela, but the focus here is on Abram and Lot.

Abram's concern was with his nephew, Lot. It is clear that there were strong ties of affection between Abram and Lot, more than the simple ties of blood and family. Abram took special pains to look after Lot on behalf of his brother. It is possible that Sarai was the full sister of Lot's father, Haran, and that this is the source of the special bond between them. Abram and his allies, Mamre the Amorite and Eshcol and Aner, overtook the Elamites near what became known as Dan, about a hundred miles to the north, and pursued them another fifty miles or so, nearly half way back to Haran, and defeated them completely. Abram's defeat of the Elamites may have occurred in about 2074 b.c. and may have enabled Shulgi to at last consolidate his power. Shulgi went on to become the greatest king of the third dynasty of Ur; his reign lasted for nearly thirty more years.

Note the contrast between the fearful man hiding from Pharaoh behind Sarai and the bold general who took on the dominant military power in that region. It is clear that Abram was a fearful man only in certain respects, but in other respects he showed real courage. Perhaps Abram was not a passionate man sexually, and the power of lust was a power he did not understand and which was therefore a fearful thing to him. But he lived in a violent world, and violence he did understand. In his battle with the Elamites, Abram was reported as having 318 trained men in his own household. That they were trained says a lot. He was a wealthy man and therefore a target in a relatively lawless land; he made sure that he was able to protect himself. Abram was a chieftain, a nomadic sheik with no set kingdom of his own. That he had 318 men in his household means that he probably had a thousand or more people attached to him as slaves, servants, or employees and their children.

He defeated the Elamites with help from his allies. The Elamites eventually recovered from this defeat and went on, about seventy years later, to destroy Ur and dominate much of Mesopotamia east of Canaan, but they never returned to trouble Abram or his descendants again. Note that there was some special tie of loyalty between Abram and these Amorites with whom he lived; it was, after all, not their quarrel. When Genesis 14:13 says that Mamre and Eshcol were Abram's allies, it means that he had entered into some kind of covenant with them. Further, it is clear that Abram was the dominant member of this alliance; it may be that this group of Amorites recognized Abram as a chieftain and owed some allegiance to him. It is interesting that, though the Amorites were among the peoples of the land who would fight the descendants of Abram in a few centuries, the presence of the people of God in the land began with a close alliance to these particular Amorites.

After the defeat of the Elamites, Abram was the dominant military power in the whole land of Canaan, with as powerful an army as any king in Canaan and having just proven his might by defeating the previous power in the region. And yet, though he was certainly the most powerful man there, though God had twice promised to give him all of the land, and though he was now in position to simply take the land he had been promised, he did nothing. What military leader in all history would have refrained from taking control of a land when he was able, especially if that military leader thought that God had promised it all to him? That Abram did not take the Promised Land for himself is exactly the same quality that kept Noah in the ark even when he saw that the ground was dry. It was God who had promised to give him the land, and therefore only God could give it to him. Abram knew, in the deepest part of his being, that God expected him to wait for God Himself to keep His own promises. Abram is the second example of the quality God desires most in His people. It is not sexual purity, it is not respectability, it is not cleanliness; important as these qualities may be, what God seeks out most eagerly in the people He chooses is what the Bible calls "humility" or "faith", the radical trust in God that is willing to wait for Him to act, the radical trust in God that does not try to accomplish by human means what God has promised to do.

Where we might rationalize it, where we could say to ourselves, "This situation is an open door from God. This must be God's way of fulfilling His promise to me. Why else would He have given me this opportunity to take what He said I could have?" Abram's understanding of God's greatness would not allow such a rationalization. Whatever God does, He is the one who must do it; we cannot do it for Him; we cannot even help Him do it. Our role is to respond when He asks us to do something and otherwise to wait quietly and patiently for Him to act. The "open door" method of discerning God's guidance is not a reliable method. For all his faults, for all his failures to understand God's power to protect him, Abram showed that he was a man like Noah, a man who understood what it means to let God be God. It is the signature of the sort of faith God looks for now as He did then, that He fosters, that He teaches. I do not mean that faith was the cause of God's love for Abram; only that He loves that quality in a person. It is the foundation of humility, just as its opposite, the willingness to do God's work in His place, is the foundation of pride.

g) Melchizedek (Genesis 14:17-24)

We now come to the most intriguing person in the whole Genesis narrative, possibly the most intriguing person in the Hebrew Scriptures: Melchizedek. There is no other single character about which we know so little but who went on to play such a significant theological role as Melchizedek. Enoch was intriguing for the brief reference to his closeness to God, but then he played virtually no role in what came later. Melchizedek, on the other hand, became an important type or symbol for the Messiah, mentioned by David and then by the author of Hebrews in the New Testament.

The story begins with the kings who seized the people and treasures of Sodom, including Lot. Sodom was a rich city, and Abram had recovered all its wealth. Bera, the king of Sodom, had escaped the Elamite army and came out of hiding when Abram returned from the battle, and his encounter with Abram is important. Bera asked him to return the people of Sodom; why? Because Abram was now entitled to them. Abram had rescued them all, and had rescued the people from the other cities as well, and had a claim to everything both as rescuer and as victor. If he wanted it all, it was his. Bera had no legitimate claim on his people or any of his property or even his throne; he made the request as a way of opening negotiations. He had reason to believe that Abram might not be interested in taking the city. They had been neighbors for a decade or so and had lived at peace with Abram giving no sign that he was interested in military conquest. But Bera assumed that everyone naturally would want more property, goods, wealth, and Sodom had a lot of it. Perhaps Bera was hoping to not lose absolutely everything.

Abram's response was extremely harsh: he had sworn to God Most High that he would not take so much as a thread or a sandal strap from the king of Sodom. It was an oath he must have taken as he set out to rescue Lot, a prayer that God would return his nephew to him, renouncing all benefit to himself. His concern had been entirely focused on Lot and Lot's family. But there was something more to his answer than his love for Lot. There was also a personal rejection of Bera himself. Abram was blunt about the reason, too: lest Bera should say, "I have made Abram rich". This was a remarkable thing for Abram to say and illuminates meaning of the whole event.

Why would Abram care if Bera claimed to have made Abram rich? What would it matter? None at all, unless Abram's real concern was with God Most High. As far as Abram's own personal reputation went, Bera's boast of making Abram rich would be simply a boast that Abram had won a battle that Bera had lost, that Abram was in fact entitled to his riches. Everyone in the land would have known it. The only motivation that seems reasonable to ascribe to Abram is that he didn't want Bera to take credit for something that God had to do.

It was the issue of trusting God in a more vivid form than it had been with Noah opening the door of the ark. Abram was like Noah in refusing to try to fulfill God's promises for Him, but he went one step further: he wanted to be sure, when God did fulfill His promises, that there was no doubt it was God who fulfilled them. It was important to Abram that no one should have any doubt that it was God who had blessed him. Though he had a *legal* right to claim the spoils, to claim the whole city of Sodom and Gomorrah and the others, as his domain, though there was no one in the land powerful enough to contradict him or oppose him, he did not want any ambiguity about how he had become blessed. He did not want to be remembered as a great military strategist whose genius had given him the land. Only God could fulfill the promise and only God could get the credit. It must not even *appear* that anything or anyone else had contributed to God's promise being fulfilled. In interpreting Abram's response to Bera this way, I am certainly reading between the lines, but I think this is the most natural way to read the text.

That Abram was concerned with God's reputation like this was something new in history. There had never been a man, at least in the records we have, who cared what people thought about God. But when God spoke to Abram, it had changed Abram utterly in invisible ways until the right circumstances arose to reveal them. It could be maintained—reasonably maintained—that the invasion of the Elamites, the choice of Lot to go and live in Sodom, and the war that Abram was forced to fight to rescue him, were all intended to bring about this one event in which Abram refused to accept even a shoelace from Bera. His statement here is just that important.

It is the Divine Choreographer at work, and this interpretation makes complete sense if it were that events ever had only one purpose. But God is too big to tie down to only one plan. Nonetheless, one of the purposes for Sodom and Chedorlaomer and Lot and the battle was that Abram and his allies could rescue them and give us another picture of faith. If simultaneously Abram's victory permitted Shulgi to establish his kingdom more securely, as I think it did, and go on to continue Ur's spectacular civilization, then we remember that God has more purposes than we can ever keep track of. The important thing to the Scripture is that we see how faith looks so that we can practice imitating it. We not only learn to let God be God, to let Him accomplish His own promises in His own time in His own way by Himself, but we see to it that everyone around us can see that there is no way to explain it away: God did something. This is evangelism. This is being a witness.

How Abram came to such a deep conviction is not clear. The Scripture calls faith a gift of grace. When God called Abram to leave his home, He gave him the kernal of faith that he needed to do what he was called to do. The whole decade, which seemed to have accomplished very little, in which Abram wandered in the land, made friends with a few Amorite chiefs, lied to Pharaoh about his wife, and separated from Lot to keep peaceful relations between them, all of that had been a process of nurturing that little seed of faith that God had planted until, at the right time, Abram knew what to not do. It was a revelation to Abram just as it is to us who stand and watch through the words in the passage.

But there is more. Abram was choosy about whom he befriended. Mamre, the Amorite, was an ally but Bera was not. He had kept his distance from Bera all along. This is the second indication that the evil conditions in Sodom were a matter of some notoriety in that area, verse 13:13 being the first. So it is also true that Abram wouldn't take Bera's stuff because he didn't want the "cooties". There may be moral ambiguity in many of the choices we have to make, it may be so difficult to tell the difference between right and wrong that we begin to doubt whether the distinction even exists; but then we see evil in its undisguised form and there is no longer room for doubt. "If you think there's no difference between right and wrong, just go down where the death squad lives" is the way Bruce Cockburn put it.

Abram's response to Bera is in direct contrast to his response to Melchizedek. Bera he would not take a shoe lace from, but to Melchizedek he gave a tithe of everything he had just taken. The spoils all belonged to Abram and his friends after the battle, and Bera had to stand there and watch as Abram gave a tenth of all his former kingdom (and of the other cities) to this king of Salem. Whatever Bera thought of it, he had no say. Abram also let Mamre and the others take their fair share of the spoils, while he and his men took nothing but what they had already eaten. But why did Melchizedek deserve a share? Why did he come out to meet them, other than the coincidence that Bera and Abram met right outside his city? Who was this guy, anyway?

The account of Melchizedek fits in with a mythical style of literature and yet squarely in the middle of a straightforward historical narrative. This story is yet another illustration of how myth and history are not incompatible with each other; sometimes they are inseparably intertwined. In the Bible myth is always breaking in on the facts of daily life; and ordinary life intrudes into myth. They cannot be kept apart, like lovers who ignore the gossip of the neighborhood for the chance to keep company with each other.

The first thing to note about Melchizedek is that he was an actual person. He was the king of an actual city that had some history in that region. Neither Mamre the Amorite nor Bera the king of Sodom were surprised that there was a city there with a king named Melchizedek. It was not a vision nor an angel. Salem continued to exist after this time and Melchizedek had successors who would turn up in the Amarna letters about six hundred years later. The kings of Salem could claim to be heirs of Melchizedek as successor kings in his city, and in this sense David became an heir to Melchizedek when he took the city and made it his capital. What then does the letter to the Hebrews mean when it says that he had neither father nor mother, neither beginning nor ending of days? In the days of Abram, a king might say he had neither mother nor father meaning that he did not owe his kingdom to his parents, that he had become king in his own right without inheriting his throne. But the passage in Hebrews seems more likely to be interpreting the life of Melchizedek as symbolic of a truth, rather than embodying the truth.

In the Genesis narrative, Melchizedek comes from nowhere; we are told nothing of his ancestry or credentials. Nor are we told of his descendants or his fate; he simply ceases to be a part of the narrative. Melchizedek is mythical as well as historical, and since he was chosen to play a mythical role in the revelation, it is his role in the narrative that is symbolic, not whether or not he had ordinary parents and ordinary children. Melchizedek had no genealogy, no father, no official place in the world, just as later the Messiah would have no father and be marginalized within Israel. Melchizedek's priesthood seemingly came out of nowhere, just as the Messiah's priesthood would seem to come out of nowhere. "The wind blows where it wishes and you hear its sound but you do not know where it comes from or where it goes. So it is with everyone who is born of the Spirit." So said the Messiah to Nicodemus. And so Melchizedek is a product of the Spirit, who raised him up from we know not where and who took him away to we know not where. It is in our not knowing where that is the key to his revelatory role, that makes him symbolic of the Messiah who came from a place that is unknowable and went to an unknowable place. Melchizedek makes an arrow pointing through David at the Messiah.

Melchizedek was a type of Christ. To be a "type" is to be a sign or a preview of what is to come. This means that there was some aspect of his life and work that represented or illustrated the life and work of the Messiah. Melchizedek was a type of Christ because later when the Christ had come his followers would look at Him and say, "Oh, I see, this is like Melchizedek". It was particularly significant that Melchizedek combined the role of king and priest. While the offices of king and priest were combined in many cultures, the Canaanite and Amorite cultures seem not to have made that identification. Only in Salem in the land of Canaan was the king simultaneously the priest.

We can also see symbolism in the fact that Melchizedek brought out bread and wine to Abram. Bread and wine is not the food of the gods—it is the food of God Most High. The gods always ate meat, but God Most High distinguished Himself in His diet as well as His character. Blood sacrifices He would require, but the food of choice between Him and His people was bread and wine, apparently from the earliest times of the oral tradition. He always had His own purposes in what He chose. Abram was participating in a sort of "proto-Eucharist", though he could not have understood the elements of the meal the way Christians do. Apparently Bera was included in this meal, or at least invited to participate. The exclusion of idols was not yet a part of the revelation, but the inclusion of the nations had been made explicit. In some unfathomable way, Bera represented those nations who would be blessed through Abram, even beyond his rescue from defeat and the coming destruction by fire from heaven.

Both Melchizedek's name and his position as king of Salem designate him as a type of Christ to whom both titles naturally apply. "Salem" means "peace" and so his name is allegorical: Melchizedek is the King of

Peace. Further the word "Melchizedek" means "king of righteousness", strengthening the allegorical cast to his identity. Finally he was a priest, a priest of God Most High, which is one name used in the oral tradition for the God of the Bible. Clearly Melchizedek had some spiritual status in that neighborhood but he was emphatically not a representative of any of the local gods. We must understand Melchizedek as being a recipient of the oral tradition, to whom God had bequeathed the earlier account in Genesis, and to whom God Most High now spoke, showing him that the man who stood before him was a man chosen and blessed by God.

That Abram gave him a tithe is remarkable. It is the first mention of a tithe in the Bible and indicates that there was some long standing cultural tradition behind the practice. Abram would have understood Melchizedek as acting on behalf of God Most High, the same God that had appeared to him. There is no record of any previous interaction between Abram and Melchizedek, and no record of any further interaction after this scene, but the same sensitivity to God's presence, which would later enable Abram to recognize angels when they were walking by, helped him recognize Melchizedek as a true priest of his God. Something in Abram recognized authority in this man, recognized a spiritual kinship, and recognized some kind of obligation toward him.

The New Testament emphasizes that all Israel submitted to the authority of Melchizedek through Abram. The unborn Levites who existed in potential in Abram gave tithes to Melchizedek through Abram, and so all Israel gave tithes to him, including the priests in Israel who received the tithes of Israel. In part this is just the ordinary course of things, that the later covenants and history of Israel would fulfill covenants and works of God that had pre-dated them. When God established a new covenant it did not supersede what came before, but extended it and perfected it. God is not a man that he should change his mind or jump from one method to another as the situation alters. Melchizedek had inherited the oral tradition and covenant originating with Noah and was a priest of God Most High, a priest of the true God who had created heaven and earth and preserved the record contained in the first few chapters of Genesis. Whatever new God Most High was about to do with Abram, it did not invalidate Melchizedek's priesthood or God's work through him. When Abram gave a tithe to Melchizedek it was to show us that He would continue the work He was doing with the Gentiles. And the work He was doing with the Gentiles—while not in the mainstream of His revelation or purposes for Abram and his descendants—was to prepare the Gentiles to recognize the purposes of God in Israel when they were accomplished. Melchizedek could well have been thinking the same words that would later be spoken by a man named John, "I must decrease and he must increase."

Melchizedek is another clear indication that God Most High had not abandoned the world to total ignorance. The fact that the tradition of Melchizedek was not directly part of the biblical tradition does not make it less valid. On the contrary, it merely reminds us of what we should have known anyway: that the Bible is a very specific revelation and not a comprehensive one. It was not God's intent that the Bible be an encyclopedic account of everything He did; in fact, the New Testament clearly indicates that even the Messiah did many things that were left out of the accounts. The purpose of the Bible is to give an intimate account of the nature of God as He revealed it in a particular series of covenants. The revelation contained in the Bible is the central act of revelation of God to the world, but it is not the only revelation to mankind. Besides the Bible, besides the Judeo-Christian tradition of historical revelation from God, there have been other revelations to those who were not in that tradition but to whom God extended mercy in showing something of Himself, even to such people as the Canaanites whom He had cursed, and the Amorites. And if God revealed Himself to Canaanites, then who can guess what He may have done to reveal Himself to others.

What do we mean when we say that Christianity is the true religion? This is a complex question, but we can say a few things as a result of meditating on Melchizedek. First, we do not, or should not, mean that all other religions have no truth about God whatsoever, or that all other people who are not Christians have no connection to God or understanding about God whatsoever. God is merciful, more so than we are, and He willingly, enthusiastically, reveals Himself all around the world with or without the help of missionaries and even apart from the Bible. That God has revealed Himself apart from the Bible does not challenge the centrality of the revelation contained in the Bible. That God has been revealing Himself all around the world all the time in no way lessens the importance of the gospel, nor its necessity, nor the importance of spreading the good news to the ends of the earth. It just means that God has done and is doing far more than we had thought. If we believe that God is love, it is what we should have expected all along.

2. The Covenant of Revelation

a) Abram's Faith (Genesis 15:1-6)

So far we have covered about a decade of Abram's life, arriving now at yet another turning point. It would seem that when God call's a person to leave his home and go to a "land that I will show you" it is a major turning point, but with God there is never just one turning point. Life is a series of turning points which serve like telephone poles that hold the strands of life above ground. At this point Abram was 85 years old and it was the year 2074 b.c.

The details of this decade of Abram's life are pretty sparse. God chose two kinds of events to preserve in the biblical record, each for the specific purpose of advancing the revelation. Most of Abram's life was like ours: just the dull routine of living, buying, selling, dealing with neighbors and family. The events God chose to have remembered were, first of all, what Abram did right that could serve to instruct us how best to think about God and behave around Him; and secondly, what Abram did wrong that could serve to instruct us how best to think about God and behave around Him. Being chosen by God is more difficult than being a celebrity. Who needs paparazzi when the Spirit is recording snapshots of what you do or do not do? At least the Spirit is not insensitive and obnoxious, but it is still difficult to be in the public eye, and not just the public eye of the contemporary tabloids but the public eye of all time and all people.

But doing such "correct" acts of faith was not what won him God's favor as we habitually are bound to think. He already had God's favor before he was called. The fact that God spoke to Abram that first time was proof that Abram didn't do any thing to win God over. Men did not try out for God's calling like models walking down the runway hoping God would pick them for the great beauty of their deep faith. Nor could failing in such a "fundamental of the Faith" lose them God's favor, like some poor guy who strikes out just at the critical time and loses the game, to forever be remember as the One-Who-Failed-Us-When-We-Counted-On-Him. God chose events from Abram's life, and the rest of the characters of the Bible so that we could understand a bit better what true Winning and Losing in Life was like. And what it wasn't like. It is not whether you or I are weak or strong that counts; it is whether God is weak or strong that counts. Abram's life shows us both how important faith is and how unimportant it is.

We have subtly altered the definition of faith over the years. Our culture uses the word "faith" to mean either a set of statements that we believe intellectually, or the act of believing things without any logical basis, (or even better, in spite of logical reasons to the contrary). The faith that Abram showed, that the Bible spotlights as the central trait of any human life, was nothing like either of these definitions. Abram did not know very much about God, he did not have much information about God to believe in, so the first definition is obviously no good. We will spend the rest of this section considering the second definition. Exactly how irrational was Abram? What exactly was he doing when he believed God? Is it impossible for a modern, scientific person to do the same thing?

Some fundamentalist Christians as well as some liberal Christians, glory in having a "faith" that is entirely irrational, as if their lack of intellectual effort was a badge of honor. Some rabid pagans caricature all religious faith as silly belief in things that can't be reasonably entertained and that are beneath any sophisticated person. In the Bible, "faith" is a synonym of "trust", not a set of doctrines, not necessarily a belief at all. It is not the conviction that God exists; it is the attitude toward God once one has the conviction that He exists. Faith can express itself in varying ways. First, it can make us choose what we don't want to choose simply because we are convicted that God wants us to. It can make us to choose the riskier alternative or the more dangerous alternative. It can make us refrain from doing something because we have the conviction that God has to do it Himself and we don't want to trespass. It can make us refrain from taking advantage of what we know we are entitled to simply because we want people to know it was a gift from God and not something we acquired by our own power. And finally it can make us hopeful because we have a conviction that God is the kind of God who likes to surprise people with good things beyond their expectations.

And so we come to the fourth time God appeared to Abram. This time He greeted Abram with "Do not fear". God had never begun a visit that way before. Why would Abram be afraid to hear from God at this point, having just won a great military victory? I think God knew that Abram was beginning to fear that God's promises might prove in vain. God had appeared to him just three times during the previous ten years, and pretty much nothing had come of those appearances. Had he misunderstood God's intent in those visits? Might God have lost interest in him? Or perhaps God was not able to bring off what He had promised? What if Abram was trusting in Someone who just couldn't be counted on to come through? Most of us have these sorts of doubts eventually. Trusting God is only easy when not much is at stake, but God never lets any of us get too comfortable for very long. He pushes us to the edge of what we can trust. He pushes us to the edge of our hopes, making us rely on Him to provide the very thing we want so much that it will be devastating if He failed. However He does it, He wants us to be in the position of risking everything that is important to us on the chance that He can bring it off. And if we "pass the test" and manage to trust Him through it all, it usually means that we go on to some harder test, some more devastating risk.

We are sometimes taught that the person of genuine faith will just believe and never doubt, that wrestling with doubt is a sign of spiritual weakness, that doubt can even cause God to change His mind about His own promises or commitment to us. This is certainly a strange view of faith, and an unbiblical one. It is a view that looks on faith as something we do to prove ourselves. The important thing is not whether or not we doubt, but what we do with doubts when they arise. Do we capitulate at the first murmuring of that murky little voice? Or do we bury the doubt, pretend it is not there, pretend that we are some spiritual hero and carry on blindly? Or do we face the doubt and master it? The first is unabashed cowardice, the second is mere posturing, the third is where strength is developed. We may be so afraid of doubts because we fear God will be angry with us because of them. But God's gentle handling of Abram was remembered and recorded just to reassure us that God is faithful to us, and that He does not find fault with our weakness. It is only by facing doubt and choosing to trust in spite of it that there is any hope of getting past the doubt, of getting to the point where we will be able to look back on the doubt and see it for what it always was.

Because doubt is not a sin, God began by reassuring him. In fact, it is the contrary. If you are following God, if you are truly exercising faith in God, you will doubt. You will come to a point of doubt because you are following God and He will take you on dangerous paths, to the very limits of what you can believe. If we fail the testing of our faith, it just means that we must go back and try that stretch of ground another time when we are more ready. If we pass the test than we go on to a yet more dangerous road. Just as there is never any question of deserving God's favor, so there is never any danger of losing it. When we fail, He will try us again.

Abram does seem to be having doubt at this point. It may seem odd, but the period immediately after a great victory is the time doubt is most likely to hit hardest, like the reaction that sets in after a sugar high. He had been in the land for ten years and apart from having a lot of livestock, what had he gotten out of it? Nothing. He could have gotten cows and goats back in Haran, and done it more comfortably. God had the right to take His time, of course, but if this was what He meant by being "a blessing to all the nations" then it was a bit disappointing. *And he didn't even have a son.* What's the point of being a blessing to all the nations if you don't even have a son to take care of your cows when you are gone? Thoughts like these must have nagged at him, and nagged at him more as the years passed.

So "do not fear, Abram" was the right introduction at that point. And then He told Abram that his reward was to be very great. Reward for what? Abram had done nothing to be rewarded for and he knew it. But it was not for something he had done. He was being rewarded because God was his shield. It was what God had done that got him a reward, not what he had done. In particular, he was not being rewarded for his faith, as if his faith were a good work that had earned him spiritual credit (this is a point that deserves repetition). Abram was being rewarded because God was determined to reward him and there was no deeper reason for it.

The root of the problem that plagued Abram was this: Abram had become very rich, but still he had no son. God had been promising to give him children, but he had been in the land for ten years and nothing was happening. In accordance with the custom of the day, since Abram had no child of his own, he had adopted a servant from his household, Eliezer of Damascus, as his heir. Eliezer had been born in his household and so had probably been with him since before he had left Ur. However long it had been, Eliezer must have become a beloved and trusted servant for Abram to choose him as his heir. Nonetheless, however much Abram may have loved Eliezer, it was a source of grief to him that he had no son of his own. Abram was clearly beginning to wonder if God was somehow unable to bring it off.

From the outside and in retrospect it is easy to see that God was waiting on children deliberately until all human hope of children was gone. Abram had done well so far in waiting on God to fulfill His promises, but

God intended to take him all the way down that road. He intended that Abram should wait until there was no human hope left. Meanwhile, God set about addressing Abram's doubts. There are many different kinds of doubt. Abram's doubt was the doubt that one might feel toward the word of a person that one still does not know very well. Abram had as close a relationship with God as anyone in the world in his day, he knew a little of God's history, and he had a little experience interacting with God himself, but they were still in the "betrothal" stage, still engaged, intending to marry but working out their future relationship. Whatever the metaphor, God was not offended by Abram's doubt. But He used his doubt to take the revelation to the next stage.

What He did was the oddest thing: He brought Abram outside to look at the night sky, and then He repeated His promise of descendants in that most unlikely place. The vision He gave Abram of the sky was not a matter of seeing such an *innumerable* collection of lights as it was of seeing an innumerable collection of *lights*. Abram was not being invited to *count* the stars; he was being invited to *measure* them, to estimate them in terms of importance, significance, value, worth. It was the quality, not the quantity, of Abram's descendants that was the point of the vision. He would have descendants like the *stars*, and the quantity was not the focal point. There are only about 6000 stars that can be seen by the naked eye on a perfect night, quite countable if one is careful. This is a number that was exceeded by Abram's descendants within five or six generations. The number of actual stars in the sky visible by any means exceeds the total number of people in the human race through all history. The point is not the number, not how many there would be, but *who* they would be.

In fact, when he looked at the sky that night he was experiencing revelation in its most basic form. He had looked at the night sky in all its glory perhaps thousands of times during his life, without the hindrance of streetlights. No doubt he carried a lot of Mesopotamian religious baggage about the stars and the various gods and myths about them. But this night, when God brought him outside his tent, he connected the dots for the first time: the God who was standing by him and speaking with him was the one who *created* those lights. He had heard the story in Genesis 1 recited throughout his whole life, the oral tradition, and now it fell into place, if not for the first time, then for the first time in this way. He saw through the words to the glory of what they meant. That is where this faith came from. He knew God could keep His promise about a son because this was the God who invented stars, this was a God beyond what he had imagined that he now imagined for the first time. He was a God who could call into existence things that did not exist.

God made the sky into something of a sacrament to Abram. From that time on, every time he looked at the night sky he would remember God's promise to give him descendants. Every time he looked at the sky he would be reminded that the God who claimed to have made those stars had also claimed that He would give such descendants to Abram, descendants who were like the stars in glory. Abram's children would be children who were like the stars. From the viewpoint of an ancient Mesopotamian man like Abram, God was promising that Abram's children would be *like* the gods.

This promise is a promise that is beyond all hope, beyond all question of proof or disproof, beyond all accounting. This is a promise that is so outrageous that it utterly transcends the question of whether it is rational to believe or not. Nothing in the world could prepare you for that kind of promise and nothing in the world could help you decide to believe or to disbelieve. In mathematical jargon, this is a question of choosing an axiom, not proving a theorem. It is the promise that hits a parent in his or her innermost being where it is the most delicate. To have a son, yes, but to have a son who will be a glory in the world; to have a son who will shine; to have a son who will not be like me, full of my stupidities and regrets and failures; who will not be doomed to inherit my weak condition and repeat my mistakes, but who will be the good man I had once hoped to be. God's promise to Abram was beyond any miracle, beyond the mere having a child in his old age, beyond even having a dozen children in his old age. God's promise to Abram was beyond mere belief or disbelief, the promise of something so astounding and desirable that it could not be imagined entirely.

But Abram believed what he could not imagine. He didn't say anything out loud. He simply believed it, in his heart, and God knew that he believed Him. This simple belief in God's word is faith, trust, in its most basic and primitive form. It is the faith "as small as a mustard seed", and it was reckoned to him as righteousness. It is important to understand that Abram's faith was not great, it was not the faith that commands a dead man to rise, or commands the Red Sea to part, or enables you to walk out and face a lion. It was humble, the germ of something that would grow.

This nearly invisible faith "was reckoned as righteousness". There are two enormously important bits of revelation we can receive from this. First of all, it means that there is *nothing* essentially righteous about faith. Where is the merit in simply believing God, who is all goodness and cannot lie? Of all entities in or out of the universe, God ought most to be believed; God simply deserves that we accept what He says and not doubt His integrity or question His competence. If faith were something good in itself, then it wouldn't have to be *reckoned* as good; it just would be. Nevertheless, though it is no more than He deserves, no more than we owe Him, He *counts* it as righteousness, *as if it were* a good deed.

Second, it means that God *chooses* to count faith as righteous. He need not have counted faith as righteous, but He decided to. When God reckoned faith as righteousness, what He was really doing was choosing a strategy. God was setting up the terms by which He would deal with people and eventually work out the salvation of the world. There was no inevitability to it. He could conceivably have chosen to save the world through some quite different method not involving faith in a central way at all, but He chose to do it this way. Why did He do it? The best answer, I think, is the one Paul gives in the letter to the Romans: He chose faith because it is nothing to brag about.

Third, God *had* to choose something to reckon as righteous. In other words, there was no real righteousness there to accept. God chose to count faith as righteousness in order to have a starting point for the relationship, for the Covenant He was about to make. There was no good thing in Abram, no foundation on which he could stand before God, so God said in effect: "Very well. Let's begin with less than nothing. Let's begin with you simply believing Me and we'll go from there." We, like Abram, have no place to stand, so He creates a platform for us out of nothing. Using the same raw materials that went into the creation of the universe, it is His style, His specialty, to make the Beautiful, the Good, the True out of nothing at all.

b) Establishing the Covenant (Genesis 15:7-21)

God established the covenant with Abram when He first called him in Haran to leave his relatives and go to another unknown land. Covenant was the term for a relationship, and there are distinctions between covenants just as there are distinctions between relationships. His intent was to establish an intimate and permanent relationship, more like a marriage than anything else, and of course that takes some time. Initially, the relationship was not spelled out, but by this point after a decade of "betrothal", when it was clear that Abram did trust God, that he did "want to get married", it was time for the formal ceremony. Covenants were relationships that continued, not just people who encountered each other briefly and went their separate ways. The idea of a covenant between two people implied a history, a future, and in Abram's case at least something of a past. When God Most High spoke to Abram that first time, He was a voice from the oral tradition that Abram had learned of but never expected to encounter.

Covenants between people were always finite, of course, because the people making the covenants were finite. Everything human ends, but when ordinary human kings made covenants they would make provisions for the covenant to be passed on to their children. Mostly human kings made covenants with kings they had conquered and they intended that their son or successor would continue to be the sovereign over the son and successor of the defeated king. Similarly, when God established a covenant it was always explicitly perpetual, it always descended to the descendants. But heretofore in this decade old relationship between God and Abram, nothing formal had been said about the next generation and what it all might mean to them. The next generation was just a promise, and a wild one at that when God took Abram out that night to look at the stars.

Abram believed God, but it was indeed a mustard seed of faith. He believed, but how could he *know* that he would have these children. He wanted some reassurance, and God Most High did not fault him for the littleness of his faith. Genesis 15 concludes with a description of God and Abram enacting a ceremony to formally establish the Covenant the next day after Abram believed God. Just as a wedding ceremony formally establishes a relationship that was previously understood, previously informally agreed upon, so this ceremony was something of a legal finalization of what already existed. It was a private ceremony, like many weddings are private ceremonies, but it was public in that it was "announced in the press", it was recorded in the oral tradition to be handed down to all generations forever. The guest list may have been short, but we can all look through the photos together.

This ceremony was not patterned after the marriage ceremonies of the time. Instead it followed the pattern of the covenants that were established between two kings when the one king had conquered the other. Something roughly like this ceremony may have been enacted when Chedorlaomer first took Bera as a vassal. Something roughly like this ceremony could have been enacted between Abram and Bera, or between Abram and Chedorlaomer, if Abram had been the conquering type. In such a ceremony, the defeated king would formally and publicly pledge his allegiance to the conquering king in a covenant ritual much like this one. As to why God Most High chose such a political covenant rather than a marital one we will consider later.

First the subject king would prepare some animals as sacrifices, cut them in half and arrange them in two rows; being a military/political covenant, it was sealed with blood. Once the sacrifices were ready, the newly conquered king would make his vows, swearing allegiance, swearing to the agreed upon tribute he would pay yearly, and swearing to any other duties his conqueror required. Then the conqueror would threaten the penalties that would befall the vassal king and his people should he fail to keep his vows. The finale of the ceremony came when the defeated king walked between the halves of the dead animals. This was a symbolic way of saying, "May I be as these animals, if I do not keep the vows I have made". The death of the animals was taken as a substitute for the death of the conquered king so that his life could be spared to serve his new lord and keep the terms of the covenant, and they reminding him of the fate that awaited him should he not keep them. The animals also reminded him that he lived only because his conqueror permitted these animals to be taken as a substitute for him.

So much for the traditional covenant ritual. The differences between those covenants and the one executed here are critically important. If you are a close observer of the niceties of ritual, they are chilling. Abram began the ceremony by cutting the animals in halves and arranging them in the proper order, as usual. But then he did nothing. He was waiting to see what he ought to do next. The obvious thing was to continue the ceremony the way it would logically be continued, but the quality that made him know not to take loot from Bera told him that the ceremony was being paused. And he didn't know his lines; he was waiting to be told what God would require of him, what tribute or sacrifices he might have to bring each year. It was a dramatic effect, by the world's foremost dramatist; it wasn't lost on Abram and we shouldn't let it be lost on us either. Abram drove away the vultures the rest of that day, waiting.

Only when the sun was going down, and Abram had fallen asleep did anything happen. Beyond the darkness of night, through the darkness of sleep, a dreadful darkness descended. Only then did something happen, but it was not Abram who did it. Rather than Abram making his vows to God, it was the reverse: God made the vows to Abram, and made them from out of the deep darkness. It was definitely out of all expectation for this ceremony, but it was not out of all expectation considering the previous decade. Abram had yet to make any vow to God except to not take anything from Bera, a vow he seems to have come up with himself. God had always been the One who made the promises, but these were not like the promises He had been making. They were promises from deep darkness about the future, the promise that his offspring (the original subject of their discussion) would live in a foreign land and be oppressed for four hundred years; and the promise that they would be delivered from that oppressor and come out of the land a wealthy nation; and the promise that Abram would live out his years in peace. How did this answer Abram's original question? How did it help him know he would have descendants like the stars? By being specific, by giving details, by making it more concrete. It was not the vague promise of descendants; now it was the promise of descendants who would suffer and be delivered, who would leave and come back again.

And then the most amazing thing happened: Abram saw a torch moving between the animals, carried by Someone he couldn't see, moving where by rights he should have been walking. Not only had God made the vows, but God had given the guarantee. In this way God pledged His own life to keep His covenant with Abram, even to the point of giving Himself like an animal as a sacrifice. If Abram failed to keep the Covenant, the whole penalty for the failure would fall on God. There is no greater enactment of grace in Scripture than here, no clearer picture of the coming Messiah. God chose the military ceremony of the conquering king to initiate His formal covenant with Abram, and then stood the whole thing on its head.

There is a point that should be emphasized here, that should not be missed by any serious student of the Bible. The animals that Abram cut up were not substitutes for Abram. This would have been their function if Abram had walked down the row as he normally should have. If Abram had performed that symbolic act it would have made these animals' blood a substitute for his own. But it was God Himself who performed the rite and the animals' blood substituted for His own blood. These sacrifices (and later the sacrifices offered under the Law of Moses) were not substitutes for the people; they were substitutes for the Messiah. Abram's life was never on the line; it was the life of God Himself, His own blood, that was on the line. There has never been any other promise from God but to give Himself for us; there has never been any other foundation for the Covenant between God and His people than the life and death of God Himself.

The additional revelation of future events was hardly to be noticed after the dramatic shock of the ritual. And while it may have reassured Abram about his son at some point, the real assurance was God's pledge to bring it all off or die. The future presented to Abram does not sound very encouraging to the modern ear. One of the two particular promises God had made, the land of Canaan, was being deferred for a very long time period indeed. Abram had been faithfully insisting that only God should fulfill the promise of land, but now it seemed he would never see it. Those of us who are trained to think in individualistic terms, in personal terms, might well be put off by a promise intended for our descendants after the year 2400 or so. What good is that kind of promise? We want our payoffs now. But the ancients thought differently than we do, not in individualistic and personal terms. Every indication from Abram's behavior suggests that he never took God's promise of the land as a personal promise, and when God established the Covenant it was all the more clear that the promises were covenantal promises rather than personal promises. As far as God or Abram were concerned, any promise fulfilled to his descendants four hundred years down the road was the same as being fulfilled to him. He *is, was, and will be* the God of Abram, and Abram *is, was, and will be* His chosen.

It was on the basis of Abram's faith that God chose to establish this second of His series of covenants, and so we might call it the Covenant of Faith. This is a reasonable name for it, but it is not the best choice. It focuses attention on Abram, on the recipient of the Covenant, rather than on the Giver of the Covenant. Others prefer to call this covenant the Covenant of Grace, and this also is a very reasonable name for it. However grace is behind and around and through all of the covenants, and it is grace that ties them all together. There is nothing that marks this covenant as more full of grace than the whole system of covenants.

If we do focus on the Giver of the Covenant, then the characteristic in God that corresponds to the faith of Abram is revelation. One reason God chose to count faith as righteousness was that He was going to channel His special revelation through Abram and the Covenant people. Belief was important on their part because His primary intent was to give them something to believe, and trust was important because He intended to lead them down some difficult roads and make His revelation in their history and suffering. For this reason I prefer to call this covenant established between God and Abram the Covenant of Revelation.

It should be made plain here that the rite of making a covenant was not fully completed at this point. There were two elements missing. Normally a sign should accompany a covenant. The lack of a sign at this point would not render the covenant invalid, but it was an irregularity. Also normally the recipient of this kind of covenant would receive a new name to symbolize his new identity under the covenant. Just as in traditional marriage ceremonies, rings are exchanged and the bride traditionally takes on the name of her husband, so in the making of a covenant there would have been some sign or token of the covenant and Abram would have been given a new name from God. It does not render a wedding invalid if the bride and groom do not exchange rings for a decade of two, or if neither choose a new name to symbolize the union. Delaying the sign and the covenant name was a way to emphasize them by having an event to spotlight them specifically. We will consider them at the appropriate time.

It is not inappropriate that I bring up the image of marriage even though the formality of the covenant was more like a political ceremony than a wedding. The idea of marriage is lurking in the background of what happened. A wedding ceremony would have not been the right form for what happened this night, even though ultimately the relationship is closer to that of a marriage. However a wedding signifies a relationship that is established between two people who are equals. The relationship that God established with Abram was not something He established with an equal.

What was performed that night included both the idea of the love and devotion in marriage and the idea of a the defeat of a hostile king. Though it was disguised in this ceremony, marriage became an increasingly explicit image for what the covenant meant as time went by. Looking at it with hindsight from beyond the terrible vision of four centuries of slavery, the

ceremony enacted on that dark and frightening night was a wedding of
sorts. God was taking a wife. God was not binding himself to the man
Abram alone, nor to the couple, Abram and Sarai; He was marrying
the people who would come from them. Nor is it unnatural that such a
wedding night would be a somewhat fearful thing. The wedding night
for most women in that culture (and probably most men too) must have
been rather frightening. Frequently the bride and groom hardly knew one
another, as in this case Abram hardly knew God. Women would join their
lives to a stranger, literally for better or worse. "Don't worry! God has a
wonderful plan for your life!" We say that and it is perfectly true. But it
may wind through a dark night and smoke and fear and a faceless voice
and a strange light passing between rows of dead animals.

c) Hagar (Genesis 16)

We now come to Abram's most serious mistake—not his first mistake,
but one that goes to the very heart of what faith is. I have tried to present
an argument that both Noah and Abram had a particular trait in common,
an attitude toward God that relinquished the impulse to step in and take
over God's work for Him. I have tried to argue that this is the essential
core meaning of faith. In both men, in spite of personal failings of the
kind we would label as sin, their basic faith in God manifested itself in
*their choosing to not take particular actions that would have been perfectly
reasonable and to their own advantage, but which they held as being reserved
for God alone to take.* Now God had used that basic faith of Abram as the
foundation on which to establish a Covenant. Now for the first time God
had joined a particular human family. And now Abram failed to live out
the faith he had just demonstrated so vividly. God's most basic promise to
him had been the promise of a son, and now Abram decided to take the
matter into his own hands and do what he could to get himself a son. He
decided to try to fulfill God's promise for Him.

The very first voice persuading him to waver in his faith was the voice
of Sarai. As a barren woman she was expected by the culture of that day to
give one of her maidservants to Abram as a wife in order to possibly obtain
children that way. The cultural pressure for her to do this would already
have been enormous; by the custom of the time, Sarai was long overdue
in making the offer. If they had been in civilization, like Ur, rather than
nomads, a court could well have forced her to give her maid to Abram as

a wife. It was a legal question, and whatever children her maid bore to Abram would legally have been Sarai's. It is possible that Sarai had already suggested to Abram that he take her maid as a wife, but that Abram had resisted the idea. Perhaps Abram had understood God's promise as being a son to him and Sarai, and his faith constrained him from accepting her offer. True, the promises God had made about a son had never mentioned Sarai, but it could have been tacit, something about the way God had called the two of them together.

But whether or not Sarai had previously suggested Abram take her maid as a concubine or not, shortly after the Covenant was formally established she renewed the suggestion and this time Abram acquiesced. He would have rationalized it, of course. All lapses of faith are rational to some extent. He would recall first that God had never *specifically* mentioned that Sarai would be the mother. Then he would think about how she owed it to him to give him a son one way or the other; all his upbringing would have said so. Then he would think about her offer, that it wasn't like he had asked her to make the suggestion. Then he would think how great a joy, a relief, it would be to have a son. The boy would still count as Sarai's legally and that could be what God had meant all along. Besides, if God was opposed to the idea, He could equally well prevent the maid from getting pregnant.

I do not blame Sarai at all. It was not likely that she had been actually physically present when God had appeared to Abram those four times, but he would have talked about the appearances with her, if only to preserve them in the oral tradition. So far as she knew, she ought to have offered her maid decades ago, and now after this new vision perhaps Abram was talking about the promised son more than usual. Meanwhile, she had acquired a slave, probably while she was in Egypt pretending to be Abram's sister, and so she offered Hagar to Abram as a wife and this time Abram accepted the offer. There was no particular sin in him taking Hagar as a concubine; God Most High had never told Abram that he couldn't have another wife. Paul would later say that whatever does not come from faith is sin, and here we see how subtle that idea can be. There was no moral or ethical constraint on Abram that made it a sin to take Hagar; sin is a much bigger (and simultaneously, smaller) question than any code of moral rules, especially after the Messiah came. So Abram "sinned", not because he did anything wrong, but because he knew this was not a way of trusting God.

God said nothing, as usual. Things might have gone all right, or at least peacefully, if Hagar had not despised Sarai. But Hagar had seen Sarai at her most vulnerable, pretending not to be Abram's wife at Abram's request, and barren. Hagar could not help thinking that something must be wrong with Sarai since even her husband treated her in such a way. A slave who despises her mistress and who then proves her own superiority in the most important way can hardly be blamed for gloating, though it was unwise. Perhaps she was counting on her value to Abram as the mother of the heir, but she underestimated both Sarai's anger and jealousy and Abram's devotion to Sarai. Though Abram had agreed to Sarai's proposal, it is evident that he was having second thoughts already. It is evident that he did not really view Hagar's child as anything like a fulfillment of God's promise. He still had little attachment to the future child, at least not enough attachment to intervene between Sarai and her maid; and he didn't do well with conflict.

Sarai must have been harsh indeed for Hagar to resort to running away when she saw Abram would not protect her. The journey back to her home in Egypt would have been long and very dangerous for a woman wandering alone. Moreover, exiling Hagar after she was pregnant was probably illegal. In Ur the system of law punished of a female slave who mocked her mistress by having her mouth scoured out with salt. It was probably performed in a way that made it much more unpleasant than it sounds. The Code of Hammurabi, the best known of the ancient codes of law outside of Moses, dates two and a half centuries after Abram, but still probably summarized the customs of Mesopotamia and the Middle East that had been traditional before and during the time of Abram. In that Code a female slave who had borne children to her owner could not be sent away or sold. If such a slave were insolent, she could be branded as a slave, ensuring that she would never be free, but not driven away. Hagar had not yet borne the child, but in that age of under-population every child was valued, born or not. On the other hand, Abram and Sarai lived in Canaan, very far from Mesopotamia, very far from any civil law or authority. Sarai was almost certainly behaving scandalously and what neighbors they had must have been gossiping in the usual delighted way; but there was no one to enforce customs, no one to whom Hagar could appeal, if Abram was unwilling to help. It was the most sordid episode in Abram's life.

Hagar got to Beer-lahai-roi. Its exact location is not known, but it is believed to have been as much as 130 miles southwest of the oaks of Mamre, along the principal route leading through Shur to Egypt. Hagar must have been traveling several days, perhaps a week, before the angel appeared to her. Genesis 16:7 is only the second time in the Bible to mention an angel, the first angel being the one that guarded the way into Eden. Thus the very first angel sent to anyone was sent to this woman, a despised Egyptian slave who had been driven away by her mistress. Usually angels frighten the people who see them, but this first angelic visitation did not have that effect. Hagar recognized the angel as supernatural, so her lack of fear did not result from mistaking the angel for a human. She thought the angel was God Himself. This is not surprising since, as an Egyptian, she was accustomed to believing in many gods and had probably heard little or nothing about God Most High until she had been bought by Sarai a few years previously. But at this point, all the biblical characters seem to have had some confusion over whether the angels were gods or not. This passage only tells us what Hagar thought about the angel without giving any hint as to the facts of the matter. Then Hagar was sent back to her mistress and told to submit to her. It would have been scary to do so, but having seen an angel would have reassured her that it would all work out all right. Returning would have been a humiliation in itself, and her humility probably mitigated Sarai's anger somewhat. Sarai also may have been feeling somewhat guilty by then.

An important point that should be made here is that Hagar's story became known. The angel gave her the name Ishmael—which means "God hears"—for her son; and then Abram used it. She had named the well where the angel came to her "Beer-lahai-roi", which means "you are a God who sees me"; and the name stuck. Finally, her story was included in the Bible and therefore in the oral tradition at this point. She must have told Abram, unless God revealed the story supernaturally to Abram or to some future generation, which seems less likely.

Ishmael was prophesied by the angel to be a wild man and there was to be strife between Ishmael and his relatives, perpetuated through the generations. Ishmael was the ancestor of the present day Arabs, and certainly there has been strife enough between the Arabs and their close relatives, the Jews. The current strife between the Arabs and Jews continues the strife-ridden relationship between the two women, Hagar and Sarai, like a family feud, now going into a fifth millenium. Some say that the story was made up in later generations to explain the hostility between Israel and the Ishmaelites, but this explanation does not hold up at all. The Ishmaelites, while never particularly friendly to Israel, did not become serious enemies until about the time of the exile, nearly fifteen centuries later, much too long a time for such an insertion to have been made and gone unremarked. It also contradicts the long standing use of the place name, Beer-lahai-roi.

The Bible uses the relationship of these two women as both an allegory and a prophecy for the relationship of the two peoples in the future. There is a deep relationship between prophecy and biblical allegory. Events become allegories when God takes them into His purpose for revelation. He then inserts a prophetic element to draw attention to the allegory He is creating. In this way God was the first to use the old teaching adage: tell them what you are about to tell them, then tell them, then tell them what you told them: first the prophesy, then the allegory, then the interpretation. Paul took up the allegory that is tacit in the story in the letter to the Galatians. He understood this bit of history as God producing historical events for the purpose of creating allegory.

In our modern interpretations of the events in the biblical history the closest we usually come to following Paul is in our tendency to draw morals or lessons from the events, but that is not what Paul did. He didn't see this event as teaching us a lesson. And anyway what would the lesson have been? "Don't make fun of your mistress or master"? It doesn't take divine revelation to invent stories with morals, and if that had been God's intent with the Bible then it was a cosmic waste of time. This event and others in the biblical narrative are allegories bearing the weight of revelation if we have the eyes to see it. When we reduce the stories to moral aphorisms then we miss nearly everything true about them.

So what is the allegorical meaning of the event? Paul said that Hagar and her son Ishmael were a picture of the people who are bound under the Law. They represented those who try to achieve God's promise by their own effort, and Paul used Hagar's status as a slave to make an equation between the two. Those who try to achieve God's promise by their own efforts are in fact mere slaves, and this is what the Law makes people into, slaves who try to achieve righteousness by their own efforts. Sarai and her son represented the people who live by the promise, for whom God fulfills His own promise without human aid. Sarai's status as the free woman became an equality in Paul's interpretation, an equality of freedom with those who do not seek to achieve righteousness by their own effort but let God achieve it for them.

Hagar was the mother of the Arab people, but in Galatians Paul used Hagar to represent both the Jews who had rejected Jesus and Christians who insisted on continuing to live under the Law rather than by grace. The allegorical meaning was entirely divorced from any ethnic reality, and in general the allegorical meaning of an event can be quite distinct from it cultural or biological context. Hagar didn't carry this symbolism by being under the Law herself (since she wasn't) nor by trying to please God by her own effort (since she didn't). *Her role in the allegory did not have anything to do with any choices she made herself.* On the contrary, her role in the allegory arose from circumstances over which she had no control, that she was a servant and bound to obedience and that her mistress gave her to Abram as a wife. *Her role in the allegory had absolutely nothing to do with her own goodness or badness.* Sarai also had an allegorical role that had nothing to do with her choices but only with the circumstance and events in her life over which she had no control. Both women were out of line, Hagar for despising Sarai and Sarai for jealousy and physical abuse, but that is irrelevant. Their lives had allegorical meaning because God had assigned them to play particular roles in the drama He was putting on; it was not personal. That someone has a "bad" allegorical meaning in the biblical narrative does not mean that that person is a "bad" person. The biblical personalities are actors on the largest stage of all, asked to perform a role to help the rest of us understand something of God and His purposes, and sometimes good people are asked to play the villain. Hagar was not playing a villain here, but she was playing a role designed to illustrate what God did not want.

Thus Hagar allegorizes legalism in general, the legalism of Judaism, the legalism of Islam, as well as the legalism of Christianity when it forgets its first love. Indeed the power of allegory is the way it naturally extends to additional contexts. Hagar is in fact a symbol of religion in general, across the board. As the revelation proceeds we can discern an increasing tension between religion and faith, even an opposition between religion and faith. Hagar represents the condition of those who seek to fulfill God's promises for Him, to make of themselves what only God can make of them: good people. She represents the people who follow a religion of human efforts that attempt to please God. In other words, she represents all religions. For if God fulfills His own promises to us, apart from—in spite of—any efforts we make, then religion of every kind collapses into worthless ritual.

I have made a point here of speaking of religion as being legalistic; by "legalistic" I mean a larger principle than merely the principle of obeying a set of laws. Legalism in its widest sense is the idea that one's actions earn merit or demerit with God, that God's favor can be earned or lost, deserved or forfeited, on the basis of what we do. Legalism is any religion whose foundation is human effort, whether it is disguised as the Ten Commandments or Karma or the Eightfold Path or the Five Pillars or human sacrifices. Christianity, when it deserts its foundation in God's grace, becomes mere religion. Modern spiritual people are fond of saying that all spiritual paths are equally valid, and the Bible absolutely agrees: all paths are equally worthless. If people are to draw near to God, it is God who must move; nothing we do can get us anywhere near God's vicinity. The Messiah did not come to found a religion; He came to abolish them all.

What the Messiah brought was not a religion at all, not a system of rules or steps to be followed in order to establish a proper relationship with God; what the Messiah brought was the *end* of religion, the *end* of human effort as the means for knowing God. What the Messiah brought was God Himself drawing near to us for once and for all. God's call to Abram was a call away from religion and into grace. One of the reasons God called a nomad as His chosen one was that all the cities belong to some god or other, some religion or other. God called Abram out of religion, though this did not become clear until later.

All of the true children of Sarai are recipients of God's grace; they trust in the God who promises and then keeps His promises Himself. The true children of Hagar are those who seek to obtain God's promises by their own effort. Grace so entirely distinguishes Christianity from everything else, that it cannot legitimately go by the name Christian when it abandons its commitment to grace. To abandon grace is to abandon the Messiah, who alone was simultaneously full of grace and truth, and who gave Christianity its name.

d) The Silence (Genesis 20)

Once God had made a covenant with Abram, you would think that everything would get more intense between them, that God would communicate more intimately and frequently than previously, and that perhaps there would be a miracle or two as God began to fulfill some of His promises. The opposite was the case. Once the Covenant was sealed there followed a period of about fourteen years of complete silence, silence while Abram contrived to have a son with Hagar, and then silence for a dozen or more years beyond that. After Abram's initial believing God's promise and God crediting it to him as righteousness, God seemed to vanish from Abram's life, seemed to forget His promise, and an old man became an older man waiting on God to do something, anything.

It is potentially a disappointing experience to get a spectacular vision and look at the stars and believe wild promises from a God who increasingly seemed very long on promises and short on results. And sure enough, it was followed by a longer period of inaction and silence than any Abram had experienced before. Abram believed God, but how long could he continue to believe God in the face of such silence? It appears to be a pattern: God withdraws into silence just when we expect Him to be most vocal. Just when He issues a call or announces some new program or policy or hope, just when we finally make what feels like a sure connection with Him, then He disappears as if He had never been. And so, in the course of time, Ishmael was born and grew and God remained silent.

The incident with Abimelech in Genesis 20 is out of sequence. Chronologically, the visit with Abimelech occurred after the birth of Ishmael but before the birth of Isaac, before the circumcision, before the destruction of Sodom. Genesis 20:17,18 reads: "And Abraham prayed to God; and God healed Abimelech and his wife and his maids, so that they bore children. For the Lord had closed fast all the wombs of the household of Abimelech because of Sarah, Abraham's wife." This implies the passage of a fair amount of time with Abimelech; they would not have noticed that God had closed all the wombs for many months, maybe even years, more time at any rate than the single year between the circumcision and Isaac's birth, more time than it would take for Sarah's condition, if she were pregnant, to become noticeable. The only way to take the account in chapter 20 at face value is to assume that it occurred between chapters 16 and 17, after the time Abraham was 86 years old and Ishmael was born, but before the time Abraham was 99 years old and the rite of circumcision was required.

Putting the events in Gerar in their correct chronological sequence would have interrupted the story of Abraham's children, and so the story was moved to a more convenient place in the narrative. The fact that the names were changed to Abraham and Sarah in this chapter does not indicate that the events in chapter 20 occurred after the events in chapter 19; moving the story to this location in the narrative required the anachronistic using of the new names so as to make the account flow smoothly. After all, Genesis does not ever claim to be a chronological account and so there is no need for us to try to make it one. There were good literary reasons for rearranging the events, reasons that do no damage to the meaning of the material or the integrity of Scripture.

During those thirteen years after the birth of Ishmael, Abram left Hebron, went to the Negev, then toward Shur retracing more or less the route that Hagar had taken the previous year. Perhaps Abram went that way because he wanted to see Beer-lahai-roi for himself. There is no reason given for his transfer to Gerar but he stayed there for what must have been several years. Gerar was something of a prosperous city in Abram's time, though as the centuries passed it played an increasingly minor role in that land. Outside of Genesis, it is mentioned only once more in Scripture in I Chronicles 14:16 under the name of Gezer. After leaving Gerar Abram returned to Hebron once again for his fifth meeting with God.

Genesis 21:32 later describes Abimelech as returning "to the land of the Philistines", which might be taken as suggesting he was a Philistine. However this time period, in the mid-twenty-first century, was before the Philistines moved into the area, at least in significant numbers. Perhaps the people of Gerar were the first Philistines in the area, the only ones to arrive for several more centuries, but it is more likely that when the oral tradition was written down centuries later, the writer added "the land of the Philistines" to identify for contemporary readers the geographical location referred to. It is the same thing modern historians may do when they write about colonial American events at locations whose place names have changed. In short, Gerar was probably not a Philistine city at this time.

This was the second time, at least the second recorded time, that Abram had asked Sarai to keep their marriage a secret, but he admitted to Abimelech that he had planned with her to compromise herself in this way even before he had left Haran to go to Canaan. After the conflicts with Hagar it must have been particularly painful to Sarai to go through this same humiliation again, and yet she did. Why she did it, as strong willed as she was, can be easily explained. The simplest explanation is that she had a genuine and deep affection for Abram that inclined her to go along with his wishes when it would have been better to object. Just as it is frequently the tendency of husbands to be too harsh and controlling of their wives, it is frequently the tendency of wives to be too willing to justify their husband's errors.

The account of this second deception details more exactly how God intervened to rescue Sarah. This time He must have been protecting her over a long period of time. However it was that He kept her from Abimelech during what was probably three years or more, the time finally came for direct action to get her out of there, and so God appeared to Abimelech in a dream. It is interesting that Abimelech seemed to understand God's character and power as well as Abram, and perhaps better. God made it clear to Abimelech that He had preserved Sarah from him not only for her sake and Abram's sake, but also for Abimelech's sake, preventing him from sinning unwittingly. Again, God's treatment of Abimelech and Abimelech's response to his dream shows that God had been active among these pagans to keep Himself remembered to some extent. Certainly the reaction of Abimelech's servants in verse 8 shows that they took God Most High very seriously. There would at least have been the witness of Melchizedek, from whom they could have learned something about God Most High.

The interaction between God and Abimelech deserves careful attention. The opening of the dialogue implies that the local pagan standard of morality demanded death for adultery, and this was the case throughout the ancient Middle East. God's words in the vision when He made the Covenant said that the iniquity of the Amorites had not become complete. It was a prophecy of the degeneracy that was to accelerate when the Canaanites arrived in the land centuries later, corrupting all around them. At this point the pagans in Gerar had a relatively modern view of sexual ethics in marriage, except for the polygamy. But to a modern person, God's first statement to Abimelech seems out of line. How could an unintentional act deserve death? Abimelech naturally protested his innocence: both Abram and Sarai had misled him in the matter. Can an act still be a sin when it is done in a state of deception; can it still be a sin to the point that it demands death? In the case of Eve, I argued that the answer was no, but now in the case of Abimelech, as harsh as it may seem, I will argue that the answer is yes. So I must explain what distinguishes the two cases.

Throughout the Scripture, and after the Fall when sin and death ruled the world, God drew boundaries for His own purposes; and the crossing of those boundaries meant death regardless of whether the trespass was intentional or not. To the ancients, even to Abimelech, such boundaries were not unheard of. They knew that there were certain places, certain objects, certain people, which were holy, set apart, reserved for God (or the gods) alone and for those He favored. Even pagan fairy tales and myths develop this concept. There were places to which it was death for a mortal to stray even by accident. Abimelech would have known the concept. God was now telling him that the marriage of Abram and Sarai was one of those places, protected, sacred, holy, forbidden. This was the couple ordained to have a son, ordained to have a son when all possibility of a son and all hope for a son was gone, ordained to have a son to bear the Covenant of Revelation and to bear God's blessing to the whole of Creation. Abimelech was in danger of stumbling inadvertently into the Holy of Holies of God's revelation and God stopped him. This was what God meant by answering yes, that even though Abram and Sarai had deceived him, even though he was innocent, it was his life, and the life of his people, that was demanded. God was speaking Abimelech's language. In so doing, He was revealing something to Abimelech, if he happened to be listening. From this point on, Abimelech, and any of his people who were involved, knew there was something holy about Abram and Sarai.

Furthermore, straying into forbidden territory, even inadvertently, is not merely a question of bad luck; it is a *sin*. God's answer to Abimelech made it clear; God had prevented him, over a long period of time, from *sinning*. We usually think of sin as deliberate, willful rebellion against God and His commandments. However, sin goes much deeper than that. Willful disobedience is sin, of course, but the problem of sin is really a problem of who we are and not of what we do nor even of what we choose to do. We can obey, and we can obey to the letter, and the state of sin goes on undiminished. It is possible to be in sin, to be under the penalty of death from sin, and to be entirely unaware that there is any problem. Neither salvation nor damnation is a matter of what one knows or doesn't know. Abimelech experienced God's grace in the only way any of us experience it: he was rescued from a certain death he didn't even know was coming.

Note again that sin behaved in a covenantal way. If Abimelech had refused to restore Sarai, not only would he have died but also all of his family would have died. In verse 4 Abimelech indicated that He understood the threat of death as hovering over his whole nation, and in his own view there was nothing unjust about his people suffering for his sin. He lived in a culture of covenants and he understood the system. But God was gracious to Abimelech and to his people and prevented him from coming anywhere near Sarai. God does not delight in the death of anyone, but is always watching for ways to circumvent it.

The deception of Abimelech was a much more serious mistake than the deceiving of Pharaoh had been. By deceiving Abimelech in regard to Sarai, Abram had put the central Covenant promise at risk. God had promised a son to Abram *through Sarai*, and it would not do for there to be any suspicion that the child to come was Abimelech's. Abram had been very reckless to deceive Abimelech about Sarai; the deception could have seriously compromised God's plan and revelation if God were not so completely in control. This consideration makes it all the clearer that chapter 20 occurred immediately after chapter 16: this episode in Abram's life was well over before Sarai got pregnant and there was never any question that Abram was the father.

Though Abram was at fault here, though Abimelech and his people had not sinned in this matter, nonetheless God would not heal the people of the land until Abram had interceded for them. It was the responsibility of the Covenant bearer to intercede for those with whom he interacted, particularly if he was the cause of their problem. By making the Covenant with Abram, God had made him into a priest to the world, a representative of God to the world, and his foolishness did not disqualify him from his priestly duties.

At no point did God rebuke Abram, either for deceiving Abimelech or for risking the Covenant. God was biased in favor of His son, Abram, and chose to overlook his sin. The embarrassment of confessing to Abimelech was some punishment, but punishment was never the issue. God never spent time looking for ways to punish sin; He was looking for ways to avoid punishment.

e) The Sign of Circumcision (Genesis 17:1-14 and 17:22-27)

And so the period of silence passed. Ishmael was thirteen years old; Abram was ninety nine, and the year was about 2059 b.c. more or less. At last, God appeared to Abram the fifth time. There were still two aspects of the Covenant of Revelation that had not been considered: the sign and the name, not indispensable but normal. The sign of a covenant is the most visible part of the covenant and we will consider that aspect first.

It would seem that Abram was at a low point spiritually, and that God Most High had waited until this opportune moment to renew His visits. Timing is a large part of communication, and God Most High is the Master. He waits to speak until we are most in need of hearing Him, and sometimes that means waiting until we are on the point of giving up. Abram was on the point of losing hope and it was time to give him another push in the right direction. By "losing hope", I do not mean that Abram was about to give up on God and His promises entirely; I mean that Abram was ready to settle for "good enough". He may have felt little attachment to Ishmael before his birth, but now he had grown to love Ishmael as an only son. He was content, happy, willing to do the legal thing, the traditional thing, and count Ishmael as Sarai's son, and just get on with enjoying his life and prosperity and happiness.

For this fifth appearance, God used a very different form of greeting than previously: "I am God Almighty; walk before Me and be blameless." The phrase that is translated "be blameless" could be translated in many different ways, such as "have integrity" or "be complete" or "be perfect". The tone was not reassuring, but demanding. He was not addressing a man who was afraid, but a man who was on the point of settling for less than God intended. Abram didn't need reassurance; he needed a pep talk. It was not that Abram had decided that God had failed, but that this partial fulfillment of His promise was really pretty good, quite good enough. Abram was old, he was tired. God had been very good to him and he just wanted to grow old in peace. It was time to retire.

So what did He mean, this God who was as short on action as He was on demands, what did He mean by telling Abram to "be perfect"? As yet God had given no commands to Abram except the original call to leave his home and go to a strange country. Being blameless before God had been easy in every sense of the word. Abram had not had to change his habits in any new or unusual way. The migrant lifestyle may have been new to him but it was certainly an ancestral tradition and he would have been familiar with it; so he had not had to make any extraordinary lifestyle changes. The only thing he had done was believe God's promise and move to a new land, one that he seems to have planned to visit in any case. Otherwise walking before God was mainly just waiting for when God might next speak. There had been no commandments to obey, no required rituals. The Most High God had left him alone, so far, and seemed easy enough to please . . . unless . . . unless He was about to spring a surprise, some unexpected assignment. And He was and He did and it was a difficult one: every male in the household, every male in his whole little nomadic nation, was to be circumcised. The long neglected sign of the Covenant of Revelation was finally being appointed and it was circumcision.

With no anesthetics and no antiseptics it was a little dangerous and quite painful. With 300+ trained warriors, and servants, and shepherds, and the sons of them all from eight days old and upwards, there were easily between five hundred and a thousand men and boys who had to be circumcised, unless some of them had been already. What if they wouldn't go along with it? Make them? It says a lot about Abram's relationship with his people that they did go along with this. They hadn't been included in the visions, they hadn't heard God Most High give the command to be circumcised. They only had Abram's word to go on, and that was enough for them. It didn't even take him long to convince them: they did the circumcision that very day. Abram had credibility. Abram was a leader that people would follow.

Though the absence of a sign did not nullify the Covenant, we would be wrong to thing it was a mere technicality that was optional, to be tacked on or left off at will. The sign of the covenant, once established, was critical enough to the covenant that it became *identified* with the covenant. It became *interchangeable* with the covenant. Genesis 17:10 says, "This is My covenant, which you shall keep, between Me and you and your descendants after you: every male among you shall be circumcised." No mention had been made of circumcision when the Covenant had first been established, but now circumcision was made *equal* to the Covenant as far as Abram's people were concerned. The sign was so central to the Covenant that to neglect or refuse the sign was considered the same as neglecting or refusing the Covenant itself.

We are not accustomed, in western culture, to taking signs so seriously. The wedding ring, for example, is not that closely identified with the marriage. Either husband or wife might well remove the ring, might even destroy the ring for some reason, without damaging or disrespecting the marriage. The closest equivalent we have in modern America is the honor we bestow on the flag as a sign of our nation. Those who feel that disrespect to the American flag is the same as disrespect to America itself have a very covenantal understanding of America.

Circumcision was the fourth explicit sign given in Genesis. Sexuality/marriage was the first, the rainbow was the second, blood was the third, and now circumcision. The Sabbath also was a sign, but since it has played no role in the revelation to this point, I am not counting it yet. Unlike the other three signs, circumcision was given only to God's people. The reason is that it was a sign of the Covenant of Revelation which was only given to this one family and not yet to the whole world. Circumcision was practiced in the Middle East in ancient times but to those people it was simply a traditional practice, with none of the meaning it had for Abram or his descendants. Circumcision was the first of the Middle Eastern traditions that God "stole", that He took from those cultures and reinterpreted and used for His own purposes. It wasn't that God lacked the imagination to come up with original symbols for His own religion. Rather, because His intent was to speak to those peoples through this Covenant, He modified their symbols to make it all more accessible to them. At the same time, circumcision was not practiced by the peoples who had already settled in the land of Canaan or by Abram's Amorite ancestors, nor would it be practiced by the Canaanites when they finally arrived. In this way, circumcision served both to make a cultural bridge to the Middle East and simultaneously a cultural barrier to the people who would live in Canaan a few centuries down the road.

What then does circumcision symbolize? What is it the sign of? Being the sign of the covenant, it was clearly a sign of the faith that was counted to Abram as righteousness on which the Covenant was established, but it was more complex than a simple one to one correspondence. The process of circumcision does not obviously "look like" God counting righteousness to Abram. In circumcision a rather intimate surgery was performed and a part of the man was cast aside to be destroyed. Circumcision made a permanent mark on the man showing that something of him had been discarded, destroyed, killed. What does this have to do with the Covenant of Revelation? What does this have to do with the faith of Abram that was counted as righteousness and provided the rationale for the Covenant? It is somewhat complicated.

The faith was Abram's faith, but the Covenant was made with all of Abram's household, with those who had a faith like Abram's and with those who did not. Faith was not required for inclusion in the Covenant.

Everyone who was born into Abram's household, everyone who was bought by Abram with his money, regardless of their spiritual state, was included in the Covenant of Revelation. His soldiers, his servants, none of them are certified as having a faith like Abram's. The eight day old baby boys born to them certainly did not have a faith like Abram's. Therefore circumcision was not a sign of the faith of the person who was circumcised. Did it have anything to do with faith, then? Yes, Paul asserted in Romans 4 that circumcision was given to Abram as a sign of the faith that he had before he was circumcised. In the context of Genesis, then, in the context of the Hebrew scriptures, circumcision was a sign of Abram's faith even when it was others who were being circumcised. Ishmael was circumcised that very day and the rite of circumcision performed on Ishmael was a sign of Abram's faith, not Ishmael's faith. So it was with them all, so it was through their generations. Throughout the centuries every Israelite man carried, and still carries, the sign of *Abram's* faith that was counted to him as righteousness.

But there is more. The physical process of circumcision would seem to point toward something that is taken away rather than something that is given. And so it does. Circumcision was a symbol—more accurately, circumcision was a promise—that God would perform in the hearts of His people a form of spiritual surgery in which a part of the person would be cut off and cast aside to be destroyed. So if circumcision is a sign of God's removal of something rather than God's gift of something, what is it that God removes? Is it not what the New Testament calls the "old nature" or the "sinful nature" or the "flesh" or the principle of death? Ultimately then circumcision symbolizes death, being crucified with Christ, but in the context of Genesis we have a long long way to go to get to that understanding. Later the revelation would place some emphasis on what would be called the "circumcision of the heart", and Paul would emphasize in the letter to the Romans that this circumcision which was inward, by the Spirit and not by the letter, was the essence of what was important.

Paul would later call circumcision a "seal". A seal is a mark of official certification, a notarization, a signature on a warranty or contract pledging the genuineness of the article. Circumcision was not just a sign of a spiritual reality, faith, which might or might not be there. It was the pledge God made that He would carry it out, that He would make it real, that the sign would not signify nothing. Circumcision was a way to emphasize that God's promises were always and only accomplished by God Himself. Here I am importing meaning from the scriptures given two millennia after Abram. The meaning of it all at that time, if they were trying to decipher it, would have been very obscure. The complete meaning of any progressive revelation always lies in the future and will always have aspects that are mysterious in the present.

In short, circumcision was a sign of two things: the removal, in some kind of spiritual surgery, of part of the man's nature; and the gift of righteousness on the basis of faith. We distinguish the two ideas theologically. We might call the spiritual surgery "sanctification", and the gift of righteousness is usually called "justification", but in Genesis the way the sign functions the two are simultaneous, a single act of God. This is a Christian perspective and not at all what the men of Abram's household would have thought or imagined. The meaning of the sign would not have been apparent to them or to Abram, but it was given to them for us. All Abram knew was that God Most High had decided on circumcision for reasons of His own, and all Abram's people knew was that Abram said God wanted them to do this. It was enough for that time.

Any male who was not circumcised was "cut off" from his people; if the foreskin had not been cut off of the man, then the man himself was "cut off" instead. Not only was he not considered a member of the Covenant, but none of his future descendants were included in the Covenant either. In this way, inclusion in the Covenant was similar to citizenship in a country: if a person loses his citizenship or forfeits his citizenship, then his future children automatically lose their citizenship as well. Consider this well: any Israelite who was not circumcised was not circumcised as a result of his parents despising or ignoring the Covenant on the eighth day after his birth. It was his parents' choice that cut him off from the Covenant (and also cut his parents off with him) or it was his parents' respect for the Covenant that established him in it. Not a single one of God's people was in the Covenant of Revelation by his own choice, though they could choose to despise the Covenant and leave it later on. But we shall see that through history God didn't always take a hard-line legalistic approach to the issue. Commandments, to be commandments, must sound more harsh than grace is willing to be.

It was necessary that those who were uncircumcised be excluded from the Covenant to emphasize the necessity of the work of God in each individual. Unless God acts to surgically remove the offending part of our nature then we cannot be admitted to His Covenant, to His people, we cannot belong to God in the way that Abram belonged to Him. If we are not, at some point, spiritually circumcised, if the truth of the sign is not accomplished in us, then the whole point of the Covenant has failed; and God, who is our spiritual Father, is the only one who can perform the surgery. What was really going on here was the introduction of a rather complex idea, what the Messiah would call "being born again". Even this act of obedience to this one command was designed to make Abram and his children aware of how their tie to God depended on His power and not on their obedience.

What then is the value or meaning of a pledge from God to a man who is free to just walk away? What did circumcision seal to those who despised the Covenant and took their children with them? What did circumcision seal to those who obeyed the command to have their children circumcised but who actually had no faith in anything? How are the sign and the spiritual reality connected? What actually happened when an infant was circumcised? Did God always perform eventually the spiritual act that the circumcision symbolized? Did the rabbi, the priest, the parent have some part in accomplishing the spiritual act by their obedience in using the sign? These are all modern theological questions regarding sacraments that would not have occurred to anyone in Abram's day, but ultimately it is all a matter of God making seemingly absurd promises like 17:7: "And I will establish my covenant between me and you and your offspring after you throughout their generations for an everlasting covenant to be God to you and to your offspring after you." The signs themselves are not what is important, they are only tools in the hands of God. It is the promise of God that is important. It is the promise of God that is powerful. God promised to be the God of Abram's offspring whether they wanted Him to be or not.

We must ask: if the sign was such an important part of the Covenant, why did God wait so long after making the Covenant to give the sign? There is an important reason why the sign of circumcision was ultimately inadequate for God's purposes: it ignored the importance of women to the Covenant. It is evident that in waiting so long He had deliberately loosened the connection between the sign and the Covenant. It hinted that the sign might not be absolutely indispensable to the Covenant. It hinted that people might be able to belong to the Covenant without the sign, like Abram had, and like all women did. It hinted that the sign itself might someday be modified to another sign (as I think it has), another sign that would display the central importance of women to God's purposes.

But I think the sign of circumcision only seems to marginalize women. It's purpose was revelatory, to point to specific concepts that needed to be clear. First it pointed to a Covenant whose foundation was faith counted as righteousness. Were women marginalized from this meaning? Granted that women do not bear the mark that carries this meaning, does this then mean that their faith will not be counted as righteousness? Or does it mean that they don't need righteousness counted to them? Or does it mean that women cannot be counted as righteous? Certainly the New Testament answers "no" to each of those absurd questions. Second, circumcision was a seal of God's pledge to remove a part of our nature, to circumcise our hearts, to sanctify us. Granted that women do not carry the mark that bears this meaning, does this then mean that God does not promise to remove part of their nature? Does this mean that women do not or cannot be circumcised in their hearts? Does this mean that women are not sanctified, or that they don't need sanctification? The New Testament again answers "no" to each of these absurd questions.

The sign is not important. It is the meaning of the sign that is important. It is the reality that the sign points to that is important. Particularly after the long passage of time before the sign was given. Particularly when the sign was changed as soon as its meaning was accomplished. For the purpose of making a clear revelation, God chose a sign that was not borne by women, but the meaning of the sign was given to the whole world, Jew and Gentile, circumcised and uncircumcised, male and female. To carry a sign is no great privilege to those who despise its meaning; they only condemn themselves in their own flesh. To be without a sign is no great deprivation to those who honor its meaning; they only show that the truth of the sign is revealed in their hearts. It seems to me that even today those who marginalize the role of women in the church are making the sign more important than its meaning.

f) The Exclusion of Ishmael (Genesis 17:15-21)

Ishmael was dear to Abram, as dear as any son is to his father. Ishmael had been Abram's only son for thirteen years and Abram had grown devoted to him. "Oh, that Ishmael might live before You!" was not mainly the wavering thought that God might not come through on this promise of a child through Sarai, it was more an expression of love for Ishmael. God had been promising him a son with Sarah for more than twenty years and now it seemed too late, but that was not the point any more. Abram had decided that it didn't matter to him. Whether or not Sarai had a son, he had Ishmael and that was enough. He was content with the way things were.

But God refused him. The Covenant, which was God's primary objective, would not go to Ishmael. Thus God answered, "No, but Sarah your wife will bear you a son, and you shall call his name Isaac; and I will establish My covenant with him for an everlasting covenant for his descendants after him. As for Ishmael, I have heard you; behold, I will bless him, and will make him fruitful and will multiply him exceedingly. He shall become the father of twelve princes, and I will make him a great nation. But My covenant I will establish with Isaac, whom Sarah will bear to you at this season next year."

The Covenant was not the only sign of God's favor to be had, not the only blessing God could bestow. Because of His love of Abram, all whom Abram loved came under His favor. There were reasons Ishmael had to be excluded from the Covenant, but he need not be excluded from everything. We must stress that Ishmael and his descendants were not excluded from the blessings and the favor and the love of God. They were to become a great nation; they were to be given land (earlier, to Hagar, the angel had said that they would live to the east of their brothers). It is important to understand God's commitment to the descendants of Ishmael, who included the Arab people, though His work among them has been different from the work He has done among the Jews. To be excluded from the Covenant meant (and still means) to be excluded from the stream of self-revelation that God was giving to the world and that culminated in the Messiah. But they were not to be left with nothing at all; God gave Himself to the Arabs, albeit not in the same way.

We must be clear on the reason God excluded Ishmael from the Covenant. Normally no child is excluded in a Covenant, and so the exclusion of Ishmael demands some explanation. From what Paul would say later in the book of Galatians as well as in the context of Genesis, the issue was the question of who would fulfill God's promises. It was critical for what God was revealing to make it clear that only God could fulfill His promises, that no human effort could do it. For this reason alone the child that was born to Abram through his own efforts with Hagar had to be excluded. It had nothing to do with Ishmael's worthiness, nor with Isaac's. It was an allegorical necessity. Abram's children, Abram's whole life, were arranged as symbols to carry the revelation. Ishmael's existence pointed to man's effort to establish God's purposes and even today the descendants of Ishmael bear this burden, the horrible burden, of believing that they must accomplish God's purposes on earth for Him. It eats them from the inside.

But why should Ishmael, and indeed his descendants even to the present day, be commanded to bear the sign of a Covenant from which they were excluded? We can't give a complete answer to the question. There is a sense in which circumcision is a witness to them against themselves, against their new religion, against their own prophet who stood outside the stream of revelation that began with Abram. There are only a few hints about the ultimate role of the Jewish people in the unfolding of God's purposes, and there are even fewer hints about the role of the Arab people. All we can say is that they are beloved by God for the sake of their father Abraham, and that they will play their appointed role at the appointed time.

There is important theological meaning in the sign being applied to Ishmael, that it was applied to him when he was thirteen years old and certainly old enough to choose for himself whether he wanted it or not. Normally the sign was applied to eight day old infants who could not choose for themselves, and similarly Ishmael was given no choice. The meaning of signs, their revelatory purpose, is a spiritual truth which may or may not be accomplished at the time they are given. In other words, it does not matter if the one who is circumcised is "circumcised in his heart" or not; the sign has the same validity and the same meaning regardless. There would be many in the Messiah's day who bore the sign of the Covenant, but not the reality of the Covenant, as both Paul and the Messiah would point out. The same can be said of the signs Christians use, baptism and the Eucharist. The human part is to use and respect the signs as they are given; it is God's part to make the signs real.

In all of these details God emphasized two points: that the Covenant relationship arises from God choosing us, not us choosing God; and that His blessings extend beyond the boundaries of the Covenant. The Covenant is critical to His redemption of creation, obviously; the Covenant is what the entire Bible is about, it is the context of the Messiah's work, it is the mystery that was hidden in God through all the ages but has now been made manifest in the final age. Nevertheless, the Covenant has never been the *only* thing that God was doing.

The Covenant people, from the very beginning, included what was probably a fair variety of ethnic groups. Circumcision was applied to Abram's entire male household, which included many hundreds of slaves and servants and mercenaries and their children. All of these people were included in the Covenant relationship with God simply because they were in relationship with Abram. Though the servants of Abraham's household are seldom mentioned individually, they were nonetheless an integral part of the community. The word for "household" in the Bible specifically included such servants. It may seem strange that the son Ishmael was out while the children of slaves were in, but it becomes more intelligible if the revelatory purpose is kept in mind.

Muslims have been taught that there were distortions in the Hebrew Scriptures and that God's Covenant passed to Ishmael rather than Isaac, but history proves them wrong. For the next 2000 years it was exclusively the descendants of Isaac to whom God revealed Himself and not to the descendants of Ishmael. It is manifestly true, simply from subsequent history, that the Jews received the Covenant of Revelation: Moses and then Joshua and then David and then Solomon and then Elijah and then Isaiah and the Jeremiah and so on until the Messiah. But to the descendants of Ishmael, as to the rest of the world, God was silent; they had no prophets and no revelation. The prophet claimed by the descendants of Ishmael was not to come for nearly three thousand years and even then he came as an outsider to the stream of revelation that God had carefully built up over those millennia.

The meaning of Mohammed was to turn the hearts of the Arab people from many gods to worship the One God. It is true that the Muslims do not know the one God in the same way we do. The Muslims as well as the Jews have misunderstood the Messiah. While the Muslims do not have the insight into the nature of God that the Messiah and the prophets of Israel brought, still they do have something, and they do have something that is true. Mixed in with the revelation that Mohammed brought them there is a barrier to their recognizing the Messiah, a veil that covers their eyes, just as there is a veil that has prevented the Jews from recognizing their Messiah. In both cases, it is God's purposes that are being fulfilled, purposes that we do not know, but that are as good as only He can be. Both of these peoples have been singled out as people who are under God's particular favor because of their father Abram and the day will surely come when all veils are removed.

g) The Covenant Name
(Genesis 16:11-12, 17:1-8 and 17:15-16)

When a conquering king acquired a new land, it was common for him to give the defeated king a new name to embody his new identity as a subject of the conqueror. This will happen several times in the rest of the Scripture when the people of Israel are taken captive, and it was naturally part of the process of God establishing a new covenant with Abram. There are a few significant differences in this covenant and the covenants in the world that we would do well to notice.

First, of course, Ishmael had already received a covenant name. He had been born a year or two after the ritual establishing the covenant was performed. Ishmael was given a covenant name just as Isaac would be given one, but Ishmael's was the first one given. The giving of a covenant name indicates a particular and special standing before God, a particular relationship to God. Though not ultimately part of this covenant, Ishmael nonetheless had a special relationship of his own to God that was distinct from the relationship of the rest of the Gentiles. Ishmael means "God hears" and it was not given for nothing; God does not make commitments like this without meaning them. God hears, He still hears, the children of Ishmael.

At this point then God changed Abram to Abraham, from "exalted father" to "father of a multitude". It was central to the Covenant that Abraham was to be not just a father but the father of many nations. Ultimately, this is the reason that the birth of Ishmael was not enough. Ishmael alone was to be the father of a dozen princes and a great nation, but it was not sufficient that Abram have a son and a lot of descendants. The goal of the Covenant was that Abram would be Abraham, the father of many nations, indeed the father of all nations, not simply the father of his descendants but the father of all descendants. This goal could only be achieved by making his Covenant descendants more than biological ones. This goal could only be achieved by making his Covenant descendants a product of God's promise and not a natural product of cause and effect. Christians interpret this passage as referring to all those who believe in the Messiah, so that by the miracle of rising from the dead, by an act beyond all possibility of natural causes, Abraham becomes spiritual father of people from literally every nation on earth. American Christians, African Christians, Chinese Christians, all of us count Abraham as our father, the one whose faith we share.

Then God took the unusual step of giving Sarai a covenant name as well: Sarah, "princess". Sarai already meant princess; the change was that she was now designated as a princess whom God Himself, and not men, had appointed as princess. She had the noble title "sister-wife", and she had been named princess by her father Terah, but now she had been crowned Princess by God. It was the fulfillment of her destiny.

But it was a male dominated world, and any attention or particular honor given to women in these accounts is significant. There are two important reasons God Most High gave Sarah her new name, that I can discern. First, it indicated that He was not making the covenant with Abraham alone, but with Abraham/Sarah the couple. Heretofore God had had no direct dealing with Sarah, but now He made it clear that she was not to play a merely secondary role in the Covenant, as if she were just another member of Abraham's household. She was not included in the Covenant merely as Abraham's wife but as co-founder. The Covenant and the promises were given to the descendants of Abraham-and-Sarah, and not to the descendants of Abraham and any other woman. Whoever did not belong to the couple, Abraham+Sarah, were not involved in this Covenant. The point of His silence, of His waiting, of much of what He had done with Abraham and Sarah was to bring them to the point where their only hope of receiving anything was through His hand. Sarah's long suffering and waiting was as much a part of God's purpose as Abraham's was. This is also why, though the other *sons* of Abraham would be excluded from the Covenant, all the *servants* of the household would be included because they belonged to Abraham/Sarah.

Another reason Sarah was given a Covenant name was to compensate for circumcision being appointed as the sign of the Covenant. Because circumcision was an exclusively male sign, the impression could have been given that women were not fully members of the Covenant, that they did not have the same standing in God's grace that men had. To counter this false impression, Sarah was given a covenant name equally with Abraham, a name corresponding to his name. She was not Sarah the assistant of Abraham, Sarah the servant of Abraham, Sarah the junior partner; she was Sarah, the *Princess*.

The child who would continue the Covenant into another generation, the child who would carry the revelation that nothing was impossible for God, that God would always keep His promises even when they were no longer possible, and that no human effort could avail to accomplish His purpose, this child was to be named Isaac, meaning "he laughs". The foolishness of God is indeed wiser than man's wisdom. At times the foolishness of God looks like skilled recklessness—a sort of divine Jackie Chan. Isaac, by his name, would be a continual reminder to Abraham of his doubt, and the folly of doubting, and of the joke God had played on him, waiting until it was too late and then pulling the rabbit out of the hat. Doubting God's ability or willingness to do the good that He promises is the ultimate in folly, and it is right that we laugh at our doubts. Imagine that! For a moment I actually thought God would fail me. How silly I was and am!

The Covenant of Revelation was given through several appearances to Abraham over the course of more than two decades, so it is worthwhile collecting all the terms of this covenant together into a single list:

- God promised to be faithful to Abraham, to be his God and the God of his children forever (17:7,8);
- God promised to make Abraham a blessing to all nations on earth (12:1-3);
- God promised to give Abraham descendants who were like the stars in glory (15:5 and 17:4-6);
- God gave Abraham and Sarah new identities, the Father of a Multitude and the Princess (17:5, 15);
- God gave circumcision of the sign of their relationship (17:10);
- God promised to give Abraham all of that land as his inheritance (12:7, 13:15, 15:18, and 17:8).

What stands out in this covenant is the way God gave Himself to Abram and his descendants. He had never done such a thing before. The central promise in this covenant, though not repeated as often as the other promises, was contained in Genesis 17:7 "And I will establish My covenant between Me and you and your descendants after you throughout their generations for an everlasting covenant, to be God to you and to your descendants after you." God chose Abraham and promised Abraham that he and all his descendants forever would worship Him as their God. God promised to be their God period, with no condition on their behavior, no provision that they had to worship Him. Whether they kept Him as their God or no, He would keep Himself as their God. It all depended on God's promise and commitment to Abraham. If it depends on God, then it does not depend on us, all or nothing.

3. Abraham's Final Years

a) Sodom

i) Abraham Entertains Angels (Genesis 18:1-21)

My approach to Scripture and interpretation views the Covenant of Revelation as the central purpose of Abraham's life. For this reason I have divided his life into three periods: his early years, leading up to the Covenant; the making of the Covenant, which took about fifteen years to complete; and his later years, after the Covenant had been made. This is an entirely artificial way to discuss his life, but I use it as a matter of convenience. Therefore since I am beginning to discuss the events that occurred after the Covenant was completely implemented, I call it his later years; but the events discussed here occurred very soon after the circumcision, perhaps only weeks.

The story of Abraham's intercession for Sodom, its destruction, and the rescue of Lot and his family begins when Abraham recognized three passing strangers as angels. With God, there are no unnecessary delays. The fourteen years of silence had been enough. Now it was the right time for things to happen. As so many important acts in the divine drama, it began quietly with three men appearing not far away from Abraham's tent. He had been taking his siesta in the doorway of his tent, when he looked up and saw them, standing some distance away. Perhaps because he had a new depth of character from all his interaction with God, a new sensitivity to spiritual things, he knew intuitively that these were not ordinary men. He recognized the angels because he could see what others could not, and perhaps that kind of discernment was also behind his hostility to the king of Sodom.

Though 18:2 specifically calls them men, it is clear that they were not. What form had the previous appearances of God taken? We don't know but the accounts do not make any suggestion that God had ever appeared like a man before this, and certainly never in a group of men. However he recognized them, this was the sixth time God had spoken to him and he was eager to respond. Abraham was very good at waiting, and perhaps he assumed he might have another fourteen years before he heard from God again. It must have been a mix of joy and relief when he saw these men; he ran to greet them.

Though there were three of them, when Abraham first addressed them he used the singular, as if he were speaking to only one of them. It is easy to read into this a symbol for the Trinity, but it is possible that he recognized one of the "men" as being special, as being an appearance of the Most High God Himself, and the other two as being subordinates. Subsequent events seem to bear out that possibility: 18:13 attributes the words of one of these "men" to God Himself, but the other two are not described in the same way as the story goes on. I do think the Trinity is prefigured constantly through the Hebrew scriptures, but not necessarily here.

Though this appearance occurred shortly after the circumcision at which God had so emphatically said that Sarah would have the child who would be heir of the covenant, when the men repeated the promise that Sarah would have a son within a year their words were met with incredulity, particularly on Sarah's part. The passage does not say what Abraham felt at this repeat of the promise, but Sarah, who was listening from the tent, was laughing, possibly with some bitterness, but certainly with incredulity. Sarah had not been involved in the visions as Abraham had, and so she should be excused. The events surrounding the circumcision would not have affected her in the same way as Abraham. He had had Ishmael to fall back on, but Sarah had had nothing. All the waiting would have been far more difficult for her than for Abraham.

God was very gentle with Sarah; He knew her. He had pushed both of them to the very limit of their ability to believe, not to find fault with their weakness when they wavered, but to help them believe Him more surely. He also meant that all who read this account over the millennia would find encouragement to believe the ridiculous promises He tends to make. So, although Sarah disbelieved His word and lied about laughing—I can't fault her for being afraid to admit she had laughed—He was very mild in His response, milder than many of us would be in His place. But He did make clear the main point of all the waiting: "Is anything too difficult for the Lord?" That is the question that is posed to all of us one way or the other, sooner or later.

Whatever we may think we would say to that question, each of us has a limit to his ability to believe. I know that nothing is too difficult for the Lord, but if He takes me out far enough on a limb I will eventually reach the boundary where doubt and fear are at least the equal of faith and trust in my heart. Whether you are strong in faith or weak, the day will come when you are on the edge of what you can believe, and when that time arrives it is important to know that it is God who brought you there, and it is important to know that His intent is not to find fault with you if you fail. Failure or success, these things mean nothing as long as you go on, as long as you get up and keep pursuing God. As in so many other areas of life, it is quality that counts rather than quantity. It is what you do with the faith that you have that is important, what beautiful thing you make of it, and not whether your faith is large or small. And it is only when we are at the edge of our ability to trust that we have the opportunity to grow. It is wise to prepare now for that time, which will surely come, so that when it does come you will be ready to make good use of it.

The meal that Abraham prepared for them would have taken quite a long time: he began by killing the animal. They arrived in the heat of the day, near noon, and it is difficult to see how Abraham could have prepared the meal very much before sunset. Also the meal that he prepared for the men was not kosher, strictly, since it apparently included both meat and milk together. This implies that, though the dietary laws were instituted by God and were required for His people, there was nothing absolute about them. We err if we think that whenever God issues a command He is issuing an absolute command which remains His will for all people in all times. This might seem obvious from a New Testament viewpoint, as when Jesus altered the dietary laws for His disciples, but it is also clear from the viewpoint of the earliest books in the Bible.

By the time the meal was over, it must have been near sunset or after. The oaks of Mamre were about thirty miles from Sodom, a guess since we do not know Sodom's exact location. Sodom was somewhere in the Jordan valley, and standing on the edge of the hill country and looking down into the valley, Sodom might have just been visible on a perfectly clear day. The hill country would have ended overlooking the Jordan and the Dead Sea, and it could be that Abraham accompanied the men at least that far, a matter of ten to fifteen miles. It is hard to see how the men, the angels, could walk to Sodom and arrive there by that same evening, at least not if they were walking like ordinary men, and so we should probably assume that the angels had spent the night with Abraham. Abraham was walking with them as a good host, but probably also because he was hoping to speak further with the One who seemed like God. Abraham seems to have had a suspicion that something was up, something important and a little scary, and he wanted to know what it was.

There were three "men" who came to Abraham, but only two arrived in Sodom; thus when the "men" turned away and went toward Sodom, Abraham was still standing before the Lord, before the third "man". The easiest way for a Christian to understand this passage is as a pre-incarnation appearance of the Messiah, Jesus. That the Most High God would appear to Abraham in the form of a man would be an odd thing to do when He would later spend so much time emphasizing to Israel that He had no such form as anything that they could see; at least it is odd apart from the future Incarnation. How can He both not have a form and yet appear in a form unless there is something complex and subtle going on, or unless He is simply not very good at communicating? Since communication is what He does best, if it seems complicated then it must be because what He is communicating is complicated. God is bigger than His creation, not like anything in it that we can see, and yet He intended to make Himself visible to us, to not only appear as something we could see, but to appear as something we could understand from the inside.

The description of God debating with Himself over whether or not to tell Abraham what He was about to do is intriguing. That this passage was put in Scripture means that God wanted us to eavesdrop on this internal conversation, and we should ask why He does. One reason was to emphasize to us that the Covenant of Revelation makes His people party to His plans. We are His accomplices, His accompanists, in His work. Genesis 18:17-19 reads, "Shall I hide from Abraham what I am about to do, since Abraham will surely become a great and mighty nation, and in him all the nations of the earth will be blessed? For I have chosen him, so that he may command his children and his household after him to keep the way of the Lord by doing righteousness and justice, so that the Lord may bring upon Abraham what He has spoken about him." Let's examine this remark very closely.

In the final analysis the reason He shared His intention with Abraham was because Abraham was *certain* to become a mighty nation, a blessing to all other nations. Why then was he certain to become a blessing to the world? Because God had chosen him. For what purpose had God chosen him? To command his household and descendants to keep the way of the Lord by doing righteousness and justice. But there was not much specific content to be commanded at that point, only the oral tradition he had received and was adding to, just these first few chapters of Genesis that we have read. In particular, there was no set of commandments indicating in any detail what righteousness and justice were. Such things would come, God would make it clear in future generations to come exactly what He meant by righteousness and justice, but in the context of Genesis all He could have meant was that Abraham was chosen to be the steward of the revelation, the oral tradition that was being expanded in his own life. He and his descendants were chosen to be the conduits of the revelation. Or in other words, he and his descendants had been given the Covenant of Revelation. And the reason he had to pass on that revelation was so that God could make him a blessing to all the nations. It was a somewhat convoluted way of saying: "Abraham is certain to be a blessing to all the nations because he is the one chosen to carry the revelation that is the blessing to all the nations." *Therefore* God *revealed* to him what He was about to do in Sodom.

This is the germ of the doctrine that is now called predestination, which is too big an issue to consider fully at this point. It was an idea like so many of the ideas in the revelation, like the Trinity and the Incarnation, an idea so deep that it had to be disclosed gradually. It is an idea that is repeated throughout the whole Scripture as the central truths always are. We will discuss the free will vs. predestination question in the future as we proceed to read the Bible. For the moment, notice that if there is *certainty* to be had, it cannot be based on free will. There is no stability, no dependability, in the free choice of men, so free will itself cannot be the whole story.

Members of the Covenant are entitled to be in on God's plans. Obviously, however, God did not tell Abraham everything, and He doesn't tell us everything either. Doubtless God was involved in doing things all around Canaan, all around the world, and still is. It would have been impossible for Abraham to carry the weight of knowing all of God's purposes, just as it would be impossible for us. What God did was to give Abraham privileged access to the information that was of direct concern to him: the people and events surrounding his nephew Lot.

ii) Abraham Prays for Sodom (Genesis 18:22-33)

God was setting Abraham up. He had walked by Abraham's tent solely for the purpose of engaging Abraham and Sarah in conversation. If He had only intended to go to Sodom, there were a lot of other roads He could have taken, or He could have taken no road at all. What He wanted was to re-emphasize to Abraham that He was serious about giving Sarah a child and to give him a specific time table; no more of just hanging out for a decade. But He had another purpose: He was there to make Abraham a part of His work; in modern terms, the Covenant had given Abraham a seat on the board of directors of God's program for world domination. He wanted to bring Abraham up to speed on the next big thing that was happening.

I wonder if it is not always the reason God shares information with us, to make us into intercessors. After all, what does it mean to be an intercessor? Doesn't it really mean that we become counselors to God, advisors on policy and procedure? Doesn't it really mean that God listens to us express our opinions on His business and then modifies His plans to a greater or lesser extent in response to us? And why would God listen to our opinions, as filled with ignorance and disreputable motives as they are? How could our opinions be other than foolish? Perhaps He listens to our foolish opinions in order to train us to have less foolish opinions. Perhaps He modifies His plans according to our foolish advice to show us the difference between wisdom and folly. Even listening to our foolish advice, He can still bring it all off in the end, He is that strong. Intercession is on the job training to run the universe.

So far as there are records, no other city since the Flood has been singled out for destruction like Sodom, Gomorrah, Admah, and Zeboiim (that these other cities were included in the destruction, see Deuteronomy 29:23). Are we to think that these were the most wicked cities that have ever existed? No, for later the Scripture will compare even Israel to Sodom. But if other cities have been as wicked as Sodom, why were these cities alone punished in such a dramatic fashion? Why did God do this thing, as if it were the standard way He intended to deal with wicked cities, and then never do it again? Or did He do such a thing again occasionally throughout history? Was the destruction of Knossos, for example, or Pompeii, the same kind of thing?

Well, no. When God does something, He is not always setting precedents for His future standard operating procedures. We are in the habit of assuming that if God chose to do something once then He will always do that same thing in response to the same situation. If another wicked city like Sodom arose then surely God would also rain fire and sulfur on it as He did on Sodom, we suppose. If He didn't do the same thing next time, then it would seem unfair for Him to spare other wicked cities after condemning Sodom. And it would bother us that we couldn't count on God to be more predictable. However, the rest of Scripture suggests that God does not care if we think He is fair or not. In fact, He rather disdains our concept of fairness as being a form of self-centeredness in disguise. And it is hopeless to want Him to be predictable.

God's purpose in the biblical record was not to set precedents for future judgment, like our concept of common Law and judicial precedent. His purpose with Sodom, as it was with all the other events in Genesis, was to communicate, to reveal. But if we think that the purpose of Sodom's destruction was to reveal to us how He intended to destroy evil, then we are wrong. Certainly the destruction of Sodom does reveal how God *feels* about certain kinds of evil, though He had made the same point more dramatically with the Flood. Still, we might think, it had been a long time since the Flood; perhaps people were forgetting the wrath of God and were getting morally lax and needed a little reminder of how angry God could get? The opposite is the case. The primary point that the destruction of Sodom was to communicate would come later when even Israel was pronounced to be like Sodom, namely that we are all in the same condition as Sodom. Sodom is a picture of what the world looks like to God. It was the same crowd demanding the crucifixion of the Messiah, metaphorically, as the crowd demanding the angels be given to them. According to the Messiah, Capernaum in His own day was in worse shape than Sodom had been. From God's viewpoint, the destruction carried out against Sodom could be carried out against us, and carried out justly and "fairly".

That He did not repeat the fire and brimstone treatment for evil shows that this is not His general plan for destroying evil. As usual, God's revelatory deeds were incomplete and intended for more elaboration in the future. The treatment of Sodom was a dramatic demonstration to show how He felt about certain kinds of evil, but the lack of other such dramatic demonstrations shows us equally that He has other and better

227

plans for dealing with wickedness in general. Sodom is frequently used as a metaphor for hell, with the fire and brimstone and sudden torment; but if Sodom is a metaphor for hell, then it would indicate that hell has no part in God's long-term plans. It was a one-time response to evil, a response whose purpose was completely fulfilled in that one occurrence, and which God never intended to repeat on a regular basis, if ever.

Then why was Sodom so singled out? Or have there been other disasters through history that were similar judgments from God? Tsunamis, earthquakes, Knossos, Sri Lanka? I think Sodom was singled out because of its proximity to the chosen bearer of the revelation, the bearer of the Covenant. God had plotted it out: that Lot settled in Sodom which established a connection between Abraham and Sodom which made Abraham break his non-political-involvement policy to rescue Sodom and Lot, and which set the stage for the intercession for Sodom. God could have used many other cities, but Sodom was handy. The real purpose in the destruction of Sodom was Abraham's intercession and what it revealed.

Other disasters through history were simply not God's judging evil; they were just disasters that came about through the course of cause and effect, with no particular punishment in view. This is not to say that God did not work out His purposes in those disasters; of course He did. I am just saying that God did not plan those disasters—volcanoes, earthquakes, or tsunamis—as punishments. Punishing wickedness is not what He is about in the world; revealing Himself is what He is about. The destruction of cities like Knossos, though they may have been deserved from a certain viewpoint, did not convey revelation, and they did not receive the intercession from God's people. Therefore those disasters were not part of God's purpose in that same way.

In the end, Abraham's intercession for Sodom was unsuccessful in that it did not result in the sparing of the city. But from God's viewpoint, Abraham's intercession for Sodom accomplished its primary purposes: God revealed to us all something of how He thinks about the role of good and evil in the world, and we children of Abraham learned that we can intercede before God, that we can intercede in a rather daring way, and not be either guilty or ignored, that we can speak and be heard by God. For though Sodom was destroyed in the end, God very clearly and deliberately agreed to all of Abraham's requests. And even though Sodom was not saved by his intercession, the real object of Abraham's concern, his nephew, was rescued. God knew Abraham's real concern even though he did not verbalize it explicitly, and answered his heart's desire very specifically. This example of intercession was intended to encourage all of us who share the faith of Abraham to think along certain lines about intercession. Considering how God reacted to his requests, what more could we dare to ask? Considering how God reacted to his requests, why do we ask for so little?

The main reason He listened to Abraham and listens to, even solicits, our opinions, is that He was serious when He made the Covenant. The Covenant relationship to God is not a pretense at relationship; it is the real thing. He knew when He made the Covenant what kind of family He was committing Himself to; and He was not like the husband-with-the-hidden-agenda who waits until after the wedding and then springs a whole list of requirements on his unsuspecting wife. He had committed Himself to Abraham and it was Abraham with whom He shared His secrets and to whom He listened. That is what covenants are all about. This dialogue between Abraham and God about Sodom is absolutely unparalleled in ancient literature. It puts all the ancient myths to shame.

Abraham's argument with God is interesting for its reasoning, and a lot of revelation is hidden in the way God reacted to the logic of Abraham's argument. He argued with God on the basis of God's justice and character. This was the first time Abraham had given any sign that he was beginning to catch on to God's global authority. Unlike other deities of Mesopotamia, which were imagined as having local or specialized authority only, Abraham was now arguing with God on the basis of God's global authority. 18:25 says, "Far be it from Thee to do such a thing, to slay the righteous with the wicked, so that the righteous and the wicked are treated alike. Far be it from Thee! Shall not the Judge of all the earth deal justly?" This deeper understanding of God's character must have grown out of Abraham reflecting on his experiences, his experience with the pharaoh, his experience with Melchizedek, his experience with Abimelech, his experience with simply waiting for God to act, as well as reflection on the oral tradition that we now have in the first few chapters of Genesis. Nonetheless, this was a major spiritual breakthrough. Not many of us would have gotten so far on so little. It is this understanding of God as the Judge of the world, as the just Judge of the world, that God was trying to elicit from Abraham by sharing His intentions toward Sodom.

God revealed to Abraham His character and His power, not by declaring it directly, but by bringing it out from the inside of Abraham.

So much of our understanding, of God or of anything else, is only there in a ghostlike sense (a Holy Ghostlike sense, if you will) until we say it out loud and make it incarnate, as it were, in our words. Many times I discover what I am thinking by listening to myself speak; it truly is out of the abundance of the heart that the mouth speaks. Abraham discovered in his intercession that he understood some things about God that perhaps he had not fully realized he understood until that moment. A really good teacher is always looking for ways to elicit the truth from the student without providing it for him, to get him to discover the truth on his own without simply giving it to him. In this way the student comes to understand the truth far more deeply and internally than he would otherwise have done. God is a very good teacher. He begets the truth in us. He knows us and we bring forth the fruit of revelation, which is truth, and then we realize that we know Him in a new way.

In considering Abraham's intercession for Sodom it is important to notice how powerful grace is. God was willing to spare a whole city of wicked people for the sake of ten whom He accepted. Even when the ten were not found, He nonetheless rescued the one Abraham was primarily concerned for, even compelling that one to be saved against his will. God would also have spared the family of that one man, his daughters and even his betrothed sons-in-law (who were, after all, men of Sodom), for Abraham's sake. Just as Ishmael was blessed because Abraham was his father, 19:29 says, "Thus it came about, when God destroyed the cities of the valley, that God remembered Abraham, and sent Lot out of the midst of the overthrow, when He overthrew the cities in which Lot lived." So Lot was spared because of Abraham's love for him.

It is worth speculating on whether Abraham could have bargained God down to one righteous person rather than ten. And if he had argued God down to one person out of the whole city, would the city then have been spared? These are speculative questions and so they are questions that can't be answered with authority. However they are also, like most speculative questions, diagnostic. The answers you are inclined to give to these questions can show you how well you understand God's character and will and grace. As an example, so that you can hone your diagnostic skills on me, I will give you my answers. To me it seems clear that God would have spared the whole city for the sake of one righteous man, but that there would have been no righteous man found there, and the end of the story would have been the same as it was. This is not to find fault with Lot. As men go, Lot was a good one, and clearly shared his uncle's spiritual discernment. He was, after all, an heir along with Abraham of the oral tradition of revelation dating back to the beginning; he had all the advantages of background and upbringing that Abraham had. But there is no one who is righteous enough to save even himself, much less anyone else.

Abraham's intercession was misguided in that it was optimistic. He thought when God accepted ten righteous men as sufficient to spare the city that surely God could find that many. On the other hand, Abraham's intercession was misguided in that it was pessimistic. He stopped at ten not only because he thought that would get him what he wanted, but also because he was not sure he could push God further. How many of us would spare a whole city of Nazis in order to spare Mother Teresa? Human nature is more concerned with making sure the bad guys get punished than making sure the good guys get rescued. Abraham was too optimistic about the goodness of people and too pessimistic about the goodness of God, as are we all.

It is striking how God's approach to His enemies is different from man's approach. God was willing to let hundreds, perhaps thousands, of wicked men walk around free just in order to spare ten who were innocent. But that was not the attitude of American leaders toward the bombing of Iraq, for example. None of our leaders seriously doubted that innocent Iraqi's would be killed in any bombing, simply due to the nature of the weapons involved; and there was no doubt that the "collateral damage" would be more than ten. Yet did we ever consider letting the wicked in Iraq simply go free for the sake of the innocent? Clearly either the argument about justice would not weigh heavily with our leaders (or with most American citizens) or else we are using a different meaning for the word "justice" than the Scripture does. For us, justice is largely a negative term meaning that the wicked get what is coming to them; but to God justice is something positive: that the innocent are not harmed, that the helpless are rescued from the ruthless. For the sake of delivering the Iraqi people from a brutal dictator who had killed thousands of innocent Iraqis we were willing to step into his place and kill those thousands ourselves. Men fight evil by becoming the evil they fight; it is the way of the world.

iii) The Angels in Sodom (Genesis 19:1-16)

God does so many strange things that we are accustomed to not even noticing how strange they are. The other two "men", the two angels, went on down to visit Sodom in person. The question about the visit to Sodom is: why did it happen at all? God did not need to enter the city in person to find out what was going on, nor did he need to send spies.

One purpose in His going was to show mercy toward Abraham and Lot. By going in person He included Abraham and Lot in the events in a direct manner. It was the Divine Condescension to go in the form of the men, but it was more than condescension; it was a careful attempt to include Abraham in the process. To repeat the point, it is the first and great privilege of being in the Covenant: we are participants in God's work.

There is also something prophetic and allegorical about the angels walking into Sodom. He visited Sodom because that is the kind of God He is, because this is what He is doing all the time in one way or another. When He judges the world, He does not stand outside of it and pronounce His verdict; He stands up from within the world, and judges by what He has Himself seen and felt as one of us. This is prefiguring the Incarnation, of course. Verse 18:21 reads, "I will go down now, and see if they have done entirely according to its outcry, which has come to Me; and if not, I will know." The omniscience of God does not mean merely that He knows all about everything; the omniscience of God is that He knows everything *from the inside*, as a participant. The omniscience of God is the full participation of God in all events, the suffering of all events, the taking of all events and all things into Himself. And whenever God brings judgment on any people or place, it is the judgment of One who has sat down among that people and lived with them. Judgment always comes from the inside.

Verse 19:4 says that all the men of the city had come to Lot's home to molest the strangers. That Lot had once been a stranger and had been allowed to settle there without being molested shows that the men of Sodom were selective in whom they attacked. What was their criterion for choosing whom to abuse and whom to tolerate? Lot had come as a man of substance, a very rich man in fact, and so to tolerate him was the same as sharing in his wealth. But these strangers had just walked in with nothing to speak of in wealth or property, so they were fair game. (Do angels ever appear as rich men, I wonder?) As usual, the poor are the ones who are helpless, the ones who are easy marks.

It is not really clear in this passage what great evil the men of Sodom did to bring about its destruction. They did convene and threaten to rape the angels; that is bad, of course, but it is not likely that they stood out in the ancient world as unusually willing to rape others. Nor was God inspired to wrath by homosexuality, as some have taught. Indeed the evil of Sodom could not have been homosexuality for at least three reasons.

First, the outcry against the city was not the outcry of moral indignation. The outcry against Sodom was the outcry of victims—people who have actually and personally suffered, not people who are merely offended. Those who imagine that homosexuality was the principle wickedness of Sodom against which there was an outcry are transferring conservative American sexual standards back onto the ancient peoples of the Middle East. All the evidence suggests that those people were less shocked at nearly anything than we would be. In the ancient Middle East same sex relationships seem to have been acceptable in many places. Second, if these people were punished for being homosexuals then we are forced to conclude that Sodom (and the other three cities) was composed *entirely* of homosexuals since everyone in the cities was destroyed; this is also very unlikely. If the totality of the cities were homosexual, who was crying out against them? Third, if they had been homosexuals, in the modern sense of having a same-sex orientation, then it would have made no sense for Lot to offer them his daughters.

On the contrary, the men of Sodom were "ordinary" men who had learned to take pleasure in abusing all defenseless people for whatever gratification they could get, sexual or otherwise. They were truly perverted, not as defined by the specific acts they craved, but in their indiscriminate willingness to violate anyone who didn't run away fast enough. They were men who were willing to use anyone, male or female, young or old, for whatever pleasure they could get. This is a very different thing from homosexuality per se. But even such sexual perversion was only the visible tip of the iceberg of evil that was the ultimate cause of Sodom's destruction.

In Ezekiel 16:49,50 we read, "Behold, this was the guilt of your sister Sodom: she and her daughters had arrogance, abundant food, and careless ease, but she did not help the poor and needy. Thus they were haughty and committed abominations before Me. Therefore I removed them when I saw it." Sodom was an example of the sort of violence that had become so common before the Flood, the rich and the powerful using up the weak and showing no mercy. It is the lack of compassion for the poor that leads directly to all the other abominations God finds so appalling. The root of Sodom's form of sexual perversion was a culture that had learned to let people starve before their very eyes, to let some people decay in poverty while others spent their days in comfort and pleasure, and to enjoy their suffering. Once a culture is able to view even one person as less than human, and is willing to let him be abased in hunger and poverty, the door is open to every other kind of abuse.

Where were the poor and the needy of Sodom during its destruction? Those people would have long known the danger of staying in that city where no stranger could even rest in the square at night without risk of his life. This is not like the dangers of, say, Central Park in New York City; Central Park is a large and private area, easy to hide in, where it is natural that criminals would assemble in the dark to be unobserved. The square of this city was public, in the center of things, impossible to hide in. All the crimes committed in Sodom were publicly approved. No poor would have stayed in Sodom; they would not have lasted long. The poor of Sodom would have long since fled out to the countryside or died or been debased and enslaved to the point of joining with their abusers. The outcry against Sodom was the outcry of those who had been raped and starved and abused and tortured, the victims who had died or fled. None of the victims of Sodom were left in the city. It was a city in wait for other victims to venture by, a Venus Fly-trap for people, something only modern horror films imagine.

Further, though it had been only a dozen or so years since Abraham had rescued the people of Sodom from being taken as slaves to Elam, and though they knew they owed their rescue to Lot's connection with Abraham, yet they forgot how much in Lot's debt they were. They had no sense of morals, no sense of justice, no sense of obligation to do good to anyone, even to someone who had saved them from slavery; they were simply ruthless in using people to gratify or enrich themselves. The angels struck the men of Sodom with blindness, but it must have been more than simple blindness. They seem to have experienced serious disorientation beyond the inability to see; they weren't able even to think, they weren't able to see with their minds, and so they could not find the door. The confusion of being in a crowd would have added to their disorientation, but their mental disorientation was emblematic of their total spiritual disorientation.

It should not be missed here that evil and the punishment of evil behaves in a covenantal way, just as grace does. It was the men of the city who came to molest the strangers but it would seem clear that their wives and their children were destroyed in the overthrow. If the oppression of the poor was the basic sin of Sodom, then the families of the oppressors would inevitably have been implicated in that oppression. But whether they were implicated in it or not, things work in a covenantal way, good and evil, and this is only another of many examples from Scripture. No one receives grace for himself alone; everyone around him is touched by it. Similarly, no one sins for himself alone; everyone around him is contaminated and suffers with him.

In 19:12 the angels mentioned a son-in-law and also sons in the plural as possible relatives that Lot might want to bring out with him. It is not clear what sons the angels were talking about since no son of Lot is mentioned anywhere else in Scripture. His two daughters were engaged to be married, but their fiancés thought Lot was joking or drunk. In any case, the sons-in-law seem to have left the house after the incident with the mob because the next morning only the daughters were there to be forced out of the city. Did the sons-in-law see their fathers in the mob and go out to help them home, or hide in case their fathers found them? Whatever sons Lot had, they must also have left his household before the morning.

Lot found it impossible to act on the angels' warning. It was not through lack of faith that he hesitated. Rather, his hesitation stemmed from being rich and having to leave his wealth behind. It is clear from later events that he lost everything in the destruction; he did not have enough left to set himself up in another city. Most likely his acceptance in Sodom had been based on his wealth all along, and without it he knew all too well what fate awaited him: rape, abuse, the most abased form of slavery. The angels agreed to spare Zoar only because Lot told them he was fleeing there. Zoar must have shared the general evil character of those cities, and so the angels spared that little city for the sake of one man who was not all that righteous and didn't go there anyway. After the destruction of Sodom Lot was afraid to stay at Zoar, and doubtless because of his poverty and of the character of the people in the city. What Lot was afraid of in Zoar is what God destroyed in Sodom, Gomorrah, Admah, and Zeboiim. It is interesting that the four cities that were destroyed were four of the five cities that Abraham rescued from the Elamites, and Zoar was another name for Bela, the fifth of the cities that had rebelled against Chedorlaomer.

Lot's character needs some comment. Mention has already been made of his sharing in Abraham's spiritual discernment. His recognition of the angels is all the more impressive considering that he had no history of receiving revelations from God nor of seeing angels. Though he apparently recognized the angels as messengers of God, there may be another explanation of his hospitality to the strangers. It could be that he was in the habit of going out into the public square and inviting in any strangers just because he knew the character of the people in the city. He could not single handedly stop the men of Sodom from assaulting strangers (one wonders how he ever came to choose to live there?), but he could protect those likely to be assaulted by getting them out of harm's way. When the mob said about Lot, "This one came in as an alien, and already he is acting like a judge; now we will treat you worse than them" it suggests that there was already some history of Lot preventing their abuse of visitors, that they had notice his interference. Perhaps it had happened once too often and now the city was determined to put a stop to it. It is another possible indication of his character that Lot's daughters were still virgins though betrothed, presumably, to men of the city. The moral state of the city was not such as to encourage chastity in any form; and as later events show, his daughters did not have particularly moral instincts.

On the other hand, Lot offered his daughters to the mob as a substitute for the strangers. It is impossible to see this as a righteous offer of a righteous man, even allowing for the savagery of an ancient culture that did not treat women as fully human. This was not a father who loved his daughters in any sense I can understand. It is just possible that his daughters never knew of this offer, and it is possible, if we are inclined to give him the benefit of the doubt, that it was part of a ruse to somehow divert the mob or buy him time. It is just possible that he had no intention of making good on his offer.

The New Testament does record Lot as being a righteous man, but it would be a mistake to take this as an endorsement of every thing he did. It would be a mistake to take this as an endorsement of any thing he did. Lot was a righteous man as you and I are righteous men or women: because God has made us so. But on the weight of this one event, if Abraham had argued God into sparing the city for the sake of one righteous man, the city would still have been destroyed. To be counted as righteous, to be pronounced righteous by the Judge of all the earth, is a different thing from being the kind of righteous man who can save others by his righteousness.

Parenthesis: The Intercession for Saddam

A modern retelling of Genesis 18 and 19 inspired by the chance similarity of "Sodom" and "Saddam"

Now it came about in those days that the Lord appeared to the President. And they were standing together before the house of the President and they were looking to the east. And the President said to himself, "Shall I hide from the Lord what I am about to do? For He has chosen me, and I am surely the leader of the greatest nation in the world and all the nations of the world will be blessed through me."

And the President said to the Lord, "Behold, I am seeking for Saddam, for the outcry against him has been great and when I get him I will know what to do with him." And the messengers of the President went out to seek the man Saddam, but the Lord remained before the President.

And the Lord drew near to the President and said to him, "Will you indeed sweep away the righteous with the wicked? Suppose there are ten innocent people in the city of Saddam. Will you indeed sweep it away and not spare the place for the sake of the ten innocent who will be collateral damage? Far be it from you to do such a thing, to slay the righteous with the wicked, so that the innocent and the wicked are treated alike. Shall not the judge of the earth deal justly?"

And the President said, "No, but I will destroy the city, even if there are ten innocent victims."

So the Lord said, "Behold, I have ventured to speak with the President. What if there are five additional casualties who are innocent."

And the President replied, "I will not spare it for the five and the ten."

And the Lord spoke to him yet again, "What if there are twenty who are innocent that are killed?"

And the President replied, "Though there may be twenty civilian casualties, be they men, women, or children, I will not spare the city."

Then the Lord said, "Oh, may the leader of the free world not be angry. What if there are thirty civilians who are killed?"

And the President said, "I will not spare the city for thirty."

And the Lord said, "Now behold, I have ventured to speak again. Suppose forty are killed there?"

"No, not for forty will I spare the city."

And yet again the Lord said, "Oh, let not the President be angry and I will speak this one more time. What if there are fifty or more who will be collateral damage? Will you spare the city for this many?"

The President replied, "No, not for fifty. And not for more. This man must be punished regardless of the price I have to pay."

And the President departed from the Lord to do what he would do, and the Lord departed to do what He would do. And behold, the fire of the President was rained down upon the city for many days and many nights. But it came to pass that before the destruction came upon the city the man Saddam had gone out from the city, with his wife and children, and he had gone to a little town. But he was afraid to stay in even a little town so he hid himself in a cave and dwelt there. And so it came to pass, when the innocent died, that the man Saddam was not harmed.

And behold, it came about that when Saddam was leaving the city through one gate, the Lord was coming into the city through another gate. And He spent the night in the city square (for there was not a lot who would give Him shelter) and He dwelt there while the fire of the President came upon the city. For He did this that the word of the Lord through the Prophet might be fulfilled, "Whatsoever you do to one of the least of these, you do it to Me."

iv) Lot and His Daughters (Genesis 19:15-38)

The destruction of Sodom is described most like a meteor shower, though others take it as a lightning storm and earthquake. The occurrence of such a meteor shower is unparalleled in recorded history, but it is not intrinsically impossible; very unlikely, unbelievable as a coincidence, but of course it is not represented as being coincidental. To those of us who are orthodox Christians, the visitors to Abraham, and possibly to Lot, included the Messiah Himself, and it was He who sent the destruction on Sodom. But was the destruction of the cities of the plain a "Christ-like" act? How can we imagine Jesus raining fire on all those people, particularly when we recall that He rebuked some of His disciples for suggesting just such a fate for a Samaritan village (see Luke 9:51-56)? Even if we do not interpret the angels as being a pre-incarnation appearance of Jesus, isn't this an inconsistency in the behavior of God, destroying one group of people with fire at one time and renouncing such an act at another time, the usual contradiction between the Old and New Testaments?

For me, there is no inconsistency between this passage and the New Testament. There is nothing that is intrinsically un-Christ-like, anymore than the Flood was un-Christ-like. If one assumes, as I do, that God comes into the world to save men's lives and not to destroy them, the angels seem to me to be working on that same agenda. The destruction of Sodom was done, not to punish the wicked but to prevent future victims, which is what I also believe the Flood was doing. The wonder is that God in His compassion does not destroy more of the world. And so we don't notice how we blame God both for punishing evil (if we aren't its victim) and for not punishing evil (if we are its victim). Either way, we accuse God of the wrong doing. It is just a convenient dodge, making the God of the Old Testament a bad God and the God of the New Testament a good one. That way we don't have to face the real problem of evil in ourselves: how is God to be merciful to us and simultaneously stop us from doing such wreckage in the lives of the people around us? When we think about the destruction of Sodom, it is all too easy and convenient to forget the point: we are Sodom.

In another sense the destruction was also the deliverance of the people of Sodom from continuing lives of relentless evil, a mercy killing if you will, the very thing advocates for physician assisted suicide want. However, I will add several points by way of softening what God chose to do there.

I do not see the destruction of Sodom as an eternal destruction, as if the rain of fire were a tongue of hell reaching up to the everyday world to carry them all into their eternal state. The people of Sodom yet have a role to play in testifying to God's mercy and righteousness and justice, as the Messiah would later indicate.

The destruction of Sodom was accomplished in such a dramatic and violent way, I think, to have it serve as a revelation, a testimony to the world that the promise to never again destroy the earth in a Flood did not mean God would stand by idly and watch the powerful abuse the weak. To a violent man, violence is the language he speaks, violence is the only warning he can heed. Sodom would have been a warning to the surrounding nations not to follow in their paths. Later in the Psalms and Proverbs, when God portrayed Himself as the Defender of the orphan and the widow, the destruction of Sodom is part of what He meant. Woe to you who grind the poor into the dirt, for God Himself is your enemy. If anything can move Him to violence it is the strong oppressing the weak.

That Lot's wife looked back at the destruction of Sodom and turned into a pillar of salt could be understood in several ways. It was not simply punishment for looking back and disobeying the angels' command; she had never been warned about disobeying angels. It is possible that she looked back just out of that common human curiosity that wants to see the calamities of others, to stop by the car crash or by the fire trucks or by the ambulance hoping to see something. To take pleasure in, or even a lively interest in watching the pain of others is not Godlike. God takes no pleasure in people's pain; pain is outside of His desire, and outside of His ultimate intent. The tabloids, the news reporters who hound the people who have experienced some great grief, these are emissaries of the serpent. Or possibly she looked back because she missed the city, she missed her status as the wife of a rich man, she missed her possessions. Perhaps she was longing for what was gone, grieving for Sodom and the life she had there, and because she was longing for the things reserved for destruction she joined them. The Bible never even mentions her name. Was she from a well-to-do family in Ur or in Haran? It is hard for the rich to lose what they have, even when an angel from heaven stands beside them beckoning.

It is easy to forget that three other cities were destroyed along with Sodom: Gomorrah, Admah, and Zeboim. It seems that Zoar was also scheduled for demolition but was spared for Lot's sake (even though Lot did not actually go to Zoar—it would seem that God spared Zoar for nothing). There is no record that angels visited those cities, or what would have happened to them if Abram had succeeded in persuading God to spare Sodom. There is a lot to this story that we are not told, but the way the story is told tells us that it is not telling us everything. We should be careful, of course, when we interpret a passage or when we speculate about a passage, that we keep clearly in mind exactly what we don't know.

The origin of the Moabite and Ammonite peoples was ignominious, the result of drink and incest. It was natural, it was easy for Lot, who had lost everything he owned and his wife and was living in a cave with no prospects, to escape into drunkenness. In his raving, maybe in despair, perhaps Lot had proclaimed loudly that he had would never again leave that cave. His daughters had given up any hope of resuming a normal life again. They had been transformed from princesses into savages, from society girls with good prospects to outcasts with no prospects. Naturally they dealt with their situation by making the worst possible choices, but to make their father drunk and try to get pregnant seems outrageous even by modern standards. Moab means literally "seed from our father". It would be fair to say that the daughters felt no sense of shame in their incest, no impulse to hide their deed from their own father, even if that had been possible. Ben-ammi means "son of my people", carrying the same idea. Abraham had no trouble learning the truth and preserving it in the oral tradition.

And so began the Moabite and the Ammonite people. Neither the Moabites nor the Ammonites exist today, and they were presumably all the posterity that Lot left. Their origin would make them easy to despise by those who imagine they have a nobler family tree, but a Moabite woman would later be chosen as part of the line leading to the Messiah, and one of the few women mentioned by name in His genealogy. In this way God took into Himself the family of Lot, perhaps as one last gift to Abraham who had spent so much love on his nephew. Lot was a man who seemingly gave up on life at this point, but why didn't he seek help from his uncle Abraham? Considering Abraham's character and devotion to Lot, it seems likely that Abraham did eventually seek out Lot and aid him, if Lot didn't die from horror and despair. There is no evidence in the Scripture about Abraham's charity to Lot except that the story of Lot was included in the tradition Abraham passed on to Isaac.

b) Isaac vs. Ishmael (Genesis 21:1-21)

If Abraham was born in 2159 b.c. then Isaac was born in about 2059 b.c., around the time Metuhotep II founded the Middle Kingdom of Egypt and when Shulgi the king of Ur was at the height of his glory. Ishmael would have been about fourteen years old. Children were weaned much older than in our culture, so Ishmael would have been in his later teens at the party thrown by Abraham for Isaac's first coming of age. It should be noted that 21:9 need not be translated as saying that Ishmael was mocking Isaac; it could be translated in a more neutral way as saying that Ishmael was playing with him, joking around with him. However, there was not much chance of a good relationship between Isaac and Ishmael. Besides the age difference, there was, of course, the on-going conflict and tension between Hagar and Sarah. Sarah was more than the typical defensive mother, and insisted that Hagar and Ishmael be driven away.

Sarah's insistence that Hagar and Ishmael be driven away had less excuse than the first time and would have been scandalous. There was no reason for it this time, no cheekiness from Hagar; it was just Sarah's need to have no competition, no comparisons. Abraham, who was genuinely attached to Ishmael, was upset as well. Nonetheless, at God's specific intervention, Abraham sent them away. It is remarkable that God intervened at this point, and to all appearances on the side of injustice. The over-riding issue with God was the continuation of the Covenant and the integrity of its revelatory role, which required that Ishmael be excluded from it. We can plead in God's defense that He had no intention of abandoning Hagar and Ishmael, but that would not have been apparent to the witnesses to the event. What would people have said when they heard that Abraham sent Hagar and Ishmael away? Would it have sounded lame to them if Abraham had told them that God made him do it? The devil perhaps, but God? Nor would it have helped if he could have explained that future generations needed to have an allegorical demonstration of certain truths. Still, God was consistently careless of His reputation in Abraham's household and in the neighborhood.

Hagar again headed toward Egypt, probably more or less along the same route she had followed nearly twenty years before. She and Ishmael arrived in the wilderness of Beersheba, twenty or thirty miles south of the oaks of Mamre. In the wilderness they ran out of provisions, particularly water, and became lost; she had not traveled as far as she had the first time she fled. Since Ishmael was basically an adult by this time, it is not clear why their journey was so much harder; perhaps there was an additional affliction such as an illness, or perhaps it happened to be one of the occasional dry years so that they could not find water once their supply ran out.

I have said this before but it is worth repeating: excluding Ishmael from the Covenant was not the same as excluding Ishmael from God's grace and favor. The passage makes it clear that God was committed to Ishmael. Being excluded from the Covenant meant that Ishmael and his descendants would not be part of the stream of revelation from God, and this is clearly historically the case. Nonetheless, they were still descendants of Abraham, still heirs of the revelation that had been handed down to Abraham to that point, and under the blessing and favor of God. So God rescued Ishmael, carrying out the promise He had made to Hagar when He gave her the name for her son, and the promise He had made to Abraham when He gave him his new name. Ishmael went to live in the wilderness of Paran, probably the central part of the Sinai. Naturally Hagar went to Egypt, her native land, to find a wife for her son. And God blessed him, and he prospered and he became a great nation even into the present day.

c) New Conflict with Abimelech (Genesis 21:22-34)

Over the next decade after Isaac's birth it appears that Abraham moved back and forth between the oaks of Mamre and the neighborhood of Gerar. Though he was already rich, he became much richer, alarmingly rich. For more than twenty years Abraham had been a formidable force in the land of Canaan, even before he defeated the Elamites. He had shown no inclination to go out empire building, but his neighbors were naturally nervous. A peaceful man can turn warlike for no obvious reason; it is always scary to live near a powerful person. After the birth of Isaac, the prosperity of Abraham became such that it was politically desirable either to come to secure terms with him or destroy him. Abimelech, if this was the same one as Abraham had previously deceived regarding Sarah, would vividly remember his vision of God's favor toward Abraham. Perhaps he wasn't sure he would be able to take Abraham; perhaps he was too wise to oppose the man who was in God's favor. It was better to be diplomatic.

When Abimelech proposed to Abraham that they bind themselves to each other by a covenant, it was entirely to his advantage rather than Abraham's. It was exactly the kind of agreement that would later be forbidden when Israel invaded the Promised Land under Joshua's leadership, but at this point in time God had no objection. It did not occur to Abraham to inquire of God whether such a covenant was advisable; there had never been any indication that it might not be. This was a lesser form of the covenant structure than a peace treaty or a marriage. When Abraham's descendants did invade the Promised Land, Gerar was never mentioned. It had faded from importance, almost faded from existence, just through the process of history.

Making the covenant with Abimelech heartened Abraham enough to bring up a sore point between his servants and Abimelech's servants. Assertiveness was not one of Abraham's traits, but this time he defended his own interests. If Abimelech had not approached him concerning the covenant, would he have ever brought up his complaint to Abimelech? It is doubtful. Even asserting his rights to the well, he still offered seven ewes as a payment for it. "Beersheba" in Hebrew means "seven well" and refers to the seven ewes and the covenant made between Abraham and this king. That the covenant between Abimelech and Abraham was made at Beersheba suggests that Abraham had included the area of Beersheba in the cycle of his wanderings, making a large circle from Mamre to Gerar to Beersheba and back again. If so, it is natural to suspect that he went toward Beersheba to learn something of Ishmael's welfare, perhaps even to see him, but there is no indication that they ever saw one another again.

d) The Sacrifice of Isaac (Genesis 22:1-19)

The narrative now skips another decade or so. Abraham has settled down in the quiet life of a rich man enjoying his new son. It is about 2045 b.c. In the outside world, Shulgi the great king in Ur is dying and Ur is about to begin its long decline; and the Middle Kingdom in Egypt is on its way to a new pinnacle of glory. Isaac is a teenager. Abraham is at peace and the events of the rest of the world are of no concern to him. He is rich and powerful, secure and content. Now is the time for another visit from God Most High, and this time one that is utterly devastating.

The sacrifice of Isaac is nearly the last recorded episode of Abraham's life. It was the last step, the last time God pushed Abraham to the limit of what he could believe. We outside observers may be incredulous that Abraham could actually believe God required a human sacrifice, but we have the advantage of knowing that God would condemn human sacrifice in very strong terms later on. And this was not the first time Abraham had been asked to sacrifice a son. When he gave the bread and water to Hagar and Ishmael, it was like sacrificing them. He knew the dangers of wandering in that land, and the fact that they nearly died shows he was not worried for nothing. Except for God's promise to bless them, he was sending them to probable death. Obviously, though, the sacrifice of Isaac raised the emotional stakes greatly. Except for God's promise to bless him, Abraham was *taking*, not *sending*, Isaac to his death.

The seventh appearance of God to Abraham, after one of God's typical decades of silence, was very different from the previous ones. No renewed promises, no comforting reassurances of the glory of the future that awaited his descendants; just a demand of the most astonishing, confusing, horrifying nature. Abraham still did not know a great deal about God's character. It was obviously not totally unthinkable to Abraham that God might require just such a human sacrifice. Some of the other gods required such sacrifices and Yahweh had never indicated to Abraham what He might want. God was being as hard on Abraham as He could have been, and He even emphasized His own hardness when He reminded Abraham how much he loved Isaac, "Take now your son, your only son, whom you love, Isaac . . ." It isn't a sacrifice unless we love what we are giving; only what is of value should ever be brought to God, and God shows no hesitation in asking for what is best and most valued.

Mount Moriah was about fifty miles to the north of Beersheba (which is indicated in 22:19 as his current residence—he moved his herds around in that area for new pasture but he was still based at Hebron) and so the three days' journey it took them would be what we would expect. Mount Moriah was associated with Salem and therefore with Melchizedek, though there is no mention of Melchizedek here. Isaac must have been old enough to carry the wood, probably a teenager. If so then Melchizedek had come out to meet Abraham returning from his victory about thirty years previously. It is just possible that Melchizedek was still alive. Further, it is natural to assume that Mount Moriah was the same as the Mount Moriah on which Solomon would later build the temple (II Chronicles 3:1). This links the sacrifice of Isaac deliberately to the burnt offerings that would be instituted under Moses and to all of the symbolism in the sacrificial system;

but it also makes Melchizedek and Salem seem rather phantom like, so very near the place of sacrifice and yet making no appearance. Indeed this whole episode is dark and full of phantoms and clouds, like the mount of transfiguration. Mountains are always dark places for mortals to visit as they get closer to God with no protection or preparation.

Isaac is a type of Christ here, and the sacrifice of Isaac is a type of the sacrifice of Christ. First, Isaac is a type of Christ in his birth; his birth was not a virgin birth, but it was like one. Isaac's birth *seemed* humanly impossible. Abraham knew that it would *almost* take a miracle for him to have a son with Sarah. God intervened and enabled the conception to happen, though in Sarah's case the conception was within the natural possibilities and just needed a bit of encouragement. This was the first of a long series of *almost* miraculous births of sons to old childless couples, a repeated symbolic chorus of promise and miracle pointing to the culmination when He would intervene with Mary in a conception that contravened nature entirely.

Second, the sacrifice of Isaac began the metaphor of the sacrifice of the first-born son. It would be repeated with variations at the Passover, when the first born of every family in Israel would be spared. The theme was only waiting for the completion, the final One to fulfill the image, another Only Son sacrificed by His Father. The sacrifice of Isaac was an allegory for the sacrifice of the Messiah. The role of the ram as the substitute sacrifice was as vivid as possible, and perfectly in line with later sacrifices. The ram was a substitute for Isaac, just as the later animal sacrifices in the Law would be a substitute for the Messiah. The symbols all tie together in the neatest possible way, as might be expected when God is the Poet.

Third, the sacrifice of Isaac was the first of many glimpses, glimpses that grow increasingly vivid as the revelation progresses, of the resurrection. If Abraham were thinking at all about the demand to sacrifice Isaac, some inkling of the resurrection would have had to cross his mind. At least, this seems to be what Paul was getting at in Romans 4:17. God had very specifically named Isaac as the heir, as the one who would continue the Covenant, as the one who would have descendants like the stars in the sky. And He had emphatically rejected the idea that any other descendant of Abraham would do.

God could fulfill His particular promises only if Isaac were alive, and therefore God must be either insane, or He had changed His mind about the promise and meant to do something different, or else He had the power to bring back the dead. The first possibility was incomprehensible. Only a modern skeptic would imagine an insane Creator of the universe. Granted, some ancient myths do portray the gods as playing with less than a full deck, but these were derivative gods, second or third generation gods. The power behind the cosmic order, while never a creator in the biblical sense, was the opposite of insane. Those "creators" were infinitely remote but they stood up against chaos, against insanity, and put things in order. The second possibility was conceivable, but since God had repeated the promise so many times, and had gone to such trouble to make the birth of Isaac as nearly miraculous as possible, it was highly unlikely. That left the third possibility, which was nearly, but not quite, as unlikely. This was, after all, God Most High, who had a taste for arranging impossible events and promising impossible things. This was the God who answered Sarah's laughter with "Is anything too hard for the Lord?"

Perhaps it is this passage the Messiah was thinking of later when He said that we must hate our own spouses and children as compared to Him. Could you kill your child at God's command even knowing, as we do now, how real the resurrection is? Belief in the resurrection changes all of our ideas about death and life, but it does not necessarily make it easier to make such choices. Death is no longer the ultimate disaster; life in this world is no longer the greatest possession to which we must cling. But the resurrection is a difficult hope to keep vividly before our imaginations. It is difficult to believe in it with more than a mere intellectual assent. To face death with a calm assurance of the resurrection is seldom required more than once of any of us who claim to believe it, but it is something that faces all of us sooner or later. Meanwhile to face *life* with a calm assurance of the resurrection is nearly as difficult, and to kill someone we love with faith in the resurrection would be as nearly impossible as a deed can be.

We have good reason to believe that God will not ask such a thing ever again. Today such a command from God to offer up our child as a burnt offering would not be believable for many reasons: there are too many specific passages expressing God's hatred of such sacrifices to think that He might want such a thing for Himself. The sacrifice of Isaac is one of those events that God arranged in the past that are, by their nature, unrepeatable. The progress of His revelation has rendered some formerly common ideas unbelievable, and other previously unbelievable ideas have been transformed into the standard fare of faith. We should understand that we do not and can not stand in the same place as Abraham; we are at a different place in the stream of revelation, and what God says to us now comes at this point in revelation, acknowledging all that has gone before. Abraham stood at such a different point in the revelation that he was capable of hearing very different things than we can hear, just as we are capable of hearing things that he could not have heard.

But if Jesus was indeed thinking of this passage when He said that we must hate our children and spouses and parents compared to Him, then Abraham's sacrifice of Isaac is an allegory of what we all must do on some level. To sacrifice someone we love is to put them into God's hands, to not cling to them for ourselves, but to watch them be taken from us, whether literally or metaphorically, and let them go. There are any number of ways such a sacrifice might be required of us, and it may not be much less difficult than Abraham's; sometimes a metaphorical deed is every bit as painful as a literal deed. An acquaintance of mine once remarked that he was not afraid of hell if it was only metaphorical, that metaphorical flames had no power to hurt. It seems to me now that such a view is silly. A wise person knows that the worst pain in life is exactly the one that fire is the best metaphor for. The pain that Abraham suffered in that long walk to Mt. Moriah with Isaac was a different kind of pain than the pain suffered by the men of Sodom, but it was just as severe, just as real. And so we see that both the evil and the good, both the excluded and the included, must suffer the pain of hell. The one suffers the pain for the destruction of evil, the other suffers the pain for the purification of good.

When Isaac asked his father where the lamb for the sacrifice was, Abraham's answer was a summation of all he believed and hoped about God: "God will provide for Himself the lamb for the burnt offering, my son." This one answer captures the point of everything that preceeded, though Abraham could not know how prophetic it would prove. Abraham's response to Isaac was not merely an evasion. Though it was certainly an evasion on one level, on another level it was the simplest and most essential truth. Even if Abraham had had to go through with the killing of Isaac, the sacrifice had certainly been provided by God. God had never before commanded such a thing as this sacrifice, but He had promised that Isaac would live to carry on the Covenant and somehow God would provide for that promise too. This is what Abraham's reply really meant, that God would provide some way to keep His word.

When, at the last possible moment, God stopped Abraham from actually killing Isaac and provided a ram for a substitute, the picture was complete. Consider carefully how the idea of a substitutionary death was portrayed in this allegory: the ram was the substitute for Isaac just as later under the Law the sacrificial animals at the Passover were substitutes for the first born of each family in Israel, and the animals sacrificed for the sin offerings were substitutes waiting for the Messiah, the Only Son of God. Thus the sacrifice of Jesus, the Messiah, the Son whom God loved, was the meaning of all the allegories, and the completion and end of all the sacrifices. We are accustomed to think of the Messiah as being the Substitute and that is true from a different metaphorical standpoint. The symbolism in this passage and in Law of Moses doesn't work that way though; the sacrifices offered from Abel all the way to the New Testament were substitutes for the Messiah, waiting until the He came. He substituted for us, they substituted for Him.

It is impossible to imagine what effect this sacrifice must have had on Isaac psychologically. You might think he would have been permanently scarred by the experience, but in fact it does not seem to have harmed him. On the contrary, he seems to have been quietly devoted to God much as Abraham was. Isaac was the only one of the patriarchs who was mentioned as walking in the fields to meditate (in chapter 24, just as Rebekkah was arriving). To be sure, the experience of being placed on the altar by his own father would have been horrifying, but he also experienced the direct intervention of God to rescue him. Isaac must have inherited some of Abraham's meekness. Although Isaac was a teenager by this time and Abraham was very old and slow, although there was no one else around, Isaac made no attempt to resist his father or to escape as his father tied him up and raised the knife. Just as Abraham chose to trust God and offer his son, Isaac chose to trust his father and God and offer himself. This is yet another way in which Isaac was a type of Christ.

The two servants had been left behind at the foot of the mountain because they might have tried to prevent Abraham from performing the sacrifice if they had been there. And why did he bring the servants along at all? Since he had no idea what was to be the outcome of the trip, I think he was preparing for the horrible climax that seemed unavoidable. I think Abraham knew he could not return home on his own, whether he carried Isaac back for burial or buried him there, physically or emotionally. He was going to need help.

The sacrifice of Isaac was a test of Abraham's faith, a test whose result God knew but which needed to be revealed and displayed for all to see.

In 22:15-18 we read, "Then the angel of the Lord called to Abraham a second time from heaven, and said, 'By Myself I have sworn, declares the Lord, because you have done this thing, and have not withheld your son, your only son, indeed I will greatly bless you, and I will greatly multiply your seed as the stars of the heavens, and as the sand which is on the seashore; and your seed shall possess the gate of their enemies. And in your seed all the nations of the earth shall be blessed, because you have obeyed My voice.' "Here God's promise to Abraham sounds conditional on his willing obedience in sacrificing Isaac, and some interpret this passage as proving that Abraham's relationship to God had always been conditional on his obedience. It is against human nature to accept a righteousness that is just counted to us; we want to earn it.

In fact the passage can't be interpreted to mean that Abraham's faith was counted to him because he obeyed the command to sacrifice Isaac. First, God had already made these same promises repeatedly over nearly thirty years. It is surely a strange view of God to understand these verses as meaning that God would have gone back on His former promise if Abraham failed him here, as if God had begun by being gracious to Abram but had reconsidered the terms and decided to be demanding and ungracious instead. Secondly, the words of the passage say no such thing. Abraham's astonishing willingness to trust God had made God all the more committed to fulfilling His promise to Abraham, and that is all His words actually say.

So what would have happened if Abraham had refused? I don't know. What I do know is that God is faithful even if we are all unfaithful (see Romans 3:4). Even among men, trying to add conditions to a promise that had been previously made unconditionally is considered dishonest. Disobedience cannot nullify a previous and unconditional promise. The promise was not founded on the power of a man nor on the obedience of a man, and therefore it could not be cancelled by the power of a man nor by the disobedience of a man. But obedience can enhance the promise; obedience, even reluctant obedience, can be rewarded by an expansion of the promise. There is no limit to how far God can increase His blessing to us in response to faith and obedience, no limit to how much further God might choose to extend His blessing beyond what He had already promised.

There is no limit to God's goodness, but there is a limit to His anger. His promises do not limit His generosity, but they do limit His wrath. It is sometimes suggested by well-intentioned preachers that there is a delicate balance in God, a delicate balance between His mercy on the one hand and His anger over sin on the other hand. Sometimes this is pictured as a balance that tips one way or the other based on how good or bad we are. Sometimes it is pictured as a balance inside of God, the Father leaning down on anger and the Son balancing Him out on the side of mercy. Either way this is a horrible misrepresentation of God's character. In truth there is no such balancing at all. His wrath is nothing in comparison to His mercy; there is no contest between the two. There is no limit, on the one hand, to His blessing and mercy and compassion and forgiveness, for they are part of His very heart; but He binds Himself with promises that limit His wrath because wrath has never been and never will be fundamental to His character. God is love. No verse ever says God is wrath.

e) The Death of Sarah (Genesis 23)

Sarah was 91 years old when Isaac was born (Genesis 17:17) and she died when she was 127 years old, when Isaac was about 36 years old, in the year 2023 b.c. It is curious that Isaac was not mentioned in the negotiations for the purchase of the cave of Machpelah, the burial site for his mother. At this point Abraham was living at his home base in Hebron, near his old ally, Mamre the Amorite, but Isaac was not living with him. Isaac, we are told in 24:62 and 25:11, frequented Beer-lahai-roi, where Hagar had first seen an angel many years before, and seemed to be living in the far southern part of the land, the Negev. He was most certainly not present at his mother's burial. There was no disrespect in this: Sarah died before he could be reached, perhaps suddenly, and the necessity of burial could not be postponed for very long.

Even by this time, having lived in the land of Canaan for more than seventy years, Abraham did not own enough land to bury his wife, though God had promised it all to him. The cave Abraham wanted for the burial was in the field of Ephron, a Hittite. The Hittites were distantly related to the Philistines, not to the Amorites, whose local chieftain was Mamre, and Abraham did not have the close ties with the Hittites that he had with the Amorites. The purchase negotiations sound odd to modern ears, but it is the way bargaining goes in many countries even today. The significant thing is that Abraham did not even try to bargain. Ephron began by offering to give the cave to Abraham, pretending to revere his powerful position among them, knowing Abraham would not accept; and then he named a ridiculously high price.

Perhaps this is another example of Abraham's lack of assertiveness, or perhaps his grief at the death of Sarah left him too depressed to go through the motions of business as usual. But it is possible that Abraham felt toward the Hittites as he had felt toward the king of Sodom. Perhaps he felt it would be a moral compromise to receive any benefit from them and he preferred to be cheated by the Hittite man than to appear to get a good deal from him. He would have looked like something of a sap. If he had been concerned about his own status or reputation, he would have sought to avoid the humiliation at all costs. He was powerful enough that he could have just taken the field by force, but Ephron risked insulting this powerful man because Abraham had a reputation for not being aggressive. People cheat anyone who doesn't fight back. Abraham knew he was being cheated, he was being insulted, but he didn't care. It seems to me that his behavior is that of a man who is concerned mainly about God's reputation. He preferred to be dishonored before men in order to be certain that no one could take credit away from God for blessing him.

Abraham was thus the first (or second if we count Noah) in the long line of people who are willing to look like fools so as not to embarrass God. It is natural for children to want to make their parents proud. What do we care what the neighbors think if our parents are pleased? Unfortunately we too quickly grow out of that loyalty. But I do think that Abraham had begun to think of himself as God's child. He didn't say so, but he acted like it. Do we—the modern children of God who carry our spiritual childhood like a chip on our shoulder—do we care that the world not get the credit for any success or prosperity we might enjoy? Not many of us avoid the stupid contests and drawings and lotteries that could make us rich. Not many of us are willing to be cheated quietly by people we don't like. Not many of us can resist charging what the market will bear, or can pass up taking the "steals" we are offered by desperate people. We may be "children of Abraham" but sometimes it is hard to see the family resemblance. If we are to prosper, let it be plain to all that it comes from God and that we owe nothing to the system of this world. Let's not rationalize our whole-hearted pursuit of wealth by saying that we can "give the glory to God". It is the world that gets the credit for such things regardless of how loudly we say "praise the Lord".

We may think of Canaan in the time of Abraham as being primitive, but there was some bureaucratic system that kept records of who owned what property. Even with no central government, property rights are important. The title to this field and cave were recorded and the records maintained over centuries. As unstable as the region was, as frequently as armies went through conquering the region for one super-king or another, there was enough stability to maintain property records and the rights of owners. When Joseph brought Jacob's body from Egypt to be buried in that cave nearly two centuries later there was no disputing the ownership.

f) Keturah (Genesis 25:1-10 and I Chronicles 1:32, 33)

The last information we have that is specifically about Abraham is contained in 25:1-10. Abraham lived seventy-five years after Isaac was born, and thirty-seven years after Sarah died. There is no indication as to when Abraham took Keturah as a concubine. The heir of the Covenant was established as the son of Sarah according to God's promise and there would be no threat posed by any new children of a concubine, especially after Isaac moved away. Abraham could have felt free to take another wife, and perhaps he did as soon as Isaac was grown and was firmly in control of the inheritance.

Keturah had six sons, all of whom were sent away when they were old enough just as Ishmael had been. This would have been against custom and against the justice of the day, just as sending Ishmael had been. These sons were surely entitled to some inheritance, but it was denied to them and there was nothing they could do to demand their rights. Abraham clearly intended to protect the interests of Isaac, even to violating the ethics of the time. The land had no central government at the time, no unifying religion, no one to enforce any code of morality unless it was the most powerful man in the country, Abraham himself. In 25:6 when it says "the sons of his concubines", probably the plural includes Hagar as well as Keturah; it seems unlikely that he had other wives and descendants that aren't mentioned here.

These descendants appear to be mentioned in order to emphasize the fact that the Covenant belonged to Abraham/Sarah and therefore to Isaac and not to the others. However, as children of Abraham they were under God's promise of blessing and His promise to be their God. Specifically the fourth son of Keturah and Abraham was Midian, whose descendants would have divided spiritual loyalties. One branch of the Midianite clan seems to have served as priests and representatives of God Most High around that whole region. Moses would encounter one such priest nearly five hundred years later. Another branch of the Midianites were hostile to Israel.

It is interesting how little God revealed to Abraham about his own shortcomings. We have noted this in previous sections, but God's slowness in rebuking bad behavior is a noteworthy facet of His character. One reason is that there are so many flaws to point out. If it were His priority to correct all our faults, He would hardly have time for anything else. Another reason is that it does not do much good to point out flaws. Knowing a certain act is wrong does not seem to keep us from repeating it. Rather than simply shaming us repeatedly by our powerlessness to control sin, God chose to provide the cure for evil while shielding us from the full disclosure of it. He doesn't care that we are never aware of exactly how much He has delivered us from; it is enough to Him that He did deliver us. There will be time later for us to realize how much we owe Him. Later perhaps He will give a more thorough revelation of our shortcomings, but not until we are ready for it and then only as much as is absolutely necessary.

One final remark about Abraham and his significance to us: the status of those who have never heard the gospel is sometimes a matter of speculation or debate, and sometimes it is a stumbling block to faith. Are the people who never had the chance to hear about Christ saved or lost or what? It is reassuring then to consider that many people who have never heard of Christ are in exactly the same position as Abraham. He was a man who had some knowledge of the traditions of the creation of the world, but who lived among pagans and was imbued with their culture. All he knew of God was that He had called him and spoken to him and bound Himself to him. Abraham had not heard of Jesus and had only the smallest hints of a coming Messiah. Who is to say that God does not similarly call people around the world to Himself even now who have never heard of Christ and perhaps never will? Who is to say how many people even now may be hearing God in their hearts though they do not realize the full import of what He is saying? Who is to say that there have not been many such mini-Abrahams through history, people who, while they have not received a Covenant of Revelation like Abraham did, nonetheless have received God's grace? The New Testament says that salvation belongs to those who have the same faith as Abraham (Romans 4:11,12), and that might well include more people than we can imagine.

B. The Second Generation of the Covenant

1. Ishmael (Genesis 25:12-18 and I Chronicles 1:28-31)

The focus of Scripture now moves to the second generation of the Covenant, to Isaac and to Ishmael. Since the Covenant would not continue through Ishmael, and little more would be said of his descendants or history, the Scripture concluded his story with his genealogy. God fulfilled His promise to Hagar by bringing twelve sons from Ishmael. These may or may not have been his personal sons, but the intent of the passage seems to be that they were. It even emphasizes that they are given in their birth-order. From these princes the present day Arabic peoples come. It is an honor to be descended from Abraham, and it is blessed in the sight of God. God, who never fails in His promises, has said that the children of Ishmael are under His blessing because of Abraham, as Israel is. His purpose is to bless everyone, all nations, through Abraham, but His blessings may come in different packages to different people. The peoples of Ishmael will be blessed through Abraham and the Messiah that comes from him, but in addition to this universal Abrahamic blessing, there is a special direct blessing to the children of Ishmael as Abraham's physical descendants.

Ishmael lived one hundred and thirty seven years, so he died in 1936 b.c. Isaac would have been one hundred and twenty three years old at the time and Jacob and Esau would have been sixty three. Ishmael and his descendants "settled in defiance of all his relatives", as it is to this day. The conflict in the Middle East is a family tradition four thousand years old; it cannot be easily solved, and it is particularly unsolvable as long as both sides of Abraham's family misunderstand the Messiah.

One question that some Christians tend to pose at this point is "Was Ishmael saved?" Especially those of us who carry a New Testament framework with us when we read Genesis tend to think of saved/unsaved as the basic two categories of people in the world. How does Ishmael fit with regard to these categories? The short answer is that he doesn't. There are problems with either answer. If we say that Ishmael was "saved", then at what point is the hope and trust in a future Messiah evident in his life? He was excluded from the Covenant that would culminate in that Messiah and was physically excluded from his kinsmen who were gradually educated in that hope. The subsequent history of the conflict between the Jews and the Ishmaelites gives no encouragement to believe that the Ishmaelites looked to their Jewish kinsmen for their future deliverance. On the other hand, if we say that Ishmael was not saved, then how is he under the blessing of God, the blessing that God promised on his behalf to Abraham? How can we speak of anyone who is without salvation as being under God's blessing?

We could just as well ask whether Abraham's household alone in the entire world was saved. The answer is that God did not say what He was doing with the other people in the world and this suggests that saved/unsaved is the wrong dichotomy to use. However God did make it clear that there were other people in the world who knew Him truly, though to a limited extent. The qualification is hardly necessary—anyone who knows God knows Him only to a limited extent. The focus of God's revelation is that He is making a revelation. The point is that Abraham received a revelation of God's character and purposes that others didn't, and that God chose to continue the process of special revelation through Abraham's descendants and not to others.

The rejection of Ishmael's descendants from the Covenant of Revelation meant that they would not be immediately in on the further revelation of God, just as the rest of us were not. We are in the habit of thinking that a relationship with God is all or nothing, but the Bible seems to describe a range of possible relationships with God. It is all more complicated than a simple yes or no, in or out, saved or unsaved. Nor has the Scripture made it clear up to this point in Genesis exactly what "salvation" might mean. At this point in the revelation, the dichotomies are between those who are receiving revelation and those who aren't, and between those who received the oral tradition and those who didn't. If anything, as far as salvation goes, the emphasis has been entirely on God's favorable intentions toward us all. We must hold off on expecting a complete answer to such questions until we have read more of the Scripture.

There is one more point to be made. Muslims have made the charge that the text in Genesis has been altered to make Isaac the heir, that in fact it was Ishmael who was the heir and through whom the Covenant continued. While it is true that some ancient texts were altered, that even some modern texts have been altered, to suit the purposes of one group or another, in this case the charge is untenable. Ishmael was undeniably a legal heir of Abraham, but he was equally undeniably not the spiritual heir of Abraham. The Covenant clearly did not continue through Ishmael, even if you do not interpret the Covenant as being a Covenant of *revelation*. Ishmael was given his due in the genealogy that follows and the list of kings that came from him and then he disappeared from the lineage of revelation. Whatever blessings God bestowed on him and on his posterity, revelation of God's nature was not one of them. On the contrary the revelation manifestly continued through Isaac to Moses and David and Solomon and the prophets all the way to the Messiah. None of Ishmael's descendants were part of this lineage of revelation. They joined the rest of the human race and deteriorated into a religion of futility.

2. Finding Rebekah (Genesis 22:20-24 and 24:1-67)

We turn now to Isaac and the continuing of the Covenant. At the end of chapter 22 we find a report coming to Abraham that his brother Nahor had been blessed with children and grandchildren. This suggests that Abraham had kept up a correspondence with his brother, and he must have heard at some point that Nahor had also left Ur and returned to Haran. The placing of this section in the Scripture suggests that he had received this news before Sarah died, perhaps only shortly before, and it was her death that fixed Abraham's mind on the future and what to do about a wife for his son. Within a few years of Sarah's death Abraham had fixed on the plan to send his servant back to his relatives to find a wife for Isaac. In all his years of sojourning in the Promised Land, with the exception of Mamre and Melchizedek, and somewhat reluctantly with Abimelech, he had kept himself aloof from the inhabitants. It was not only the king of Sodom, but it was the Hittites among his neighbors and apparently many others. Abraham had been conscious of a barrier between himself and most of his neighbors nearly since he had arrived and this antipathy crystallized into a strong desire that Isaac not marry one of them. Even Mamre's family was not acceptable, or Melchizedek's. It became fixed in his mind that Isaac must marry a relative.

Isaac was nearly forty years old by this time and living independently of Abraham and unmarried. Isaac could have chosen a wife for himself at this point; the father arranged marriages for his daughters but not for his sons. Nonetheless, Abraham took the lead here. Because it would be strange for Abraham to arrange for Isaac's marriage without consulting Isaac, it seems likely that after Sarah's death he went south to stay with his son for a while. In this way, sending the servant back to Haran could have been a joint decision. The way Abraham spoke to the servant in 24:3 implies that it had become the servant's duty to seek out a wife for Isaac, as if Abraham were too feeble or too ill to make such a journey. Abraham in fact lived several more decades after Isaac was married, so if Abraham was thinking of the possibility of his impending death, then he was premature. Even if Abraham had felt well, he would probably not have made the journey back to Haran in person if only because of his age. Probably Abraham had few duties at this point; Isaac would have assumed most or all of the duties of the head of the household by then.

Consider the identity of the servant that Abraham sent with this most important task. Naturally he would send his most trusted servant; it also seems likely that this most trusted servant would have been the one he had adopted sixty years previously to be his heir if Sarah had had no son. Could it be that Abraham was sending the very servant who had been done out of a great inheritance to find a wife for the one whose birth had been the cause of that loss? Whoever the servant was, he was a man of integrity and entirely devoted to Abraham. Repeatedly we see the loyalty of Abraham's household, and that is the best of character references.

The servant took an oath to seek a wife for Isaac among Abraham's relatives, and if he failed to find a wife among those relatives, he promised at least to never take Isaac back to Haran. Hence, as he reflected upon his life, the promises God had made to him, and the future he had in mind for Isaac, the most important priority in Abraham's mind was that Isaac not leave the land of Canaan. If a wife could not be found among his relatives in Haran, then a wife could be found in Egypt, or perhaps Mamre's family would be acceptable as a second best. But why was Abraham so concerned that Isaac not go back to Haran, (as one of his grandsons would do a century or so later)? It is not clear. Perhaps he had been directed by God not to allow Isaac to go back there for some reason. When Isaac's son Jacob did go back there, he found his family almost more than he could handle; a person as meek as Isaac might have been trapped there.

The servant's trip back to Haran took place in about 2020 b.c. and this suggests an interesting possibility. At about this time Ishbi-Erra, from the city of Mari, came to power and began plotting the overthrow of his lord, Ibbi-Sin, the king of Ur. Mari, and Ishbi-Erra's base of operations in Isin, were between Haran and Ur. Since there was some ethnic tie between Haran and Ur, perhaps there was a danger that Isaac might get enmeshed in the conflict, particularly because of Abraham's history with the Elamites. The political intrigues of this era are little understood, but a good general guideline is that one should stay out of a nation's internal conflicts, especially if one might be mistaken as sympathetic with one side or the other. The servant could more easily "move under the radar" than Isaac himself. This is entirely speculation generated by the chance coincidence of dating.

Abraham told the servant that God would send his "angel" ahead of him to prepare the way before him and give him success. It is not at all clear what Abraham had in mind when he said this; and probably he did not know exactly what he meant either. He had had many visitations from God, but only two, the one concerning Sodom just before Isaac was born and the one in which he was prevented from sacrificing Isaac, were described as being angelic. The word translated "angel" simply means "messenger". Abraham was just beginning to try to understand the appearances he had received and this was the way he described what he understood. Angels are a part of the on-going revelation and at this point their nature was left obscure, as in fact it still is.

Abraham's servant took a great many valuable gifts for the bride and her family, but it does not mention him taking any security measures, guards and so on. Abraham had plenty of trained soldiers in his household, so perhaps the protective escort went without saying. It was a dangerous time on the fringe of a decaying empire, and even the most frequented trade route was a dangerous one. Still, the servant arrived without mishap in Aram-naharaim, near Haran, where Nahor was dwelling. What the servant found there was Rebekah, the daughter of Isaac's cousin Bethuel.

God's eagerness to guide the servant correctly was apparent in that He answered the servant's prayer even as he was speaking it. But if we are praying for what God wishes to give us then there is clearly no need to ask for it over and over again; and if we are praying for what God does not wish to give us then we would be foolish to ask for it repeatedly. Therefore the way we see prayers sometimes practiced in churches, with great loudness and zeal and repetition, suggests that we neither know what we are doing nor what God is doing. Sometimes our prayers seem more like attempts to nag God into doing what we think He doesn't want to do. Abraham's servant had the faith of a child: he just asked.

Furthermore, when his prayer was apparently answered instantly, the servant was still cautious. He did not assume that just because everything appeared to be a direct and even a dramatic answer to his prayer, that it was in fact the answer to his prayer. He was not to be tricked by mere appearances, mere coincidences. His mission was too important to permit him to jump to conclusions too hastily. It is a lesson worth learning. We could all be more cautious and discerning, not because God is unreliable but because our perceptions are unreliable, because we are so prone to leap ahead of the Spirit, because we are so prone to make assumptions about what God is doing, or has done, or is about to do based on superficial appearances.

We are the opposite of careful. It is considered by us a sign of superior faith to hop right in. But if we are serious about what we ask of God, then let's be serious enough about the response that we examine it with caution. This is not a sign or doubt or unbelief in God; it is humility, an admission that we are easily fooled. God is not offended when a person, who sincerely wants to follow Him, checks out everything carefully. He knows how gullible we are, and we please Him when we can admit it, when we learn to rely on Him and not on our own understanding. It is a subtle thing, relying on God rather than on ourselves. Some feel that caution and careful investigation is a way of relying on ourselves. Some feel that an energetic trust in the circumstances is what real faith is all about. Humility is a tricky thing, but it is the real point.

Rebekah took the man's gifts and, in her excitement that he had come from a distant relative as well as at his obvious wealth, she ran off and left him alone by the city's well. He knew she would come back, of course, and that she would bring a male relative to escort him back to their house. The future course of Laban's history might lead us to think that he was quite taken with the gifts the stranger had given his sister and was thinking of the potential gain that might be had from a rich relative. Laban was a young man at this time, just beginning to take over control of the family estate. He greeted the servant in the name of the God of their family, the God of the oral tradition they held in common; doubtless one reason Abraham sent back to his relatives for a wife was the common spiritual heritage. As it turned out, having a common spiritual heritage was no protection against dishonest business practices, but that would all come out later.

The servant knew how the feasting would go once it got started, Middle Eastern hospitality being what it was. The feast could go on for days. Because he had such a sense of urgency in his mission he was somewhat abrupt with his hosts. He insisted on telling the complete story of his mission before the feast could be begun. It is not clear why he felt such urgency; perhaps it was just the nerves of a responsible servant who wouldn't be able to rest properly until this important job was done. Or perhaps there was a sense of premonition of coming events in that region (whether such events transpired or not, Laban would prosper over the next seventy years). In any case, Rebekah's brother and father agreed to the marriage once they had heard the story. The culture of that time and place was a fratriarchal one in which the oldest son took over the family affairs when he came of age. Laban was probably assuming the leadership of the family and his approval of the marriage was necessary. Rebekah did have some say in the matter; though the male head of the household commonly arranged marriages, the woman could veto the arrangement under most circumstances. Since this was a very sudden match her wishes were consulted. The passage does not indicate how old Rebekah was, but she must have been fairly young to be still unbetrothed, perhaps half the age of Isaac.

On the next day the feast was to continue, as much as ten days more, while Rebekah prepared to leave, but the servant of Abraham could not rest. Again he behaved in an abrupt, even a rude, manner. He insisted on leaving at once. On this matter, Rebekah did have the deciding voice; it was she who would be inconvenienced by a hasty departure. It was also important that her willingness to go to Isaac should be made clear. The servant had been commissioned to bring back a wife who was willing to come; it would not do if Rebekah was not fully committed.

It took a great deal of courage for Rebekah to go with the servant of Abraham to a distant land to marry a man she did not know. If she had been afraid she could have delayed. On the other hand, she did know that her husband-to-be was very rich, and later events showed that she was an ambitious person who seized opportunities as they came up, who even made opportunities for herself when there were none. Indeed, Rebekah was cut from the same cloth as Laban, and they were both as unlike Abraham and Isaac as close relatives can be. And what prospects were there for Rebekah in Haran? Probably only limited ones. Later scripture describes Laban as a crafty man, but a man whose fortunes were waning despite all his craftiness. For Rebekah to have resisted this marriage would have meant keeping her fate in Laban's hands, and Laban mainly looked out for his own interests. But Rebekah was not Laban's sister for nothing; she knew how to take care of herself, how to look out for her own interests. So Rebekah seized the opportunity and did not spend a lot of time saying good-bye to a brother for whom she probably had little affection.

Isaac was out meditating in the field in the cool of the evening when the caravan returned. When Rebekah knew the man she saw ahead of them was her husband-to-be she put on a veil as was the custom of that day. And so Isaac married Rebekah and took her to Sarah's tent, a sign that she was the new matriarch of the clan, and another indication that Abraham had come to visit him after Sarah's death. And he grew to love Rebekah after the fashion of arranged marriages, and was comforted after Sarah's death. Subsequent events do not flatter their marriage as being ideal; but they did find some happiness together.

3. The Birth of Jacob and Esau (Genesis 25:11, 19-26)

Isaac resembled Abraham in character. He was a quiet man, not at all assertive. His life was not as eventful as Abraham's. God made two recorded appearances to Isaac (not counting when the angel rescued him), compared to seven for Abraham. This does not mean that he lacked the spiritual depth that Abraham had, however. On the contrary, the small amount of information we have indicates that he had both the same personal flaws and the same spiritual discernment that Abraham had. He was the only one besides Abraham among the patriarchs that was recorded as interceding in prayer for someone else, in his case for his wife Rebekah (25:21); and he was the only one mentioned who had a habit of meditating in the field at sunset.

Isaac fought no great battles, interceded for no cities, and never was called on to sacrifice his sons, and so we may imagine he had less on the ball spiritually than Abraham. But I believe that his near sacrifice as a boy had had a profound effect on his spirituality, deepening and maturing him more than many visitations and visions would have. It is not how many visions we have that make us godly, but how much we get out of them. In being rescued from Abraham's knife, he deepened spiritually a great deal in a short time. It was a profound experience. True, Isaac did no great deeds, but great deeds are not a sign of deep spirituality as Enoch proved.

It is a misguided ambition, one not encouraged by the Scripture, to want to do great deeds for God. Let's resist arrogance in any form. Great deed assignments are what God does, and they don't usually go to whom we think they will.

Abraham did not die for thirty-five years or so after Isaac and Rebekah were married. During that time Isaac and Rebekah settled in Beer-lahai-roi, while Abraham probably returned to Hebron. They may have been too rich jointly to live together. Abraham, who had seemed very ill when he sent off the servant to look for Rebekah, must have made a good recovery and gone on to a vigorous life with Keturah. Isaac and Rebekah had been married nineteen years before Isaac felt the need to pray for Rebekah's barrenness. The struggling of the twins within her womb was unusually intense and alarmed Rebekah. Her inquiring of the Lord was the occasion of the prophecy regarding Jacob and Esau. It is not known how she would have gone about inquiring of the Lord; such things usually have some ceremony attached, but there were no priests, no precedents. The answer that God gave her told her that the behavior of the babies in her womb was itself a prophecy of their future, that they would be always rivals of one another and that the older twin's descendants would produce a nation that was the servant of the descendants of the younger twin.

It is possible, of course, that this is an insert from a later time, a reading of their subsequent history back into the events surrounding their birth, but it doesn't seem to be. Why would a fictional account of the founders of the two nations be so honest and negative about them? The founders of America were disinfected as completely as the records would allow, and not as much as they would have been had there been no widely disseminated documentation. If the story of the twins' birth is an insert from later generations to exalt Jacob over Esau, why would they then continually portray Esau as the cheated one and Jacob as the cheater? If the story of the twins' birth is an insert from later generations, why would they then have presented their own father Isaac as biased against Jacob and in favor of the one they intended to discredit? If later generations inserted only the prophecy, and the rest of the story is original, then they achieved only a rather lame justification of Jacob at the cost of discrediting Isaac. Further, if one were intending to insert a fictional prophecy to strengthen a nation's claim to pre-eminence, one might clean up the ancestor's life a bit as well. Jacob was relentlessly portrayed as a scoundrel. There is no evidence in the account that anyone was trying to make Jacob look good; it is quite the contrary.

I assume Genesis was an oral tradition passed from generation to generation as stories around a campfire, as it were. If later generations of Israelites had wanted to modify the story to glorify their ancestral founders, there was nothing to stop them from doing it; no one could have stood up to contradict them. It was Isaac that would have had to add these chapters of Genesis to the oral tradition and it portrays him as biased in favor of Esau, against Jacob and against God's choice. The account would then have been passed on to Jacob for preservation and it is important that neither patriarch felt entitled to dress up their own account or hide their flaws. Indeed, the account of the prophecy is in deliberate contrast to their actual lives. The whole history of Jacob and Esau is a deliberately and carefully drawn portrait of God choosing an unscrupulous man over a "good" one. Only God insisting on truth can well explain what we have here. They were given the job of bearing the revelation that was being enacted in their lives and God held them to it. They did not dare embellish the truth however embarrassing it might be.

Nor would such an insert ever have been imagined as necessary. Israel was forbidden to take land away from the descendants of Esau. Though later several of the Israelite kings were powerful enough that they took tribute from Esau's people, there was never the possibility of occupying their land as they had done with the Canaanites. Even more than for the Canaanites, it is hard to see why the ancient Israelites would have ever felt the need to rationalize their relationship with the descendants of Esau.

Jacob and Esau were born in about 1999 b.c., during a time of great innovation and brilliance in Egypt under Mentuhotep III, and while Isin and Larsa were competing to dominate Mesopotamia. So far as civilization went, the balance had tipped toward Egypt and away from Mesopotamia, but Isaac and his family were out on the fringe where the action wasn't.

4. Isaac's Later Years (Genesis 26:1-33 and 35:28,29)

Assuming that the events of chapter 26 occurred after the birth of the twins, there was a severe famine in the land when they were young. During the famine from the previous century Abraham's instinct had been to go to Egypt to seek pasture, but God warned Isaac not to go down into Egypt.

Why would God warn Isaac not to go to Egypt? There are many possible reasons why He might, reasons that we have no way of knowing. But there is an interesting possibility. In about 1985 b.c. there seems to have been a coup in Egypt. Amenemhat I, who had been the vizier, seized the throne from his master Mentuhotep IV and there was a period of violence and disorder at the beginning of his reign. It is tempting to hypothesize that this is the date of the famine and Isaac's dream and his relocation to Gerar. If so, it is also about the time Abraham died and going to Gerar would have put Isaac nearer to Abraham at his death.

In addition, there is a collection of letters written by an Egyptian farmer, Hekanakhte, to his family that seem to date from approximately this time. These letters suggest that there was a famine in Egypt as well and so there may have been no relief from the famine there anyway. Furthermore the Egyptians had been growing more suspicious of foreigners just preceding and during Amenemhat's reign. He sent his army against Asiatic peoples living in the delta early in his reign, and so Egypt may have been unsafe as well as unhelpful for Isaac. Isaac had gone to Gerar already, intending to leave for Egypt from there, but God's appearance changed his plans.

This was the first recorded appearance of God to Isaac in his adult life, the first since the angel had prevented his death. At this point God renewed the covenant He had made with Abraham, summarizing it all: that He would bless him, that He would give him all of those lands, that He would give him many descendants, and that all of the nations of the earth would be blessed through him. And why did God renew this covenant with Isaac? Because *Abraham* had been obedient to Him—not because Isaac had been obedient. He didn't even give Isaac anything to obey. Abraham was portrayed as being obedient to God's charge, His commandments, His statutes, and His laws but all these laws, commandments, and statutes boiled down to a single law regarding circumcision, and the one command to sacrifice his son. The list of Abraham's obediences here sounds more like a formulaic list, a means of expressing approval of Abraham rather than a statement to be taken at face value. The translation is somewhat misleading; literally the text in 26:5 means "hearkened to My voice" rather than "obeyed Me". Abraham was the man in all the world who *listened* to God. The point was that however Abraham had managed to please God, Isaac was to reap the benefits of Abraham's favor, and the Covenant was renewed to him in an entirely unconditional manner.

At this point, shortly after he had heard from God for the first time, Isaac told Abimelech that Rebekah was his sister. He used the same lie that Abraham had used eighty-five years or more previously, and even more a lie since she was not in fact his sister. Clearly he got the idea from his father, from the oral tradition, from the stories he had been told by Abraham to be preserved. Isaac was literally walking in the footsteps of the faith of his father Abraham. It is barely possible that this was the same Abimelech as had been deceived by Abraham, but more likely he was a successor, Abimelech being a title rather than a personal name. Previously the Abimelech had attached Sarah to his harem pretty quickly, but this Abimelech took no such action and did not seem to be contemplating it. Possibly this was because it was the same Abimelech but now an old man rather than a young man; or possibly not. According to 26:8 Isaac had been in the land for a long time, with no real threat from anyone, before Abimelech saw him fondling Rebekah and knew immediately what was going on.

But why would Isaac try the same deception again and in the same place? It had not worked out very well for Abraham. And why would Rebekah agree to such a hair-brained scheme? Further, this lie was complicated by the presence of his fourteen year old twin sons, if my chronological guess work is correct. But Isaac seems to have inherited Abraham's paranoia, and perhaps he panicked at some point and simply could not think of another story on the spot. How many of us say foolish things in the heat of a moment knowing very well that they are the lamest of things to say? I imagine him having just returned from the burial where he had stayed with Abraham during his final days and perhaps had been told all the stories one more time. It could have been fresh in his mind, the events from his father's life in that same city. Whatever the cause, Isaac did say what he said and might have gotten away with it if he had not been indiscreet and been caught. He may not have consulted with Rebekah before he told the lie, either, forcing her to either contradict him or play along. The course of her life would show that she was not averse to a lie or two if it was to her advantage.

And why had the men of Gerar filled in all the wells that Abraham had dug in his lifetime, rather than use them? It appears that Abraham did not move around as much after Sarah died and perhaps never visited Gerar again. Perhaps the men of Gerar did not want him to come back, despite the covenant they had made, and to discourage his return they had filled in all the wells he had dug. Perhaps it did keep Abraham out, but it didn't keep Isaac out. After some time Isaac was as settled in Gerar as a nomad gets, and he planted some fields and reaped a hundred fold. We need not take this as an exact figure, but the intent is clearly to indicate that he made a huge profit. Even more to the point, he made a huge profit reaping a harvest during a famine. Isaac was so blessed with an increase of material possessions when everyone else was declining that Abimelech and his people became afraid of him and asked him to leave their land. Fighting over water rights was a symptom that the land was too crowded with their many animals. But Isaac shared his father's non-assertiveness; rather than argue with the servants of Abimelech, he preferred to relinquish his rights and try again somewhere else.

When Isaac had withdrawn as far as Beersheba God appeared to him a second time, the last time, and repeated His promises. This was the first time Isaac was recorded as building an altar to God though it might not have been the first time. It is noteworthy that God introduced Himself as the God of Abraham. From this time to the present day it has become part of God's name by which He is known everywhere in the world. He is the God of Abraham; His bond to Abraham was a permanent and a public bond. Just as a man leaves his father and mother and cleaves to his wife and they become one flesh, even so God left Himself, as it were, and joined Himself to His people, and they have become one (and we might say they have become one flesh though this is for a future chapter of revelation), and they have taken each other's names. In this way, symbolically, when God joined Himself to the people of Israel it was God who left heaven, who left Himself, to come in to His new family and He took Abraham's name as His own.

Abimelech came after Isaac for the purpose of making a covenant, just as his predecessor had gone after Abraham ninety or so years previously. The original covenant between Abraham and Abimelech would not have been forgotten, but Isaac had not lived in the neighborhood of Gerar until the famine as far as we know, and perhaps Abimelech felt nervous about Isaac's willingness to keep the agreement his father had made. Note that Genesis 26:28,29 says, "And they said, 'We see plainly that the Lord has been with you; so we said 'Let there now be an oath between us, even between you and us, and let us make a covenant with you, that you will do us no harm, just as we have not touched you and have done to you nothing but good, and have sent you away in peace. You are now the blessed of the Lord.' "This strongly suggests that this Abimelech knew something about the Most High God and honored Him as a god. Abimelech had no idea that a covenant with God Himself was possible, but he could recognize the hand of God's favor and wanted to be closely associated and allied with it. Also it suggests that Abimelech had recognized Abraham as the "blessed of the Lord", and recognized that this distinction had now passed on to Isaac. When Isaac and Abraham made these covenants with Abimelech, God was already beginning to fulfill in a small way His promise to make the descendants of Abraham a blessing to every nation.

The only other detail from this passage we might mention is the alternative story given about the source of the name of Beersheba. There is no reason to see conflict between the two accounts, 26:33 and 21:31. Many places in the ancient world had several names, and Isaac typically gave the same names Abraham had given to the wells he dug again, and sometimes for similar reasons.

The focus of Scripture now turns to Jacob and Esau, the third generation of the Covenant. Though Isaac lived a long time, and played some role in their lives, the burden of the story passed to the next generation. We are only left to note the death of Isaac at the age of 180 years, in the year 1879 b.c. Isaac lived until Jacob was 120 years old and was still alive when Joseph was sold into slavery. Meanwhile, the Covenant and the oral tradition and the revelation of God proceeded according to His purposes in the next generation.

An oral tradition, indeed even the concept of a written revelation such as the Bible, composed over many centuries by many people, assumes that knowledge of God is something that can be accumulated and stored up, rather than begun from scratch with each new generation. It is not evident how the details preserved in Genesis were selected for remembrance; one must assume that God Himself somehow made His will known as the events went by. For the most part, the events that were preserved were embarrassing to the people involved and to their immediate families, so it is quite clear that God was impressing on them what was to be preserved, forcing a certain character on the overall account. It is not explicable as the result of merely human authorship.

C. Jacob and Esau

1. Jacob Buys Esau's Birthright
(Genesis 25:27-34; 26:34-35; 27:46; and 28:6-9)

When the twins have grown up, they are introduced into the biblical narrative in terms reminiscent of Cain and Abel. Esau was a man of the field, a skillful hunter, parallel to Abel who cared for the sheep and lived outside; Jacob was a quiet man who stayed inside, parallel to a gardener like Cain. And Jacob was parallel to Cain in more than externals. Jacob was jealous of his brother, the older brother who would inherit a double portion of the inheritance because of a few minutes head start in being born, and who was his father's favorite. And Jacob figuratively killed his brother, cheating him out of everything he was entitled to as the first-born. And yet in the story of Jacob and Esau it was Jacob who found favor in God's eyes; it is as if we read the story of Cain murdering Abel and God rewarded Cain. Sometimes bad guys finish first, and finish with God's full support and blessing. The story of Jacob and Esau lands us squarely in the middle of the mystery of God's choice, the mystery frequently called Predestination.

Not only does a covenant relationship rely entirely on God's initiative, it also relies on God's sovereign choices. Within the Covenant God reserved the sovereign right to exclude or include. Romans 9:6-13 takes up this theme and expands on it. One of the points of both the examples, Isaac/Ishmael and Jacob/Esau, is that God's choice was made before the individuals were born. Their choices and their characters were not part of that decision. In particular, God did not narrow the Covenant to Isaac because of any virtue in Isaac, nor because of any flaw in Ishmael; God excluded Ishmael from the Covenant simply because he had the wrong mother, because of the meaning he was assigned in the long metaphor of revelation. And in another particular, God did not narrow the Covenant to Jacob because of any virtue in Jacob, nor for any flaw in Esau. God excluded Esau from the Covenant simply because of the meaning he performed in the long metaphor of revelation.

Esau is first described as despising his birthright, his inheritance rights as the elder. When brothers would divide their inheritance, the eldest would get a double portion, as if he counted as two people. Thus, if there were four brothers, the inheritance would be divided into five equal portions and the eldest would get two of them. So Esau was entitled to inherit two-thirds of Isaac's property but Jacob only one-third. Esau traded this advantage for a bowl of soup. Some commentators have argued that Esau was despising the spiritual components of the birthright even more than the material components, and that this is the real cause of Esau's exclusion from the Covenant. This view seems to be based on Hebrews 12:16. As the eldest, wasn't Esau the rightful heir to the Covenant of Revelation, the rightful heir of the oral tradition preserved from the creation of the world, and the rightful successor to Isaac in continuing that revelation?

No. In fact there is no indication at all that the Covenant was ever meant to operate by headship being passed from the father to the eldest son. The leadership in the Covenant people would always be something of a random selection from various tribes and never from eldest sons of previous leaders. Even the later kingship over Israel did not automatically go to the eldest son. Furthermore there had been no indication to this point that anyone besides Ishmael would ever be excluded from the Covenant. All that had been said to Rebekah was that there would be two distinct nations arising from her, and that the descendants of the younger would rule over the descendants of the older; there was no need to think that the older would be excluded from the Covenant.

On the contrary, there is no reason to think that Esau despised anything except the material blessings he was entitled to as the oldest son. And there is no reason to think that Jacob was coveting anything of Esau's except those material blessings. We can try to spiritualize/demonize the twins but there is little or no evidence in the passage itself to support it. As events unfold, the characters of both Esau and Jacob belie such an interpretation. If we try to make Esau into a bad guy and Jacob into a good guy, it may be because deep down we are uncomfortable with the thought that God should pick someone like Jacob over someone like Esau without a secret and good reason. Surely God, who looks at the heart, saw a heart of flesh in Jacob and a heart of stone in Esau and that is why He did what He did, we think to ourselves. But no; God chose Jacob because He chose Him, with no reason given except the one given in Romans 9: God was demonstrating that His choice does not depend on works, on the deeds of the person, but simply on His call. Perhaps it was displeasing to God that Esau despised the blessing he was entitled to as the eldest son, the riches in camels and goats and sheep and servants; but the taking advantage of one's brother when he is exhausted and fainting and not in his right mind was certainly displeasing to God as well. Jacob did worse than Esau: though he did not despise his inheritance, he did despise his brother.

There is a further question: just how binding could their deal over the inheritance have been? Who would have known about it? At some point, Esau's selling of his birthright must have been made public, and it must have been made public by Esau himself. What good would Jacob's word alone have been, particularly if Esau had contradicted it? Who would have believed that Esau had sold his birthright for a bowl of soup? At some point, Esau must have admitted what he had done. The jaded among us would say that this just shows how dumb Esau was. Perhaps so, but it also shows that he was honest, even honest about dumb things he had done that would only serve to hurt him. The selling of his birthright speaks more good about Esau's character than bad.

This was the event that got Esau the nickname "Edom", which means "red", after the color of the soup he got from Jacob. The name would become a barrier between the brothers, always reminding Esau of his mistake, always reminding him of the dis-service Jacob had done him. Who gave him the nickname "Edom", anyway? At birth, Esau had had an unusual amount of hair and of a reddish color, and the name Esau is related to the Hebrew word that means "hairy one". The nickname, Edom, could have been applied at birth, but 25:30 attributes it to the bowl of soup. Though it must have been Esau who admitted what he had done, it must have been Jacob who gave him the nickname. It must have been Jacob who first began calling him "Red", mocking him, rubbing salt in the wound of Esau's foolishness, inviting others to laugh at his stupid older brother who was willing to buy a million dollar bowl of soup. Others might have taken the nickname to refer to Esau's red hair, but from Jacob it would have been a barb, and Esau would have known it: "What a doofus" is what Jacob meant. Thus Jacob planted the seeds of bitterness in Esau. First he cheated Esau, and then when Esau had made his foolish bargain known, Jacob made sure to give him a name that would humiliate him every time Jacob used it. Esau was a bit thick, a fool who was dominated by his needs of the moment rather than a rational consideration of his true situation, a man who was insensitive and impulsive, and who held a grudge; but Jacob was a snake.

The next recorded event in Genesis after the episode with the soup is the marriage of Esau to the two Hittite women, who caused much grief to Isaac and Rebekah. The women were Judith the daughter of Beeri and

Basemath the daughter of Elon, daughters of Hittite men. In 28:8 they are said to be Canaanite, but in this case the word is being used generically for an inhabitant of the land that would later be called Canaan. The word would have naturally been used in later years when the oral tradition was written down and when the Canaanites dominated the land. However, this was the century in which there were a large number of actual Canaanites moving into the land. The marriage occurred when Esau was forty years old, so in the year 1959 b.c. It is easy to think of Esau's marriage to the Hittite women as yet further evidence that he was not interested in the spiritual aspects of his family, but this interpretation of Esau is not quite fair. It is true that Esau was ignoring his family history; his grandfather Abraham had never been close to the Hittites. But once he realized how important his choice of wives was and how greatly they offended his parents, he tried to remedy his mistake by marrying an Ishmaelite woman, Mahalath, the daughter of Ishmael himself. Clearly, the problem was not that he did not care; he was just a bit clueless. On the other hand, Jacob did not give any thought to going back to Haran for a wife; he only went to Haran as a convenient dodge to escape his brother's wrath.

And how important was it that they not marry the natives of the land? Important, yes, but not so important that their descendants would ever go back to Haran again looking for wives; Jacob was the last to make that journey. Judah would later marry a Canaanite and then marry his son to a Canaanite woman who then became part of the Messianic line; marrying a Canaanite was certainly not a fatal mistake. It is not clear whom Judah's brothers married, but at least one other also married a Canaanite. The exact cause of the grief these Hittite women brought to Isaac and Rebekah is not stated, but it was more than simply their nationality. They were Hittites, but worse, they were obnoxious Hittites. In them, perhaps because of their personalities, the clash of cultures reached a boiling point over the decades.

The timing of the events recorded here is not clear, particularly how the events with the twins fit in with the events in Isaac's life. Isaac lived in the neighborhood of Beer-lahai-roi with Rebekah for a while, probably until the twins were born in 1999 b.c. and for a while afterwards. Then at a time of famine he moved to Gerar, just before 1985 b.c. and stayed there for an extended time during which he pretended Rebekah was his sister; then he went to Beersheba (coincidentally the place where God had rescued Ishmael in Isaac's youth), from which Jacob fled to Haran

(Genesis 28:10) in about 1920 b.c. (this is based on the dating of events in Joseph's life and working backwards). Esau married the Hittite women (in about 1959 b.c.) but whether at Gerar or Beersheba is not possible to tell. Somewhere in this sequence, Jacob bought Esau's inheritance, but we also cannot determine where in the sequence it fits. The book of Genesis does not claim to be a chronological account, and as the book covers the lives of increasing numbers of people it naturally departs from a strict chronological order. My preference is to think Isaac's family moved to Beersheba before Esau's marriage and before he sold his birthright. What does it matter? Lots and none at all. It matters a lot just because it is part of taking the Scripture seriously; and none at all because no great spiritual principle hinges on it.

I have been reading between the lines here, which also seems to me to be part of taking the Scripture seriously as long as we don't lose sight of what we are doing. As best I can make out, there is simply nothing in the text that presents Jacob in a good light. On the contrary, the text is relentless in exposing Jacob's character. With each event, Jacob must decline in our estimation, as if we were being invited to judge him. The point, of course, is not to get us to judge Jacob, but to help us to understand how differently God judges than we do. It should be a relief.

2. Jacob Steals Esau's Blessing (Genesis 27:1-40)

It must have been roughly forty years after Esau's marriage that Jacob stole his blessing (this is based on the timing necessary to events in the latter part of Genesis). This would make Jacob and Esau about 80 years old and Isaac about 140 years old, about the year 1920 b.c. Isaac had another forty years left to him but his eyes were already failing badly. As a rich man there were ways he could compensate for physical infirmity, even blindness. Still, a hundred and thirty year old man must think about the likelihood of his own death, or so he was thinking in 27:2.

Unlike Esau, Jacob had not married. It would have been unusual in that culture for a man to not marry, but the biblical account gives the strong impression that Jacob was very much under the power of his mother, that she was possessive of him, and that she was ambitious for him. And Isaac's favoritism toward Esau would have increased Rebekah's power and influence over Jacob as well. For Jacob to marry would have diminished her power in his life and she may have contrived to delay it. Seventy-six is not too old when the general lifespan goes past one hundred, but it is getting very late. Jacob was a sedentary man, as far as a man could be in that world, content to let his older brother take the lead in managing their collective property. As eldest, Esau would have been in charge of the family affairs, and Jacob let Esau run things while he hung out. Jacob was self-motivated primarily in looking out for his future material interests.

When Rebekah overheard Isaac and Esau discussing the blessing, she seized the opportunity. Rebekah was not one to dither but Jacob, on hearing the plan, was plainly a hypocrite: he hesitated to deceive his father because it might *look* like he was trying to deceive his father. Rebekah was the forceful one, pushing Jacob on to do the deed. She persuaded Jacob by taking full responsibility on herself; if the deception resulted in a curse rather than the blessing, then the curse would land on her rather than on her son. Jacob was a superstitious man, as his later story repeatedly shows, and felt safe with her promise of being a curse magnet. Clearly, while he might be under her power, he had no great affection for her. He was only concerned about himself.

To modern materialist ears, Jacob and Rebekah both sound rather superstitious. What is the big deal about a blessing or a curse anyway? Just words. Did the blessing of Isaac have any more power to ensure Esau's future than reciting limericks? Would a curse from Isaac have any real power either? Isn't their behavior here not only an example of family politics of the worst kind but also an example of how the ancients believed in some unscientific things? Our age is no longer able to tell the difference between superstition and faith so we will pause here to consider the difference.

I would distinguish the difference between superstition and faith this way: superstition is naturalistic—it sees a link of cause and effect between two events for no valid rational or scientific reasons; faith is trust in God. Superstition is frequently a matter of "post hoc ergo propter hoc": because event A happens after event B, therefore event A must have been caused by event B. Superstitions frequently come from tradition but sometimes they just come from imagination. Faith usually comes from a previous conviction that God has spoken, or the conviction that God has a certain character and acts in a certain way. Superstition is a conviction that rests on human invention; faith is a conviction that rests on a prior understanding of God. Those who believe that all understanding of God is merely human invention will naturally not be able to distinguish the two.

There is a difference between believing in the power of Isaac's blessing and believing in the oracle from before their birth. The oracle did not make its prediction based on any link of causes and effects, but only on God's choice independently of any events. The oracle was an announcement of God's will and therefore did not portray itself as having power of its own. The blessing of the father on his eldest son is iffy: it could be taken as having power in itself, a cause of whatever future blessing comes to the son, a superstition; or it could be taken as an act that God honors and respects and, for His own purposes and our best good, will enforce or not in His wisdom—in short, a matter of faith. True faith would not ascribe power to the words themselves, as if there was a mystical or spiritual force that makes such things invariably effective in shaping the future. True faith recognizes that God may choose to put His authority and weight behind the words, by inspiring the blessing along lines that He has ordained and by making His power available to fulfill the words.

Rebekah believed the oracle, apparently, probably because she believed in God and that He communicates with us occasionally. So Rebekah was a woman of faith on that score. But then she used her faith to justify lies and deceit and schemes. She tried to fulfill the oracle by her own means; what Noah had refused to do when he would not leave the ark, what Abraham had refused to do when he would not take the spoils of Sodom or conquer the land, she did and worse. Rebekah became the mother of all who use their faith as an excuse for evil. She has many spiritual children.

Isaac, on the other hand, presumably believed the oracle. The rest of the account paints a picture of a man of faith. But Isaac's clear preference for Esau over Jacob, and his insistence on giving the blessing due the firstborn in spite of the oracle to the contrary, suggests that he may have been trying to circumvent the oracle. Perhaps he thought he could mitigate some of the prediction of the oracle by throwing a little "positive energy" on the other side of the equation. If so, Isaac's faith was defective but in a very different way from Rebekah's. She thought she could help the oracle, and Isaac thought he could hinder it. Neither is fully a trust in God and His purposes.

From my standpoint, the high estimation Rebekah, Jacob, Isaac and Esau placed on the power of the blessing was merely superstition. A mature faith would have known that Isaac's blessing had no more power to overrule the oracle than any other human words. But superstition imagines that mere words or rituals or symbolic acts can have a power over events to the point of either accomplishing or circumventing God's will. When Rebekah contrived to steal the blessing reserved for Esau, she acted on the basis of superstition, and when Isaac decided to give to Esau the blessing which the oracle had set aside for Jacob, he acted on the basis of superstition.

In the context of the Covenant, however, which is passed down the generations, what the father said to the children before he died was of great significance exactly because it was the Covenant that was being passed down. The father's blessing was the human side of the divine order in the Covenant. When Isaac did place his blessing on the deceiver, the words even echoed the covenant promises to Abraham and Isaac, particularly at the end of the blessing: "Cursed be those who curse you, and blessed be those who bless you." Isaac's intent was to pass on the Covenant blessings to his older son, to establish Esau as the leader of the Covenant tradition. It was part of the culture to pass everything on to the eldest son, and so it was natural for Isaac to imagine the Covenant worked the same way. It was natural but also went against his own experience: he was himself a second son. He should have known better, but his love for Esau seemed to outweigh even his own memory.

God could have easily foiled Rebekah's plan to steal Esau's blessing. Isaac recognized Jacob's voice immediately. A blind man quickly becomes acute in the sense of hearing and relies on that sense heavily. It would normally have taken something more than feeling some goatskin and smelling the scent of Esau's clothes to convince someone as suspicious as Isaac, so it seems that God made him more willing to believe than he would normally have been. Moreover, Jacob left Isaac in the nick of time to escape; if Esau had been quicker by just a few minutes, Jacob would have been caught in the act of deception and would have received a curse instead. It was not just that God *allowed* him to get away with it. The ease with which Jacob deceived Isaac was from God. The accidents involved in the hunt and the incidental route to finding the game and bringing it back to the camp could easily have been shortened if He had wished, but He did not. There are no coincidences in timing; this was God's choreography. God cooperated with Rebekah's scheme. Why?

First of all, God permitted the theft to succeed because God had already decided to bless Jacob and not Esau. The blessing that Isaac inadvertently conferred on Jacob conformed to what God had determined to confer on Jacob anyway. God interfered—not to fulfill His word, but to repeat His word—even using Jacob's lies to do it. It might seem somewhat scandalous that God would use such questionable means to establish His will, but that is because we aren't thinking clearly. In fact, God uses absolutely everything that happens to accomplish what He wants in the end. It is a great comfort to know that He takes the tawdriness of life and makes it accomplish elegance.

Secondly, God did not actually allow Jacob to get away with stealing the blessing, as we shall see shortly. In fact, He did not allow Jacob to get away with cheating Esau out of his inheritance either. God had tolerated superstition and even idolatry in His people for one reason or another, but that does not mean He just let them slide. There are always consequences in doing what is wrong, whether we know it is wrong or not, just as there are always consequences in ignoring the law of gravity whether we know the law of gravity of not. But God knows how to be patient, none better.

In the case of Jacob and Esau God took great care to bestow His favor on the less deserving of the two and to do it in a public way that we would have to notice. I believe that Jacob and Esau lived for exactly this purpose. The lives of these two men were the substance of the revelation He was making. The Covenant of Revelation was to continue through Jacob, and so God set about revealing Himself to Jacob and making the lives of both Jacob and Esau act out a metaphor of His character. One reason for God choosing the more unsavory of the two brothers was to make this point: that God's work depends on His power and not on our worthiness. He had already taught us that He does not need our help in fulfilling His promises; now He showed us that He didn't need our goodness either. God did not and does not choose His people because of their "goodness". We would like to believe that He chose us for our fine qualities, but that is just our pride speaking. In particular Christians are not, and have never been, particularly good people. If anything, my experience suggests that we may be worse than the average.

In fact Jacob was as nearly an atheist as a man of the ancient world could be, for the man who believes that the gods are irrelevant is twin brother to the man who believes they don't exist at all. He doubtless had heard of the oracle, but he showed little interest in the God who had given the oracle. It was not that he did not believe in God; it was that God or the gods were very far away and not fully part of life. And the little belief he had was entirely in the realm of superstition. Jacob was a sort of Mesopotamian Deist.

Though Jacob did nothing to try to win God's favor, though He did not seek God's favor, though Jacob's character did not win God's favor, nonetheless God loved him and was gracious to him. God's graciousness to Jacob was revealed as graphically by the way God disciplined him as it was by the way He shielded Jacob from the consequences of his own self-centeredness. From this point on, Jacob could hardly turn around without God meddling in something he was doing, without some trouble coming on him at God's instigation, without God blessing everything he did in some unusual way. Whereas God did not reprove Esau's behavior or say anything to him good or bad, He interfered repeatedly in Jacob's life. From the time he had to flee Esau's wrath, God was actively "teaching Jacob a lesson".

God began to reveal that He desired certain behavior and was willing to discipline, train, teach, instill such behavior into His people, even though He might wait seventy-five years to begin. In other words, He revealed Himself as being something like a Father, a careful and a patient Father, but an inexorable one. The Covenant with Abraham and Isaac was a Covenant of Revelation, and one thing that revelation means is correction. God did not intend merely to tell us cool things about Himself; He also intended to tell us something about ourselves and what He thought about the way we behave. It makes sense, if one is planning to teach about character, to choose people whose character gives ample room for comment. I might add that He was so subtle with His moral instruction as to be nearly inaudible, a still small voice. He never came right out and said "Thou shalt not . . ." He never pointed out the moral in anything He did. He merely interfered and left Jacob and His people to figure it out for themselves. God was so very slow at teaching people how to be good and not to be bad that it looks very much as if He didn't think it was important. We shall see, as we read on, whether this is true or not.

I must repeat what I said previously. Esau may have despised the material benefits of his birth, but the Scripture does not say that he despised the spiritual benefits or the Covenant. On the contrary, Esau was deeply grieved that his blessing had been stolen; he loved his father and wanted his blessing perhaps more than anything in the world. It was Jacob who despised the spiritual benefits of the Covenant by his actions. It was Jacob who treated the blessing of the Covenant as a commodity that he could steal and treated God as a blind and impotent force that could be manipulated to his own will by tricks. There is no evidence in the least at this point in Jacob's life that he respected or valued or honored either God or the Covenant. The Scripture would later describe Esau as godless, but this godlessness came, not from Esau turning away from God, but from God turning away from Esau. The difference between Jacob and Esau, even at this later age of their lives, did not lie in what they wanted or what they did or what they thought. The difference between Jacob and Esau rested exclusively in how God treated them: "Jacob I have loved but Esau I have hated" is the way it would be put by Malachi, but another way to say it would be "Jacob I have disciplined but Esau I have ignored".

Isaac sought to circumvent the theft of the blessing, but all he could do was to give Esau a violent and rebellious spirit that would throw off the rule of his brother. Actually neither blessing, nor even the oracle, had any immediate effect at all; nor did they have any long-term effects in the lives of the two men, Jacob and Esau. Esau never did become a servant to his brother, nor did he throw off Jacob's yoke, nor did Jacob's yoke ever have a tangible existence. If the blessings of Isaac meant anything then, in Esau's case, they had prophetic significance only. Esau's heritage became mixed with the Horites, a people who lived in the land of Seir to the south and east of the land of Canaan, and Esau's descendants came to dominate them to such an extent that they became known as the Edomites.

There was intermittent conflict between Israel and Edom all the time that Edom existed as a distinct people, which was not long. Conflicts commonly arose from the hostility of the Edomites toward Israel and not the other way. Thus we come to another instance of institutionalizing the bitterness of brother against brother, a bitterness which the two of them resolved to some extent in their later years but which continued in their descendants. Isaac wished things for Esau that he shouldn't have wished. In the end, Isaac's "blessing" of Esau, giving Esau a violent and rebellious spirit, did come to pass, but only served to alienate Esau from the Covenant and isolate his people to the point that they soon ceased to be nation at all. Isaac's blessing was far more negative, as a prophecy, than the oracle alone would have been. Whatever else the "wrath of God" may be, it is most commonly God letting us have what we want.

It is hard to take Isaac's blessing to Esau in any way other than as a rejection of God's will revealed in the oracle. All that came of Isaac's "blessing" on Esau was the confirmation of a mindset within Esau, a bitterness and further alienation from his brother. Ultimately the result was Esau's estrangement from the Covenant, eventual violence between the descendants of Jacob and the descendants of Esau, and finally the disappearance of Esau's heritage from the earth. It need not have been that way. God had not hinted that Esau was to be excluded from the covenant, nor that being ruled over by the descendants of Jacob would be demeaning. That all came as the result of Isaac and his misguided love for his favorite son. It was not long, however, until Isaac was at least reconciled to the fact that the Covenant was passing on to Jacob; when Isaac sent Jacob away to Haran to find a wife, his words were the Covenant's own words.

3. Jacob's Flight to Laban (Genesis 27:41-28:22)

Esau was enraged by Jacob's deception, but he was completely self-controlled in his anger. This contrasts with his lack of self-control when he returned from the hunt hungry and traded his inheritance for a bowl of soup. Physical desires were too hard for him, but emotional desires were within his power. He calmly plotted to murder Jacob at a good opportunity, when their father died so as not to distress him. Of course Esau did not know that there would be more than forty years before Isaac died. Even Isaac thought he might be getting close. However Rebekah did not want to take any chances; it would be better to put Jacob at a safe distance and rely on time to soothe the anger of Esau.

It was a wise plan, and Esau's wives presented the perfect rationale to talk Isaac into agreeing to the plan: send Jacob to Paddan-Aram, to Rebekah's family, to find a wife so they wouldn't have any more of those Hittite women in the family. Even after thirty or so years, by my chronology, or perhaps especially after thirty years, the relationship with the Hittite women increasingly irritated Rebekah and Isaac. Rebekah had been gone from her brother Laban for ninety years and probably had lost touch with what was going on in her family, but it seemed like a good bet that they were doing well and would at least be able to offer Jacob a safe hiding place in addition to getting him a wife.

When Jacob left for Paddan-Aram, the insensitive Esau finally noticed that his parents did not get along with his wives. He just had simply not noticed there was a problem even after decades, but Jacob's departure finally brought it to his attention. Esau really did not mean to displease either of his parents. He wanted to please them and to make up for his mistake with the Hittite women he found an Ishmaelite woman to marry. The Ishmaelites were close relatives and there might be less friction. That was the best he could have done, short of following Jacob to Paddan-Aram, but as the eldest he would have had duties managing the family property, especially if Isaac was sick and blind, and it would have been more than awkward being in close company with Jacob. For all these reasons a journey to Paddan-Aram was out of the question for Esau. Esau really was a dutiful son; he was just kind of an oaf, clueless but with good intentions.

The most likely guess would have Jacob leaving for Paddan-Aram in about 1920 b.c. when he was nearly eighty years old. This timing fits well enough with later events. Mesopotamia was in a state of turmoil and the city-states of Isin and Larsa vied with each other to dominate the region. It was a time of shifting alliances with no clear power in charge, but their focus was on the centers of power and not on the edges of world. The fringes of Mesopotamia, which was where Paddan-Aram was, were on their own until some super-power arose to interfere with their lives. We don't know the political climate of Paddan-Aram at the time, but it may have been reasonably, though briefly, stable.

The main problem with dating this narrative is that it would have been unusual for Jacob to be unmarried at eighty. As I mentioned in the previous section, one gets the impression that Jacob was very much dominated by his mother and such people often find it difficult to make their own choices. Marriage could be perceived by the mother as a threat to her influence and therefore to be postponed as long as possible. Such a story is not unheard of in our day, but we don't know enough about that culture to judge its likelihood in that context. In more modern times, even a man as forceful as General MacArthur had a mother who was more than his match. If Jacob had not had to flee from Esau, how long would it have been until he married? And we can imagine the sort of wife his mother might have picked for him. The Bible does not portray the relationship of Jacob and Rebekah as at all healthy, but dysfunctional families were not an invention of the modern age.

Jacob arrived in Bethel, but probably not on his first night; it was nearly sixty miles to the north. He seems to have arrived at that spot coincidentally, not realizing it was the place his grandfather Abram had built his second altar to the Lord after his arrival a century and a half before. It was one of those divine coincidences that dot the process of Covenant history, underlining its unity. There, on his first night away from home, God appeared to Jacob for the first time. This is also the first time

God chose to communicate in a dream. Previously the text had described God as "appearing" to Isaac or to Abraham, without being specific about how it happened. This time it is specifically a dream. The dream of the ladder going up into heaven with angels ascending and descending echoes through the millennia, until the Messiah promised the same vision to His disciple Nathanael with his waking eyes.

In the dream, God reaffirmed all the promises He had made to Abraham and to Isaac, thus firmly indicating that the Covenant would be passed on to Jacob. Giving a vision to Jacob and not to Esau does not mean that Esau was being excluded from the Covenant, but it does mean that Jacob was being chosen as the leader for the Covenant people, the primary guardian of the revelation. The Covenant itself was not transferred from generation to generation by the giving of visions but by birth. Esau was as much a part of the Covenant as Jacob, or as anyone else born into that household, including the slaves and the children born to them. But Esau was estranged both by Jacob's underhandedness and by Isaac's imprudent favoritism and only continued to grow more isolated from his heritage in his old age.

Jacob's response to the dream is embarrassing even to read. Having heard the Covenant promises of God, the same that had been made to Abraham and to Isaac, the same promises he must have been told of by his father and grandfather, Jacob might have felt awe, he might have felt gratitude, he might have felt humbled. He might have but he didn't. Jacob's vow in response was more like slapping God in the face. God had promised to care for him and protect him unconditionally; Jacob turned it upside down and made his response to God a conditional one. God humbled Himself by seeking out this son of Abraham and Isaac, ignoring Jacob's deceitful character. Jacob sent God back for His resume: only if God was able to pull it all off would Jacob worship Him.

So Jacob was saved by grace, but God was put on probation! Why did God not give Jacob a good swat to remind him who was the creature and who was the Creator? How many parents among us would take such cheekiness from our children without responding in some harsh manner? Yahweh took it because He meant what He said. He did not respond to Jacob in the manner he deserved exactly because He was gracious. In other words, God had had a lot of practice being spat upon before He came in the flesh to experience it physically. To be more emphatic, the crucifixion of the Messiah was just the material realization of a process that had been going on for millennia.

This is the context of the second time tithing is mentioned in the Bible. The first mention of the tithe was when Abraham gave a tithe to Melchizedek. There was clearly a custom somewhat common in the ancient world that when thanksgiving or vows were made to God a tenth was a fair amount to give. The origin of tithing is lost in ancient history just as the origin of burnt offerings is lost. While burnt offerings go all the way back to Cain and Abel, however, it is not clear how early the practice of the tithe began nor where it came from. One thing is clear: although God intended to incorporate the tithe into His official worship eventually, He had not made a point of requiring or expecting tithes from Abraham or Isaac. It was never described as being part of their lives. At the beginning of the Covenant of Revelation tithing was apparently peripheral and unimportant. Though Jacob promised a tithe, it is not clear how or in what form he ever actually presented it to God. Since there was no priesthood, no rituals, and no precedents at this point we can't say how he intended to keep the promise. There is no reason to doubt that he kept his vow, but there is no record of him actually keeping it.

Still, for all his arrogance Jacob was profoundly impressed that God was indeed present in that place. Jacob did not know God very well; he was apparently still thinking of the finite and localized gods of the Middle East. And his awe of God was the awe that bows before the unpredictable and powerful, not the awe that comes from love or gratitude. Doubtless he had heard of God's appearances to his grandfather; he was in on the oral traditions and the family stories of God's intervention, but he just didn't get it. He was like so many of us; the stories about God are great, inspiring, comforting, part of our heritage; or else they are quaint and interesting but don't actually intersect our lives. It is fine to believe in the God of our fathers, but to directly encounter God is not what we expect, and sometimes not exactly what we want. It catches us by surprise, throws us off guard, and without thinking we find ourselves treating God like a shabby and uncouth cousin we haven't thought of in years, an unwelcome intruder.

From this experience Jacob named the place Bethel, the "house of God". The account of Abram's visit there used the name Bethel because the account was written down later when Bethel had replaced Luz as the common name for that place. In giving this name, Jacob realized that God could be present even when he was unaware of Him, a very important truth to learn. We would all benefit by understanding this same idea. For those of us who are susceptible to spiritual desires, we want to feel God's presence, we want the experience of Him here and now. But if we don't feel anything, it doesn't mean He isn't here. We are all clueless, like Jacob, unobservant fools stumbling through our lives and hardly ever aware that Bethel is where we always are, with angels ascending and descending all around us.

4. Jacob with Laban (Genesis 29-30)

God does not always gift wrap blessings. Jacob the deceiver—and worse than a deceiver, a hypocrite—was sent away to a man who could out-deceive him, his uncle Laban. Laban was Rebekah's brother in ethics as well as parentage, a crafty man, a schemer. Laban doubtless remembered how when he was young the rich servant of Abraham had visited them and taken away his sister. Now he was old, more than a hundred years old, and though he was rich, he had found it to be true that the rich are never rich enough. It would seem that his children ran to sons (as Jacob's would); Leah and Rachel may have been his only two daughters in his old age. Perhaps his greed for more was the result of his property being split into many pieces when he died and it was the welfare of his sons that worried him.

Though he might not be able to share his sister's and nephew's wealth directly, Laban was a very superstitious man. He could tell that God Most High had been with Abraham and Isaac, and was presumably with Jacob as well. Like many superstitious men, he did not care about God or the gods, but if he could manipulate the people the gods blessed he could siphon off some of that divine influence. If he couldn't share the wealth directly Laban figured he could stand near enough to the blessings to skim off a bit for himself. I do not mean Laban was a particularly evil man; he was most like a modern business man with a bit of magic and spiritual susceptibility thrown in. He was a superstitious version of the woman who reminded Jesus that even the dogs eat the crumbs from under their master's table. Laban didn't see Jacob as a master, of course; rather he saw him as a dog to whom some Master was throwing a lot of bread. Like so many, Laban's faith was a form of mercenary allegiance, a belief that tried to exploit God's kindness to others for his own profit. Compare Laban's faith with Abraham's faith, the faith which was counted as righteousness. Abraham trusted God, in a rudimentary way he loved God, and he seems never to have particularly sought material blessings at all. Laban loved himself and sought to use the gods as a business asset. It never occurred to Laban that he could or should get to know God directly, or that there were other than material blessings that were desirable.

It had been a hundred years since Rebekah had left Laban. Jacob told Laban all that had taken place since Rebekah had left with Abraham's servant, nearly a century of catching up, including his own personal history. Jacob the deceiver was so naive; it never occurred to him that other men might be as deceitful as he was. Laban knew he had had an argument with his brother and was not eager to go back home for a while. So after the customary month of feasting it was natural for Laban to offer Jacob a job. Now that Jacob was independent of his mother for the first time, a month with Laban was enough to show Jacob what he really wanted. He would work seven years for Rachel, and those seven years seemed like nothing to him with the prospect of marrying Rachel at the end.

It seems that Jacob sincerely loved Rachel; she was probably the first human being besides himself that he had genuinely loved—his love for his mother would have been a selfish kind of love, not a matter of the heart; in fact, his love for his mother was probably quite strained, with a large dose of resentment and anger mixed in. Possibly Jacob was merely falling for the first pretty face he met, having escaped his mother. It may have started that way, but it does not seem to have continued that way. Seven years of living in Rachel's household had not dimmed his desire for her and it would have, had the attachment been mere infatuation. Rachel would not have known Rebekah, of course, but doubtless knew of her. Being unwed and the younger daughter, Rachel was probably not much more than a teenager, sixty or more years younger than Jacob as I count the chronology, but such a marriage would not have been as unusual then as now.

It is difficult to imagine Jacob not recognizing that it was Leah who was brought to his tent on his wedding night, but that is because we are used to lights everywhere we go. Also, Jacob had been drinking a lot of wine, no doubt. Even so, the deception that Laban and Leah together perpetrated on Jacob should certainly go down in history as one of the most astonishing. It certainly beats the deception Jacob had perpetrated on Esau by a long shot. It is also difficult to see how they could have deceived Jacob without Rachel knowing it. It seems most likely that she was kept in the dark until the last minute and that Laban restrained her somehow. In Leviticus 18:18 we see that the marriage of Jacob to both Leah and Rachel would be forbidden under the laws of Moses, so Jacob is yet one more of the patriarchs who would not have measured up to the moral code of the Law.

How humiliating it must have been for both Rachel and Leah. Leah had been waiting in the wings for seven long years, unwanted, while her younger sister was betrothed. Laban had certainly been seeking other opportunities for her during those seven years; it is not plausible that he had planned to substitute Leah all along. If another viable marriage opportunity had presented itself during those years, surely he would have taken it. Though Laban could afford a decent dowry by the standards of the time, though he was rich enough that he would have made a good connection, by the end of the seven years no such marriage opportunity had come up. And why not? Laban must have been the sort of man that his neighbors did not want to be connected with. Would marrying Leah have seemed like marrying into a crime syndicate? Something kept Leah, the daughter of a rich man, single and it wasn't merely her "weak eyes". Laban estimated Jacob's character shrewdly and correctly. The scheme that finally occurred to him had a strong financial appeal, a way to marry off both daughters without even the cost of a normal dowry and get more out of Jacob at the same time. The excuse that Leah was the older was lame, but Jacob was at a disadvantage.

But what was Leah feeling when she went along with her father's plan? How Leah must have suffered during those years; by the end of that time she was getting embarrassingly old to be still unmarried. It could not have been satisfying to her to marry someone who didn't want her, to marry by guile rather than honestly. And yet if she hadn't gone along with the plan she would have had to face her father alone. No one would have been there to help her. All she had before her were either dismal prospects of a miserable home life and the slim hope that she would eventually win Jacob's affection, or else a father who had failed to find her a husband and who could not be trusted to have her interests at heart. And what was Leah's problem, besides a scheming father, that made her undesirable? She "had weak eyes"; it is not clear what the passage means by those words, but with no glasses available she probably had to squint to see anything; perhaps she had a lazy eye or her eyes were crossed and there was no way to treat the condition. Societies from ancient days have been very harsh in their treatment of women, and our own culture is no kinder.

And so the foundation of a truly dysfunctional family was established. There now began a time of intense competition between Jacob's two wives, these sisters, whose marriage to Jacob had transformed them from sisters to rivals. Jacob's clear preference for Rachel only made Leah's resentment worse. Jacob's family, as it grew over the next seven years, had conflict built into it, saturating it, from the beginning. Naturally the politics between the wives was handed down to their children. This family was a psychologist's nightmare and takes "dysfunctional" to a whole new level. Nonetheless, it was this family that God chose as the foundation of the future nation of Israel. God's choice of this family as His own family outweighed all the damage and dysfunction. Reflecting on the very poor prospects that Jacob's family had for any happiness and goodness on the human level should give us some hope regarding ourselves. Things are bad with us, with our families, but God is merciful and can draw out grace from the most hopeless of situations.

Considering the culture of that time and place, the rivalry between Leah and Rachel naturally expressed itself in the production of children. The value and status of a wife was determined by the number of male children she bore, and so Leah and Rachel were both eager for this tangible sign of their worth. And God became a player in the game as well. It is so like God that He would bless Leah because she was unloved, because she was judged for a simple defect without regard to her character or humanity. There is no indication in the passage that Rachel was at fault, other than the fault of being born with more beauty. Still, God is the Equalizer, who raises up what is lowly. He does not like to see people treated badly for no good reason—the poor, the lame, the blind, the deaf, the orphan, the widow—and that attitude extends even to those who fail to measure up to some arbitrary standard of beauty or worth or romantic preference.

Jacob had agreed to work another seven years for Rachel; Laban had judged his nephew's desire for Rachel rightly and he fully meant to keep Jacob doing his work as long as the Lord would bless it. During the second period of seven years the rivalry of Leah and Rachel resulted in eleven sons and a daughter. At first Leah was the clear winner with four sons in rapid succession: Reuben, Simeon, Levi and Judah. Indeed for all eleven sons to be born in this seven-year time frame, everything must have been done in rapid succession. Leah must have borne them during the first four years, and this was rare in itself. The long period of nursing was a natural form of birth control that tended to spread out the time between births. Childbirth was dangerous at that time and births in rapid succession more so.

But when Rachel saw that she was having no children, she gave her maid, Bilhah, as a wife to Jacob, just as Sarah had given Hagar to Abraham. Bilhah then bore two sons, Dan and Naphtali, in rapid succession, probably while Leah was still bearing. As the fifth year wore on and Leah did not get pregnant again immediately as usual, she resorted to the same scheme and gave Zilpah to Jacob as a wife. Zilpah then bore Gad and Asher in rapid succession. Asher was probably born as the second set of seven years were ending.

But shortly after Leah gave Zilpah to Jacob a curious thing happened. Leah's son, Reuben, was out in the field; he was perhaps four years old. Whether he was sent by Leah to look for them or not, Reuben found some mandrakes. In the ancient Middle East, the roots of mandrakes were believed to be an aphrodisiac; they were sometimes called "love apples". It could be that Leah had shown Reuben how to recognize them and sent him out looking for them thinking they might help her get pregnant again. When Rachel saw the mandrake roots, she also wanted them. That night Rachel knew Jacob was coming to her tent. Probably more often than not, Jacob slept with Rachel because he loved her. Rachel was thinking that the mandrake roots might help her finally conceive. Leah was not willing to share with her husband-stealing little sister, but Rachel offered to trade the night with Jacob for the mandrakes. She could delay being with her husband one night if it gave her an advantage when she did have him.

But then it was Leah who became pregnant even without the aid of mandrake roots. She bore Issachar and then Zebulun, probably just as the second set of seven years was ending, six sons in seven years. This episode with the mandrakes is polygamy at its worst. Sexual politics has ruined monogamous marriages, and it is exponentially worse in a polygamous union. Buying her own husband for a night would have been as humiliating as the wedding night had been, but Leah and Rachel were growing adjusted to their family. Leah might be humiliated by using the mandrakes to get her husband to come to her, but she could boast about her four sons. Rachel might be humiliated by having no children at all, but she could boast about how much her husband preferred coming to her.

It was at this time, at last, as the seventh year was beginning, that God finally blessed Rachel with what she desired most. Joseph was born just as the seven years were ending so in about 1906 b.c. Dinah was probably born to Leah the following year, but there is no way to be sure. 37:35 suggests that Jacob had other daughters than Dinah, but none are mentioned by name. It would not be unusual for daughters to be left out of these old genealogies, but Dinah would have been included because of later events.

Naturally, when Jacob's time of service for his wives was over he was ready to leave and told Laban so. But Laban had "divined" that the Lord was blessing him because of Jacob. In other words, though he had been well off when Jacob had arrived—Jacob said Laban had little before he came but "little" is a relative term—Laban had become much richer under Jacob's care of his possessions. Laban could have been satisfied with what he had already gotten out of the deal, which had been greatly to his advantage. Still, Laban was a greedy man and now he was determined not to let the advantage slip away without squeezing the last few shekels from it. He determined to cheat Jacob one last time.

Later, when Jacob was plotting with his wives to escape from Laban he would tell them that he had had a dream, his second one, from God telling him to ask for the striped, speckled, and mottled among the sheep and goats. Thus inspired, he made a deal with Laban that would have seemed ideal to that man. It was a deal Laban thought he could easily manipulate to his advantage. All he had to do was to initially separate those sheep and goats from the herd he entrusted to Jacob. Jacob would only have the white sheep and goats and, though the science of genetics was unknown, Laban knew that the offspring look like the parents. It wasn't rocket science. In the normal course of events, Laban knew Jacob would end up with almost nothing.

However, luck, such as it is, was not with Laban; luck, such as it is, is only one of God's many disguises. The account of how Jacob put the striped sticks in front of the flocks while they were mating is difficult to appreciate. He added to the dream the idea that the sticks would cause the coloring, for the striped sticks were no part of the vision he described to his wives. This was clearly a superstition that Jacob had acquired somewhere, that the presence of the sticks with alternating white and dark bands could affect the color of the lambs and the kids, that the sticks had the power to affect inheritance. Jacob's grasp of genetics was considerably less than

Laban's, but it was not genetics that was behind the coloring of the flock. Genetics is partly a statistical process anyway and God has always found ample cover in statistical processes.

God did not even try to straighten out Jacob's ignorant ideas, though Jacob's insistence on finding a "natural cause" would have competed with God for the credit, at least by the way a modern person looks at things. By blessing Jacob's activity and causing the kids and lambs to be striped and speckled, God would appear to be encouraging this kind of superstition, but God takes His time correcting our errors. Wasn't He missing a valuable teaching opportunity with Jacob? Apparently He didn't think Jacob needed that kind of lesson at that point. For the most part God continues to let our foolishness stand uncorrected. Remember how lenient He is toward your ignorance whenever you are tempted to enlighten your more ignorant brothers and sisters. If God corrected all of our foolishness, how quickly we would grow discouraged under the constant necessity of His reprimands. And if God is so lenient toward our foolishness, maybe we shouldn't spend so much of our own time and energy trying to correct the so-called foolishness of the world. Perhaps God could give us other priorities.

Clearly Jacob had come a long way in fourteen years in humility and faith in God Most High; a long way but not very far. He had progressed from not caring for God to trying to do God's work for Him. He was trying to use his own great insight into the way things worked to help God fulfill the promise in the dream. But if he could not help Him fulfill His promises, neither could his help do anything to hinder Him from fulfilling them. I wonder if all the help we sometimes try to give God is equally superstition. How much of what we believe is just silly, regardless of the thin coating of rationality we give it? We think we know cause and effect, but how can we know any causes when the original Cause gets involved? This is a picture of the sum total of human wisdom: putting striped sticks in the ground to make the laws of genetics work the way we want.

5. Jacob's Escape from Laban (Genesis 31)

When a cheat realizes his plans are failing, he grows angry with his intended victim. After six years of the new deal they had agreed on, it had become clear to Laban and his sons that the deal had gone sour, that all the good animals belonged to Jacob and belonged incontestably to him due to their coloring, that God was taking away what was Laban's and was giving it to Jacob. If Laban did see God's hand in Jacob's share of the flocks then he profoundly under-estimated God's *immediacy*. He still thought he could manipulate events in his favor with or without God's cooperation. He had no idea just how directly involved in events God was willing to be. Laban is interesting as an example of the kind of spirituality that is so normal in the world, believing in God but not in His presence or power. He was part of the oral tradition that had preserved the first part of Genesis, as all of Abraham's family had been, and there is no reason to think that he was worse than the usual representative of the "seed of the woman". Again, it is an eye-opener whom God is willing to use to carry on His work in the world.

Since God had apparently revealed to Jacob that the striped, speckled, and mottled animals were the right animals to request for his wages six years previously, God's appearance to him at the crisis calling him to go home was the third visitation from God to Jacob. Jacob's attitude toward God had certainly altered from Bethel. For one thing, he knew that Laban outclassed him as a crook and that he was going to need some real help to get away. He was also beginning to be worried that he and his family were in actual danger from Laban and his sons. So when God told him in a vision to get out of there, it was reassuring to him, and all the more since he had fully realized that he owed all of his prosperity to God. It is interesting that when God spoke to him and told to leave Haran that He reminded him of his promise at Bethel, that if God would provide for him that he would worship God as his own God and give Him a tithe of everything. God intended to finish His probationary period and to hold Jacob to his word.

By this time, Rachel and Leah had both grown alienated from their father, who had been willing enough to try to cheat them as well now that they belonged to Jacob. It must have been one of the few times Jacob's whole household was united in pursuing a single task. Reuben, the eldest, would have been about twelve or thirteen, Judah would have been about ten, and Joseph only about six, so his children would not have been a great help if it came to fighting. Jacob had been an older man when he fled from Esau, and was now in his mid-nineties, and he had never been vigorous like Esau had been. Though twenty years of hard work might have made him more vigorous, this would still have been a strain for him.

The description of Jacob's cleverness in fleeing from Laban when Laban was not looking sounds sarcastic: how clever of him to not tell Laban that he was planning an escape. Clearly, Jacob was not the great general that his grandfather was. Moreover, though Jacob had acquired servants, they would not have been trained as soldiers as Abraham's had been. His household was not prepared for fighting; so he did the only thing he could think of, getting as large a head start as possible and putting the Euphrates River between himself and Laban. It was a desperate move, but it was also courageous. A timid man would have tried to talk his way out, counting on family ties to protect his family. Laban would probably not have actually harmed Jacob or his family, but neither would he have let Jacob leave with more than a modest portion of what he had agreed to. Laban was not ruthless, but he was greedy and manipulative and craftier than Jacob; he was not above taking Jacob's possessions by force.

It was inevitable that Laban would catch him; Jacob's stealth had only bought him a three-day advantage. Jacob would have had to move slowly with his children and herds, while Laban took only men who could hurry. Even so Jacob had made it to the hill country of Gilead before Laban found him. In other words, Jacob had gotten most of the way to his home—not that he had much hope of a warm welcome when he got there—and this suggests that Laban had some difficulty finding him. Verse 23 says that Laban took seven days to find Jacob searching through that sparsely inhabited land. Jacob's household was too big to keep unnoticed, but there were a lot of out-of-the-way places to hide. He clearly didn't take the main trade route, and he was perhaps more clever at covering his tracks than we might give him credit for. Jacob made very good time over the ten days of his flight, and Laban was not a great tracker.

What Laban intended to do when he caught Jacob is not clear. Perhaps his intent was as evil as it sounds from the text, but he still had some respect and fear of God, especially after the warning in this first vision he had ever had. So his arrival at Jacob's camp was one of bluster rather than serious threat. Laban continued to maintain his innocence; he continued to pretend that he had meant only kindness toward Jacob. He had brought what amounted to an army; he clearly had the power to do whatever he wished and Jacob could do nothing about it and Laban made sure to point that out. His kind intentions toward Jacob might have been doubted because of the rather threatening presence of his men, but his kind intentions were evidenced by his not using force when he could have. He was determined to at least make Jacob look like the one who was in the wrong, even if he was afraid of going against God, so he seized on the one legitimate gripe that he had: he had been robbed. Rachel had stolen Laban's household idols. Though Laban didn't know who had done it, he wanted those idols back. It was the only legitimate excuse he had for detaining Jacob.

Idolatry was thus a commonplace, even among the people that carried the oral tradition. Laban was part of that tribe that knew about the Creation and Fall and Flood and Babel. In 35:4 we see that it was also common in Jacob's household for individuals to have their own gods. Jacob may not have told his servants much about the Covenant, and they might not have heard very much even about the oral tradition. Rachel and Leah were heir to the oral traditions, but not to the history that God had shared with Abraham. None of them knew, not even Jacob knew, that the God of Abraham and Isaac was the only true God, that idols were nothing, and that idols were offensive to God. God had not told them any of this and still did not tell them. He simply let them keep their idols, biding His time until the right opportunity to take the revelation further. Only because the search was not conducted thoroughly, and Rachel was a quick thinker, did Rachel get away with it.

But why did Rachel take her father's idols? It was another superstition, the idea that possessing the idols of Laban gave her some power over him, perhaps some protection from him as well. Hence, when God intervened to protect them, from her viewpoint her theft of the idols was being justified: her trick had worked and stealing the idols had indeed helped to rescue them. Laban did tell them about his vision from the night before, so on one level she knew that God Most High had intervened. And yet superstition has deeper roots than that. It is likely that she attributed their deliverance mainly to the idols, rather than the God whom she had heard of but never seen.

Furthermore, Jacob didn't know what she had done (eventually she would tell him since the story was preserved in the oral tradition) and had offered to execute whoever was found with the idols. Rachel's life was in danger and so God again protected the life of the guilty, an idolater and thief, without any word of rebuke or correction. Later we will see that the issue of idolatry was very important to God, that it was one of the two or three most important issues to Him; and yet He could bide His time here. God's priority has always been to behave with integrity, according to

His own gracious character, rather than to demand that His own moral standards be obeyed. He won't clear the guilty—this is utterly true—but even more importantly He won't violate His own nature to punish the guilty.

Thanks to God's intervention, however, Jacob did get away from Laban and the two made peace with each other. It is not known where the spot is that they made their covenant together. One significant thing that should be noticed about their covenant is how Laban made his vow to Jacob: in the name of "the God of Abraham and the God of Nahor, the God of their father". Abraham had come from a family, as already alleged, that had a strong oral tradition and allegiance to God Most High. That oral tradition would not simply have disappeared once Abraham was called; it would have continued on as long as God kept it alive. When God does something special and new it does not mean that He abandons all that He had been previously doing. On the contrary, God worked outside of the Covenant to keep alive some knowledge of Himself in the world. Laban handed down his small part of the revelation, and God continued to work outside the Covenant among Laban's family and others that are not mentioned here.

It is worth noticing 31:47. Laban and Jacob already spoke different dialects. Abraham had left Haran one hundred and eighty years previously certainly speaking the same Aramaic that the rest of his family spoke, but after almost two centuries his grandson had already begun speaking a dialect that would become Hebrew. At this early stage, it would have been only just beginning to separate into a distinct language, and he and Laban were still mutually intelligible to each other. In subsequent centuries, after a lengthy stay in Egypt, Hebrew would become completely distinct from Aramaic. It is the natural evolution of language. There would be no further close contact between Jacob's descendants and Laban's, and the day would come when the Aramaeans, of which Laban was part, would do harm to Jacob's descendants.

6. Jacob Prepares to Meet Esau (Genesis 32:1-21)

Getting away from Laban was scary enough, but seeing Esau again after twenty years was worse. Laban had been cheating Jacob, but Jacob knew he was the guilty one in his own home. It is one thing to break free of a bad man who has been using you, but it is quite a different kind of fear, and a worse fear, to return to a man whom you have wronged and who can reasonably be expected to be violent. Jacob had apparently not received any word from home since he had left. Rebekah had said she would send for him when it was safe to return but she had not done it. What was he to think of that? Did it mean that Esau was continuing to hold a grudge after twenty years? It is almost certain that Rebekah had died, and perhaps not long after Jacob had left. There is mention only of her tomb but no mention of her death anywhere in Scripture. She disappeared from the narrative as soon as Jacob left for Haran. But Jacob had to assume the worst, that Esau still hated him and intended to kill him.

The first recorded event after Laban and Jacob parted company was the encounter with the company of angels near Mahanaim. Actually, Mahanaim means "two companies", so it would seem that there were a large number of angels involved in this encounter, unless one of the companies is the company of his own household. The name could also refer to his dividing his household into two companies to meet Esau. It is interesting that until Jacob angels had always come individually, three together at the most. But Jacob's first dream included many angels ascending and descending a ladder, and now he saw an army of angels. Because of their numbers, these angels cannot be easily understood as a pre-incarnation visit by the Messiah. Whatever angels are, they are not just some disguise that God assumes.

It would have been interesting if some detail had been included to indicate how Jacob knew they were angels rather than men. Wings? Radiance? Halos? More intriguing, as well as more importantly, is what the angels were doing there and why Jacob was permitted to see them. Angels are apparently not always visible when they are present, so God must have wanted him and the rest of his household to see these angels. It seems that these angels were there to reassure Jacob, that if there were hostilities between Jacob and Esau, God was prepared to intervene on Jacob's behalf. Whether this was Jacob's understanding or not, he continued to take all the precautions that he could think of for the coming reunion. Jacob was seriously afraid of Esau with or without angels as bodyguards.

By this time, Esau was living in the land of Seir, to the south of the Dead Sea and between seventy-five and a hundred miles south of where Jacob was camped. During the two decades of Jacob's absence Esau and Isaac had separated into two households, just as Isaac and Abraham had separated into two household even before Isaac was married. Perhaps when Esau moved to Seir, Isaac had also moved to Hebron, Abraham's main home. Jacob would not have wanted to risk surprising Esau, so he decided to send a message to him from this comfortable distance. It might have been better to meet Esau at Isaac's home, but there was no guarantee that Isaac would be a protection and there was no guarantee he could make it there without Esau hearing of it.

It was horrifying to hear that Esau's immediate response to Jacob's message was to begin assembling his men, four hundred of them, to come to him. These men were probably trained soldiers; Esau was more the type to follow Abraham's military example than Jacob was. What else could such a response mean but hostility? Esau was coming with a great force to meet him and destroy him; even after twenty years, the anger was alive in Esau's heart. Though Isaac was still alive (Jacob wouldn't necessarily have known it), perhaps Esau was tired of waiting for his revenge and meant to get it immediately regardless of the consequences with his father. Something had to be done to mollify Esau. Jacob knew that his household could not fight and he knew that Esau had just cause to be angry.

So Jacob divided his household in the hope that one part of it might escape if the other was attacked. Jacob's prayer in 32:9-12 is perhaps the main point of his long sojourn with Laban. His character had been transformed by his experiences there. The arrogant man who had run from Esau had become a humble man, a weak man who knew his weakness and knew the necessity of depending on God. What God might have tried to accomplish twenty years before by rebuke and punishment He had accomplished by letting the years and experience work through him. For those who see this account as revelation, the events of those decades had been designed exactly to produce such a change in Jacob's character. This is the meaning of God's discipline: that He brings people and circumstances into our lives to cause us to grow in certain ways. It is the way we are: we find it very difficult to learn anything by being told. Experience is the best teacher because it is usually the only teacher we will listen to.

What of Laban, then? Doubtless, Laban also learned much in those years with Jacob. For one thing, Laban learned something about the reality of God, that He was not just a family tradition but also a real presence who might interfere in earthly events in unexpected ways. Perhaps Laban was not changed in the same way nor to the same degree as Jacob, but in his own way he had been the recipient of a revelation as well. Laban was not called to be a bearer of the Covenant, but he was called along with all the rest of us to be blessed by the bearers of that Covenant, and blessed he was.

On the next day after receiving the news of Esau's approach Jacob did the most sensible thing he could do: he sent Esau a present, a lavish present, to try to mollify his anger. There is nothing like receiving valuable gifts, especially from someone who has cheated you, to make you feel better. Even better, he divided the gift into smaller parcels, each lavish in itself. In this way, Esau would repeatedly encounter a gift from Jacob, each gift would go a little way to easing his anger, as well as slowing him down a bit. Jacob guessed wisely that an anger that had been nurtured over twenty long years could not be assuaged by a single gift in a single moment, but might be chipped away a little at a time.

Furthermore I suspect that this gift to Esau matched in value the share of the inheritance he had cheated Esau out of for the bowl of soup. God may choose the most unsavory of men for His covenant, and He may be very slow to address their unsavoriness, but He need not let them go uncorrected forever. Esau was also loved by God, and He didn't let His man cheat his own brother. If this gift to Esau was payback for the cheater, it is important to note that God didn't feel the need to point it out to Jacob. God's priority was to compensate Esau; whether Jacob recognized the moral or not. God leaves His lessons hanging in the air, as it were, and if we don't get the point, eventually someone will. He is patient.

The gift to Esau took a whole day to arrange, so it had been a day and a half, roughly, since Jacob had heard of Esau's approach. At this point Jacob was still camped at Mahanaim on the northern side of the Jabbok, a river which runs west to the Jordan and which would form the future boundary between the kingdoms of Sihon and Og when the Israelites returned from Egypt. There was danger Esau might arrive that night before he got the gifts if he made all possible speed. Just as important, what route would he take? Esau knew Jacob was on the north of the Jabbok and would aim for that point. If he came along the eastern side of the Dead Sea, then he would arrive to the south of the Jabbok and have to cross at Peniel; but if he came along the western side of the Dead Sea, then he would follow the western side of Jordan and cross it to the north of the Jabbok. Jacob apparently expected the western route, so in the evening he moved down to the ford at Peniel and put his wives and children on the southern side of the Jabbok where they would be somewhat hidden from Esau if he arrived in the night and attacked before he got the gift. Everything Jacob owned was on the south side of the Jabbok, but Jacob himself stayed alone on the northern side to be there to meet Esau if he arrived early. If Esau was early then perhaps killing Jacob would satisfy him and he would leave Jacob's family alone. It was a dangerous situation, but it was about to get weird.

7. Jacob Wrestles with the Angel (Genesis 32:22-33:17)

The man who came to wrestle with Jacob appears in this narrative out of nowhere. Like the serpent in the garden, like Melchizedek meeting Abram, like the three angels walking past Abram on the way to Sodom, this nameless man came unaccountably and suddenly from nowhere. Again the mythic and the historical intersect. The wrestler was called a man in this passage and was called an angel in Hosea 12:3,4, and he is frequently interpreted as a pre-incarnation appearance of the Messiah. Why did they start wrestling? Clearly the man picked a fight with Jacob. I think that initially Jacob thought the man was Esau. Perhaps he was a hairy man who smelled of the fields; in the dark he may even have looked like Esau. But at some point in the wrestling Jacob recognized the hand of God in the hand that was pinning him down. Suddenly it all became much more serious.

And so they wrestled through the night and day was about to break. The identity of the man is mysterious, but his motivations were even more so, regardless of who he was. Why did God appear to Jacob and wrestle him? Or if not God Himself, why did God send an agent to wrestle with Jacob? And once Jacob recognized the supernatural character of his adversary, why didn't he give up? What did he hope to gain by wrestling with God? Wouldn't it have been more humble, more righteous, more reasonable, once he recognized the man as being from God, to surrender to His power? But Jacob refused to quit until the man blessed him. What made him think fighting with God should get him a blessing? Doesn't God prefer that we submit humbly to His will?

One reason Jacob might not capitulate was that the strange man had started the fight in the first place. Perhaps Jacob was thinking something like, "All right, if God wants to fight then let's fight." It does not sound like the kind of thing many Christians would think, and it does not sound much like what we know of Jacob's character. We are accustomed to believe that submission to God is the highest good, the thing that He wants, the sign of great spirituality. The harder God pushes us the more we are supposed to accept. If He pushes us into the mud and we are supposed to lie in a huddle and let Him pick us up and throw us back again if He chooses. God's will be done. That would have been a natural mode of thought for Jacob as well. "Don't fight with gods" is a maxim recognized in the most primitive religious circles.

The thing is, Jacob's belligerence seems to be what God was looking for. There had never been a doubt about who would win the fight; Jacob was elderly and had never been a fighter anyway. When the stranger wished to put an end to it he merely touched the socket of Jacob's thigh and crippled him; he could have done that at the beginning, at any point. When the dawn was approaching and "he saw he had not prevailed against him" it was not an admission that he couldn't beat Jacob. It was an acknowledgment that Jacob was not going to quit fighting without some serious injury. Even after Jacob was crippled, he would not let go until he had gotten a blessing from him. It was evident that the stranger was going to have to really hurt Jacob in order to stop the fight. Jacob wanted that blessing regardless of the pain.

And he got it. Mind you, God did not have to bless Jacob; He could have reprimanded him for being so stubborn or He could have cast him to sleep or injured him in a more debilitating way, like blindness. As strange as it may seem to think it, apparently God had been rather hoping that Jacob would not give up the fight.

I think what was going on here was that God made Jacob pay for the blessing he had stolen from Esau. It was important for Jacob to know, before he saw Esau again, that the blessing he had stolen was meaningless, worthless. All blessings come from God and God was not to be tricked into blessing a man, even one that He had already decided to bless. So God fought with Jacob as Esau could reasonably have fought with him twenty years before. Perhaps the angel even appeared in the form of Esau when he came to him; but whether He did or not God was substituting for Esau. He was saying to Jacob something like, "Do you really want My blessing without cheating? Do you want it enough to fight for it? It can't be truly yours by means of a lie." I also think that at this moment, God's Spirit softened Esau's heart toward his brother. When the sun arose, Esau was in the right frame of mind to receive Jacob's gifts; God had taken all his revenge for him.

And what was the blessing Jacob received? A new name. The angel asked his name, not because he couldn't remember, but because Jacob needed to remember it. We all remember our names, of course, but when Jacob spoke his own name he would have said, "Supplanter" or "Deceiver"; to give his own name was to confess his sin, it was to call to mind why he had fled from Esau, why he had been forced to flee from Esau, why he justly feared to see Esau again. And in place of that name, God gave him a new name, a new identity. No longer was he Supplanter; now he was Wrestler-with-God. *Jacob* would not have to meet Esau ever again. Now it would be *Israel* who went back to meet Esau, a man with a new identity who was not guilty of cheating his brother, a man who had been forgiven.

But God was doing more than just giving Jacob a new name, more than just comforting him in his fear. God was announcing that Jacob had indeed become a different person. The Jacob who had fled Esau was a person who had little regard for God. That Jacob would never have wrestled with God. That Jacob would make God prove Himself (sound familiar?) and God had done it. God had proven Himself worthy of Jacob's devotion. God had proven His desirability, and now Jacob knew for the first time that he wanted Him. He was a different man, with a different name and a different identity and a different relationship to God. He had fully embraced the Covenant that belonged to him by birth.

But God was doing more than just revealing to Jacob how much he had been changed over the years. God was taking a new name for Himself as well. In other words, He was taking another step in revealing Himself. From this point on He would be known all over the world as the God of Israel, the "God of the One Who Wrestles with God". Not only is a certain kind of wrestling with God desirable to Him, it is a part of His essential nature to seek out such people and to be their God. These are the people He wants to be the God of, the ones who will wrestle with Him until dawn, who will not let go until He blesses them.

With this episode we have touched on one of the essential differences between the biblical Jewish and Christian tradition, and the Muslim tradition. The word "Muslim" means "one who submits to God" whereas "Israel" means "one who wrestles with God". The relationship of Allah to a Muslim and the relationship of Yahweh to a Jew or Christian are very nearly opposites in nature. It is no wonder that the Jew/Christian and the Muslim cannot easily understand one another. Allah and Yahweh are two completely different understandings of the one true God. Allah desires submission above all. Yahweh desires engagement above all. The Muslim revelation is not just discontinuous from the biblical revelation in time; it is discontinuous from the biblical tradition entirely.

But the name Israel was also a prophecy about the character of the people He had chosen to be His people. They would prove to be a rebellious people, a stubborn people, a people who always put Him to the test, and who wrestled with Him continually. There is the wrestling of a man like Jacob who sought to hold on to God, and there is another wrestling of a man like Saul of Tarsus who sought to destroy Him. It is God's pleasure to find people who will struggle with Him rather than people who don't react to Him at all. There is a place for wrestling, there is a place for submission, but there is no place for indifference.

The other side of the coin to Jacob wrestling with God is that God wrestled with Jacob. God loved Jacob and therefore He wrestled with Jacob. God never wrestled, even metaphorically, with Esau. This is what the latter prophet Malachi would mean by saying, "Jacob have I loved, but Esau I have hated." The evidence that God loves us is that He strives with us; in fact this is a more reliable sign of His love than His blessing is. The apostle Paul says something similar in Romans 1 when he repeated the phrase "Therefore God gave them up . . ." The essence of God's wrath is abandonment. The abandonment that is wrath is not a matter of feeling, but a reality that is usually, perhaps always, not felt. It is no evidence of God's attitude toward you how you are feeling about His attitude toward you. To feel abandoned by God is not to be abandoned; in fact, it is probably the opposite. To feel abandoned by God is to feel that He is missing and to feel regret and longing for His return, and He does not abandon those who long for Him. On the contrary, the one who is abandoned by God in fact is the one who misses Him not at all, who is oblivious to the abandonment, who is content to live alone.

God is the One who wrestles with His people, a new aspect of the Covenant relationship, a new quality of God revealed for the first time. It was to emphasize the importance of this new revelation about the Covenant that God changed Jacob's name to Israel. The new name showed that Jacob had a new dimension to his intimacy with God that had been given to him by God Himself. God would not be content to reveal Himself to His people by mail; He would look at them face to face; He might get angry, but when He did get angry He would fight with them rather than walk away from them.

But dawn began the day in which he would have to face Esau, so he made his final preparations. He would go in the front with his wives and children in groups behind him, the first group being Bilhah and Zilpah and their four children, then Leah and her six children, and finally Rachel and Joseph. When Israel did see Esau, it was not as the blessed one, the one who would rule over his brother, and the one who had the double portion. Instead, he was the one who bowed to Esau, the one who gave gifts to Esau, the one who called Esau "lord". God had foreordained that Esau would serve Israel but that did not mean what the world might mean by it. Since the beginning the people of God submit to each other, the greater to the lesser, the ruler to the ruled, the parent to the child and the husband to the wife and the master to the slave. The kingdom of God has never been like a human kingdom.

Though Israel and Esau met peacefully, and were reconciled, they had never felt close or comfortable with each other and never would. Israel refused Esau's offer of an escort and his offer to leave a bodyguard (Israel obviously had no ability to protect himself). Hebron, and Isaac, would have been a logical destination. But Israel was exhausted from his traumatic escape and return and did not want to travel far, and he had never been close to his father. Israel had little intention of actually going to Seir whatever he said. Instead he moved a few miles further west along the Jabbok and established a long-term camp at what became known as Succoth, to the east of the Jordan. Initially he was probably just looking for a place to rest and to recover from what had been a difficult trip, as well as to find the best available pasture. There is no record in the Bible that the twins ever saw one another again until Isaac's death, and never again after that. Though there was forgiveness for the sins of the past, there was no closeness between them. The only brotherly love we have encountered in three generations of this family history is Abraham's love for Lot.

8. Jacob's Later Years
(Genesis 33:18-20; 35:1-21; and 35:22b-27)

I will now use Jacob's new name, except in the title of the section. Later in Scripture "Israel" is the name applied to the nation as a whole rather than to the individual, so when we get to Exodus, I will resume calling the man "Jacob", and use "Israel" as the national name. It may be confusing, but I want to use "Israel" for this particular man while I finish discussing Genesis because I wish to keep clearly in view what God did at Peniel. The focus of Genesis now turns to the children of Israel, but there are a few details of the life of Israel that we will consider first, even though they will be out of chronological sequence. Then we can then turn our attention fully to the twelve sons.

The camp at Succoth was probably only a short term resting place. Within a year or two Israel journeyed on to a more permanent dwelling at Shechem near the oaks of Moreh across the Jordan and twenty miles west, one of the sites visited by Abram when he had first arrived in the Promised Land. At Shechem Israel bought a piece of land to make into a permanent camp, and he built an altar to "God, the God of Israel". He must have told his family about wrestling with the stranger and about his new name. It was an event obviously worthy of incorporating into the oral tradition without even being told to do so.

Israel showed no hurry to get back to his father or mother. He had left his family at Beersheba but would have heard that Isaac had moved on to Hebron and that Rebekah had died. He seems to have lived near Shechem for around ten years, at least until his older children were adult and potentially dangerous. Probably he visited his father at some point shortly after his arrival in Canaan, but the visit was not recorded. His relationship to Isaac was not a close one, so there was no hurry to get back "home". Besides, he was fundamentally a nomad as his father and grandfather before him.

The events in Shechem primarily concern some of his sons so we will skip chapter 34 for the moment. But the events in Shechem were of such a nature that Israel could no longer feel comfortable living in that land, and the inhabitants of that region were terrified of him as well. Fortunately God directed him to move twenty-five miles south to Bethel, perhaps in another dream or perhaps not. It is clear that Israel wanted and needed to leave the area, but whether he would have done so without authorization is not clear. Israel was still something of a ditherer, and I think God gave him a necessary push.

Bethel was the place he had first camped when he fled from Esau and where he had had the dream of the ladder going up to heaven with the angels ascending and descending. In sending him back to Bethel, God was bringing final closure to that episode of Israel's life. Israel, remembering the dream and his certainty that God Most High was present at that location, had everyone in his household, wives and servants, bury their household gods before he moved. This would have included Laban's household idols; if he hadn't learned of Rachel's theft he would have learned it now. It also included their earrings as well, which were sometimes worn as amulets or charms for magic.

God had not commanded him to get rid of the idols; he took this action on his own initiative as a better appreciation of God's glory began to dawn in him. Israel was just beginning to feel that God Most High did not mix well with other gods. Returning to Bethel, he wanted to especially devote himself to God Most High out of gratitude for the blessings he had received. He may have planned on coming back for the idols and jewelry later. We don't know if he ever did, but he was leaving part of his flocks and herds at Shechem anyway, probably under the care of Simeon and Levi who were about twenty years old, so he easily could have done so.

At Bethel God again met with Israel, and again it does not seem to have been in a dream. This time He formally renewed the Covenant promises He had made to Abraham and to Isaac. Specifically God repeated the promise that Israel's descendants would be great and that they would inherit the land. The other promises of the Covenant had not disappeared, but were tacitly included. A man who fails to mention something may have forgotten, but God never forgets. Also God again changed Jacob's name to Israel, just in case there was any doubt that the angel he had wrestled was speaking on God's behalf. Thus all three of the patriarchs received their names directly from God, and Ishmael as well. This marks the end of God choosing the names of His people, with a few notable exceptions. Israel's children are not recorded as being given special names by God, nor is Esau, but that does not mean that they didn't have special names that only He knew. God has always done and said too much to have it all recorded. In the book of Revelations, in 2:17, the idea that God has a secret name for each of His people is specifically mentioned.

The only other event at Bethel of note was the death of Rebekah's nurse, Deborah. It is easy to miss it in the narrative, just one verse, but I think it is important. It is not clear how Deborah came to be with Israel at Bethel; she would still have been with Isaac at Hebron after Rebekah's death, thirty miles to the south. Probably Israel had visited Isaac much earlier, as a son should, without moving his whole household to Hebron, and had brought Deborah back with him. Being Rebekah's nurse she had probably played an important part in raising the twins, but perhaps she had been more especially involved in Israel's childhood. The description of Deborah's death is striking; she was so mourned that the tree marking her grave was given a name: Allon-bacuth, the Oak of Weeping. We can only wish that more details of her life were given so that we could have another example of another heroine to study. But then the details of her life were no doubt not the kinds of things that can be easily written about. It was not heroic deeds that made her a heroine to her people but how she lived, blessing the people around her by the quality of her character.

Sarah and Rachel were particularly mourned when they died; Israel mentions burying Leah; only Rebekah was passed over in silence. Of course, the purpose of the narrative here was not to be a complete obituary and the narrative was focused elsewhere when Rebekah died, presumably while Jacob was in Haran and after Isaac moved to Hebron. Still it is significant that there is no mention of her death in the Bible, no mention of her funeral, no mention that Isaac mourned for her. Rebekah took the curse for the plot to steal Esau's blessing on herself, and I think she did bear some of the consequences. After Jacob's flight, Rebekah is only mentioned one more time in Genesis 49:31 when Israel reports that Isaac had buried her in the same cave as Abraham and Sarah. This makes Deborah's inclusion all the more significant, not only the absence of any reference to Rebekah but the unusual honor given to Deborah. Rebekah's character, what we know of her as an ambitious and ruthless woman, caused strife and bitterness in the lives of her family; and so she was not particularly missed nor mourned when she died. Israel thought of Deborah, not Rebekah, as his mother.

After Bethel, Israel decided to move to Ephrath, which is Bethlehem, more than half way to Hebron where Isaac was dwelling. On the way to Bethlehem Rachel died giving birth to Benjamin. As Rachel had been the favorite wife at the beginning, she still occupied that favored position in Israel's affections and her death was a severe blow to him. His devotion to Rachel was so great that he had real difficulty recovering and he transferred all the weight of his love to Joseph and Benjamin. In this way a family that was already dysfunctional became more so, for the jealousy of the other brothers toward Joseph and Benjamin could only lead to trouble.

Finally, after all of these things Jacob came to Isaac at Hebron, where Abraham had lived so long. It isn't clear how long Jacob stayed at each place, but Jacob was living either at Bethlehem or with his father Isaac when Joseph was sold into slavery. The later narrative relates that Jacob still had flocks at Shechem, and it is possible that he moved from

Shechem to Bethel and then to Bethlehem and then to Hebron because his possessions were becoming too great and needed to be spread out more. Perhaps he left part of his flock at Shechem under the care of older sons, and the same at Bethel, and so on. Thus Jacob's holdings were becoming so great that he was occupying a wide part of the land. It seems reasonable to construct events so that Jacob was with Isaac during the last ten years of Isaac's life. Isaac may have been present when the brothers reported Joseph's death, and may have heard of Joseph's dreams, and would have seen the strife and envy among his grandchildren. I do wonder if he regretted some of his indiscretions as a father, or if he even realized that so much of the strife around him was in part his own doing. And I wonder what he thought of Joseph's dreams. After all, he knew about the prophecy to Abraham about being enslaved in a foreign land. And I wonder if he missed Esau.

9. Esau's Descendants (Genesis 36 and I Chronicles 1:34-54)

Chapter 36 wraps up the story of Esau by giving his genealogy. 36:5,6 suggest that Esau did not move to the land of the Horites until after he had married Basemath the daughter of Ishmael, which would mean that he moved after Jacob had fled to Laban. Probably his and Isaac's combined wealth was too great. If so then after Jacob left, the inheritance was split up and Esau took his share from Isaac and just moved away. Presumably Esau honored his deal with Jacob and took only one part out of three of the herds with him rather than the two parts out of three he would have been entitled to.

The names given for Esau's wives here in verses 2 and 3 disagree with the names given in 26:34 and 28:9; there is a copying error somewhere. Most likely the error is to be found in chapter 36, which seems to have been inserted when the oral tradition was written down to tie up loose ends. There would have been little need, and little opportunity, for the oral tradition itself to keep a list of Esau's descendants. This chapter was probably obtained from the official records of the kingdom of Edom after Israel had escaped from Egypt, centuries after these events. The discrepancies in the genealogies are irritating, but you have to have an obsession with the details to notice them at all. They seem to me to have nothing to do with the revelation or its integrity.

The Horites lived in the land that was called Seir, named for their dominant clan, just south of the Dead Sea and not far from what had been Sodom. The Horites have only been mentioned previously in Genesis 14 as one of the tribes casually conquered by Chedorlaomer and his allies before they proceeded to punish Sodom. Once Abram had defeated Chedorlaomer, the Horites were left in peace, and Seir was the first of their chiefs. It seems likely that Esau took a fourth wife just as he was moving to Seir, namely Oholibamah, a great-granddaughter of Seir himself. If so then he was connected to the most powerful family of that land by marriage.

In 36:20 we find a good example of how the word translated "sons" was being used in a loose way to mean a descendant in general, for Anah is listed here as a son of Seir and in verses 2 and 24 he is listed as the son of Zibeon the son of Seir. The genealogy is confusing. Esau's son, Eliphaz, then took Timna, the sister of Lotan and daughter or Seir, as a concubine. This make Esau's son's concubine, Timna, the great-aunt of Esau's wife Oholibamah, possible but weird, a twisting of the generations. Timna is important as the mother of Amalek, a grandson of Esau, whose descendants became notorious for evil and for their enmity toward Israel. However, both Timna and Oholibamah are listed as chiefs who descended from Esau—possible, but not likely on the face of it. The genealogy recorded by the officials of Edom do not appear to have been kept very carefully.

Esau's descendants became closely intertwined with the descendants of Seir and many of them became chiefs themselves in the land of Seir. Eventually, Esau's descendants came to predominate in that land and it became named for Esau by way of his nickname, Edom. Thus Esau simply drifted away from his heritage; though God blessed him and made him a nation, it was at the cost of losing his identity and blending with this other people, the Horites. Eventually the nation of Edom would be absorbed into the surrounding nations and lose its distinct identity entirely. However, an outside observer in those centuries might not have been sure who was the blessed of the two brothers. While the descendants of Israel went into Egypt and became slaves, the descendants of Esau grew into a strong nation just south of Canaan. A century or two after the death of Isaac, it would have appeared that Esau had been blessed and Israel had been cursed.

D. Joseph and His Brothers

1. Reuben (Genesis 35:22, 37:18-35, 42:21-22, 42:35-38, 46:9, and 49:3-4)

With Jacob's children, the Covenant quit narrowing. The Covenant continued to each one of Jacob's sons, which is the normal way a covenant works. Covenants were handed down from generation to generation. The core of the Covenant of Revelation was God's promise to be God to Abraham's descendants, and this means the renewing of the Covenant with each generation. God promised to be their God period, no conditions, forever; and He has never failed to come through on a promise. No explanation is required when the Covenant passes on to the next generation, however unworthy they may be. Only the opposite requires comment: how can the Covenant have failed to be passed on to these children?

I have argued that there were discernible reasons God first excluded Ishmael and then excluded Esau from the Covenant: Ishmael in order to show that human effort could not accomplish God's will, and Esau in order to show that God's favor does not depend on how good we are. In other words, they were "excluded" from the Covenant of Revelation because they were included. It sounds paradoxical, and that is all right. Their lives were revelation itself. When they departed from the Covenant of Revelation they performed their part of the revelation that was being handed down in the Covenant of Revelation. If this sounds like a sort of spiritual catch 22, it is to some extent because we equate "being in the Covenant" with "being saved". I see salvation as a rather different issue than the Covenant.

Then what does it mean today if the children of Christian parents walk away from the Christian faith? My response is: "I don't know, exactly". But there is a little that I do believe I know. The Covenant relationship the Christian lives in is the same as the Covenant Abraham stood in and its central promise is the same: God will be the God of our children. And that is true whether they reject him or not. It depends on His promise, not on child evangelism, not on the faithfulness of the parents, not on the choices of the children. Our children are holy because He is holy. It is a matter for faith, as sometimes the next generation in our families may well resemble the succeeding generations of Israel. We are not so different from Abraham or Israel. It is enough if we are like Abraham or Israel. It is the most familiar of stories: a dysfunctional family that produces a new generation of dysfunctional people. But where dysfunction abounds, grace abounds all the more.

The Scripture now turns its attention to giving us some idea of the character of these men, especially of Joseph and the four eldest sons. The timing of events is tricky. The details that are given are just precise enough to fit together, and this is the chronology as best I can determine it. Jacob must have stayed at Shechem for eight or nine years after his arrival. Then he would have spent a little time in Bethel, leaving some of his flocks at Shechem and perhaps some flocks still at Succoth. Joseph had taken the duty of courier, taking messages to his brothers at Shechem or Succoth. This was the year that Joseph was seventeen, 1889 b.c. Israel and most of the family were at Bethel and about to move on to Bethlehem when Joseph began giving bad reports about his brothers and having some strange dreams. Rachel was pregnant and Joseph's dreams included her and her baby not yet born. Shortly before the twelfth son was born, Israel moved his camp to Bethlehem and on the way there Rachel died giving birth to Benjamin (Rachel was in her mid or late forties by this time). In his grief, Israel was all the more inclined to favor Joseph and Benjamin and the family tension grew even worse. It was at this point that Joseph was sold into slavery. Joseph would have remembered his brother Benjamin only as a baby. Shortly after Joseph was sold, Israel moved on to Hebron and at last reunited with his father Isaac.

Reuben was the oldest so we will consider him first. He was about thirteen years old when Jacob arrived in the land of Canaan and around twenty-one when the family left Shechem. In order to be sure of adequate pasture for their many animals, Israel left some of the flocks at Shechem, probably under the care of Simeon and Levi, for reasons we will consider in the next section. As the eldest, Reuben was beginning to assume the duties of head of the family and was probably largely in charge of the larger flock when they split up. He would be entitled to two out of thirteen parts of the total inheritance when it was divided, once Rachel's second son was born. We are only given four brief glimpses of Reuben, for though he was the eldest and was acting head of the family, he did not play a central role in the events that were to follow. He was doubtless a good manager of their property, but younger brothers dominated the spiritual history of the family, for better and for worse.

Episode one occurred when Reuben was a young man, shortly after Rachel's death. It is not clear if this is before or after Joseph was sold, but my feeling is that it is before Joseph was sold, in 1889 or 1888 b.c. In a very terse passage we find him seducing or raping his father's wife, Bilhah, the maidservant of Rachel (35:22). Doubtless their camp was not one conducive to privacy, and so his liaison with Bilhah became known to Israel, and probably to the rest of the family as well. Family politics is strongly suggested here. Bilhah was the maidservant of Rachel, the rival wife to Reuben's mother Leah, and it is striking that the sin with Bilhah occurred immediately after Rachel's death. How much bitterness there was between Leah's children and Rachel's, especially Joseph, is evident in the ensuing history. It is not far fetched to think that Reuben intended to insult Joseph by going in to Bilhah, though there is no way to know. Perhaps instead Bilhah was stunningly beautiful and tempted or even seduced the youthful Reuben. It is not clear whether she was a willing participant in the adultery or not, but her willingness is doubtful. In that culture, she would have been risking death to have an affair with her step-son. Reuben's later behavior does suggest that he carried the weight of guilt.

Though Israel heard of the sin, there is no evidence that he took any disciplinary action against Reuben at the time. Nor did he take any action against Bilhah. In part this can be explained by his being still in a time of intense grief over Rachel. Israel does not seem to have done well with confrontations and, unless he had suspected Bilhah of being a willing participant in the deed, he would have been inclined to do nothing. Many years later he would express his verdict, but at the time he left it alone. And so also did God.

It is clear, however, that Reuben's offense was severe by the moral standards of that time and place. In Mesopotamia, or among the Amorites, it would have been scandalous for a man to sleep with his father's wife. Later, under the Law of Moses, Reuben would have been put to death (see Leviticus 18:8 and 20:11), making him the third of the patriarchs to be condemned by the future legal code of Israel. Even the later and nearly unshockable Romans would have been shocked by this. Reuben committed the same sin as the man who was put out of the church of Corinth, the one that Paul discusses in I Corinthians 5. In short, I believe Reuben essentially assaulted Bilhah as a calculated insult to Joseph, and that immediately afterwards, perhaps especially because his father did not punish him, his guilty conscience was devastating.

It was not long after the episode with Bilhah that the other sons of Leah conspired against Joseph. Reuben apparently was not present when the brothers decided to kill Joseph, but he arrived just in time to divert their plans from murder to mayhem. On the one hand, Reuben's quick thinking certainly saved Joseph's life. He planned to return to the pit later and rescue Joseph, and so he might have prevented the entire crime. He may have hated Joseph still, but I think it was his wounded conscience that made him unwilling to participate with his brothers.

That Reuben felt he had to save Joseph by stealth rather than by exerting his authority probably shows both the weakness of Reuben's will and the dangerous character of his brothers. Though Simeon, Levi, and Judah were Reuben's full brothers, was their hatred for Joseph so great that they would have hurt even their own older brother? Simeon and Levi had already proved their capacity for ruthless murder, which we will discuss shortly; Judah was more practical, more calculating, ultimately more ruthless. On the whole it seems doubtful that Reuben would have been in real danger, but it also seems that Reuben did not have the guts to stand up to his brothers. It may be that his guilt concerning Bilhah had ruined his self-confidence as well. He hadn't been punished, but he was certainly suffering the consequences.

The third episode involving Reuben happened in Egypt during the famine on their first trip to buy grain, when Joseph had their money secretly returned to them. This would have been about twenty years later, Reuben would have been in his mid-forties. But the guilt for what they had done to Joseph still plagued the thoughts of the brothers, especially Reuben's. Reuben and his brothers all assumed that their difficulties were due to some kind of divine punishment for their sin against Joseph, and Reuben was saying, "I told you so". The interesting thing is that they were wrong. God was not punishing them.

True, their plight was a consequence of their sin; Joseph was taking some revenge and they were in his power though they didn't know it, but it was not God's doing. God does not search for really clever ways of punishing people for their sins. He does not devise intricate schemes over decades to pay people back. If you want schemes, you must go to the devil who is well-known as a schemer. God does not need to plan pay back for evil. The merely natural consequences of our actions, that only a fool thinks he can escape, are quite torture enough. If you do evil to someone and that person has an opportunity to get even with you, then he probably will. God is mercy itself and counting on Him for mercy is the necessity of our lives; but your brother can't be counted upon for mercy and you are foolish to do so. You will naturally be paid back for the evil you do, and that is true even in an atheistic universe and even to an intellectual who doubts there are standards for good or even.

The last episode involving Reuben finds him back at home and talking over the trip with his father. As the oldest, whatever had happened on the trip was Reuben's responsibility and so whatever blame there was for Simeon's imprisonment was his. By this time Reuben had two sons of his own, probably Hanoch and Pallu (we are never told whom Reuben married). Reuben offered his own two sons as surety for Benjamin's safety if they were to go back to Egypt again, but Israel summarily refused him. Reuben had no credibility left with Israel, and when the second trip into Egypt finally had to be made it was Judah who took the initiative. After the disastrous first trip to Egypt, Reuben never again took the lead in family affairs. Reading between the lines, it seems that Reuben's heart was not in it; he was a broken man.

Near Israel's death, when he was pronouncing his final blessings on his children, he removed Reuben from the privilege of the firstborn as punishment for his affair with Bilhah. Israel gave the rights of the firstborn to Joseph by adopting Joseph's two sons as his own, thus ensuring that Joseph's descendants would get the double share of the inheritance. In a sense, Israel was just ratifying what God had already announced through Joseph's dreams, making Joseph the head of the family. Israel may have been remembering Joseph's dreams when he made the decision, deliberately carrying out what he knew God had predicted. After all, he and his own brother had fulfilled such a prediction and his own father had tried to prevent it with complete futility. Maybe he was learning from Isaac's mistake. Israel's last words seem to be aimed at Reuben individually but are also prophetic of Reuben's descendants, that they would also be removed from leadership among the clans of Israel as Reuben himself had been removed from leadership. Were all the descendants of Reuben excluded from prominence in Israel because of Reuben's sin? It would seem so. The descendants of Reuben play little role in Israel's history. On the personal level, Reuben seems to have never fully recovered from what he did to Bilhah. He was a broken man, yes, but it wasn't God who had broken him, nor Israel. He did it to himself.

2. Simeon and Levi
(Genesis 34:1-31, 42:24, 46:10-11, 49:5-7)

Next in age after Reuben are Simeon and Levi, who need to be considered together. Their story begins with events at Shechem shortly after the return to Canaan. They had been in Shechem for eight years or so, Simeon and Levi were about twenty years old and Dinah, their full sister, was about fifteen or sixteen. Dinah grew up there and became friends with some of the young women in the city. The prince of Shechem saw Dinah grow up and as she became a woman he fell in love with her. This was not a spontaneous moment of desire, as I read it, but something that had been growing for a while. It grew to the point that, when an opportunity presented itself, he forced himself on her. This is not an uncommon story from that or any time. Princes, even princes of small city-states, are accustomed to take what they want. It isn't clear how much Dinah resisted him, but it is clear that force was involved and that he violated the propriety of the day. It was considered an offense against Israel and his family, a serious insult, but it would not have been considered the crime it would (or should) be in our day.

But the prince, Shechem, wanted to do the honorable thing because he genuinely loved Dinah. Admittedly, rape is not a promising beginning for a lifetime commitment, but we must give Shechem some benefit of the doubt here, even admitting that the average behavior of men does not attain to a high standard. He behaved more honorably than one of David's sons would later behave (see II Samuel 13). Perhaps he had not originally intended marriage; perhaps he was only acting on passion when he forced himself on her, but his feelings for her were deeper than mere lust. In 34:3 it says, "He was deeply attracted to Dinah the daughter of Jacob, and he loved the girl and spoke tenderly to her" (literally, he "spoke to the heart of the girl"). Whatever his original intentions, he recognized her as a woman he wanted to marry and so he had his father speak to Israel.

Israel reacted calmly; but by this time his older sons were coming into their duties as managers of the family and they were not so calm. Since Reuben is not mentioned, he was probably away at the time. Their possessions were large and it could be that even at this early time in their return to Canaan they had had to split up their flocks to find enough grazing land and Reuben would likely have been in charge of the other flocks, perhaps back at Succoth. Wherever Reuben was, Simeon and Levi were the ones who took the lead. Family politics was involved in their reaction as well; Dinah was their full sister, and it is doubtful they would have reacted as strongly had she been a half-sister. The other full brothers of Dinah would have been old enough to be involved and so they probably were away. Judah would have been about nineteen but there is reason to believe that he had separated from the family; but that is a different story. Issachar and Zebulun were not much older than Dinah but old enough to be involved had they been present; we may assume they were away with Reuben. It would seem that Simeon and Levi carried out the whole plot by themselves.

Though the king, Hamor, recognized their anger as justified and did his best to conciliate them, Simeon and Levi remained furious. But they pursued their revenge in a calculated and cold-blooded manner, not in passion but with a kind of calm insanity that justified punishing everyone vaguely associated with Shechem. They seem to have hit on their scheme fairly quickly and it was easy to pull off. If the Prince really wanted Dinah, then let him be circumcised. Further, if they really wanted this joining of their families, then let all the men of Shechem be circumcised. It had to be done to remove the religious barrier to intermarriage; otherwise forget about it. Thus Simeon and Levi used the Covenant and their supposed devotion to God Most High to deceive the men of the city. They were good liars. This is what it means to take the name of the Lord in vain.

Shechem and Hamor fell for the ruse completely, and set about persuading the rest of their countrymen to join them. The man, Shechem, was apparently a good man by the standards of the day as well as the prince, and had won the genuine respect of his people. The argument he and his father used on the men of the city was the wealth that Israel possessed which could be theirs to share by intermarriage. Like his father and grandfather, Israel was as rich as a little mobile kingdom could be. By all means then, let a rich man become one of us and then we can share in his wealth, they said. Clearly Israel must have had other daughters, and there must have been daughters of the other members of his household; he was a village in himself.

Simeon and Levi slaughtered the men and boys of Shechem in cold blood while they were in pain and helpless, to avenge their "honor". They took all of the women and daughters as slaves and concubines and all the material possessions as their own, just as if there had been a war. Some of these women may have become wives of some of the sons of Israel, perhaps of Simeon at the least, though we are not told. Dinah's friends, if they were married, were now widows, and if they weren't married, were now orphans; and in either case they were now slaves or concubines of her brothers or her servants. It is not said how Dinah felt about it all, about Shechem or his murder, about her former friends. There is no word of what became of Dinah later on. Is it at all likely that Dinah agreed to Simeon and Levi's plan? I don't know. Did they care about her feelings on the matter or consult with her? Perhaps I am too cynical about men, but I do not think they did.

Israel did not rebuke Simeon or Levi for the massacre. On the contrary, his reaction suggests that he was only concerned with the possibility of reprisal from the surrounding cities rather than the moral issues involved. Never the general his grandfather had been, he complained of having too few fighting men in his household. Israel's new Covenant identity had not given him a much deeper moral insight, at least not yet. Justice is something we must grow into, even Christians. Too often we assume conversion is the completion rather than the beginning of righteousness.

But it was far worse that God said nothing either. On the contrary, God intervened to protect the family from any immediate consequences by casting the neighborhood into a panic. We must be careful how we think about this episode. There are two conclusions that we might easily make unless we are careful. First, we might think God approved of the massacre. After all, in a few centuries He would have the Israelites wage a total war against the people of the land, including Hivites like the men of Shechem. Second, we might conclude that God used a double standard when He judged people. His own people could pretty much get away with murder, literally, whereas those who were not His people were held strictly accountable for their offenses and liable to harsh consequences. This opens up questions that need to be considered at greater length, so I will finish discussing Simeon's and Levi's lives and return to the massacre in the next section.

I must suspect that Simeon was the brother who most relentlessly bullied or badgered Joseph. In any event, when Joseph first met them buying food during the famine and had them in his power, he chose Simeon to put into prison. Ultimately Simeon had six sons: Jemuel, Jamin,

Ohad, Jachin, Zohar, and Shaul. The last son mentioned, Shaul, was listed as being the son of a Canaanite woman. By this time the Canaanites were a majority in the land but it is possible that the passage means a Hivite woman, and perhaps a woman Simeon took in the massacre. The fact that Shaul was singled out as being of a Canaanite might suggest that the brothers mainly married non-Canaanites. Levi had three sons: Gershon, Kohath, and Merari but it is not stated who their mother was or when they were born.

Just as Israel did not get off entirely from cheating Esau, Simeon and Levi did not get off entirely from the massacre of Shechem. On his death bed, Israel cursed them and their children for their deeds, rather than blessing them. They were to be dispersed among the other brothers when they came to inherit the Promised Land. Interestingly, for Levi's descendants this scattering among the others was the result of being appointed to the priesthood. Simeon's descendants were simply scattered with no priestly compensation and perhaps this is an indication that Simeon was the real leader of the massacre and drew Levi into it as an accomplice.

Nonetheless, the priesthood was in part a punishment on the descendants of Levi for his participating in the massacre of Shechem. Giving the priesthood to the Levites was one way in which his descendants could make some restitution for the massacre, though not of course to the victims. When we go on to study the priesthood, and the role of the descendants of Simeon and Levi in the nation of Israel, it will be important to remember the words of Israel in 49:6: "Let my soul not enter into their council; let not my glory be united with their assembly; because in their anger they slew men, and in their self-will they lamed oxen." Taking this as a prophecy means that God was also pronouncing this verdict, that His glory would not be united to their assembly. For all the glory of the priesthood, it was not God's glory that was united to it. The priesthood could not have endured. It was founded without God's full heart in it, and its glory had to fade away and die. Furthermore, the priesthood would inherit the tendency of Levi: in anger it would slay men; even the Messiah was slain by the anger of its counsels.

But as usual the consequences of the massacre of Shechem were mainly only tangibly experienced by the descendants of the criminals. This is a theme we have seen already, and will see repeatedly through the Bible. The effects of evil, as well as of righteousness, pass down through the generations. In fact, it seems to be mainly in the succeeding generations that we see the full effects of evil and of grace, whether in the conflicts between Ishmaelite and Israelite, or between Edomite and Israelite, or more immediately in the children themselves. It seems odd to me that many who agree that the effects of our evil deeds descend to our children are offended by the suggestion that the effects of grace also descend to our children, as if the power of grace were weaker than the power of wickedness. Perhaps it is a matter of pride: we are quite willing to attribute the evil in us to original sin and the nature we inherit from our parents, but unwilling to attribute God's favor toward us to His favor toward our parents. The blame can reside with our parents but we want God to love us for ourselves.

To begin the discussion of the massacre at Shechem, let's put the event in its starkest terms. God was not simply silent about the massacre, He was supportive. As they moved on to Bethel, God caused the fear of them to fall on the whole neighborhood: the surrounding cities were all afraid they might be attacked next. If God was offended at what they had done, why did He respond this way? God's policy, ever since He had called Abram, was to support the family regardless of what they did, whether He condoned their actions or not. When Abram and Isaac lied about their wives, when Jacob deceived his brother, when Jacob's household kept their idols, every time God had turned a blind eye to any wrong that they did. He never corrected or rebuked or punished them, but instead He cushioned them against some of the immediate and natural consequences of their actions. And He did all of this even when their deeds were ultimately abominable to Him. His protection of them after the massacre at Shechem was just a continuation of His previous policy, so we must examine God's larger policy toward His people in order to understand this event.

We must broaden the discussion to the larger problem of revelation. When God chose Abram and his future descendants His purpose was to reveal Himself cumulatively and in some detail over a long period of time. It is reasonable to think that correcting their behavior would be a natural part of that revelation. But in revelation, as in any communication, there is a correct order to how information is presented. Restricting our attention to Genesis alone, we might conclude mistakenly that God approved of the massacre. Having the rest of the Scripture we know that God *did not* approve of massacres and *did* intend to correct their behavior. It would seem then that God thought it was premature to make a point of the immorality of this violence. But how could it possibly be premature to rebuke murder? This question really has to do with discerning the central and ultimate point of the revelation; we must look behind the event.

To those who think the primary purpose of the revelation is to tell us the difference between good and evil, commanding us to be good and threatening us if we are bad, the massacre of Shechem is a stumbling block. From such an assumption, we can only conclude either that somehow the massacre of the entire city of Shechem was morally acceptable, or else that God Most High and His Messiah disagreed on the question. There are plenty of people who have unwittingly fallen into each error, and there may be some who have contrived to fall into both errors at once.

The first error amounts to this: the Bible teaches that it is good to do bad things to bad people, that when we do bad things to bad people we are not really being bad because they are bad and we are good, but when they do the same bad things to us they really are being bad because they are bad and we are good. In other words, this error is the same as thinking that the Bible teaches moral relativism, a conclusion that most of the people who fall into this error wish to avoid.

The second error imagines the Bible presenting us with a God whose character and moral standards change over the years, either because the "God of the Old Testament" is a different God from His Messiah, with a sort of Divine Multiple Personality Disorder; or else because God made a mistake in Genesis that He later discovered and corrected; or else that He is an old ditherer, like the Canaanite god El, probably slept through the massacre and couldn't make up His mind what to do about it. It is one of the ironies of biblical theology that taking the events of the Bible as paradigms for moral behavior leads inevitably either to moral relativism or to compromising God's character. We only get away with such non-sense because we are not accustomed to following our beliefs through to their conclusions.

The belief that the primary purpose of the revelation is to make a statement about good and evil, to discourage evil deeds and encourage good deeds, is simply wrong. We gained the knowledge of good and evil at the Fall; we don't need to be told what is good or what is bad. We know enough of good and evil already for our own consciences to condemn us; we don't need the details. God did not spend all of that time and energy writing the Scripture to give us lessons with tidy morals, as if He were writing Sunday School curricula. Instead the primary purpose of the revelation is to reveal grace as the foundation of all contact between humans and God, grace as the foundation of all interactions between humans, grace as the link that holds all things in creation together, grace at the source of all hope for the future. Grace is such an impossibly alien concept to our nature that it took all those thousands of years of revelation and we still barely get it.

The first step in explaining grace was to give some clear cut examples of what grace means in its starkest terms, in which His people commit atrocities, offenses which were repulsive to Him and to us, and His kindness to them in the face of those atrocities. When He picked the chosen people He was looking for a family that could be counted on to make all the mistakes in the Book, whose founding members would nearly all have been condemned to death by the Law that was to come, and who would inevitably be guilty of the most heinous of crimes. In other words, any family would do. He was looking for the worst of sinners so that He could be gracious to them so that no one would ever think he was too evil for God to save. The book of Genesis picks out the events it does to emphasize this supremely important fact: that His love and commitment had absolutely nothing to do with anything they did or did not do. That this point would be missed and misunderstood by every generation from Moses onward, including our own, only shows how necessary it was to emphasize the point.

Hence, I suggest, God ignored the immorality and the scummy ethics of the patriarchs and their families because He felt that we could not understand the call to holiness until we had some inkling of the power of grace. He was right, of course. He did not hurry on to the commandments and the law. He took the whole book of Genesis so as not to slide past the grace, so we could get a good long drink before we hit the desert.

All the same, it was rather hard on the Canaanites in Shechem. What about God's grace to those people? It wasn't very fair to them, was it? It certainly looks as though God played favorites, and this is the second difficulty of the passage; it is especially difficult for modern people. We live in a culture that has elevated tolerance to the level of the ultimate virtue. There is a modern idea that all people are God's children equally, that God playing favorites is unthinkable. From such a viewpoint, much of the biblical story is repulsive. God, the One in the Bible, is in big trouble with respect to public opinion in our culture. So is this a problem with Him, or is it just a matter of putting the right spin on things, or is the problem with us and our standards?

It seems to me that the Bible would answer that there are two causes of God's bad reputation in the modern world, due to this passage and many others like it. One cause is that revelation is hard. Its subject matter is difficult; God is intrinsically more complicated than nuclear physics and we insist on making Him a sort of divine tautology. If He is not as simple as 2+2=4, we lose all patience and refuse to go on to the spiritual equivalent of algebra. The revelation is too big for us to take in one bite or to summarize in one aphorism, and it had to be given piecemeal over many millennia and mainly in cultural contexts very different from ours. By isolating one event from the totality of revelation we will invariably misunderstand. Sound bites distort, and so does quoting a verse out of context, or letting the meaning of a passage get away from the Scripture itself. We cannot fully understand the massacre of Shechem until we understand the letter to the Romans, and we cannot understand the letter to the Romans without meditating on the meaning of Shechem.

But the second cause of God's low rating in our culture is that we use the wrong standards for judging Him. We are historical imperialists, as if we had arrived at the final perfection of society and could rightly demand all previous history, and even God Himself, to meet our standards. We are quite willing to reveal to God what He should have said rather than trying to hear what He actually did say. To the modern person, so tolerant of everything but God, I insist that the Bible asserts *both* that all people are God's children ultimately and essentially (like we want it to), and simultaneously that some people are more particularly God's children than others (unlike what we want). God is *both* inclusive and exclusive and we will not fully or truly understand God without keeping both ideas in our minds at once.

If we ignore the exclusivity of God because it is culturally offensive, if we ignore the bias God shows toward His people and against others, then we will fail to appreciate the possibility of intimacy with God, an intimacy that is so deep as to be automatically private and exclusive. On the other hand, if we ignore the inclusivity of God because it is theologically offensive, then we will fail to appreciate the true character of God as the Creator and Lover of all things, and we will fail to recognize our neighbors when He includes them in our lives. Admittedly it is difficult to hold on to both ideas at once, but that is the nature of truth.

The men of Shechem who were murdered by Simeon and Levi were behaving more honorably, more justly than Simeon and Levi, and God loved them. There is no statement in this text that God loved the men of Shechem but we know He did because of later testimony in the Scripture that God is love, that He loved and loves the world. We might prefer more compelling evidence of it in the immediate context, and we might prefer that His love for people be a bit more safe. But the way He is is the way He is and we have to cope with Him as He actually is and not with Him as we wish He were.

The Bible does not give a complete resolution of exclusivity with inclusivity and we must each of us choose how we will respond to God's silence on the contrast. We can turn away from God in disgust that He could stand by in silence as Simeon and Levi murdered so many people; it is reasonable, ignoring that we are condemning God for the same crime we have committed and for which He did not condemn us. Or we can use the passage to justify our own hatred and violence; also reasonable if we ignore the fact that we aren't the creator and center and judge of all things. God does not make it easy for us. But the most reasonable course is to admit that we do not understand why God did what He did and why He didn't say what He didn't say, but we trust Him nonetheless. That is faith.

God is the One who ultimately chose to include this story in the Bible. His honesty about the massacre might be called obsessive. He wants us to know what He did even if it casts Him in a bad light. And He did not tell us everything, even the just causes—if there are any—that might make it easier for us to believe Him. It is important, before you decide whether to turn away from God or to misuse the Scripture to justify your own evil heart, that you should at least be clear that not all of the story has been told here. The Shechemites got a bad deal and they are dead, but death is not the end of the story. They are not merely gone, and the most important part of their story is yet to be told.

Whether we like it or not—and admittedly there is not much to like about it—the Scripture leaves us with the promise that all the loose ends will be tied up after the world is ended and we are all finished with our lives. It is a frustrating answer, but it is also a reasonable answer: we are in the middle of a play speaking our few lines, but the meaning of the few lines we have will only be clear when the play is over and we can all get off the stage and see the whole story from beginning to end. So we are presented with the necessity of choosing whether to trust God or not, whether to trust Him despite the evidence that tends to incriminate Him, whether to throw in our lot with the very One who may be the biggest Scam Artist of all time and who even has the gall to tell us the story of His scurrilous background while asking for our trust. But He does not, He will not ever, make it easy for us.

The closer we are to the heart of God the angrier we can allow ourselves to be, the louder we can argue. Why did God have this event recorded at all, why include it in the revelation? Didn't He ever hear of pleading the Fifth Amendment, of refusing to testify when the evidence would tend to incriminate Him? Why deliberately make it so hard for us to trust Him, to love Him, if that is what He really wants? Why give us a part of the picture that only makes us hesitate and doubt? His revelation may be a gradual one, but it pulls no punches. He put the account of the massacre at Shechem into the Scripture, and when we read it, it is like meeting an angel in a dark place who picks a fight and throws us to the ground and hopes and hopes and hopes we will fight back.

3. Judah (Genesis 37:25-28, 38:1-30, 43:1-10, 44:14-34, 46:12, and 49:8-12)

With Judah we have more personal detail because Judah was the chosen ancestor of the Messiah. God ordained, through Judah, to fulfill His promise to Abraham to bless all the peoples of the earth, and to keep His promise to the serpent to raise up the Savior who would destroy the results of death. Chapters 37 and 38 show Judah as an unscrupulous person, willing to kill and then to sell his brother whom he hated; but they also show a man, like Israel, with whom God wrestled. We will split up Judah's life into two sections of these notes in order to keep them short, but it does not divided up very naturally this way.

Judah would have been about ten years old when the family arrived in Canaan. He would have been about eighteen at the massacre of Shechem, old enough to participate and willing enough if he had been there. It appears that before the massacre Judah had essentially left home. There is no reason given why he would have left, but in a family as dysfunctional as this one it is easy to see how it could happen. Judah, in this interpretation, was a restless and independent child who finally had had enough of his family. When an opportunity came, however it came, he moved out and went to live with a native of the land, a man named Hirah. 38:1 means that in this general time frame between the massacre and the selling of

Joseph, Judah spent much of his time with Hirah and was married to a daughter of another native named Shua. Shua is said to be a Canaanite, and by this time he could be the genuine article. Hirah lived in the vicinity of Timnah, half way between Bethel and Bethlehem but offset twenty miles west. He was an Adullamite, a man from Adullam, a city just ten miles west of Bethlehem.

Judah was close enough that he could visit his home whenever he wished. If Israel had been the forceful type, he might have tried to make Judah stay home, but he wasn't. More likely he put Judah in charge of a portion of the family flocks and herds to at least make his absence practical. Thus it was quite possible for him to be present when the anger of the brothers boiled over against Joseph three years after the massacre. It was Judah who came up with the idea of selling Joseph rather than killing him; what was the profit in murder, anyway? Judah was not morally better than Simeon and Levi, just more practical. His anger and hatred did not control him. He used it in a businesslike fashion.

Judah married the daughter of Shua, who is never given a name, as early as his eighteenth or nineteenth year. This timing is necessary to fit in the subsequent history of Judah and his children before the whole family left for Egypt. She must have had the three sons in fairly rapid succession, Er and Onan before Joseph had been sold, and Shelah some time afterward. I would hypothesize that after Joseph was sold—possibly because of suppressed guilt and further alienation from his family—Judah moved further away from them all. By the birth of Shelah, he was living in Chezib (=Achzib) in the southern part of the land that his descendants would later possess, about sixty miles from his father Israel. We are told later that he kept some of his flocks at Timnah so he had become rich enough by himself to have to split up his property.

By 38:6 we jump to Judah's eldest son Er as an adult and married to another native woman, Tamar, as arranged by Judah. From 38:12 we know Tamar was from the area around Timnah where Hirah lived and possibly Hirah helped Judah arrange the marriage during one of his visits to his friend. This must have been near the end of the time of plenty, just before the seven years of famine, when Er was about twenty years old. Er was so evil that God killed him outright, and considering what God had tolerated up to that point, he must have been evil indeed. Er was the first, but not the last, person recorded in the Bible as being evil enough that God Himself felt it necessary to destroy him. If Er and Onan and Shelah's mother was a Canaanite, this could be the first indication of how evil the influence of a Canaanite marriage could be, and why it would be such a serious issue later.

The same was true of Judah's second son, Onan. According to the custom of the day, as well as the later Mosaic Law, Onan was expected to take Tamar as a wife and raise up children for his brother Er, indicating that Er maintained status as one of the people of God in spite of being so evil. Er still had a right to a heritage in Israel and it was Onan's duty to preserve his brother's name. Further Er's continued standing among God's people is underlined by God's anger at Onan for refusing to do this duty. Onan seems to have refused to raise up a child for Er from simple selfishness, but he did not refuse in so many words. He was underhanded, pretending to try to impregnate Tamar but ensuring that no pregnancy could result. He was thus an evil man pretending to be a good man. When God executed him, He must also have somehow made known to Judah what his son had done and the story was preserved in the oral tradition.

Nonetheless Er and Onan were still members of the Covenant people; they were still what we would call "saved". They may have been so evil that they could not be allowed to live, but they were never purged from the Covenant relationship to God. In fact in Genesis 46 when the Scripture lists the descendants of Jacob who went up to Egypt it specifically includes Er and Onan, even though they were dead. When the summary of Leah's children is given the total is 33 and that includes both Er and Onan, and they are included in 46:26 in the total of Israel's descendants who went to Egypt. Three times Er and Onan were included in the count, even though they were dead, even though they had been too evil to live; they still had a standing among God's people in spite of it all. Grace works all the way to the end, and can even work through a necessary execution.

Judah by now was afraid that his last son was in similar peril of execution as well, either because he knew Shelah's character was as debased as his brothers' or because he had a superstitious idea that Tamar was at fault. Judah tried to protect Shelah by sending Tamar to stay with her father until Shelah grew up. Shelah was younger than Onan, probably on the order of fifteen or sixteen, and Judah used his youth as the excuse, but it was really just that he was afraid. Judah was probably no more superstitious than any of his day but this was, after all, the Covenant of Revelation. He was a target to be spoken to.

When several years had passed and Shelah had grown up enough and Judah's own wife had died, he visited his old friend Hirah for the time of sheep shearing, in Timnah near Tamar's home. It was just as the years of famine were beginning, about the year 1869 b.c. Judah would have been about forty years old and Shelah was eighteen. Tamar knew that Shelah was old enough to be married now but that Judah had not sent for her. When she learned that Judah was coming but that Shelah was not, it became clear to her that Judah had no intention of giving her to Shelah. Perhaps her father had also begun making discrete inquiries as to what was going on, or perhaps he had begun thinking about what else to do with her.

She had limited options open to her if she did not marry Shelah. Women in such circumstances were sometimes forced to become prostitutes by their fathers, though that would become illegal under Moses. Being married to Judah's sons cannot have been very pleasant, but her situation was hopeless. It was a desperate enough to justify a desperate plan: she decided to disguise herself as a temple prostitute (to which life she might be forced in any event), set up her tent on the road that Judah would take into Timnah, and lure him in. She would be wearing the veil of a temple prostitute and Judah would not see her face clearly enough to recognize her.

This plan was a long shot but then remember Jacob's wedding night. Many things could have gone wrong. What if Judah ignored her? What if she didn't get pregnant? What if some other man got there first? But if one is engaged in a desperate plan, one cannot worry about all the details that might go wrong. Oddly enough, and against all reasonable expectations, her plan worked perfectly: she obtained Judah's seal, cord, and staff—any one of which would have identified him, he did not recognize her, and she became pregnant.

We must say that God was with her. God brought her to Judah's attention, God brought her to Judah's attention in such a way that he would want to go in to her, God protected her from strangers who might have gotten there first and ruined it all, and God brought about her pregnancy. All of these coincidences require some very intimate participation from God. How could God get involved in such a sordid scheme? Yet He obviously did. The circumstances leave God very little wiggle room; the plan could not have worked at all without some cooperation on God's part.

We could say "He *allowed* it all to happen but never *aided* its execution". Such a grasping at straws is frequently used by well meaning people trying to get God off the hook, but it assumes a totally different character for God than the one He has.

If God is anything, He is a *participant*. Any interpretation of Scripture that portrays Him as a *bystander*, an *allower of events*, is suspicious. Isn't this what it means to say that He is the living God: that He is active in daily events? From the very beginning, from the very first animal to be killed for its skin for clothing for Adam and Eve, God has shown His willingness to be totally involved in the dirt of creation and there is no reason to think that He ever changed His mind. In fact, the Incarnation is a striking assertion that He is still involved personally in the sordidness of the Creation. Furthermore, God was proud of His involvement in the affair. He *italicized* His involvement in her scheme by choosing Tamar and this pregnancy to be part of the line leading from Judah to the Messiah. And then He made sure the event was remembered in the oral tradition. And then He went out of His way to be sure Tamar was mentioned in the Messiah's genealogy in Matthew. He wasn't just permitting this scheme, He was immersed in it. These were His own ancestors that were coming together; hence, the whole sordid plot is intimately interconnected to His own plot.

There is another problem with the story of Tamar and Judah that should be mentioned. Tamar disguised herself as a *temple* prostitute, one who was involved in the worship of Astarte. Astarte was deliberately mispronounced as Ashtoreth in the Hebrew Bible to confuse the name with another word that means "abomination". Astarte is the same as the goddess Ishtar, the evening star, the goddess of love and fertility. Probably there were no self-employed prostitutes; the pagan temples seemed to have monopolized the profession. There are two different Hebrew words translated as "prostitute", one in 38:15 and another in 38:21-22, but it is not clear what the distinction of meaning is; they are both translated as πορνη in the Septuagint, from which we get the word pornography. Tamar may not have intended much with the idolatrous aspect of her role; she simply wanted to lure Judah. But Judah was certainly implicated in the worship of Astarte by visiting her. Even though she was not actually a priestess of Astarte, Judah did not know it and his intention was to go to such a priestess. Hence we have the very brother chosen out of all the brothers to be the ancestor to the Messiah involved in the worship of the fertility goddess, and a direct ancestor of the Messiah was conceived in this idolatrous circumstance. This is the heritage that God chose as His own.

It must have seemed strange to Judah when the temple prostitute vanished. Not only did she vanish, but no one in that neighborhood could even remember a temple prostitute ever being there. As mystified as Judah must have been, it would only have been embarrassing to pursue the matter so he dropped it. Three months later, Tamar could hide her pregnancy no longer. She still counted as a married woman, though she had not been given to Shelah as a wife (the worst of both worlds, married but with none of the privileges or protections of marriage), so she would be counted as an adulteress. Adultery was a capital offense, even among these heathen. Even if her father had wanted to protect her he could not easily have done so. Instead, he took the only socially acceptable course open to him—he sent her back to Judah for judgment and execution. But Judah had only to see his ring and staff to realize what had happened.

At this point, he might have tried a cover up. If he had acted quickly to execute her while all her evidence was in his possession, he might have contained and controlled the story, as we now say. But Judah spared her life. He had understood himself as a sinner possibly for the first time. He knew it was his own sin in not giving her to Shelah that had driven her to do what she had done. He knew that if she had committed a crime, his was worse. He knew that she was more righteous than he was. And knowing all this, he could not bring himself to judge her. This is quite a turn-around for a man whose conscience seems never to have bothered him before.

It is interesting the relative weights that he assigned to the two crimes. On the one hand, Tamar had disguised herself as a temple prostitute to seduce her father-in-law; and on the other hand, Judah had postponed her right to be married to his third son. Why was Judah's crime worse than Tamar's? Our own culture would judge Tamar's as the more heinous of the two, but our culture's perspective, ironically and unlike the Scripture, regards nearly all sexual sins as being worse than other kinds of sins. However, I think that Judah's reaction was not really one of comparing the degrees of the two crimes. When one's conscience is finally breached, it always feels like a log, not a splinter, in the eye. Realizing his own guilt for the first time in his life blinded him with the sudden realization that evil is evil, that guilt is guilt, that there is never a valid comparison between my sin and your sin. How can a judge who is guilty of anything at all ever pass judgment on the criminal who is guilty of anything at all? The answer Paul gives in Romans 2, and that Judah now grasped, is that he can't.

These events surrounding Judah's sons and daughter-in-law, were all disguises of God's angel wrestling with Judah; and when Tamar sent him his ring and his staff, his thigh was put out of joint. He was wounded; the only question was whether he would hold on until he was blessed. And he did. He chose the path of confession, repentance, and justice. He spared Tamar but did not have sexual relations with her anymore. He brought her under his protection, and treated her children as legitimately his, but he did not count her as his wife. A modern man would have perhaps thought that since Judah had already had his daughter-in-law against all custom and against the Law that would come later, then there would be no further guilt incurred if he had kept her as his wife. That is not the way the ancients thought about it. On the contrary, it is never inappropriate to discontinue what should never have been done in the first place if it is possible to do so without further harm being done. Judah had obligations to protect her, to care for her and her children, but he could not continue what should not have been.

It is in the second trip to Egypt that we again see Judah. Judah may have encountered the beginning of self-doubt when God executed his two older sons—parents tend to feel guilt for raising an evil son; but it was Tamar's deception that finally forced him to face his own character for the first time. Judging by his later actions on behalf of Benjamin, humility and repentance had taken root in him, and this is why I think the events with Tamar took place before the brothers went to Egypt the second time, though Perez and Zerah were born a bit later, not long before the whole family moved to Egypt. By this time, Tamar's pregnancy was well-known in the family, and some of the benefits of Judah's recent encounter with his own guilt can be discerned. He assumed leadership of the family, in part because his two older brothers, the two not in prison, had been discredited. Judah's offenses had been committed in isolation from the rest of the family, but both Reuben and Levi still lived under the shadow of their past. So it was Judah that offered to bear the blame personally if anything happened to Benjamin during the trip, as Reuben had tried to offer.

Israel seemed to have no concern for Simeon's welfare, and in the past this would have stirred up old grievances and bitterness in Judah, but he had been getting beyond all that. Seeing the wickedness of your own heart, if you genuinely see it, makes it easier to look past the failings of others. Israel should have loved Simeon as much as Benjamin, but he didn't; and if Israel didn't love Simeon as much as Benjamin, then he didn't love Judah as much as Benjamin either. So what? Judah could see his father's weakness as being like his own. The old offenses didn't seem so unforgivable anymore.

But the real test of Judah's new found repentance and humility came in Egypt as Joseph again set up his brothers and framed Benjamin for a crime. Joseph could guess how it would be with Benjamin, how Israel would have put Benjamin in Joseph's former place as the new favorite and how his brothers would have been made jealous of him just as they had been of Joseph; he would guess that one of them had probably had to offer to be responsible for Benjamin's safety; and when Judah assumed the role of spokesman he would have known that it was Judah who was on the line for Benjamin. So much the better. Joseph could remember with justifiable bitterness how it had been Judah's idea to sell him as a slave, how Judah had turned away from his pleading; now was the time for revenge. He tightened the noose by offering to send them all back except for Benjamin, putting Judah in the worst possible position. And just as Joseph suspected, the story came out: Judah had offered himself as surety for Benjamin, and Joseph got to hear the one who plotted his sale into slavery offer up himself as a slave in place of his younger brother. The wheel had turned full circle and Judah was paying for his crimes in the most perfect possible way. The rest of the scene belongs to Joseph's story and will be examined in due time. For now let's stop and just consider Judah.

Was this whole sequence of events God's judgment against Judah for the sale of Joseph? Yes and no. First of all, Judah only suffered the consequences in his imagination; he never actually experienced being a slave and never actually suffered as Joseph had done. But he had begun to understand exactly what he had done to Joseph and that if he did become a slave it was only the justice due him. This was the culmination of the whole process of Judah being brought face to face with himself, the culmination of a process of discipline, of wrestling with the angel. More than any material blessing could have done, the events with Tamar and then in Egypt demonstrated God's love for Judah and His commitment to him. God does not punish us for our sins the way we punish our children. The punishment of sin, the way we do it these days in our families and in our society, is utterly stupid because it teaches nothing, it accomplishes nothing, except to inflict suffering. God has no interest in making people suffer. His discipline is to show us how to see our choices the way He sees our choices. This is another reason the Covenant with Abraham should be called the Covenant of Revelation—it is not that direct verbal revelation is always involved, but for those in the Covenant life itself is a revelation.

We have already mentioned Genesis 46:12, that Er and Onan retained their standing among the people of God; they "went to Egypt" even though they were dead. We could further note that there are two sons of Perez listed among those who went to Egypt, though Perez himself must have been but a baby at the time. Doubtless, the children of Perez were listed here because they were of particular interest to the line of David and the coming Messiah. They went down to Egypt with Jacob, not because they were born at the time, but they were present in potential in Perez the infant. That is a stretch, I know, but the book of Genesis is intrinsically a stretch. This is yet more evidence, by the way, that the genealogies were not meant to be taken as timetables.

Finally we must look at Israel's deathbed prophecy over Judah. Israel's words look forward to David the King, but they also look beyond him to the Messiah. Judah was given the pre-eminence over his brothers, and that must have astonished Judah as much as the others. At the time, they were all bowing to Joseph, and Joseph had been elevated to the position of first-born when Israel adopted Manasseh and Ephraim as his own, so it would be naturally expected that he would have the blessing of the first born as well. By this time the famine had been over for a dozen or more years and the authority of Joseph was not so great under the next Pharoah, but it must have been something of a surprise that spiritual pre-eminence did not go to Joseph's family. Joseph had the spiritual credentials in the dreams and the great work God had done through him. Judah was just a sinner, with a long list of crimes to his credit. But Israel had been chosen over Esau, and Judah was now chosen over all the others.

And it was clear that rule was what was in view. The image of Judah's descendants as a lion is a kingly image, and the scepter of course has to do with a king. The image of the Lion of Judah began here and has become for us a name for the Messiah. Furthermore it was not just the submission of his brothers that would come to the line of Judah, but the obedience of the peoples, the obedience of those who were outside the family, was prophesied as well. The Jews as the chosen people, as a nation among the nations of the world, did not yet exist. The children of Israel were simply a clan, a very large extended family, not a nation. The world was not yet divided into Jew and Gentile, and the term "peoples" would not have the same meaning for them as it would have later. Yet it still conveyed that the authority of the descendants of Judah would extend beyond their own circle.

"Shiloh" is the word that is most obscure. Some translate "shiloh" as "tribute", but we do not know what the word means. It would be the name of a city in the territory of Ephraim eventually, but its meaning here is more likely a personal name. So the rendering of 49:10 could be "The scepter shall not depart from Judah, nor the ruler's staff from between his feet, until Shiloh comes, and to him shall be the obedience of the peoples." The context of the prophecy as a whole suggests that it is a Messianic reference. The last verses of the prophecy continue with an image of peace and prosperity, of abundance of wine, and later the land of Judah would be known in Israel as the source of the best wine. Though we do not understand this passage in any detail, the overall thrust of its meaning is clear: a future king will come from Judah to whom much of the world will owe allegiance.

4. Joseph

a) Joseph as a Youth (Genesis 37:1-17)

We know nothing much about Joseph until he was seventeen and the dreams started. He and his family had arrived in the land of Canaan when Joseph was about six years old and he would have been about fifteen years old at the time of the massacre of Shechem. By the time the Scripture turns attention to Joseph in chapter 37 the family was probably living at Bethel after the massacre at Shechem. Joseph's mother, Rachel, died in childbirth shortly after the dreams began and his only full brother, Benjamin, would have been very young when Joseph was sold.

Israel was the worst sort of parent, openly showing favoritism to Joseph over his older brothers. 37:3 says that Israel loved Joseph so much because he was the son of his old age, though in fact the brothers were all born in a very short period of time and Joseph was hardly younger. Israel's age was not the real reason; the reason was that Joseph was the only son of Rachel and the last son. Israel was a nearly a hundred and ten years old, and Joseph was sixteen or seventeen, when Rachel became pregnant again unexpectedly. Rachel herself was in her mid-forties, possibly fifty; she was not too old, but with her long history of childlessness, she and Israel would have been surprised and delighted.

Joseph was, of course, employed in tending the family's flocks even as a young boy. The family flocks were so large that they had been divided into two or more herds, particularly after they had seized the property of the entire city of Shechem. Doubtless, most of what they had seized at Shechem stayed near Shechem and they may have had another herd still at Succoth. Shechem was fifty or sixty miles to the north of Bethel. Joseph apparently was used to carry messages from one part of the family to another when they were separated, and in this context he brought a bad report to Israel about his brothers.

It was the rivalry between Leah and Rachel, Israel's open favoritism toward Rachel, and Leah's bitterness that drove the family's dysfunction. Hence Joseph would have had the most conflict with the sons of Leah, but with all of his brothers to some extent. From 37:2 we see that Joseph was helping the sons of Zilpah and of Bilhah, while the sons of Leah had charge of the other flocks at the goodly distance of Shechem. The sons of Leah were kept away from Joseph for the sake of peace. Joseph was all too willing to exploit his position as his father's favorite. He tattled on his brothers, criticized them to Jacob, and foolishly related dreams that could only upset them. They were jealous of Joseph, and the special robe Israel had made for him would have only aggravated the problem. It is not entirely clear what the Hebrew words mean, whether the robe was special because it was many-colored or because it was full-length. In either case, it was an expensive article of clothing and conferred special honor on Joseph in a culture in which only the privileged would have two changes of clothes.

The dreams were the last straw for Joseph's brothers. Dreams were taken seriously in that culture—the Middle East had had professional dream interpreters from the beginning of the historical records—and Joseph related them simply to get at his brothers. For a long time, as much as a year, the dreams continued to be a hot issue among the brothers, increasingly a source of anger. It was dangerous to relate the dreams to them: Simeon and Levi had already shown how ruthless they could be, and Judah seems to have been alienated from the family and increasingly tied to the people of the land. But Joseph was counting on the strong family loyalty demanded by that culture; he felt safe within his family to harass his brothers as much as he could. And he was not the last to discover that blood-ties are no protection against bloodshed. The second of these dreams portrayed Joseph's mother Rachel, symbolized by the moon, as bowing to him. Hence these provocative dreams came before Rachel's death and as much as a year before the brothers finally broke down and sold him into slavery; perhaps it took that long to find a good opportunity. Their revenge on Joseph was a long premeditated act, and not merely a crime of passion.

Dreams and the interpretation of dreams were to mark Joseph's life. From his earliest years he had a connection to the realm of the spirit through dreams and it is certainly implied by the passage that these dreams in his youth came from God. The two dreams described in Genesis 37 each portrayed the rest of his family as bowing to him, as being under him in some sense, the very thing most likely to cause trouble with his brothers. The question is, why did God give him those dreams at that point, dreams whose relating could only cause further trouble in a fragile family? The simplest answer would be that God was *engineering* Joseph's sale by his brothers, that God intended to stir up enough bitterness that they would be pushed over the edge of what they could endure and commit a rash and evil deed against Joseph. To be sure, God meant it for good and would accomplish a great deliverance because of it. The problem with this interpretation of events is that it sounds like "the ends justify the means". Does the Scripture intend to teach that God can and will do anything He wants to do, even if it is what we call evil, to accomplish His purposes, because He can make it come out all right in the end?

We could back off a bit and say that God was just testing Joseph at this point, that He sent the dreams to see how Joseph would react (as if He didn't know), that He didn't mean Joseph to relate the dreams to his brothers and precipitate a crisis (as if the whole series of events to follow were out of God's control and He was just hanging on for the ride). But backing off would be a mistake. We are always mistaken when we back away from questions about the Bible with no other motivation than trying to protect God's reputation. When we try to protect Him, we only introduce new weaknesses to be attributed to Him that He didn't invite. In the case of Joseph's dreams we can get God off the hook of being an interfering, stop-at-naught manipulator, but at the cost of making Him out to be a rather simple-minded duffer, muddling along while He tried to figure out what to do next. It is better to let Him choose the accusation He wishes to face.

As usual He presents Himself in an unflattering light, with no compromise toward our sensibilities, with no hesitation to offend our ideas of what we think He ought to be like. The best defense against God's honesty is to get in the habit of not thinking much about what He says; this is the traditional response to His word. But if He has opened Himself up to these charges, I think the least we can do is take Him to trial. There can be little doubt that when He gave those dreams to Joseph, He knew that Joseph would relate them to his brothers and that for his brothers it would be the last straw. He did not have to test Joseph to see what was in his heart, nor did He have to test Joseph's brothers to see what they would do. But it was important for Him *to show us* what was in Joseph's heart and in his brothers' hearts.

This is part of what it means to be one of the Covenant people of God—our lives are a revelation to us and to the rest of the world to show both what we are like and what God is like in relation to us. If Jesus really came in to the world to save sinners, He needed a few examples to communicate that fact. He needed some people whose sins and weaknesses could be displayed before the universe so that He could show what it meant to save them, so that the rest of the world could see and turn and be healed. When Abraham, Isaac, Israel, and his sons were adopted into the Covenant of Revelation, their lives went on display to the whole universe through the Scripture for our benefit. When we become Christians, we also volunteer for that job, though on a less dramatic scale since our lives do not get written up in Scripture. Even so, our neighbors look at our lives to learn what God is like, and we waste so much of the opportunity trying to look respectable, when we ought to be trying to look like we are saved by grace.

It is certainly true that God could have rescued the world from the famine that was to come in some less dramatic fashion, one that would not have involved so much suffering and bitterness between brothers. But the point was to stage a show, a show that would show us what He wanted to reveal. So is God a manipulator? Absolutely. He manipulated history for His own purposes, and He chose a people whose lives He would particularly manipulate to teach all the rest of the world who He is. He chose Abraham and his descendants, not because of their great faith but because of their great weakness: the perfect lives to reveal a strength and power and goodness that did not come from people but from God. Then He gave them opportunity to behave as they would behave and He poured out all His goodness into it.

It follows, by the way, that the Scripture does not give us graphic pictures of the weakness of people, of their failures, with the idea of teaching us a moral. *See, children, this is to teach us to not be jealous of our brothers and sisters and not to brag about the gifts God has given us.* If we only see the Scripture as a series of morals it becomes one of the single most boring books ever written and it is no wonder so few read it anymore. Nor does the Scripture hold up the failings of these people to give us someone we can judge, as if we needed more practice in judging. The single most important thing to understand before you read the Scripture is this one fact: the lives of these men were not written down so that you or I could grade them or feel superior to them or make them into lessons to teach our children; they were written down so that we could recognize ourselves as the kind of people God saves, so that we could see in their story the very corruption and stupidity and weakness we find so difficult to face in ourselves.

So Joseph told his family about his dreams, and that was a bad idea, and it is probably just what you or I would have done in his place. In fact, isn't it exactly like many things we are all doing right now? I want my brothers and sisters to know when God has given me a blessing or a dream or a calling or a vision. Why do I want them to know? Because I want them to be encouraged by what God has done for me or promised me? So when my testimony makes them feel more left out, more ignored by God, that is an unintended consequence? Is our real desire to bless others when we tell them about the great things God has done for us, or do we have a more insidious desire? I admit that my experience within churches has made me cynical, but it is a nearly invariable pattern that the loudest insistence that all the glory should go to God "inadvertently" draws all the glory onto the person who is speaking. And, God forgive me, I have done the very same thing, though in serpentine fashion I can occasionally manage to do it with a bit more subtlety. Joseph is not someone I can judge; he is someone who helps me judge myself.

The second of Joseph's dreams deserves particular attention. The second dream portrays the sun, the moon, and eleven stars as bowing to Joseph. The striking thing about this dream is its interpretation. First of all, the interpretation was obvious to all who heard it: the sun was

Joseph's father, the moon was Joseph's mother, Rachel, and the eleven stars were his brothers; no one had any doubt as to the interpretation, and it was consistent with the previous dream. Unlike the dreams Joseph would encounter in Egypt, this dream and the first one seem to be intended as clear revelations to the family and not as puzzles that would require a special gift to interpret. On the contrary, the slowest of them would know immediately what it meant; God might as well have slapped them, it would have been just that subtle. Given the clarity of the dream's meaning, it is surprising to note that the dream would never be fulfilled.

The dream clearly came before Rachel's death, and before Benjamin's birth, so at the time of the dream Joseph had only ten brothers and not eleven, and when he did have eleven brothers he had no mother. There was never any time at which the dream could have been fulfilled in detail. So what did God mean by giving Joseph a dream which was not only never to be fulfilled in its details, but which could never have been fulfilled? Was it not from God? Or was it not a revelation? If it wasn't a revelation, was it a sort of accidental half-revelation? Did God make a mistake in it? Or is God not as concerned with the details of His revelations as we are? We must choose between some unpleasant alternatives with this dream, it seems.

The best way to answer these questions is to think about the alternatives. What would we have God do? Our doctrine of revelation tends to require Him to give only dreams which He intends to fulfill in complete and vivid detail; we are a very insecure culture and we want to know that every loose end is tied up before we will venture out in trust. So we would require God to give Joseph a dream in which the moon was not present, in which no reference was made to Rachel at all. What would we have Him do about the eleven stars, then? The dream was probably given shortly before Benjamin's birth, so the presence of eleven stars rather than ten would have been easy for the family to account for. And yet if the new baby were included in the dream but his mother left out, wouldn't that have raised uncomfortable and irrelevant questions? A baby brother without his mother bowing to Joseph would have been unsettling. Leah might be left out without causing comment, particularly since there is only one moon to be had for the dream, but Rachel was Joseph's own mother and her presence would have been required. The previous dream was set in the context of the harvest and the workers of the harvest which would have naturally left Rachel out; further the first dream did not include a specific number of sheaves of grain, so the question of the coming child did not arise in that dream.

Since leaving Rachel out of the dream would have been unsettling and irrelevant to the point of the dream, God chose to put her in so as not to bring up issues that were beside the point. At any rate, this is my reconstruction of the rationale behind the dream, and the principle of revelation that I would derive from the dream is this: when God reveals anything to us, He sticks to the point He is making, and He arranges the irrelevant details so as not to confuse us with peripheral issues. We may want Him to take the same kind of care with the details that He takes to make His point, but in the end we would only be confused or disturbed or sidetracked by such details; they would hinder our understanding rather than helping. If God had hinted that Rachel was about to die, Israel and Joseph's brothers would have lost the main point of the dream. Did God lie to them? If you think so, then perhaps you don't understand what telling the truth means the way God understands it.

I realize, of course, that this is not adequate as a complete answer to the question. God could have given a different context for his dream, leaving the question of Rachel out of the context entirely, or He could have chosen a different time to give the dream, maybe after Benjamin was born. But He didn't do those things, and no one seemed to care that He didn't. Israel and his family understood the purpose of revelation better than we do; they were a bit more humble in the way they received the dream, they were less demanding that it be packaged according to their specifications. Meanwhile, the rest of the Scripture seems to be written in accordance with the principle stated above: the details that are irrelevant to the point, or that would confuse us, or that would hinder us giving our full attention to what He wants to say, are simply left to sort themselves out.

b) Joseph in slavery (Genesis 37:36 and 39:1-18)

When Joseph was sent out the last time with a message for his brothers, they had moved the flock to Dothan, no doubt in search of water or better pasture. Shechem was nearly sixty miles from Israel's camp at Hebron, and Dothan was another thirty miles beyond that. They were so far from Israel's camp that they were safe to carry out nearly any scheme against Joseph without danger of any rumor getting back to Israel. Dothan was on one of the principal caravan routes from Mesopotamia to Egypt so it was not unusual that the Midianite traders came along. The caravan that happened by is twice described as Ishmaelite (37:25,28) but once as Midianite (37:28). It was probably a large commercial operation, one with merchants from many tribes, including Ishmaelite and Midianite. Both Midianites and Ishmaelites were descendants of Abraham, nomadic merchants with similar cultures, and could easily have conducted joint business ventures. If Ishmaelites bought Joseph, by the time they got to Egypt he was in Midianite hands.

It was Judah who had the idea of selling Joseph. After all, he said, they shouldn't kill him, their own flesh and blood; it would be much better to sell him as a slave and make a little money at the same time. Reuben had gone off to attend to some duty or other and did not get back until it was too late; whether he could have prevented the sale of Joseph is a matter for speculation. Later events show that Joseph's slavery was in accordance with God's will, so Reuben's absence may have been arranged so that he not be there to rescue Joseph, and the crime of the brothers would go unchecked. The price given for Joseph corresponded to the same price given in the Law of Moses in Leviticus 27:5 four hundred years later, noteworthy for those who are interested in economics; inflation had not been invented.

Joseph was sold into slavery early in the reign of Senusret II, in about the year 1888 b.c. Senusret II came to the throne suddenly at about this time, when his father, Amenemhat II, was assassinated. Potiphar, a wealthy and important official in Pharoah's court, bought Joseph. He was the captain of the bodyguard and would have had jurisdiction not only over the personal guard for the Pharaoh but also over the prison, which was in his house; and he was in charge of all executions. If this dating is correct and Joseph arrived shortly after the assassination of Amenemhat II then Potiphar may have been newly appointed as the captain of Pharaoh's bodyguard, the previous one having failed in his duties.

Over a period of years Joseph's faithful service won the favor of Potiphar, who put him in charge of his whole household, of "all that he owned" is the way it is phrased. I think this means that Joseph was in charge of the private property of Potiphar and that his authority did not extend to the parts of the household that were the official duties of Potiphar, like the prison. There was a chief jailer who was in charge of the prisoners, and there may have been other officials with other duties within Potiphar's house that were not under Joseph.

For some reason Joseph's character was shaped positively by his slavery and his experience serving Potiphar. Rather than becoming embittered and, as a result, becoming a slouching servant, or a calculating servant, Joseph became a man of character, a man of morals in a land in which morals did not abound (is there a land anywhere in which morals do abound?). Rather than wrecking whatever bit of faith Joseph had in the God of his fathers, his hardship seems to have strengthened and matured it.

Except in the theological sense, it was not a foregone conclusion that his hardship would mature him. In general, there is nothing necessarily ennobling about hardship; some are embittered, some are crushed, and some are ennobled. Some are able to understand hardship as discipline; some cannot see beyond the pain to any good thing. Some see an angel in the stranger who picks the fight with them, but some see a demon. Some find that God's discipline makes them cling to Him more tightly while others only want to escape Him. God brought Joseph into slavery in Egypt exactly because Joseph was the type of man who would be ennobled by suffering, and prepared by it for the role he would have to assume in the future. There is great reward for those who can submit to hardship without becoming embittered, as Joseph did. It is the mark of the work of God that hardship produces gentleness and wisdom. It is the mark of wrestling with an angel.

Within the limits of his slavery Joseph prospered. God took a direct hand in his prosperity, and during this time with Potiphar Joseph was learning to manage the affairs of a household. He was gaining the administrative skills that would be so necessary to him later. He was also healing a bit from his brothers' ill treatment of him. The best treatment for such injustice is time and a period in which things work out, a time in which you can relearn how to "feel good about yourself". This may sound like modern pop-psychology self-image stuff, but there is something to it. Joseph had to learn to respect himself again, and this time in a healthier way. There is the self-respect, the "good self image" that Joseph had as a youth, in which he defined himself by comparison to his brothers and fed off the preferential treatment he got from his father. Now he was learning a better kind of good-self-image defined by the quality of the work that he did and by a simple trust in God's favor toward him.

Don't be misled into thinking that God showed favor to Joseph because Joseph was obedient and faithful as a servant; don't reverse cause and effect, as we always want to do. Joseph did not earn God's favor; he received God's favor and God's favor transformed him, one degree at a time, into a better man. God had extended His favor to Joseph when he was still a spoiled brat bragging about his dreams. He had chosen to send Joseph into Egypt and He had chosen to bless all of Joseph's work before he had done any of it.

But more subtly, Joseph was getting to know God. He was learning who God was in a way that no one before him had had the opportunity to learn. Perhaps it is the other side of the coin to being a dreamer, but Joseph was apparently given to reflecting on the meaning of the events in his life. He did not waste his time just drifting through life, but he considered what had happened to him, and what it all meant. Joseph, perhaps as part of his sensitivity to dreams, saw God as being behind everything; and so reflecting on things automatically meant reflecting on God.

It appears that he remembered the oral traditions that were part of his family heritage; not being written down, they were more easily fixed in his memory. It is ironic that he did not truly get to know God, the God of His traditions, until he was immersed in the Egyptian religious culture. The Egyptian religion, unlike the religion of the Middle East, was worthy of being called a religion. The myths of Mesopotamia and Canaan tended to be ad hoc and incoherent, more for magic and manipulation of events than for worship. Perhaps this is unfair to them, for there was a strong tradition of spiritual devotion to the gods of Mesopotamia; but their ideas of their own gods were quite primitive, very anthropomorphic, hardly more than projections of humanity onto the sky. The Egyptians, on the other hand, were very sophisticated spiritually, and their religion was more like modern Hinduism than like the pagan religions of the west.

Certainly by the time Potiphar's wife set her sights on him, Joseph had matured in his understanding and devotion to God beyond what anyone in his family had. Where did he come by his understanding that adultery with Potiphar's wife would be displeasing to God? Was it because adultery was condemned by all cultures? Or was it that he was devoted to Potiphar, who showed himself to be a kind master? Or was it something more profound? How did he learn to think that *his God*, who was clearly not an Egyptian god, cared about his behavior toward an Egyptian's wife? Certainly, adultery would have had grave consequences for him if it were discovered, but the fear of consequences is frequently not powerful enough to deter the crime. Joseph's standard of morality came from something more than his upbringing and more than practical question of his vulnerable status. His insight must have been something that God had taught him in the quietness of inner reflection, a matter of the heart and not a matter of the law. Joseph had received new revelation from God, not by means of a verbal revelation, but by an inward, invisible and inaudible working of the Spirit. He knew God; he could not point to any commandment—there were none—but he knew, or thought he knew, how God would feel about an affair with Potiphar's wife.

Joseph had learned to care about what God thought about things, what God thought about the events in his life and what God thought about right and wrong. And here I mean God Most High, the God of his fathers, not the Egyptians' gods. In his slavery, Joseph had become convinced that God Most High, of his fathers' tradition, was an ethical God, a God who had opinions about right and wrong. This was hinted at, to be sure, in the oral tradition he had inherited, but Joseph picked up on those hints to a degree that the rest of his family had not. The details of the moral code that his God preferred had not been spelled out; Joseph had only his own conscience, his cultural traditions, and the possibility that God would speak to him as He had spoken to Abraham and Isaac and Israel. By this point in his life he had become accustomed to considering the events in his life and the choices he made from a spiritual perspective, so when Potiphar's wife suddenly confronted him with the temptation to adultery he had a spiritual mindset in place to evaluate her offer.

It would certainly have been dangerous to agree to the woman's advances, but as Joseph discovered, there was also danger in refusing her. Potiphar's wife was relentless in her pursuit of Joseph, and it is difficult to see how the other servants could have helped noticing her advances to Joseph. The house was full enough of servants that there was usually a manservant or two around, and wealthy women tend to keep their female servants about them very closely. Servants always knew what was going on with the lord and lady; secrets couldn't be kept in such a household. The mistress knew that her secret would not be betrayed; it would have been dangerous for any servant to even hint to his or her master what was suspected or heard.

In 39:10 it says that "he did not listen to her to lie beside her or be with her"; not only was he refusing the adultery she wanted, but he was refusing the context that could lead to adultery. He not only refused her outright suggestions, but having decided the right course of action, he refused any course of action that might set him up to betray his decision. We do not discuss how to resist temptation these days, but it is not enough to "just say no", as excellent as that advice may sometimes be. That something is a temptation means that there is an inward impulse toward giving in to the temptation, an inclination against our own resolve, and that is what we must guard against. A resolve to resist is not sufficient because our resolution is exactly what is at stake; we must act to protect that resolution and ensure that it will not fail, to put ourselves beyond the reach of the power temptation will have over us.

Potiphar's wife watched for opportunities to seduce Joseph, and inevitably one arose in which all or nearly all the servants were away. It is hard to see what Joseph could have done to protect himself. Leaving most of his clothes behind may have been necessary but it was not helpful for his alibi. He reacted out of desperation and just ran, but to where? He could not go to his master; it is not likely that his master would have believed any story Joseph would tell him about his wife. Raising the subject with his master would only put Joseph in a bad light no matter what he might say. When Potiphar's wife determined to seduce him his fate was inescapable.

When Joseph ran, she could simply have given up on him, of course, and pursued some easier prey, but her pride had been hurt. She wanted to hurt Joseph in return, and that is why she made the scene with the other servants. She summoned the men servants, all of whom were under Joseph's authority, but all of whom also knew that Potiphar's wife's power went beyond any delegated authority. Then she told them what had happened—that is, she gave them the official story that she would expect them to verify to her husband. She wasn't so much informing them of what happened as telling them what to say; but surely they knew better; they weren't blind or deaf and they knew her character, but they also knew the consequences should they contradict her.

Potiphar's wife's role was not exactly like that of the serpent deceiving Eve. There was no subtlety involved. She skipped the part about, "you won't really die" and went right to the "isn't this a delicious idea". There was no attempt to trip up Joseph with confusing questions, no sweet assurances that everything would be all right. Eve had to be deceived, but since the Fall we generally come "pre-deceived" as it were. But Joseph's training in Potiphar's house had wakened him, it had opened his eyes enough that he wasn't just a hapless victim wandering past. A little subtlety might have captured her prey, but this one was wearing a kind of armor against such a head-on attack. This time the intended victim ran rather than falling for the ruse, so there was what we might call a spiritual victory. And the result of this spiritual victory was . . . death of another sort: disgrace, probably a beating, and prison. This is the beginning of the theme of sacrifice and resurrection. Since the Fall, no choice right or wrong, escapes death. Choose to do right or choose to do wrong, either way you die. The difference lies in the quality of the death involved. One kind of death is just death, and the rottenness of it is all there is until decay has finished it off. Another kind of death leads, against all hope, to a new kind of life. Joseph's fall into disgrace is an allegory of this second kind of death. He went into the tomb, the dungeon, but he did not stay there.

c) Joseph in prison (Genesis 39:19-40:23)

It was certainly a case of injustice, though it was not as severe as it could have been. Prison was a merciful punishment for Joseph's crime; a flogging of a thousand lashes would have been the usual punishment, a punishment not designed to leave the culprit physically functional afterwards. But either Potiphar was a particularly merciful man or he had a secret suspicion that Joseph might not be the wrongdoer here. But Potiphar believed his wife; he had to try to believe his wife. Even if he had suspected her of having an unfaithful character, it would have damaged his pride too much to admit she might be the one to blame, that she might prefer a slave to her noble husband.

So Joseph suffered a fate even more ignominious than that of being sold as a slave to begin with. At least when he had been sold by his brothers there had been some reason for it; he despised them as much as they hated him. He certainly had never tried to win their brotherly love. He knew on some level, that to some extent he had brought them to it by his obnoxious personality. But to be thrown into prison for something he not only had not done but had been strenuously trying to avoid doing: it was simply unjust and he knew it.

Here again Joseph had the opportunity to become bitter. *See! He had obeyed God but it hadn't paid off. He had sought to honor God, and what he got out of it was just more of the same mistreatment as was common all over the world. There was no justice, and if God did exist then He was either too weak or too busy, or else not really all that good. Maybe God did prefer the rich people, the Pharaohs, and the chief guards. Maybe God was playing favorites here, like He had done at Shechem, only now Joseph was the one getting the short end of the stick.* Or so we would be tempted to think in his place.

But Joseph did not become bitter. For some reason, the unfairness, the cruelty, the sense of the injustice of the thing, only made him trust God more deeply. Now why is that? Why does hardship cause some to spurn God and others to cling more tightly? I can only think that it is the grace of God; it is the internal grace of the Holy Spirit and that is all there is. Or put another way, Joseph could either choose to see God as abandoning him or he could choose to give God the benefit of the doubt and continue to trust Him in spite of the evidence, and he chose to trust. This description does not do justice, I think, to the way Joseph actually *experienced* the imprisonment. It was not so much a choice as a lack of choice: what else could he do?

To cease to trust God, for those who have trusted Him, is like stepping off the edge of a cliff; there is nothing beyond such a choice. It would be the end. Choosing to renounce God, for those who have once trusted Him, is like committing suicide. We usually talk of "choosing God" as if the choice were a free one, but I don't think it ever is. To those who reject God as untrustworthy, the whole spiritual thing is like the smell of decay, revolting and disgusting and they run from God like they run from a sewer. To those who accept Him and trust Him, it is the same as choosing life over death, sweetness over pain, plain sight over blindness. This gives us more credit than we are due, in most cases. More usually I think it is like choosing the last thin string of hope over letting go in despair, because our grasp of God's sweetness, or light, or life is tenuous a lot of the time. Still, for those of us who choose Him, there is little doubt as to what must be done.

While Joseph did not become embittered, there is no doubt that he felt bitterness. It was not that Joseph didn't feel the way an unbeliever would; it was that the balance of his heart was on the other side of the equation. Joseph continued to be faithful in jail. Faithfulness had become a habit to him during his long years as a slave and now he became a faithful criminal. And his faithfulness as a prisoner was faithfulness to that same master who had thrown him into prison in the first place, for though there was a chief jailer who was his direct overseer, it was Potiphar that he really served and in whose house he still served. What did Potiphar's other servants think of it, the slave who had once been their overseer now humiliated in the prison, and humiliated, as they well knew, through no fault of his own but just to satisfy the lady's pride? Joseph probably had no contact with Potiphar's wife while he was in prison, and very little contact with the other household servants, and just as well. How might Potiphar's wife have mocked him, quietly, with her little secret? She could find another slave to seduce, but he was doomed to prison forever.

Joseph's degradation was complete, but he did not give up the integrity he had found as a slave. Again God blessed Joseph in his work, however much Joseph's feelings may have tormented him. Over the years he was entrusted with increasing responsibility until he was in charge of all his small domain once again. What a remarkable person Potiphar must have been as well. The charge against Joseph would have been the worst charge possible from Potiphar's personal viewpoint, and yet Joseph won his favor a second time. Not many people could have bestowed a second favorable opinion on a man with Joseph's reputation, and this reflects well on Potiphar. It also suggests that Potiphar suspected his wife, even if he couldn't admit it.

It is easy to imagine how Joseph's feelings could have rebelled even against his success in the prison, just as his feelings could have rebelled against his success in Potiphar's household. What was the point of being put in charge of Potiphar's household? He was still a slave. What was the point of being in charge of the prisoners? It didn't change the fact that he was still a prisoner himself, that he still had no meaningful future. He was in his late twenties, he had been a slave and a prisoner for eleven long years. His life was passing by in this meaningless way, when the chief baker and the cupbearer to the pharaoh came under his care and had some strange dreams.

The cupbearer and the baker were put in confinement in Potiphar's house because that was the king's prison, the prison for those who had somehow offended Pharaoh and who might be executed. Potiphar was in charge of executions and so he would be the one to arrange the beheading of the baker later on. It was Potiphar himself who put Joseph in charge of the cupbearer and the baker. They were somewhat special prisoners and Potiphar wanted to be sure that they were treated right, and Joseph was the right one to choose when special prisoners needed special treatment. Imagine him noticing one morning that they seemed to be feeling a bit low, and then imagine him taking the time to inquire about it. How many slaves would do that for a fellow prisoner? It was not part of his job to cheer up prisoners, to coddle them; but he did it because that was who he had become.

It is interesting that they responded to Joseph's question by saying, "We have had a dream" rather than "We have had dreams". It is as if they knew that these dreams were the same in some strange way, though different in detail. When Joseph heard of their dreams, his response was diagnostic of all that had happened to him over a decade or so of slavery: "Do not interpretations belong to God? Tell it to me please." What is the big deal about interpreting dreams? Doesn't the job of interpretation belong to God? If so, God could as easily share the information with Joseph as with anyone else. Why not give it a shot? If no interpretation was forthcoming, then it wasn't, and they could go on with their lives. There was no false humility about Joseph, the kind that leads to a hopeless inability to even try. He could have said, "Don't interpretations belong to God? But I'm just a prisoner like you. There's no way He would tell me anything. You need to find a real interpreter." But Joseph had no pride to be hurt, nothing to lose. If God didn't give him the interpretation, so what? Would anyone think less of him?

And Joseph must have been wondering about his own dreams from when he was a teenager. What had happened to those dreams? Had they meant anything? Whether they did or not, Joseph still felt an odd connection to dreams; he knew intuitively that dreams, his own and others', were part of his life. But Joseph had no doubt, when he heard the dreams, that he knew what they meant. How did God manage to tell him the interpretation? There is no way, for those of us who are on the outside, to know what it feels like to be told something by God. In modern, western concepts, it must have been a subjective feeling of Joseph's that he understood the dreams, and subjectivity is one of the worst of sins a western mind might commit. At some point, though, we have to simply decide that Joseph just knew, that he knew he knew, that it was different from merely holding a strong opinion or feeling. We can only understand how he knew if we happen ourselves to have a conviction that is unassailable, something that is beyond doubt even though it is unproven, something axiomatic. Joseph gave them the interpretations somewhat dispassionately, like a caring physician might give out the diagnoses to two patients, one destined to recover and one destined to die.

When Joseph was first sold into slavery, there was a destination marked for him, the very man he would need to help him accomplish his work.

Any other owner and there would have been no Joseph, no interpreter of dreams, no rescue from the coming famine. No other master would have thrown Joseph into contact with the baker and cupbearer in the right circumstances. It is clear, reading the story, that God was behind all the events that had occurred in Joseph's story, and that at this point God sent dreams to these two disgraced men so that Joseph would interpret the dreams, and so that one of the men would remember the Hebrew dream interpreter when the right time came.

It is inspiring to read such stories and to be awed at the care God took to accomplish His purposes here. But what is so surprising about it? Why are we moved, inspired, horrified by the fact that God can manipulate historical events, that He can cause the right person to be present and in need of a slave at the right time, that He can arrange two officials to get in trouble and meet Joseph, that He can send dreams to whoever He wants whenever He wants? If you buy that God created all things, then a little manipulation of daily events is not a very strenuous undertaking. What is rather frightening is that He took all that care and trouble to do it. He is an artist, a dramatist. It could all have been done in a thoroughly boring fashion, but God has style. He wanted this to be a good story. And like any really good story, there are some incidentals to the story that merit reflection.

First, consider the whole story from the viewpoint of the chief baker. His role in God's story was to have a dream predicting his own execution, and then to be executed, just so that he could be remembered as an example of Joseph's ability to interpret dreams. It isn't fair, is it? Was he a bad person? Was he a worse man than the cupbearer? Was that why the cupbearer got to be the one who lived, who was restored, and who was in the right place at the right time to mention Joseph? Or is the reason both more and less arbitrary than the simplistic one? I do not think, and the Scripture does not encourage us to think, that bad people are given bad roles to play in the script of life, and that good people get the good roles. It is more complicated than that; more complicated in the sense that we will not be able to figure out the rule for the assigning of the parts. In the end, the baker was killed because God chose him, appointed him to that role, and the cupbearer lived because God appointed him to that role. It was arbitrary from the viewpoint of people who are not privy to the Playwright's designs or conversant with the craft of running a universe.

On the other hand it was as far from being arbitrary as it is possible to be. It was no more unfair than Joseph's imprisonment had been, and it was also no more arbitrary. That we do not know what was going on does not mean that nothing was going on. It is this same unfairness that forces us into a dilemma: we have to choose how to think about God's meddling with the affairs of the world, just as Joseph was forced to decide how to think about it. If God meddled like that in ancient Egypt, then no one is safe; there is no way to feel safe anymore; there is no way to know that He is not meddling in my life right now, that my parents, my children, my grief, my disappointments and successes, are not just part of some design in some bigger story I don't know. If He is a meddling kind of God, then there is nothing we can do to stop Him. The dilemma is always the same: either we choose to grow bitter on behalf of the baker and our own griefs, or we choose to trust. There is no answer given when we ask for a reason. My suffering, your suffering, the suffering that goes on all the time around us is either pointless or it isn't. In either case, it is useless to ask questions that will not be answered. We must all fall into despair or else fall into hope.

Second, consider the whole story from a more personal angle. It has become a tiresome cliché in our day to say, "God loves you and has a wonderful plan for your life." It is no doubt true, but it is neither informative nor helpful. The fact is that that "wonderful plan" for your life may be to give you a role like that of the baker. The Wonderful Plan for your life may not look so wonderful while it is going on. The Wonderful Plan for your life may feel much more like the proverbial Bitter Pill. We do an injustice—actually we lie—when we tell people that God has a wonderful plan for their lives and imply that it will seem sweet and good to them as it unfolds. Maybe it will and maybe it won't. But woe to that evangelist who leads a person to Christ and leads him to believe he will now have an easy and pleasant life and leaves him to grow offended at the reality when his misconceived hopes fade away. Woe to the Christian witness who makes it sound as though we are all called to be Josephs. Woe to them all, but most of all woe to the evangelist who misleads.

Of course, when the play is ended, when the curtain is brought down and we see our role in the finished product, I believe we will all stand up and give the Writer and Producer and Director a standing ovation. But the truth is that until then it can, and probably will, seem pretty grim and meaningless. We all experience sooner or later what it means to be stuck in the prison with Joseph, or find to our horror that our dreams mean we are about to die. That is when we must choose to trust or not.

d) Joseph Becomes Master of Egypt (Genesis 41)

But the chief cupbearer forgot Joseph. The pharaoh during Joseph's imprisonment was probably Senusret II (the Greeks called him Sesostris II). My theory is that Senusret II died shortly after restoring the cupbearer to his office; perhaps it was his death and the succession of the new pharaoh that drove Joseph from the memory of the cupbearer for two years. Another possibility is that the cupbearer and the baker were put in prison because Senusret II died. The cupbearer probably functioned like a taster to check for poison, though that is not known. It may be there was a conspiracy theory that led to their imprisonment, but that the cupbearer was cleared of suspicion. The dating in the Bible tends to tie down selected dates pretty securely and the events in between them have to be interpolated between the two ends. The latter half of Israel's life floats a bit and I have dated it by the best fit between Joseph and his dreams and secular Egyptian events, and then working backward. There is considerable slack in my estimates of the dates, in other words.

We do know that the Middle Kingdom pharaohs competed for power with the other great lords and nobility of Egypt. These lords were known as nomarchs, and ruled over the provinces, which they called nomes. Early in the reign of Senusret III the power of the nomarchs was significantly broken and the pharaoh became absolute ruler over Egypt. Genesis 47:13-26 could be a description of how these nomarchs lost their power. Furthermore, Egypt was usually hostile to foreigners, but at this particular point in their history there were an unusual number of Asiatics (mostly Canaanite) in Egypt, and relations were relatively good with foreigners, except for the Nubians to the south. Historians disagree on the dating of ancient Egypt, but the ones I am following place the beginning of Senusret III in 1878 b.c. It was about two years later, then, in 1876 b.c., that this Senusret began having bad dreams.

God's timing seems a bit strange here. Why did He put the baker and cupbearer in the prison two years in advance of when they were needed? Was He playing mind games with Joseph, raising his hopes only to seem to let him down (say the cynics)? Didn't He do the same thing with Abraham, promising him a son in his old age and then going to Palm

Beach or somewhere for thirteen years? It seems to be becoming a pattern with God to make big promises, big plans, big announcements, and then disappear for a while just when we are most expecting something to come of those promises, plans, and announcements. The book of Genesis merely introduces this unappealing aspect of God's personality; the rest of the Scripture verifies that it is indeed a habit with Him. It is as if time meant nothing to Him; or lots.

This is too much of a pattern with God to be a mere accident. His timing is so flawless, getting the right people together at the right place against all the odds, that to be habitually late with every single promise demands some thought. We all know people just like that, who are always late, and the appearance is that they just don't care if other people have to wait for them. They are simply rude or else rather godlike. God is too deliberate about it for it to be coincidence. It must be either a calculated insult or else He has a different attitude toward timing than we do. It must be that God is always late in order to always arrive on time. He is always late because He loves time and He loves timing and He loves *waiting* for the right time. There is no more important spiritual duty, no more *artistic* duty in anyone's life, than waiting for the right moment. Isn't the pause the essence of all drama as well as all comedy? God simply has a better sense of the aesthetic moment than we do.

Our attention is definitely centered on the present moment. We want things when we want them: now. It is the most frequent trial some of us have to face: to be in line at the store or the bank, to be on hold, to wait at the doctor's office, to have to pause the video while we wait for someone to get something from the fridge, to sit there while the computer gets itself unfrozen. But God delights in waiting; and He delights in making us wait as well. Waiting is where the action begins; waiting is where all of the preparation for action occurs. The person who can wait well is the person who is ready for action when the time comes. The person who cannot wait is never really ready for anything. It is one of spirituality's most important lessons and if you aspire to become a truly and deeply spiritual person, you must learn how to wait. What Joseph did during those two years was what he had been doing all along. Day-by-day he practiced choosing to do a good job, choosing to do his best, choosing to hope that God would not leave him forever. He practiced so well that when Pharaoh had his dreams and grew troubled in spirit, Joseph was ready to do what he had to do without being destroyed by it.

One striking contrast in Joseph's character before and after his thirteen years of slavery was his humility. He was very full of himself when he was young as the spoiled favorite of his father, but his years as a slave, as a prisoner, and then suddenly as the second in command of all Egypt, had proved to him who he really was and was not. In particular he had learned the difference between what he did and what God did, between what he had to do and what God alone had to do. In other words he was walking in the footsteps of the faith of his great-grandfather, he was letting God fulfill His own purposes in His own way without trying to do it for Him. This is no where more clear than when he stood before Pharaoh.

He refused to take credit for his ability to interpret dreams and "gave all the glory to God". This, of course, is only what we owe to God; it is only the plain fact of the matter, but it is not so easy to remember in the excitement of the moment. Too often praise is thinly veiled boasting. The line that separates praise from bragging is all too easy to cross. The account of Joseph, however, portrays him as genuinely humble. He put God forward from the beginning, before he had either failed or succeeded, before he heard Pharaoh's dream. He had done nothing yet, but he wanted Pharaoh to know that whatever happened, it would only happen because of God. He could have said, "Yes, God has gifted *me* with the ability to interpret" or "God has appointed *me* to help you out here, O Pharaoh"; either statement would have been literally true, but they would both have been false because the focus of both sentences would have been praise for himself disguised as praise for God. Instead Joseph told the "truth, the whole truth, and nothing but the truth": "It is not in me. God will give Pharaoh a favorable answer."

There would have been a theological barrier between Joseph and Pharaoh. Joseph would no doubt have been speaking to Pharaoh in the Egyptian language and he was apparently using the generic word for God, but what he meant by the word and what Pharaoh meant by the word would have been quite different. Pharaoh would have seen himself as a descendant of the great god Amon, the sun god, whereas Joseph would have been thinking of the God who had been appearing to his family for several generations. In Egypt this was the time when the cult of Osiris was reaching its full importance in Egyptian religious life, and this Senusret was one of its major devotees. This cult taught that all people—at least all Egyptians—and not just the Pharaoh and his family, had a "spiritual force", what they called a **ba**. It taught that all Egyptians, and not just the Pharaoh and his family, had some future expectation of a good after-life.

Pharaoh would have experienced some spiritual dissonance as he spoke to Joseph. After all, if Pharaoh were a close relation to Amon, then why did Amon use some foreigner to speak to him rather than directly or through an Egyptian magician or wise man? Further, while Pharaoh may have been liberal (for an Egyptian) toward foreigners, slaves and criminals were another matter. Why then, Pharaoh might ask, was Amon giving the interpretation to such a foreigner as this slave/criminal? Clearly Pharaoh would only have consulted with Joseph if he were forced to. His spirit was troubled, distressed, driven to distraction over the dreams and he could find no help or relief in Egypt. It was desperation that sent him to Joseph.

But the theological barrier only worked in one direction: Joseph had no problem. His increasing understanding of God Most High was not put off balance by the Egyptian religion, sophisticated as it was. For one thing, they needed him, their gods seemed to need his God. Nor did Joseph feel the need, as a modern Christian probably would have in his place, to correct Pharaoh's understanding of God; indeed, Joseph had even at this point almost no understanding of how his God and the other gods were connected. He did not have theological maturity; he was simply connected to the God of his fathers and could let the details sort themselves out.

And Joseph was entirely ready. No doubt he wanted to get out of prison, but there was no hint of desperation in him. He had been humbled, he had been taught how to wait, and he does not seem to have thought this might be his ticket out. His answers to Pharaoh would have been palatable, not at all designed to challenge his spiritual beliefs. His demeanor would also have struck Pharaoh favorably and made it easier for him to see this foreigner as exceptional. The Egyptian religion was filled with elements that were irrational and even inconsistent with each other—magic and superstitions and rituals that did not have to make literal sense. The Egyptian religion was deeply (one might say terminally) metaphorical. If Amon chose to speak to a foreigner, then that would just be one more odd thing to add into the mix. It was difficult to swallow, but not as hard in the Egyptian religion as it would have been in a more rationalistic religion like our modern western ones.

Joseph's manner, while humble, was also authoritative. He was not guessing what the dreams meant. He was not interpreting the dreams like a person might who was decoding some language of specialized symbols. He knew what the dreams meant; how he knew is a matter for fruitless argument. Joseph had no doubt that he saw the meaning of the dreams in a complete way and so when he spoke to Pharaoh it was with a plain-spokeness that would have been utterly convincing. It must have blown them away in a superstitious time and place to encounter such simple certainty. Magicians and wise men of every age know to hedge every prediction they make for their own safety. They must protect their reputations and their lives with vagueness. Joseph had no such need. And his certainty was such that he could follow up the interpretation with a concrete proposal for a strategy to meet the crisis in an intelligent manner. Joseph was clearly the man of the hour and Senusret was no fool.

Joseph's interpretation of the dream raises certain questions, however. It is interesting that the interpretation ascribed both the years of plenty and the years of famine directly to God's will, but gives no hint of any reason for them. Why did God think that a severe famine, a severe famine over a large chunk of the world, was so necessary at that particular time? It was not as a punishment for evil, like the Flood had been, since He warned them and sought to protect the people from the effects of the famine. Was it just a means of getting Israel to move to Egypt? Surely an easier and less damaging way could have been devised if all He really wanted was to get Israel moved. Or was God simply caught in the flow of cause and effect with little choice in the matter, a Creator who had lost control over His domain? That would be a pathetic image for the Scripture to present, considering how it emphasizes His power everywhere else.

Further, the repeating of the dream was to show that the decision to send the years of abundance followed by the years of famine was a non-negotiable decision. This implies that sending the dream in only one form would have left some room for haggling about the details and perhaps, by making some appropriate sacrifice or penance, avoiding the whole scenario. This is an important point. When God sends a prophetic warning about some disaster or other, He apparently does not always mean it absolutely, like Fate or Calvinistic Predestination. Other gods of the ancient world were both more vague and more whimsical and flexible in their intentions, more open to discussion. Joseph's interpretation suggests that sometimes God Most High is open to discussion and sometimes He isn't, that He may sometimes reveal plans that are open to negotiation.

It is just as well that no one asked God to give a reason for the famine since none was ever given. There are too many variables in history for us to think that the sequence of abundance and famine in Egypt was simply unnecessary and merely a dramatic way to get the children of Israel into Egypt, God showing off. True, Joseph's role in managing the resources of Egypt would have gotten his family off to a good start with the Egyptians, but there must have been a greater significance to the events than that, especially since they would just end up as slaves in any case. There are too many details we don't know to guess God's purposes here, but one thing is clear from a purely theological perspective: when God meddles directly with history, He is revealing something. And pointedly, He was not just engaged in revelation to the Covenant-of-Revelation people. This was revelation on some level to the Egyptians as well. This was revelation on some level to everyone who ended up hungry and had to run to Egypt for food.

Note that Joseph apparently did not take any action against Potiphar, but more especially he did not try to get even with Potiphar's wife. Potiphar seems to have been a reasonably good master to Joseph and who could blame him for believing his wife? But Joseph could reasonably have held a grudge against the woman who had framed him and humiliated him. It may be that he restrained himself from revenge against her because any action against her would have hurt Potiphar as well. Or maybe his restraint was just a matter of wisdom, recognizing that the reach of even a powerful foreigner in Egypt was not that long. But I am inclined to give Joseph the benefit of the doubt here. I don't think he wanted revenge anymore; the pain of being falsely accused and imprisoned had been greatly soothed. The real pain he still bore was the memory of being sold into slavery to begin with. So he could forget Potiphar's wife; his success would be punishment enough for her as she wondered what he might do. Revenge never helps heal the pain anyway.

Naturally Pharaoh gave Joseph an Egyptian name, Zaphenath-paneah, which seems to have meant something like, "God speaks, he lives". It is interesting that Joseph's wife was Asenath, the daughter of Potiphera, the priest of On (On was another name for the city Heliopolis, a center for the worship of Amon). Pharaoh might naturally have thought of marrying him to a priestly family since he spoke for God; he may have even been trying to resolve a bit of the theological conflict he felt by trying to absorb Joseph into their system. The Egyptian religion was particularly good at absorbing new ideas, like a pool can absorb a rock thrown at it and be entirely unchanged. The conflict in religion, the conflict between Joseph's deepening understanding of God Most High and the Egyptian spirituality was not very visible; it would have been difficult to put into words in the Egyptian language, and God did not push the question. The conflict did not seem to cause Joseph much worry, and did not seem to contaminate his family life. The incipient conflict in theology would be a battle that could be fought later, literally. In the meantime though, Joseph's faith was not diluted by the Egyptian influence, and God did not seem worried that it would be.

Assuming that Pharaoh's dream was fulfilled immediately, then the years of plenty would have lasted between 1876 and 1870 b.c. so that the famine lasted between 1869 and 1863 b.c. During the seven years of plenty Joseph became the father of two sons, Manasseh and then Ephraim. For comparison of chronology, Joseph's two sons were being born at roughly the same time that Judah's two oldest sons were being executed.

A famine in Egypt would normally be caused by a failure of the Nile to flood, which would be cause by a drought through a large portion of east Africa. For this reason, famines in Egypt were rare. Such an wide-spread drought over Africa would have no particular effect on the surrounding nations. Hence this famine went far beyond the failure of the Nile; it was a disaster over the Middle East and half of Africa, and perhaps over an even larger portion of the world. We don't have evidence to confirm such a famine, even in the Egyptian records, and I will discuss why that might be when I get to Exodus. Whether the famine was felt in areas remote from Egypt or not, that stage of civilization was very vulnerable to starvation: the food supply averaged out to just enough year by year. Seven years of famine was potentially a civilization-destroying famine.

e) Joseph Deceives His Brothers (Genesis 42:1-45:3)

As the first year of the famine was proceeding, in 1869 or 1868 b.c., Israel sent the ten older brothers of Joseph down to Egypt to buy grain. In most of the world, the food supply was seldom more than sufficient, so a famine would be felt quickly. Isaac had died while Joseph was in prison. Though Benjamin would have been about twenty by this time and old enough to go on the trip, Israel was still playing favorites. To keep Benjamin at home for fear of what might happen to him was another way of saying that if harm came to one of the older brothers then it would be acceptable. Israel didn't really mean it like that, but it would have felt like he meant it that way. The older brothers were growing up though, and what would have caused bitterness twenty years previously was not as large an issue as it would have been.

The famine was not a total absence of all food. They had almonds, raisins, and dates, but they were lacking in the foods that are staples, particularly grain. Large herds are good to have, but for a shepherd eating much meat is like eating the future. It takes a long time to build up a herd. Further, if grain was in short supply, then grass was probably also in short supply and so the herd would already be having a difficult time. Milk production would have been down as well. As a source of protein and calories, grain and beans or peas have been the primary sources ever since men switched to agriculture from hunting.

Each of the brothers brought his own money; this suggests that each of them was buying grain for his own household, and the family wealth had been divided into eleven separate camps according to the inheritance laws. The money they brought was not what we think of as money, but was gold or some precious metal that could be weighed and traded for goods. Some wealthy merchants of the time would have made their own coins with their gold, but most traders, like Israel's family at this point, would not have had coinage.

Surely Joseph was expecting a visit from his brothers. At first perhaps he didn't know that the famine extended as far as Canaan, but as the first desperate Canaanites came to him he must have thought about his family and how they were doing when so much of the rest of the world was starving. He would have been on the look out for them. So when Joseph's brothers arrived it is not surprising that he recognized them at once even though it had been twenty years since he had seen them. Ten brothers from the land of Canaan would have been noticeable anyway.

Joseph would not personally have dealt with everyone who came to buy grain; that would have been too big a job for him. But it would have been more important to have close control over foreigners who came to buy grain. The grain had been stored primarily for the welfare of the Egyptian people and Pharaoh would have insisted that his overseer make sure that if grain was to be sold to foreigners enough was saved for the Egyptians. We can reasonably imagine that Joseph had a staff specifically assigned to interview all foreigners, and they may have been told to be on the look out for people like his family. He would have wanted to be there if anyone from his family did come, and it is likely that he was remembering his own dreams from his youth. It is also natural that Joseph's brothers did not recognize him in Egyptian dress, ruling the land. Who would have thought?

Given that Joseph would have been expecting his brothers, his harsh treatment of them appears to be planned, not a spontaneous act as if he had been caught unprepared and didn't know how to react and went by instinct. It would be a natural human response to get even and, though Joseph stands out as one of the most exemplary characters in the book of Genesis, certainly he was an ordinary human with a fallen nature. Speaking harshly to the brothers would have also been consistent with the overall Egyptian attitude toward foreigners at that time. To give them a taste of what they had done to him, he threw them into prison for three days, the prison in the house of his old master, Potiphar, that he knew so well. He may have wanted to get even with his brothers (especially Judah, Simeon, and Levi), but he didn't want to harm his father or Benjamin. So he chose one of them, Simeon, probably the one who had treated him the worst, bound him before their eyes and sent them home with both food and their money.

Joseph's tears were for himself; he remembered what it felt like when they turned away from his pleading. He was not yet ready to forgive them, however. He knew they would have to come back eventually and he made it as uncomfortable for them as possible by putting their money back in their bags. Of course, he didn't want to take money from his father, but it was not that scruple which made him return the money. He wanted to alarm his brothers, to make it awkward for them to return, to make it necessary for them to return to Egypt as people who must look guilty. It was a subtle revenge, but perfectly fitting to the circumstances.

The brothers were quick to guess what was going on, and Reuben was quick to say "I told you so". Even after more than twenty years their consciences still hurt them regarding Joseph, and they were quick to ascribe their troubles as punishment for their guilt. They were right that their troubles were coming upon them because of their crime in selling Joseph, but they did not know the real process behind it all. Hence they were both right and wrong in regard to their situation. They interpreted it as the judgment of God against them. They may have thought, briefly, that some man had put the money back and must be trying to make them look like thieves, but who would want to do that? There was no reason to think the man in command would have done such a thing, no reason to suspect anyone of wanting to do such a thing. It must have been God who was out to punish them for their sin.

But they were wrong. It was because of their guilt, but it was not God who was punishing them. At least not in the sense that God wanted Joseph to treat them this way. Revenge is so thoroughly forbidden in the rest of Scripture that we must understand that Joseph was not acting on God's behalf here. They were suffering the natural consequences of their crime, though through a tortuous chain of events that would not naturally have occurred. It was not God who was behind it, but it was God as well.

Reuben was the first to offer his own children in exchange for Benjamin shortly after their return. As the eldest he was responsible to take the lead, but as the disgraced eldest he was refused. But Judah was in the middle of his spiritual crisis at this point, tricked by Tamar into coping with his own short-comings. Judah had come a long way in spiritual maturity, in coming to grips with his own sinfulness. His greater depth of character is evidenced by his willingness to put himself and his children forward as guarantees for Benjamin's safety, though it was not his place to do so, and though that kind of offer doesn't actually make any sense.

In all of the family discussions about a second trip into Egypt, the welfare and fate of Simeon was not mentioned at all until Israel finally sent them off. Israel did love Simeon and did mourn his loss, but he was terrified of losing Benjamin. The nine brothers could not help but notice that he was willing to leave Simeon in prison, possibly for life, rather than risk Benjamin, and if so then he would equally be willing to leave them all in prison. It was his favoritism that had started the conflicts to begin with, but now, at least with Reuben and Judah, there was some healing of the old bitterness. It was not that Israel had changed or apologized or even realized that he had hurt them; nothing had changed for the better externally. But internally they had gotten beyond their bitterness. It is not that they were beyond the pain, but they were beyond the resentment. Their father's betrayal of them no longer dominated their choices. They were free.

In the end hunger drove him to risk Benjamin where love of Simeon could not. And so the nine brothers returned to Egypt with Benjamin, probably near the beginning of the second year of the famine. They tried to defuse any trouble they might be in for the returned money by bringing double the money and taking the previous payment to Joseph's steward before they even saw Joseph. It would have been puzzling when he refused to take the money. It could only add to their apprehension when Joseph had them brought to his own house, rather than to his "office". As harsh as Joseph had been on their first visit, it would be impossible for them to trust in Joseph's good will. It must have looked to them like some kind of trap, though they had been effectively trapped as soon as the donkeys (not camels; camels were for professionals who traded over long distances) set foot across the border. But they were in no position to refuse the invitation. They might have been reassured when the steward brought Simeon out to them: surely the man wouldn't have released Simeon if he only intended to arrest them all again. Simeon had been in a position to hear gossip about Joseph and even to learn what was really going on if he had known the language. But Joseph would have taken care that no one talked to him.

At this point Joseph was about thirty-eight years old, Benjamin was about twenty-one, and they had not seen each other in twenty years. It was not the *memory* of Benjamin that moved Joseph so deeply. It was the *idea* of Benjamin that stirred him. To have a real brother, a real family to which he could belong, which he could love and be loved by; only having such a family could heal the pain of being sold as a slave. Even so, simply seeing Benjamin once again, from a distance, as it were, only made it worse, only made him more fully aware of what he didn't have. He had to run from the room to cry because he was in such inner turmoil. He wanted to just accept them, I think, to let the past be the past and move on, but he couldn't quite let it go, and he really didn't know if they could be his family, not again, but finally. He was angry, he was in great pain, and he was determined to play out this charade to the end.

The Egyptians could not eat with Hebrews, just as later the Jews could not eat with Gentiles, so to keep up the pretence Joseph had to eat apart from the brothers. But even as thoroughly adopted as he was, second in command of Egypt, son-in-law to an Egyptian priest, he could still not eat with the Egyptians. He could hold power and marry into a prominent Egyptian family, but power cannot overcome some barriers, and the racial barrier between Joseph and the Egyptians would always be there however long he lived in Egypt, however much authority he had. The brothers did not detect that barrier, however. A person trained in twentieth century detective fiction might have noticed that Joseph did not eat with his own staff, and might have deduced that Joseph was not Egyptian, and then might have remembered the dreams of an obnoxious kid brother from years before, but of course they didn't notice or didn't think. We wouldn't have either in their place, despite our mystery-story background.

But what really might have given the ruse away was when he seated the brothers in order of their age, grouped according to who their mother was, and then gave Benjamin five times as much food as the rest. Sherlock Holmes would have deduced immediately that the great second-in-command over Egypt was in fact Joseph, but not these guys. But Sherlock Holmes did not believe in magicians, whereas they did. Joseph was supposed to be an Egyptian seer, so that explained how he knew the order of the family and the half-brothers from the full brothers, and it made them even more afraid. Even so, the brothers didn't remember those obnoxious dreams that egged them into selling Joseph in the first place, they didn't connect the few dots they had, and neither would we have. How many of us notice or think about what is going on around us? How many of us are on the alert for any mystery in our lives, especially when we are afraid? Very few of us. Things like conspiracies don't happen to ordinary people like us. If Joseph's brothers thought about it much—and they probably didn't—then they would have ascribed it to the man's magical powers, divination or whatever.

Joseph's revenge was perfect. He knew his father, his father's favoritism, and he figured that his father was now pouring it all onto Benjamin. He would have figured how things stood with the other brothers bringing Benjamin, how they would have had to guarantee his safety to their father. So he framed Benjamin for stealing his cup of divination to give him an excuse to arrest Benjamin. He wanted to put them into a position where at least the older of the brothers would have to face the prospect of slavery and prison in exchange for the brother who stood in Joseph's place. But to make the trap as painful as possible, he let them think for a short time that they were getting away and that all was well. He timed his steward to overtake them just as they were beginning to relax about the trip and to think that they would make it home OK.

The brothers should have been a bit more cautious in answering the steward. They knew they weren't guilty of taking the cup, but then again all their money had been returned on the first trip. How had that happened? Who had put it back? Truthfully, they had no idea what they might find when they opened their sacks, and their past experience should have warned them to be careful. Once burned, twice careful, but once burned was not enough for them. Finding the cup in Benjamin's sack was the crown on Joseph's revenge. What hope had they of ever escaping?

Joseph received them harshly, boasting of his ability to divine. It was enough to scare the brothers that he was the lord over all of Egypt, but that he was a magician of real power as well would have perfected their fear. All that remained was for him to close the trap, and as he was probably hoping, it was Judah that approached him to intercede for Benjamin. Levi would have been the other primary instigator of Joseph's troubles, but it was Judah who had actually sold him. At first Judah offered that they all stay as his slaves in place of Benjamin, ten in exchange for one. But Joseph wanted to tighten the screws a bit. He wanted them to face the prospect of going home to their father deprived of his last son, like they had gone home to him twenty years before without Joseph. He wanted them to face the prospect of confessing to their failure to their father, like they should have done twenty years before. He wanted them to remember what they did to him and to show some remorse. He wanted to know if they regretted it.

It was Judah's speech that did it. Judah proved to Joseph that he had grown to love his father, that in spite of the favoritism, in spite of the injustice to himself, in spite of any resentment he could reasonably feel, he had learned to forgive his father and love him even in his dysfunction. Then Joseph knew there had been a real change in Judah, and that there was real hope they could become a family. Then Joseph was able to forgive his brothers.

f) Joseph Revealed (Genesis 45:1-20)

It was, I think, the process of deceiving his brothers that enabled Joseph to see his brothers as his brothers and genuinely forgive them. We are all obliged to forgive our brothers, but if our "brothers" are literally our brothers and if the pain we carry is severe, then the act of forgiveness may take a bit of working out. I don't think Joseph perceived the obligation to forgive the way we are taught in the New Testament. He had grown closer to God than anyone before him, he understood God's character more deeply than anyone before him, but that is not to say that all the subsequent revelation would have been simply wasted on him.

So I don't think Joseph intended to be reconciled with them when they first showed up. Seeing them, even though he had anticipated it, would have freshened the pain, reminded him vividly of the crimes of the past. He wanted to make them suffer for a while the way he had suffered. We can't, we shouldn't, condone what Joseph did, but neither can we judge him harshly. It was natural to want to get even and he had never been told that God doesn't like it. However I think Joseph was also torn by the conflicting desire to be part of a family, even though his family wasn't a very promising one. For better or for worse for each of us, our family is our family and we must make the best of it or give up. Though it may have taken a while, Joseph did come to the point where he didn't want to give up.

The key for Joseph ultimately depended on three of his brothers, on Benjamin, Judah, and Simeon: Benjamin as his full brother, the closest brother to him even though he had never really known him—he needed to see Benjamin and he needed to see his brothers behave toward Benjamin as they should have behaved toward him; Judah as the brother who had conceived and carried out the plan to sell him—he needed to see some sign that especially Judah regretted what they had done to him; and Simeon, the brother who probably had been the most cruel, he simply wanted to hurt. I do not mean to make it sound like Joseph was a monster. He was a man like you or me. Everything I have described about Joseph is imagination based on what I know of myself and have seen in my neighbors.

But Joseph had the power and the luxury of manipulating events until he was ready to forgive. Most of us who are hurt don't have the privileges he had and must work out our pain in a more subtle way. We have to learn to forgive without the props. Forgiving the people who have hurt us is so critical that sometimes it is justifiable to use tricks to help ourselves forgive, but there is always the danger that tricks will get out of control. Joseph was gambling with his brothers, even with his father who was old and under a lot of stress. The story of Joseph deceiving his brothers was not put in the Bible as a model to imitate. Revenge would be so emphatically forbidden that the techniques Joseph used should never lure us into imitation. But what we can do is spend energy looking for ways to get over it. We can't forget the pain, but we can refuse to let it control us. We can refuse to let the past rule the future, as if the process of cause and effect were overpowering and we had no input, no causes, we could insert into the stream. Though we shouldn't use Joseph's methods, we still want to end up where Joseph did. Once he had broken down, once he finally got to the point of letting go of the past, it was complete. No longer would he bear any anger against his brothers.

It is also clear that one key to Joseph's recovery was his understanding that God was behind it all. Joseph said in 45:5, "Now do not be grieved or angry with yourselves, because you sold me here, for God sent me before you to preserve life" and then in 45:7,8 he said "God sent me before you to preserve for you a remnant in the earth, and to keep you alive by a great deliverance. Now, therefore, it was not you who sent me here, but God; and He has made me a father to Pharaoh and lord of all his household and ruler over all the land of Egypt." It was when he was finally able to forgive his brothers that he finally and fully realized the truth of the matter, that all things come from God, even those things which seem evil to us. He wasn't saying that God made his brothers sell him, or that God approved of slavery or of his brothers selling him; but he was beginning to understand that there was nothing that could happen to him that was outside of God's goodness.

It is ultimately the problem of predestination, which is so confusing to think about but which those who go through some pivotal event understand from the inside. Admitting that God predestined something seems to mean believing that He caused it to happen, that He wanted it to happen, that He approved of it. But Joseph understood God a little more deeply than that. He understood that God maintained all things, even all evil things, and that His glory consisted in always making the evil turn into good. So God predestined evil to happen to Joseph, yes, not as the instigator of evil but as the redeemer of evil. For if evil can occur without God's predestining it, then the evil has become as powerful as God, outside of His authority, and there is no redemption. If evil can exist without God's creating it from nothing and keeping it in being, then evil has become like God, a self-existing being, and there is no hope left to us. To disbelieve in the predestination of evil is logically equivalent to disbelieving in God's power to redeem. Or so it seems to me.

But I think there is something else universal about the parable of Joseph's suffering. His suffering was not ordained for his benefit only, nor even primarily. He was not sold into slavery because he was such a spoiled brat that God had to teach him a lesson to make him a better person. It is the self-centeredness of our faith that imagines God has us in view when He calls us to suffer. Sometimes it is the only way we can find to cope with great tragedy: God has inflicted this pain on me because I need it to become a better person. No doubt tragedy suffered in faith does make us better people, but the truth is that our suffering is usually—I want to say it is always—for the benefit of others, cosmic rather than personal in scope. Joseph did have one benefit that we will usually not have in our suffering, however: he got to see what it was all for. To Joseph, the perennial question, "Why do I have to suffer?" was actually answered to some extent. Most of us have to deal with our tragedies without seeing the years of famine that even one other person was delivered from through us.

What particularly strikes my imagination is how the brothers must have felt. I cannot picture myself in Joseph's place, but I can put myself in the brothers' place. Very few of us are the victims who suffer and who emerge through all their pain as the Hero and Savior of their people. I am not there, anyway. Joseph was very clearly a type of the Messiah to come, for the Messiah would be sold into slavery figuratively and by His own Father, He would serve faithfully as a slave, be wrongfully accused and condemned, be thrown into the prison of death by the betrayal of His own brothers, and suddenly against all the odds rise out of the prison to be given all authority and accomplish the preservation of those who were facing a spiritual famine. The metaphor Joseph's life provides for the Messiah is worth meditating on, as it was intended. But if Joseph is a type of the Messiah, the brothers are types of us.

Suddenly the events of the previous year popped into focus for them: the money returned in the bags, the way the ruler had spoken harshly, the way he had kept Simeon in prison, the way he knew the order of their births, the preference he had shown to Benjamin, the way he ate separately from the Egyptians though he was their master, the whole course of events they had been caught up in were suddenly pulled inside out and they saw what had been going on. This kind of event is what is central to all good suspense stories, the mind-altering event that transforms the way we see all that came before. Thus God invented the suspense genre. Literary devices imitate God every time. The brothers were caught in history's first plot twist.

And it must have frightened them totally. It must have been like their worst fears all materializing before their eyes—at least for the older brothers; it is not clear if the younger brothers knew much about what had happened to Joseph, but the older sons of Leah were trapped. There was no way to hide their guilt and there was no escape from the consequences. All the doors were closed for them and they had no hope left. It must have been astonishing, unbelievable, when Joseph spoke gently with them, when they realized they were not to be executed on the spot, or be thrown into prison. And the Scriptures indicate that they didn't really believe it even as much as seventeen years later when Israel died. When Joseph did not take his revenge they just assumed that he was waiting until their father died so that he would not be hurt by the harm Joseph planned for them; that had been the scheme of their uncle Esau, after all. Their punishment, unintended by Joseph but the natural and just consequence of their crime, was to live in guilt and fear for the next seventeen years.

The only people really happy when Joseph revealed himself to his brothers were Pharaoh and the Egyptians. This is a mark of the impression that Joseph had made at the court. He was not just faithful and respectful when he was a slave, but as a master he had won the admiration, and even the love, of the people who saw him day by day, just as Abraham had won the devotion of his servants. This is as revealing of Joseph's character as his years of slavery were. A man can be faithful as a slave out of simple selfishness, to get ahead; but a man who is in Joseph's position, the ruler of all the land, all the people, can easily come to believe that he can do as he pleases. Any latent selfishness or greed or pride will certainly come out in that situation. But Joseph was a good man; his humility was his submission to God and that did not change when he moved from earthly slave to earthly master. Slave and master had become just roles to him; the point of either of them was whatever God decided to do next. Therefore the Egyptians loved him and honored him.

It is important to note in all of this that God never directly punished the brothers for their sin against Joseph. The consequences to them were all natural ones: guilt, needless anxiety, Joseph's anger during their two visits to buy grain. But God Himself did not punish them nor did He condemn them nor did He rebuke them. It is the pattern in Genesis, and one that we need to consider carefully, that the only times God intervened to punish sin was on a global or community level in the Flood and at Sodom. We view so much of the Scripture in the light of the Law, we so commonly picture God as a policeman on the prowl for crime, ready and even eager to punish any infringement of the Code, that it is hard to see without wearing those spectacles. But before the Law, when God was simply acting on the earth and setting up all things in a context to lead to the Messiah, He was the opposite of a policeman. He simply let most events go without comment. "Should not the judge of all the earth do right?" we could ask with Abram; "Should not the judge of all the earth get busy and do a bit of judging? That's what we pay Him for."

When we read the Law back into Genesis, when we insist on forcing Genesis into the mold of the Law, it colors our understanding of God's character and purposes and makes us misunderstand everything that comes after. It is what comes first that is foundational. He put off introducing the Law for a purpose, because it was not the foundation of His relationship with the human race or with the world. Instead we should allow Genesis to color our understanding of the Law. The Judge of all the earth does not want to condemn or punish sinners, to trap miscreants. His first priority was to devise a way to get out of pronouncing our final sentence.

g) Israel Moves to Egypt (Genesis 45:21-47:12)

Joseph loaded his brothers, but especially Benjamin, with many gifts, not only food but also fancy clothes; "changes of garments" could be translated "garments for changing", meaning fancy clothes for wearing on special occasions, such as when being presented to Pharaoh. Day to day clothes were not changed very often; clothing in general was too expensive to be worn the way we wear it. But Joseph clearly favored Benjamin giving him money and more clothes, and he made it clear to the others that they had no right to be jealous. "Do not quarrel on the journey," he told them, reminding them that they had no cause to complain if he did give preference to Benjamin over them. Not only was Benjamin his full brother and therefore naturally the object of extra gifts, but considering the past they could not have expected any presents at all. But I think Joseph was not mainly expecting them to be jealous of his generosity toward Benjamin; the more likely cause of quarreling now would be the blame game, of who did what and whose fault was it.

By this time Jacob was 130 years old. Both Rachel and Leah were dead, but he could hardly be said to be alone with eleven sons nearby and Bilhah and Zilpah still alive as well. And yet his companion and true love, Rachel, was gone and her only remaining son was on a dangerous trip into Egypt. He knew he could literally lose everything, all his sons. He had been left feeling desolate and vulnerable. So how could Israel be expected to believe the news? It might even have been dangerous to tell a very old and presumably delicate man such good news. Can someone actually die from the opposite of shock at bad news, from the shock of good news? Twenty years of grief made it unbelievable anyway and that would have cushioned the drama of the moment. And he was naturally also afraid to believe. It feels dangerous to believe such overwhelmingly good news because the risk of disappointment is so horrible. It was the generosity of the gifts from Joseph that finally convinced him.

And so it was that in about 1868 b.c. Israel moved to Egypt. There were still five years of famine left and so there was a practical reason for his moving. He packed up all he could—a lengthy process for someone that wealthy, but after all they were nomads—despite Pharaoh's message that they should just leave their possessions behind and count on being recompensed in Egypt. They could have traveled only slowly, so it was perhaps two days of traveling before they reached Beersheba, twenty-five miles to the south, and there God appeared to Israel for the fifth and last time in this world, before He met him again at the top of the ladder He had first shown him.

From the words that God spoke to him it is clear that Israel had some reservations about going to Egypt but it is not clear why he did. He would have known the oracle to Abraham at the establishing of the Covenant, that Abraham's descendants would go to a foreign land and be enslaved, though the foreign land had not been specified as Egypt. It could be that Jacob did not connect the future foreign land of their enslavement with Egypt and was just nervous about leaving his home; for a nomad he had been pretty settled in Hebron for more than two decades, and perhaps his advancing age made him afraid to leave what had become familiar. Or it could be that he did connect Egypt with the land of their enslavement and was apprehensive about the future on that account. God promised Israel to personally accompany him into Egypt and to personally see to it that he (that is, his descendants) were brought back to the land of Canaan.

The way God worded His promise suggests that He knew Israel was still unclear about the scope of God's authority in the world, that God Most High was not merely the God of Canaan but also had authority and presence in Egypt. It was a deeply embedded concept in the Middle East that gods were settled in their own cities and lands. The universal god was always imagined as so remote and uninvolved that he hardly counted as a real god. And though we tend not to think about future generations much in our culture, though we tend to not care much what happens to our remains after we die, the ancients did care a lot. It was important to Israel to know that he would be buried in Hebron with Leah and Isaac and Abraham. We moderns do not think of the afterlife as anything in particular, and certainly not as a condition in which we will feel or think or be aware of anything that has to do with this present life. We emphatically don't believe in ghosts and carefully segregate the future life from the present life as if we were trying to avoid contamination. It is characteristic of our culture to emphasize the present world and to avoid thinking much about death or what comes after, even if we do believe in an afterlife. But Israel expected to have some sense of what was happening to his descendants and of what was happening to his remains; he expected to be involved emotionally in the future of his children.

We have already mentioned something about the list of descendants of Israel who went with him into Egypt. In 46:26 we are told that 66 direct male descendants came with Israel when he went into Egypt, but there are three problems with that total. First of all, the total included Er and Onan, whom God had killed five or six years previously; the significance of their inclusion in this list has already been discussed in the section on Judah. Second, though Perez the son of Judah must have been a young child when they moved to Egypt, the total included the two future sons of Perez. Third, the total included ten sons for Benjamin but at the time Benjamin was only about twenty-two years old. Perhaps Benjamin had five to ten wives by this early age? Furthermore, there is a discrepancy between this list of Benjamin's descendants given here and the list of Benjamin's descendants given in Numbers 26:38-40. In Genesis, Ard and Naaman are listed as Benjamin's sons whereas in Numbers they are his grandsons; also the list of Benjamin's sons in the book of Numbers includes three names not mentioned in Genesis and leaves out six names given in Genesis. The genealogy in Numbers also leaves out a son of Simeon and a son of Asher.

These discrepancies are not serious problems unless you insist on taking the genealogies as strict chronological and biological accounts, which I don't. The sons missing from the later account in Numbers may have died childless in Egypt; contributing nothing to the census being taken at that point they would naturally have been left out. It is also possible they were actually grandchildren since the genealogies are not careful to completely distinguish each generation. It has been suggested that the list was inserted later, when Genesis was being written down, not as a genealogical record, but as a list of those ancestors whose descendants became numerous enough to be counted as distinct clans. This is a reasonable theory except that the presence of Er and Onan on the list would argue against it. On the other hand, the list does point out that they had died, so they were included for particular reasons that over-rode the purpose of the list (I think to emphasize their continued standing in the Covenant despite their evil character). On the whole it seems most logical to me to interpret these 66 descendants of Israel who "came with him into Egypt" as the totality of the male descendants, dead or alive, that he had when he died seventeen years later, but this interpretation is suspect as well.

It is important to understand that just as this list included some who did not actually move into Egypt, so it does not include many in Israel's household who did move with him. Not only the women that were not listed, but also many, probably hundreds, of servants who had joined the household of Jacob. All of those people would be sorted out and incorporated within Israel as they lived in Egypt, attaching ultimately to one tribe or other. The tribes of Israel were not neat, airtight packages; they contained many who were not descendants of Abraham through Isaac. The Covenant may have been exclusive of the descendants of Ishmael and of Esau and of the other children of Abraham and Keturah, but then it smuggled a lot of them back in. Ishmael was sent away to found a people of his own, and Esau wandered away, but anyone who stayed was included in the Covenant people of Israel.

The brothers, other than Benjamin, had a narrow range of ages, at this time between their mid-forties to their late thirties. Judah seems to have taken the lead in organizing the move into Egypt, but it was Joseph who had thought it all out. He did not want his family to live too close to the Egyptian court; for one thing, he knew well the Egyptian distaste for foreigners. Though he had procured Pharaoh's favor, he knew that Pharaoh's successor would probably not be so positive. Even a great deliverance such as Joseph had managed would fade in memory all too quickly; foreigners just did not have a great future in Egypt. Goshen was good pastureland and had the advantage of being remote from the court and in the general direction of Canaan. Joseph must have ruminated on what he had heard of God's call to Abraham and Isaac and doubtless he knew of the oracle to Abraham that his descendants would become slaves in another nation. It would be easy for Joseph to figure out that it would be Egypt that would enslave them. He wanted them to be as separate as possible from the Egyptians, segregated together in an area that would help preserve some ethnic identity as their status deteriorated.

Furthermore, I think he was trying to protect his family from the strong lure of Egyptian culture. The Egyptians were by far the most complex and impressive culture of that day and were imitated by everyone exposed to them, much like the American culture has been imitated recently. The Canaanites, who were growing numerically in Egypt, did exactly that, imitating Egyptian customs to a large extent. They tried to become as Egyptian as they could but would never be accepted by Egyptians as being truly legitimate. Joseph secured his family's isolation from Egyptian culture by emphasizing their occupation as shepherds. The Egyptians were so oriented toward agriculture and the Nile and so prone to prejudice against outsiders that they tended to despise any custom alien to their way of life. Though it was a part of their culture, animal herders had the lowest social status. Herding was not a necessity for the Egyptians as it was in most nations, and they could afford to look down on it. Joseph wanted to ensure that even this Pharaoh would want to keep his distance from his favorite's family.

The capital of Egypt had already been moved from Thebes to Itjtawy (the ruins of Itjtawy have not yet been found) by Senusret's great-grandfather. It was at this presently undiscovered site that Joseph presented his family to Pharaoh as required, choosing five brothers only so as not to be too much of an imposition. Then he presented Israel to Pharaoh. The interview was a matter of court manners and protocol, a necessary formality, but doubtless Pharaoh had great interest in seeing Joseph's family. However, the interview concluded with Israel blessing Pharaoh, probably not part of the usual protocol. After all, what need did Pharaoh have for a blessing from this wandering animal herder? It wasn't an insult to the Pharaoh, but it may have seemed beneath his notice.

And yet Israel's blessing of Pharaoh is the most theologically significant part of the procedure. It was not merely a formality from God's viewpoint. It was not merely polite well-wishing because Israel was the bearer of the Covenant and as the bearer of the Covenant his blessing carried God's blessing as well. From this point on, Egypt was under God's particular blessing. Even as idolators, even as the oppressors of the chosen people, even in the midst of the plagues, Egypt nonetheless enjoyed the warmth of God's favor on them. Egypt was bound up with God's promise to Abraham that he would be a blessing to all peoples. The Arabs, the Edomites, and now the Egyptians all became a special people to God, and this in spite of conflict and warfare and hostility and enslavement. They all became part of God's overall plan of revelation, though it is not yet clear how it is all to be worked out. This point is emphasized as the Scripture goes on, particularly by the prophet Isaiah (see Isaiah 19:16-25) a thousand years after Joseph died.

The land of Goshen is still the most fertile and productive part of Egypt. In 47:11 Pharaoh called it "the land of Rameses"; this suggests that he intended them to settle in that part of Goshen near the city of Rameses. This was on the principal trading route which ran along the coast of the Mediterranean to the land that would be Philistia and beyond it to Mesopotamia. It was probably along this same route that Joseph had been brought to Egypt to be sold as a slave. Pharaoh also bestowed the care of the royal livestock on Joseph's brothers; as we shall see Pharaoh's herds were newly acquired, and now the benefits of doing service for Pharaoh would belong to Joseph's family.

h) Joseph in Charge of Egypt (Genesis 47:13-26)

We now have a short description of how Joseph managed the land of Egypt during the famine. First he sold grain to the Egyptians for money, that is, for gold, silver, and other precious metals to be had in the land. Money was still informal by today's standards. But this famine was the worst ever and the money was gone before the famine was gone. The next year the people of Egypt came to him to beg for food since no one in the whole land had any money left, but Joseph knew what to do. He traded food for all the livestock in Egypt during that year. And since all the livestock in Egypt became the property of Pharaoh, Pharaoh suddenly found himself in need of people to care for all those animals and Joseph's brothers got the job. They were the right people in the right place at the right time, and Joseph might have introduced them as shepherds hoping for just such an offer.

The following year, with all the money and animals gone, the people had to sell their land; they were abandoning their drought stricken land and moving into the cities anyway. By this stage of the famine the land was mainly barren, but Joseph knew it would bloom again eventually. Along with their land, the Egyptians had to sell themselves to Pharaoh; from that point on the Pharaoh became the undisputed master of all of Egypt. No longer would the nomarchs, the Egyptian nobles, vie with him for power. From this point on in the history of the Middle Kingdom, the Pharaohs were the sole masters, and they owed it to Joseph. And when the famine ended the people paid the Pharaoh twenty per cent of everything they grew on the land as they had agreed. The power of the Pharaohs of the Middle Kingdom would never again be challenged by anyone. When the Middle Kingdom failed, it was not through the power of external rivals but through the internal weakness of the rulers.

5. Epilogue

a) Israel Adopts Manasseh and Ephraim (Genesis 47:27-48:22)

The central story of Genesis is done now, but there are a few details and loose ends to tie up. The Victorian novelists frequently inserted a chapter at the ends of their books to summarize what happened to the main characters after the main story was done. The last few chapters of Genesis are similar to that kind of epilogue. There were also some details that the sequels the revelation would pick up on that needed to be put in place.

So Israel lived seventeen more years after moving to Egypt; we therefore date his death in about the year 1851 b.c. still within the reign of Senusret III. Before his death there were two events that shaped the context of the events in the next volume of the revelation. First Israel adopted Joseph's two oldest sons as his own. That Manasseh and Ephraim were not Joseph's only sons is indicated in 48:6, but any other sons are never mentioned by name as sons of Joseph; they were absorbed into the genealogies of Manasseh or of Ephraim. It is not clear when the adoption happened. In 48:12 when Joseph presented Manasseh and Ephraim to Israel, he "removed them from his knees". If this phrase is taken at face value, then Israel adopted them shortly after he moved to Egypt, when the two boys were under ten years old. This makes sense of the fact that he only brought his two eldest; the other sons were likely quite young and he didn't want to burden his father in his illness.

There is another possible interpretation however. The account of the adoption in chapter 48 follows the legal form for adoptions documented from Ugarit a few centuries after this time. Ugarit was to the north of

Canaan, not far from Haran and the homeland of Abraham, so it is reasonable that legal forms might be similar. It may be that "removed them from his knees" was legal terminology for the transfer of parental authority. Verse 47:29 suggests that Israel had several periods of illness before he died, and that it was not the first of these at which he adopted Manasseh and Ephraim. If this was near his death, then Manasseh and Ephraim may have been in their mid-twenties. If the adoption did occur later when the two sons were adults, it may have been arranged between Joseph and Israel, so that Joseph knew what was happening. There would have been little financial gain in the adoption since Joseph's heirs would certainly have had advantages the other brothers' children wouldn't have. The advantage to them of adoption by Israel was status within their own people. Very clearly it was important to Joseph that his children be raised in his own heritage and not in the Egyptian heritage.

Israel began by telling Joseph of his last vision just before coming to Egypt, that God had appeared to him again and had repeated the promise concerning the land of Canaan. It was important to him to emphasize that they were not to stay in Egypt, that it was important not to get too settled there, that they must remember that they were destined for another land, the very thing Joseph had probably been thinking himself. It is interesting how much the land of Canaan had come to mean to them since they actually owned very little of it: the cave at Hebron and the lands around Shechem. The cave would somehow be remembered as theirs over the centuries of their slavery, but apparently the city of Shechem was abandoned. Canaanites lived there but no one rebuilt the city until the people of Israel took the land. It was to become part of the inheritance of Manasseh.

Israel was going blind just as Isaac had and so he did not recognize Manasseh and Ephraim. But that he asked who they were may not be an indication of his blindness; he knew who they were, but he asked the question as part of the formal legal procedure. Joseph brought them forward for the blessing so that the older son would be in front of Israel's right hand and the younger in front of his left, but Israel crossed his hands. This would confer the blessings of the first born on the younger of the two, though the words he said were directed equally at them both. Joseph assumed it was a mistake and tried to correct him. It upset him to disregard the birth order even though the history of his family should have made him a bit more flexible on that issue. But Israel was not merely making the mistake of the blind; he knew what he was doing. By crossing his hands, placing his right hand on the younger, he prophesied that Ephraim's descendants would be greater than Manasseh's.

The way Israel talked about God in the blessing (48:15,16) is worth considering. Here is the first use of the shepherd as a metaphor for God. The metaphor was sometimes used in Mesopotamia to talk about the king, but it was not used to describe the gods. It is difficult to over-emphasize how incredible this metaphor was. What other religion in the ancient world could have applied that metaphor to their gods? The gods of the ancients were typically either savages or beasts or humanoid monsters or fools; at the best a few gods and goddesses were benign enough to be considered decently human, enough to gain some gratitude and worship from human admirers. But the metaphor of God the Shepherd would not easily have arisen in any other context but Israel. It was one of the points of His history with Abraham, Isaac, Israel, and Joseph to bring this metaphor to birth.

And isn't it entirely appropriate as a metaphor? Hadn't God Most High behaved exactly like a shepherd with His little flock of people? First He made them into shepherds themselves so they would be able to abstract the ideal of a shepherd from their own experience. Then He guided them around the land to places they could live safely, protected them from all dangers, and made sure they had room and nourishment enough to grow. God had been working for generations to create this metaphor in Israel and had finally brought it forth; this is revelation.

And note how offensive this metaphor would have been to the Egyptians, who despised shepherds. It is the routine through the whole revelation that God presents Himself in the most humiliating terms, and especially terms that would make Him scorned in the Gentile world. From shepherd to crucified criminal, He has not changed His approach. The humility of God would be a stumbling block to the Egyptians, as it would be to nation after nation since then. The revelation inspired within Israel on his deathbed would only further repel the Egyptians from the Covenant, of course, if they heard of it. But isn't this the typical manner in which people are excluded from the Covenant? Isn't it always because they are either repulsed or bored by the kind of God they find there? People are excluded from the Covenant, not because God judges them, but because they judge God.

Israel also referred to God as an angel, an angel who had redeemed him from evil. The evil he was thinking about could have been many things: Esau's anger, Laban's guile, the famine, the conflicts with his children, Shechem. Probably he was not thinking of what we would call sin, but by this time he would have recognized his own failures as a father and as a man; sinfulness before God did not play a significant part in their thinking until after Moses. As for calling God an angel, the concept of "angel" was still not clearly defined. Whether an angel was God Himself or some other creature that He was using as a messenger was a question that had not even been thought of.

In 48:22 Israel used a play on words: the word for "portion" (or "mountain slope" in the ESV) sounds like the name "Shechem". Israel used the word for "portion" to refer obliquely to Shechem as land which he "took from the hand of the Amorite with my sword and my bow", not quite a fair description of a massacre by deceit, but it still may be what he meant. Before the massacre, when he had just arrived in the land, Jacob had purchased some land outside of the city of Shechem for which he had paid one hundred coins (see 33:19), and future generations would understand Israel's remark to mean that he was giving all of that land to Joseph (see Joshua 24:32). The future city of Shechem would be on the boundary between the inheritance of Manasseh and that of Ephraim.

b) Israel Blesses His Children (Genesis 49:1-28)

After the adoption, Israel summoned all of his children together to give each of them his last word. In Israel's mind, he was prophesying, but sometimes his last words to particular sons are not at all like what we would call prophecies. Sometimes, as in the case of Reuben, the last word was more in the nature of a rebuke. Sometimes the last word appears to be simply a word-play based on the individual's name. For the most part, these blessings/prophesies are difficult to interpret. Many of them seem to require some inside knowledge into the events of the centuries to come. Some of them seem to refer mainly to the geographic regions where their descendants would settle. However some words are clearly prophecies, particularly the one concerning Judah, and are just clear enough to be interesting. We have already looked at the words he spoke to the four oldest children of Leah, to Reuben, Simeon, Levi, and Judah, so we will now just consider what he said to the other eight.

Israel blessed the last two sons of Leah in reverse order, the sixth and then the fifth; there doesn't seem to be any significance in this rearrangement. Whatever the blessing on Zebulun meant, it does not refer to the location of the future inheritance of his tribe; their territory would be between the Sea of Galilee and the Mediterranean Sea, but would not include a coast and would not be near to Sidon. How we are to take this blessing is not at all clear, but it lacks the prophetic character of the word he had just spoken to Judah. Nor does the Bible specifically endorse it as an authentic prophecy. However it is evident that this blessing was actually spoken and recorded before Israel entered the Promised Land; otherwise someone might have been tempted to "fix it up", as it were. It is a clear encouragement to trust the integrity of the text that we have. The tribe of Issachar was predicted to become a people who would inherit a good and pleasant land and would prefer maintaining their comfort rather than their liberty. The metaphor for such a tribe could be fittingly chosen as the donkey which lives in some comfort but is really a slave. Again this lacks the prophetic character of the word to Judah.

Moving on to the children of the maidservants, the blessing on Dan, the oldest son of Bilhah, is intriguing for its imagery. As a tribe, they were to perform the role of the judge, and here Israel was playing on the meaning of the name Dan. This could be partially fulfilled in the person of Samson, but it really seems to be meant more broadly than that. It is interesting that the image used for this tribe that would judge Israel was the serpent. One might think that the serpent would always be a metaphor for evil but it is not so in this case. In this instance, the serpent was the metaphor of choice because of its ability to overcome what is much greater than it is: it frightens the horse and the rider so that they fall over backwards, and it accomplishes this without any actual fighting, by inspiring fear. Dan was to be a tribe that would be like that snake. Again, it is not clear how this blessing worked out in practice, except that it provides a good picture of Samson.

For the blessing on Gad, the older son of Zilpah, whose name means "with fortune", Israel used a pun, a similar sounding word that means "to press" or "to raid". The future for Gad's tribe would have more to do with conflict than good luck or possessions, but in their conflicts they would give as good as they got. The younger son of Zilpah was Asher, which means "with my happiness". This time Israel ignored the meaning of the name entirely. Instead he predicted "fat bread" for Asher's tribe, meaning a fertile soil that would provide the best of food in abundance. Asher did receive some of the best land in Israel, and Solomon would trade some of their produce to Hiram, the king of Tyre. There does not seem to be any larger meaning than this.

The blessing on Naphthali, the younger son of Bilhah, is entirely obscure. I can't even guess as to its meaning, either its immediate meaning or any long term prophetic meaning it might have. This is a prophecy for the scholars, but so far as I know no one has much clue concerning it. The message contained in the words is a very personal one, and it may be that no one besides Naphthali, or his descendants, ever knew what it meant.

Israel waxed eloquent when it came to Joseph, his favorite son; some things never change and Israel's clear preference for Joseph was one of the constant marks of his later life. He pronounced every blessing on him that he could, from the heavens to the depths, of fertility, of the surrounding hills, from above, below, all around, the past, and the future. Joseph's two sons did produce two of the largest tribes; the two tribes together would dominate the northern kingdom. Ephraim was so important that the tribe became virtually synonymous with the northern kingdom of Israel, as Israel had suggested in 48:16. When he referred to Joseph as "distinguished among his brothers", it was not just his current position as ruler over the land of Egypt that he had in mind, but a future distinction as well.

The words pronounced on Benjamin are very warlike, and one is immediately reminded of Saul, the first of the kings of Israel. The wolf seems like a very appropriate metaphor for Saul, who hunted David like prey, but whether there is more to its meaning than this is unknown. It is true with these blessings, and with other words of the future prophets and poets of Israel, that much of the wording was poetic in meaning, and included metaphors and images that are unfamiliar to us. They probably cannot be completely understood by us however much we study them. 49:28 says that Israel gave to each son a blessing that was *appropriate* to him. So those who were not to go on and play a central role as Israel's history unfolded were given a somewhat "generic" blessing, and those like Judah and Joseph who were to go on and play important roles were given substantial prophecies. But the truth is we know too little of their subsequent history and lives, and the appropriateness of Israel's words is lost on us.

c) Israel's Death (Genesis 49:30-50:21)

And so Israel died in about the year 1850 b.c. and was taken back to the land of Canaan to be buried with Leah, with Isaac and Rebekah, with Abraham and Sarah; it was his last request. He had been in Egypt for seventeen years but his title to the cave at Machpelah, that Abraham had purchased from Ephron the Hittite, was still known among the Canaanites (there was efficient and systematic record keeping in the Middle East even at that early time, even on the outskirts of the great cities, even though the Canaanites had moved in and taken over from the Amorites) and there was no problem in going back to his old home and reclaiming the site. The Egyptians had long been involved with a colony at Byblos on the Mediterranean coast, less than a hundred miles north of Canaan, so they were a familiar presence in the land from both directions.

The famine had been over for twelve years, so it is unlikely that Joseph still had authority or duties in the government of Egypt. Nonetheless, he retained some official role in the court of Pharaoh and was not simply free to come and go as he pleased. He had to obtain Pharaoh's permission to take his father's body to Canaan for the burial. Joseph still enjoyed the favor of the Egyptians and the Pharaoh, though, and easily obtained Pharaoh's approval. That Joseph spoke to the household of Pharaoh rather than to Pharaoh himself suggests that he no longer saw Pharaoh regularly. He had not been fired, but his job had disappeared from under him when the crisis was over. He had been retired, but was known as a great man and diviner, at this point in his mid-fifties, probably serving as a dream interpreter and magician along with the Egyptians trained in the occult.

Israel was embalmed in the Egyptian fashion, the only other Israelite to be embalmed besides Joseph. Finding these mummies today would be a great find indeed. The Egyptians mourned for Israel for the seventy days of mourning, as if he had been an Egyptian prince. The Canaanites, who were in awe of Egyptian civilization, were impressed at the great honor they showed to Israel. Most of Pharaoh's court went to Canaan to bury Israel and honor both Joseph and Israel. The funeral went on for a full week, the usual time frame. Certainly the local Canaanites were impressed by the presence of so much Egyptian royalty, who usually came to their land only with an army. They must have wondered why the Egyptians honored a foreigner like this; we do not know how much of the story of Joseph was remembered or known outside of Egypt. It was not remembered for long even inside of Egypt.

It would seem that Joseph's brothers, since they were all in Canaan for Israel's funeral, could have just stayed there and circumvented the years of slavery. It is curious that they went back to Egypt. They were quite a bit richer in Egypt than they had been since they were now in charge of Pharaoh's herds. This may have been the determining factor in their return. But they did carry with them the oral tradition of their family and some of them may have thought about the prophecy to Abraham about being enslaved. Joseph's brothers were not the sort of men to meditate long and hard on the family spiritual inheritance; Joseph was the only one likely to have done much meditating and he had to go back. In the end they may have gone back to the land of their future enslavement without thinking much about what it meant.

It was natural for the brothers to think, with Esau as a precedent, that Joseph had been just waiting for his father to die before he took his revenge. Now was the time to do whatever was necessary to avert his anger, his perfectly justified anger. In suspecting Joseph of such intentions, they judged themselves. We must know a sin pretty thoroughly from the inside in order to suspect someone else of it. They were afraid Joseph would do to them exactly what they would have thought of doing to him had they been in his place. Do unto others as you would have them do unto you, but always remember that others may do unto you as you would have done unto them if you had had the chance.

But Joseph had long ago forgiven them; he had dismissed the whole thing from his mind, and it distressed him to think that they thought he might still hold a grudge. He had grown to genuinely love his brothers. His years in slavery, his toying with them when they came to buy food, and his seventeen years of living with them in happy and prosperous times had healed him of his bitterness. He was beginning to realize, on a spiritual level, that for better or worse his family had been chosen by God for some reason, and he had been chosen by Him to save their lives. Was he to turn around now and bring up old grievances? He was beyond that point, and it grieved him that his brothers were still afraid of him.

Joseph's reply to his brothers is the fitting and perfect end to the book of Genesis. It is the high point to which the first phase of revelation had been aiming. "Am I in God's place?" Who before, of the whole human race, had thought of asking that question? Perhaps Noah; perhaps Abraham.

But human history shows clearly that we are all only too eager to act in God's place if we get the chance. Joseph, and Joseph the first of all, saw revenge for what it was. To take revenge for the evils done to you is to put yourself in the place of God, to act as judge over your brother (in this case literally), as if being a victim were the only qualification for being a judge.

Even worse, to take revenge is to judge God. Joseph, and Joseph first of all, saw how supremely powerful and good God was. His brothers had meant evil to him and no mistake; Joseph never romanticized his brothers motives or tried to excuse them. They had done evil to him and no mistake, but God had meant it for good. It had all come about because of God, and God had been the power behind it, making an evil thing into a good thing. To take revenge would be to pronounce judgment on God, to condemn Him as mistaken, or as too weak to bring forth the good that He intended; or else it would be to judge the good He brought forth as an inadequate compensation for the suffering he had endured. To put ourselves in the place of God is to judge God as insufficient for our needs.

d) Joseph's Last Days (Genesis 50:14-26)

Joseph rounded out the first phase of revelation that had been going on since the Fall, the revelation of grace. God's sovereignty is the other side of His grace. Grace without sovereignty, without power, is just wishful thinking. "Go, be warmed and filled", He might say to us, but we would go away hungry because His good will toward us would be unable to accomplish our salvation. Similarly, sovereignty without grace is horrible, tyrannical, the power of master over slave. It is the marriage of the two that make up God's character and being. This is one of the major points of the revelation through the centuries narrated in Genesis.

Joseph died at the age of one hundred and ten in the year 1796 b.c. Senusret III, Joseph's Pharaoh, had died in 1839 b.c. just more than a decade after Israel. He had reigned over Egypt for thirty-nine years during which Egypt had prospered greatly, due in great part of course to Joseph. Senusret III was succeeded by his son, Amenemhat III, who also had a long and peaceful and prosperous reign of over forty-five years, and died within a year or two of Joseph's death. During his reign the Middle Kingdom of Egypt reached its cultural zenith. His son, Amenemhat IV came to the throne in 1794 b.c., just after Joseph died, and was probably an old man when he came to the throne. He was succeeded by his wife, Sobekneferu, and with her short reign the twelfth dynasty came to an end, about sixteen years after Joseph's death. Thus the steady decline of the years, the change of fortunes, and the terribly short memory of men quickly brought about an Egypt that did not remember the deeds of Joseph, and did not distinguish his family from the other tribes of Asiatics that filled the land of Egypt. The stage had been set for their enslavement and the next phase of revelation. Meanwhile the descendants of Israel settled down and became numerous and prosperous and eventually began to make the Egyptians nervous

One last comment. There are no Egyptian records of Joseph's existence, and that is significant. The Egyptians kept careful, though biased, records. It is necessary to account for Joseph's absence. I think two reasons can be given that go a long way to explain it. One is the Egyptian hatred of foreigners, which was only briefly set aside during this one century of their history. Joseph's memory would have been loathsome to later Egyptians and it is quite possible his name was simply erased. The other reason is that Joseph served in the capital, Itjtawy, whose ruins have not yet been found. It is just possible that when we do find those ruins that we will find his name mentioned there. Itjtaway continued to be the capital of Egypt for a while as the political unrest engulfed the land subsequent to the decline of the Middle Kingdom, and then it disappears in the years of confusion. Whether it lasted long enough to have Joseph's name erased is not yet known.

AN OVERVIEW OF GENESIS

Originally this book was written to be the first chapter in an "overview of the Bible". Obviously it has gotten out of hand and no longer even qualifies for the title of "Overview of Genesis". However, it is perhaps useful to take a few paragraphs and try to summarize the main points of Genesis and where it fits in to the Bible as a whole. In other words, I will try to give a genuine overview of Genesis at this point.

How it fits into the Bible as a whole should be easy enough to answer: it is the beginning. Genesis lays the foundation for all of the themes that are found in the rest of the Scripture together. There is nothing important in the Bible that does not begin in Genesis. The incarnation? Genesis is imbued with an incarnational perspective, easily noticeable by anyone who knows the concept. Redemption? Ditto. Grace? Even more of a ditto. Perhaps a better image than the revelation as a building and Genesis as its foundation, would be the image of revelation as a tree. Then Genesis is the trunk of the tree, and all the other branches sprout directly from it.

The plot is the easiest bit to get a handle on. It begins at the beginning, as it should, but before we are off to a decent start everything falls apart. This has been a standard plot outline for human novels ever since. The body of the novel, like the body of history, like the body of revelation, consists in putting Humpty Dumpty back together again, or destroying the Ring of Power, or in facing that final confrontation with Voldemort. We were alive and now we are dead; how are we ever to come back to life?

Genesis does begin at the beginning, but then it immediately skips to the middle. The existence of evil begins outside of the physical universe where we can't look. The story of God's response to evil starts outside of time where we can't look. So the plot of Genesis starts with a handicap like all stories and novels since. No story can give all of the background; at best a story can give a patchwork account of the previous history of our characters to explain how they got into the pickle our plot will then follow. Similarly, Genesis can't really proceed in an orderly fashion from the very beginning. It has to give a patchwork account of the previous history of a Creator who springs into action and sets everything up and then, in the greatest inexplicability of all time, let's it all fall apart. But Genesis does give us this brief glimpse of the cosmic past in a totally masterful way, setting the stage for the greatest of all paradoxes: the all powerful, purely good Creator who let His perfect creation fall into evil. "What is the meaning of life?" is the question it raises and does not answer: life is this paradox, and we can feel in our bones how true to life this non-answer is.

Genesis sets the stage for the drama to follow but it does much more than raise the pertinent questions: it creates The Pertinent Question. One might say that it invents The Pertinent Question: if God is so good and so all powerful, how did *everything* get so badly ruined? Where would all those philosophy classes be if it weren't for Genesis? If we had never been told that God was purely and simply and completely good, or if we had never been told that God was the all powerful Creator, then we could have relaxed into a comfortable dualism and been content with the "force". Genesis sets the stage and stacks the deck against the very God it presumes to reveal. It forces us into the corner that the rest of the Bible will squeeze us further into. It impales us on the horns of a dilemma so that the only viable option to go between the horns. It forces us, it was designed to force us, to decide if we believe or if we don't. There is no question that the God we are being asked to believe in is as strange and unbelievable as can be. And it all starts with Genesis.

Genesis lets the unanswerableness of this central question lead us into a more answerable second question: what's to be done about it? To this second question Genesis gives only the beginning of an answer: the promise of a Hero. This has now become the standard fare of novels as well. To obtain this hero, a particular family must be chosen to be His family, and here the story gets a little bizarre. The family that is chosen to bring forth the hero is not a very promising family: a couple who are already passed their prime, who seem to need fertility counseling more than anything else, and a man who is not particularly forceful or dynamic. They finally have a son against all odds who is also pretty non-descript and who marries his cousin who then alienates everyone with her scheming and deceit. She at least has twins but she and her husband soon have them hating each other and playing off one parent against another. Finally the least admirable of the two has to run away from his furious brother. He seeks refuge with his uncle, a con artist who tries to take him for everything he has. After two decades this twin manages to create, on a larger and more dramatic scale, all the family politics and ruthlessness that made him what he had become. But his next to youngest son, a spoiled brat who is sold as a slave by his own brothers, against all odds turns out to be a hero with a small "h". While working out some of his personal issues he saves the day and turns out to be a nice guy after all. He is kind of a practice hero for the real one that is still to come. And thus ends the first part of the revelation. It ends on a hopeful note but with the orchestra playing sinister music and a hard glint coming into the Pharaoh's eye as the scene fades out.

So much for the plot. What can we say about the "lessons" to be drawn from it all? What is the appropriate sound bite to come away with? What is the central cool aphorism we can print on our bumper stickers? Practically speaking, how does Genesis shape the way we live today? Let me just say that I don't think Genesis was given to us to "teach us lessons". No doubt it is true that we can learn wisdom from it. No doubt we can derive principles from it that will help us make better choices. But as worthwhile and noble as these things may be, they are not its purpose. Genesis was given to us to help us *think* about God and ourselves more correctly. Once we begin to think more truly, once our imaginations get trained to see the universe through the eyes of Genesis, we will naturally begin to fall into patterns of behavior that conform to our better understanding. This is how we are designed to work: first to understand, then to reflect, then to behave accordingly. Reversing the procedure does not usually work well.

Rather than asking, "What lesson for today can we draw from this book?" we would do better to ask "What is the dramatic premise, where is the dramatic pause, that drives the story in Genesis?" Deliberately I am making the question sound pretty obscure and academic. I do this because we must ask our questions deliberately, reflectively, carefully, attentively. If the question itself wakes us up and makes us think then there is more hope we will be awake to notice the answer. But really it is just a fancy way of asking what the book is about, of asking what direction we should approach the story from, of asking what we can expect to get out of it if we do our work correctly, of asking why we should bother reading it in the first place.

The clue to help us find the answer comes from the opposite end of the Scripture. In one sense, the book of Revelations is the opposite end of the Scripture; certainly it is the opposite end physically and in time. But in another sense, the polar opposite to Genesis in so far as *revelation* goes, in so far as theological meaning goes, is the letter of Paul to the Romans. Here we see clearly that the dramatic pivot of Genesis is chapter 15 when Abraham believed God and it was counted to him as righteousness. This event is the pinnacle of the story, or the hinge on which it all turns. This is the primary event of all the events, the one we need to understand in order to understand all that came before and all that came after. This is the "moral" to the story from which all the other morals spring. Get this one right and the rest will begin to fall into place.

ABOUT THE AUTHOR

Carroll Boswell was born in Texas and was raised as a Southern Baptist in the Deep South. He became serious about faith in college while attending a Congregational church and then a Presbyterian church. For a time, Carroll attended Covenant Seminary in St. Louis and though his experiences at that seminary were entirely positive, it became clear to him that he was not called to the ministry. He pursued the discovery of his actual calling over many years and down many blind alleys. His professional degree is a PhD in mathematics, but he always pursued theology and biblical studies as an amateur in the older sense of the word—as one who pursues something from love.

Carroll served as an elder in two very different congregations: first in a Presbyterian church (PCA) as a ruling elder for four years, and then again in a non-denominational charismatic church. Currently he is a member of the parish of the Episcopal Church in which his wife is the priest. Carroll and Kathryn have been married 38 years as of 2011 and have ten children ranging in age from 13 to 37. They spent ten years living on what had been an Amish farm, without electricity or plumbing, raising sheep and children and a garden.

Carroll brings his rather checkered denominational past into full use in his approach to the Bible, which tends to fall in between the various theological and denominational schools. His training in the mathematical sciences may be noticed in his organizational style. His home is in upstate New York, where—despite the climate—he spends as much time at gardening as he can spare. When he is not studying the Bible or gardening, he enjoys reading nearly any type of book and writing poetry.